CONTEMPORARY
INDIGENOUS
COSMOLOGIES AND
PRAGMATICS

CONTEMPORARY INDIGENOUS
COSMOLOGIES AND PRAGMATICS

FRANÇOISE DUSSART &
SYLVIE POIRIER
Editors

UNIVERSITY *of* **ALBERTA** PRESS

Published by

University of Alberta Press
1–16 Rutherford Library South
11204 89 Avenue NW
Edmonton, Alberta, Canada T6G 2J4
Amiskwacîwâskahican | Treaty 6 |
Métis Territory
uap.ualberta.ca

Copyright © 2021 University of Alberta Press

LIBRARY AND ARCHIVES CANADA
CATALOGUING IN PUBLICATION

Title: Contemporary Indigenous cosmologies
    and pragmatics / Françoise Dussart and
    Sylvie Poirier, editors.
Names: Dussart, Françoise, editor. | Poirier,
    Sylvie, 1953– editor.
Description: Includes bibliographical refer-
    ences and index.
Identifiers: Canadiana (print) 20210309288 |
    Canadiana (ebook) 20210314184 |
    ISBN 9781772125825 (softcover) |
    ISBN 9781772125924 (EPUB) |
    ISBN 9781772125931 (PDF)
Subjects: LCSH: Cosmology. | LCSH:
    Indigenous peoples—Religious life. |
    LCSH: Indigenous peoples. | LCSH:
    Spirituality. | LCSH: Religions.
Classification: LCC BD511 .C66 2021 |
    DDC 202/.4—dc23

First edition, first printing, 2021.
First printed and bound in Canada by
Houghton Boston Printers, Saskatoon,
Saskatchewan.
Copyediting and proofreading by
Kay Rollans.
Indexing by Judy Dunlop.

University of Alberta Press is committed to
protecting our natural environment. As part
of our efforts, this book is printed on Enviro
Paper: it contains 100% post-consumer recy-
cled fibres and is acid- and chlorine-free.

University of Alberta Press gratefully
acknowledges the support received for its
publishing program from the Government
of Canada, the Canada Council for the Arts,
and the Government of Alberta through the
Alberta Media Fund.

CONTENTS

INDIGENOUS COSMOLOGIES, ENTANGLED RELIGIOSITIES, AND GLOBAL CONNECTIONS

A Theoretical Overview

FRANÇOISE DUSSART & SYLVIE POIRIER

IN THE LAST FEW DECADES, anthropologists and other social scientists have shown growing ethnographic and analytical interests in the indigenization of global religions and the local entanglements of Indigenous and global traditions. There is now a growing literature analyzing the ongoing Indigenous creative drive to revisit their cosmological expressions and ritual practices in order to meet the pragmatics of their changing (and increasingly interconnected) worlds (see, e.g., Goulet, 1998; Hefner 1993; Brock 2005; Niezen 2000; Bousquet and Crépeau 2012; Poirier 2013; Charlesworth, Dussart, and Morphy 2005; Schwarz and Dussart 2010; Laugrand and Delâge 2008; Laugrand and Oosten 2010; Laugrand and Crépeau 2015; Harvey and Whitehead 2018).

While scholars have often stressed the so-called Indigenous attachment to their "traditions," Indigenous peoples' cosmological and ritual expressions have nevertheless always been characterized by a fair degree of openness, flexibility, and creativity, and thus anchored in dynamic modes of trans-actions and trans-formations. Indigenous peoples have reconstructed themselves through the Christian colonial project. Such "cosmologies in the making" (Barth 1987) are the products of Indigenous peoples' ongoing and multifaceted encounters, dialogues, frictions, and negotiations amongst the knowledge and values inherited from their ancestors, Christian and Charismatic churches, "political modernity" (Chakrabarty 2000; see also Friedman 2002) and the globalizing world (Tsing 2005, 2008). In continuity with the colonial encounter, the responses of Indigenous peoples to neocolonial and globalizing forces are informed by their ontological and epistemological principles and cultural backgrounds, including in the domain of cosmology. In this volume, we pay specific attention to the ways Indigenous peoples are exploring, despite many constraints and much suffering, in order to (re)produce and (re)configure their worlds and their identities at the cosmological and ritual levels, as well as their sense of being "at home in the world" (Jackson 1995).

In this volume, we engage with the concept of indigeneity as defined succinctly by Francesca Merlan (2009, 304):

> Indigeneity *is taken to imply first-order connections (usually at small scale) between group and locality. It connotes belonging and originariness and deeply felt processes of attachment and identification, and thus it distinguishes "natives" from others. Indigeneity as it has expanded in its meaning to define an international category is taken to refer to peoples who have great moral claims on nation-states and on international society, often because of inhumane, unequal, and exclusionary treatment.*

The question of what constitutes "indigeneity" raises complex issues often fraught with debates over what indigeneity means, how it is lived, and how colonial histories have shaped it. The authors in this volume provide ethnographic examples highlighting the complex ways in which Indigenous people articulate their Indigenous identity through forms of resistance and engagement, even at times embracing essentialist notions of Indigenous categorization, as they are confronted with a global world. In their seminal volume, Marisol de la Cadena and Orin Starn (2007, 4) have underlined how indigeneity "is at once historically contingent and encompassing of the nonindigenous." Thus, being

Indigenous is not "a fixed state of being" (11). It is relational, emergent, and in dialogue with whatever is contrasted with it.

With a focus on contemporary Indigenous cosmologies, the chapters in this volume examine the fluidity of the relationships between Indigenous and non-Indigenous ontological worlds. They look at how performances of indigeneity unravel locally and globally and are thus open to change. They consider, moreover, the ways in which these dialogues and changes take place for people who are too often perceived to not control the means and forms of their representation globally (Tsing 2005). As highlighted in the recent edited collection by Graham Harvey and Amy Whitehead, Indigenous cosmologies are tethered to place, kin, and multifaceted relationships. We focus most specifically in this volume on the relational ontologies of Indigenous cosmologies in contrast with the dualistic ontology of the modern Western tradition. We pay attention to the processes of change and "the negotiation of indigeneity within this mobile, networked global world" (Harvey and Whitehead 2018, 1:12).

Such reflections on contemporary, changing Indigenous worlds and cosmologies, as well as pragmatic actions and forms of engagement in the global world, have been the raison d'être of the ERSAI (Équipe de recherche sur les spiritualités amérindiennes et inuit),[1] a research group created in 2005 under the initiative of Robert Crépeau (Université de Montréal). The present volume was conceived after a ERSAI panel organized by Françoise Dussart and Sylvie Poirier at the 34th Conference of the International Society for the Sociology of Religion (ISSR) held in Lausanne, Switzerland, in July 2017. The original title of our panel was "Indigenous Contemporary Religiosities: Between Solidarity, Contestation, Convergence and Renewal." The contributors to this volume include twelve anthropologists and one scholar in Indigenous arts. Among them, Robert Crépeau, Frédéric Laugrand, Ingrid Hall, Laurent Jérôme, Anne-Marie Colpron, Antonella Tassinari, Sylvie Poirier, and Caroline Nepton Hotte are members or collaborators of ERSAI. The remaining contributors—Françoise Dussart, James MacKenzie, Kathryn Rountree, Ksenia Pimenova, and

Petronella Vaarzon-Morel—presented papers at the ISSR conference. These contributors draw on timely ethnographic experiences among and works by Indigenous peoples in the Americas, Australia, Malta, and Russia to explore how contemporary Indigenous peoples mediate cosmologies, secularisms, and histories; how conversions often turn out to be double gestures of commitment; and how cosmological and ritual plurality, which we here call "entangled religiosity," has become the new normal in Indigenous worlds. Overall, the goal of this volume is to consider the complex connections among religiosity, politics, activism, and resistance within specific, local contexts, as well as the ways in which globalization shapes these processes.

Relational Ontologies

Indigenous and non-Indigenous scholars have always stressed the paramount value and reality of relationships and relatedness in Indigenous world-making and ways of being (see, e.g., Deloria 2006; Myers 1986; Alfred 2005; Starblanket and Stark 2018; Simpson 2008; Blaser et al. 2010; Harvey and Whitehead 2018). Indeed, "most Indigenous cosmologies build on the notion that relationships constitute the very fabric of reality: without relations there is no world or life" (Blaser et al. 2010, 8). More recently, and still in contrast with the dualistic ontology of Western modern thought, these relationships have been conceptualized as "relationality." As Blaser et al. (2010, 7) note: "In Indigenous people's own ontologies and epistemologies, relationality in varying forms rather than separation flourished"; thus, in Indigenous worlds, "being well is therefore relational; it happens through balanced relations with one's family, one's community, and with other human and non-human entities." While there are various ways to express the meaning of relationality, at the ontological level, "a core principle is that all the things of the world are made of entities that do not preexist the relationships that constitute them" (Escobar 2018, 75; our translation).

In Indigenous conceptions and experiences, relations and relationality are thus constitutive not only of local forms of sociality, but also of being-in-the-world (Bird-David 2017). They are central to the production of the person (human and other-than-human). In other words, the inner logic of Indigenous cosmologies and socialities, as well as local forms of (inter)subjectivities and historicities, express themselves in complex relational patterns (Myers 1986), including relations with human and other-than-human kin, the land, the spirits and ancestors, and various forms of sacred power and knowledge, both local and "foreign." Such relationality continues to guide Indigenous cosmological (re)configurations and ritual practices. In these relational ontologies (Dussart and Poirier 2017a; Poirier 2008, 2013; Harvey and Whitehead 2018; Escobar 2018), "relationality is ontologically primary" (Scott 2017, 52; see also Vaarzon-Morel, this volume). Furthermore, in Indigenous worlds, relationships and relationality nourish an underlying and deep sense of care and responsibility, which is addressed, in one way or another, by the contributors to this volume. Also addressed are the ways in which the colonial encounter, the conversion to Christianity and more recently to Charismatic churches, and the hyperconnectivity of the global situation[2] have engendered the proliferation of relations emanating from different worlds and cosmologies. Managing these diverse sets of relations at the cosmological, ritual, and political levels is indeed, to use an Australian Aboriginal-English expression, "hard work."

Apart from Irving Hallowell's (1960) classic text on Ojibwa ontology, "ontology" was, for a long time, not part of the anthropologist's conceptual tool kit. Since the 1990s, anthropologists such as Eduardo Viveiros de Castro, Philippe Descola, Tim Ingold, and Bruno Latour have hastened the "turn to ontology" and offered novel and contested avenues to think about differences, alterities, and relational worlds (Poirier 2016b). "Ontologies, as we wrote elsewhere, are not only metaphysical and concerned with theories of being and reality, but have real practical, political, aesthetic, and phenomenological implications" (Dussart and Poirier 2017a, 8; see also Clammer, Poirier, and Schwimmer 2004). Within our discipline, the ontological turn has given rise to significant debates about the meanings and uses of the concept of "ontology" (Venkatesan 2010; Henare, Holbraad, and Wastell 2007). The turn has highlighted the ongoing crisis of alterity and difference that stems from globalization and the hegemonic character of Western modernity, which tends to "normalize" ontological and cultural differences. Anthropologists who engage with the ontological turn investigate not so much the diversity of worldviews—that is, varying representations and cultural constructions of the same world—but the multiplicity of worlds themselves, and thus the different ways of being human and of making worlds. This also implies that "rituals and performances are not 'symbolic' or 'representational' of something else. They are *power*" (Harvey and Whitehead 2018, 2:2; emphasis in the original). Thus, the ontological perspective offers conceptual tools to seriously consider other ways of being-in-the-world and to reconfigure our understanding of cultural encounters and spaces of interculturality in today's context. Approaching differences and alterity through an ontological perspective requires taking some distance from the naturalist ontology and Western/modern model of a universal human nature and its various cultural expressions. The authors in this volume adopt an ontological perspective and highlight the differences with cultural others and/or the social construction of Indigenous subjectivities to bring us closer to understanding subjugated knowledges and worlds.

Alongside relationality and relational ontologies, cosmologies are one of the core concepts of the volume. Anthropological inquiries demonstrate the ongoing importance of cosmologies to an understanding of contemporary worlds and their varied entanglements (Abramson and Holbraad 2014; see also Harvey and Whitehead 2018). We consider the concept of cosmology far more encompassing than those of "religion" or "spirituality" (Laugrand 2013). *Cosmology* refers to local theories elaborated by social groups about the origin, composition, and dynamics of the cosmos; about its spatial and temporal proprieties; about the beings, objects, and powers that constitute it; about the nature of the relations between all these "existents" and forms of agencies; and finally about the place that humans occupy within it (Poirier 2016a). Cosmologies convey within their narratives particular ontological and epistemological principles. Indigenous cosmologies are always *in the making*: they are knowledge in movement and "a dynamic source of change" (Abramson and Holbraad

2014, 21) inscribed in a local historicity. To ensure their transmission and reproduction, cosmologies must be open to the world and able to integrate new elements. We agree with Allen Abramson and Martin Holbraad (2014, 15) when they write that such "cosmological openness" illuminates "the plethora of actual ways in which foreign forms (e.g., mines, money, medicines, white persons, white gods) are not only incorporated into customary 'ways of life' but are radically re-signified within and through existing cosmological frames," ontological principles and cultural idioms. Marshall Sahlins's (1985, 1995) and Michael Taussig's (1983) seminal works were particularly eloquent on these issues. In Indigenous worlds, these processes of cosmological reframing and reconfiguration have accelerated during the colonial period and conversions to Christianity. They continue to accelerate today in the face of neocolonial and neoliberal forces and global encounters and connections.

Furthermore, by proposing to consider "seriously" other cosmologies and rationalities, the anthropology of ontologies, alongside symmetric anthropology (Latour 1993) and reverse anthropology (Wagner 1975), has contributed to the disenfranchisement from the concept of "belief" that was paramount in classical anthropological studies of nonmodern and Indigenous ontologies and cosmologies (Viveiros de Castro 2009; see also Latour 2009). More often than not, Indigenous cosmologies were indeed considered to be fictional, false, untrue narratives and representations that had somehow to be corrected and replaced. Indeed, and as underlined by Dipesh Chakrabarty (2000, 111) in relation to the Bengali people, "gods and spirits are not dependent on human beliefs for their own existence; what brings them to presence are our practices." Indigenous cosmologies and ritual practices, as demonstrated in this volume, are sources of knowledge, power, and change; they are guides and templates for dealing with the imponderables of life; they are expressions of Indigenous responses to global forces and of their struggles to promote their own life projects; they are "sites of tension and creation that are present-oriented as well as future-oriented in their concern with creative and degenerative forces" (Abramson and Holbraad 2014, 21).

Cosmologies are reproduced, transformed, and legitimated through people's experiences, which include dream experiences, rituals, and pragmatic actions.

Entangled Religiosity: Cosmological and Ritual Plurality

When we examine contemporary Indigenous peoples' engagements with monotheist worlds and Western modernity, the concept of religiosity seems, from our perspective, more relevant than that of religion. Whereas we understand religion to focus on specific dogmas, religiosity focuses instead on experiential and performative dimensions (Whitehouse 2000). Although the two words share the same etymological root—namely *religare*, "to bind"—*religiosity* further evokes a dynamic process always *in the making*. The notion of religiosity includes the conceptual, ritual, and experiential dimensions of the cosmological fact. It conveys how the dialogic and dialectic relationships between creativity, knowledge, power, and authority orients Indigenous ways of being and knowing. Religiosity acknowledges the openness and fluidity of Indigenous perspectives and practices. Indigenous peoples are confident in their living, multifaceted "traditions" as "means and measure[s] of innovation" (Sahlins 2005, 47)—the more so as they are confronted with the need to affirm, define, and redefine their place, their identity, and the meaning of indigeneity in a hyperconnected world (see especially, this volume: Hall; Nepton Hotte and Jérôme; Pimenova; Rountree; Vaarzon-Morel).

Indigenous religiosities in the past or in the present have always been in movement, open to new elements and forms of power, and reinterpreting these within their own relational ontologies and "cosmological openness." Early anthropologists, with the notable exception of Franz Boas,[3] evaluated a ritual/cosmological corpus as more or less traditional, more or less authentic—but according to what frame of reference? From a "pristine time" before contact, before Christianization? Sahlins's innovative anthropological work makes it easier to understand the ongoing and unpredictable processes of local ontological and cosmological reconfigurations in the face of the proliferation of global encounters and connections.

As Sahlins (1993, 2) writes: "The very ways societies change have their own authenticity, so that global modernity is often reproduced as local diversity." Indigenous peoples are tethered to their dynamic engagements with ongoing cosmological and ritual inventions, reinterpretations, and reproductions—what Bousquet and Crépeau (2012, 8) have called "transformative continuities," that is, "the local and contextual updating of the forces at play" (see also Laugrand and Crépeau 2015; Lear 2006, 154). As Laugrand and Denys Delâge (2008, 7) have aptly argued, Indigenous "traditions" have for a long time borrowed without bothering about questions of homogeneity or authenticity. In brief, Indigenous cosmologies have always provided the means for change and innovation.

The different ethnographic examples in our volume (see especially Laugrand; Vaarzon-Morel; Tassinari; Crépeau; MacKenzie) seem to indicate that engagement with Christianities do not prompt a "systematic reorganization of personal meanings" but rather provide "a new locus of self-definition, a new, though not necessarily exclusive, reference point for one's identity" (Hefner 1993, 17). Christian ideologies and behaviours are here not those of conversion as "rupture" or "radical change" as seen in other cases but rather are in a constant state of flux (Robbins 2007; Keane 2007; see also Hann 2007, 390; Schwarz and Dussart 2010). As Jean and John Comaroff (1991, 250) have argued, transformations of social identities and ritual practices in the Evangelical encounter may be gradual, fragmented, and erratic in ways that challenge the idea of conversion itself, which retains a common-sense European connotation (see also Asad 1996, 264). As illustrated in the case studies in this volume, such performances of localized Christianities are processes through which Indigenous peoples rethink their entangled cosmologies and pragmatically engage in the definition of their own contemporaneity[4] (Bousquet and Crépeau 2012). In such entanglements, processes of continuity and discontinuity are not necessarily mutually exclusive. Indeed, our aim in this volume is to draw attention to the fluidity of change and continuity in these contexts—that is, to how Indigenous peoples live and reimagine their identities as embroiled with traditional organizational models, which themselves have been impacted by different settler-Indigenous histories (Macdonald 2008).

To these timely considerations on Indigenous living traditions and cosmological and ritual openness, we add another vector: that of "plurality," and thus of entanglement. We understand the concept of "entangled religiosity" as the local co-existence and management of plurality at the ontological, cosmological, and performance levels. The concept of entanglement, as we write elsewhere, "suggests also no coherence and ordering, no given direction and fixed categories, no boundaries, and leaves room for principles of uncertainty and unpredictability" (Dussart and Poirier 2017a, 6). The authors in this volume analyze some of these complex and subtle relationships and negotiations in the forms of various entanglements, interactions, and frictions (Tsing 2005, 2008) between continuity, transformation, and plurality in the ritual and cosmological realm. Entangled religiosity is about mediation precisely because mediation puts the emphasis on the politics of difference and the negotiations of co-existence (Engelke 2010). While social scientists, beginning with Max Weber, envisioned a secularized world, the chapters in our volume illustrate how contemporary entangled religiosity is a defining feature of life and of differentiation all around the globe. Contemporary Indigenous cosmologies are the multifaceted expressions of processes of transmissions, trans-formations, and trans-actions in a given cultural and historical context—of co-existence and entanglements between varying and at times radically different ontologies, but also between local life projects and global opportunities and constraints.

In Indigenous worlds and cosmologies, the ontological and epistemological principle of ancestrality is a paramount source of knowledge, power, inspiration, and guidance (Ingold 2000; Poirier 2008, 2013; Jérôme and Poirier 2018).[5] Ancestrality refers to an encompassing reality that binds together land, kinship, and spirit realm (Harvey and Whitehead 2018). Ancestrality also refers to the immanent and ongoing presence of a broad spectrum of spirit beings and agencies, local and "foreign" (at least initially), and often identified with specific places. Such a spectrum includes the spirits of the ancestors and of dead relatives, but also spirits of animals and plants, shamanic powers, Catholic Saints, and Christian deities, as well as other powerful "foreign" figures or objects that have been locally appropriated. A range of these may co-exist within the same spacetime (this volume: Colpron; Tassinari; Vaarzon-Morel; MacKenzie). They are existentially coeval with the living. As illustrated in this volume, the contemporaneity and tangibility of the ancestors, spirit beings, and sacred powers are thus constantly (re)confirmed through a range of experiences and pragmatic actions.[6] Ancestrality and the spirit realm act also as principles of regeneration and renaissance. Despite becoming entangled with secular modern, neoliberal, and state ideologies, ancestors continue to play an active role in the production of the person (this volume: Laugrand; Tassinari; Nepton Hotte and Jérôme; Vaarzon-Morel) and in shamanic experiences and powers (this volume: Colpron; MacKenzie).

Ancestrality also refers to kinship. The importance of kinship in Indigenous worlds has long been demonstrated. Entangled religiosity is a process through which Indigenous peoples reify and remodel kinship and genealogical relations, as well as local forms of subjectivity and sociality. Together with the land to which it is, mostly through corporality, closely tied, kinship is one of the main expressions of the ontological principle of relationality alluded to above. Today, ancestrality and kinship continue to provide a framework of reference to creatively model and remodel the person and cultural identity (this volume: Vaarzon-Morel; Laugrand; Tassinari; Pimenova; Crépeau). At the local level, Indigenous peoples often deal with the co-presence of at least two modes of personhood and (inter)subjectivity: the relational (or dividual) self and the sovereign (or individual) Christian and modern self (Strathern 1988, 1992; Poirier 2008, 2013).[7] Such unavoidable encounters are not without creating ontological angst (Vilaça 2015), tensions, and frictions within communal and family networks. While Indigenous peoples seem to resist the process of Western forms of individualization or the "hyper-individualisation of agency" (Abramson and Holbraad 2017, 12), this does not mean that local forms of subjectivity and sociality are not impacted. Despite their marginalized positions in any one nation-state—or maybe because of them—ancestrality and

kinship networks fuel more sustainable forms of belonging and solidarity. Entangled religiosity is one of the political means through
which Indigenous peoples negotiate their relationships with modernity
and the global world.

The co-existence and entanglement among different cosmologies,
spiritual powers, and ritual practices are inherently political and inex-
orably linked to processes of identity politics. From an Indigenous
perspective, the political sphere is often perceptibly different from how
non-Indigenous people conceive political modernity. Political domains
and regimes of power and authority are not limited to the human realm.
Rather, as this volume highlights, the Indigenous political sphere invites
in ancestors and other-than-human agencies with whom humans share
a "common cosmos" and engages them in relations of communication,
mediation, and alliances. Following the works of Isabelle Stengers (2003)
and Bruno Latour (1999), such reality has been called *cosmopolitics*—
an alternative to political modernity (see also de la Cadena 2010;
Poirier 2008).[8] In other words, worlds are "predominated by an ethos
of inclusiveness and co-existence (where positionality and negotiation prevail) as opposed to the ethos of exclusiveness characteristic
of the modern constitution and ontology (where relativism and hegemony prevail)" (Poirier 2008, 76). This distinction renders their
encounter and co-existence challenging and the outcomes even more
unpredictable.

Locally, cosmological and ritual plurality may give way to different
situations defined by peaceful co-existence and entangled responsibilities, but also tensions, struggles, contestations, and constant
reactualizations. In their relationships with non-Indigenous and state
institutions and organizations, and within unequal and neocolonial
relations of power, Indigenous peoples are constantly negotiating,
mediating, and managing differences. In the domain of religiosity, as
in other domains of collective life, contemporary Indigenous peoples
strive to maintain a "relative autonomy" (Morphy and Morphy 2013;
Dussart and Poirier 2017a) and a relational ontology of care towards
the land and "all their relatives"[9] (Simpson 2008; Starblanket and
Stark 2018; Pasternak 2017). Howard and Frances Morphy (2013) urge

us to go beyond an understanding of the different forms of relations between Indigenous and non-Indigenous peoples and the settler-state. They propose that we move away from seeing such interactions as just intercultural to better understand how Indigenous people· embedded within specific historical processes and unequal relations of power resignify their "relative autonomy." We suggest that such relative autonomy can be read as a strategic relationality, within which Indigenous agents maneuver their differences, engage with their own life projects, and project themselves into the future. In this volume, for example, Crépeau shows how an Indigenous community controls the narrative of the end of time and of the advent of a new era. Nepton Hotte and Jérôme, as well as Pimenova, discuss how, when dispossessed Indigenous peoples wish to (re)connect with their pasts/imaginaries and customary orders, these pasts and orders remain grounded in place, kinship, and ancestrality.

Managing Modernity, Alterity, and Plurality

Within a contemporary globalizing economic and political context, this book's contributors engage not with an anthropology of Christianity, but rather with the entanglements of Indigenous and Christian cosmologies, which have now become co-existing, living "traditions" in most Indigenous communities. To these we may add New Age cosmologies present in the form of, among others, shamanic tourism (this volume: Colpron; Rountree), as well as secular modern and state cosmologies (MacKenzie). Such explorations within Indigenous contemporary religiosities and cosmologies, we argue, offer insights into the interrelationships of local and global processes as they affect the lives of Indigenous agents worldwide. We argue also that analyzing the conditions for the co-existence of multiple cosmologies and ontologies present challenging anthropological, ethical, and political projects (Poirier 2004; Cowan, Dembour, and Wilson 2001; Dussart 2010; see also, this volume: Laugrand; Rountree; Pimenova; Crépeau).

The different forms of Western modernity impacting Indigenous peoples in the past as well as the global connectivity of the neo/post/colonial times continue to promote entangled religiosity and opportunities.

As mentioned earlier, entangled religiosity engenders, in a world of unequal power relations, multifaceted sites where we can find harmonious co-existence and frictions as well as possibilities to go back and forth amongst different religious organizations and movements. Indeed, the predicament of modernities and the rise of Charismatic churches and New Age movements among disenfranchised and postcolonial subjects are irrevocably linked. At the crossroads of a contradictory juxtaposition of Indigenous and mainstream moral economies, Christianities and New Age movements often appeal to peoples' desires to challenge authority structures, hegemonic categories, and institutional inequalities as formulated in the Comaroffs' (1991) seminal work.

This volume thoroughly explores the motivations and strategies of contemporary Indigenous peoples to negotiate and manage indigenized exogenous elements. The contributors provide insight into the flexibility of Indigenous religiosity and practices and into concurrent intercultural (mis)understandings. For example, in their respective chapters, Pimenova, Vaarzon-Morel, and Hall discuss how processes of modernization promoted by national and local policies, socioeconomic and religious institutions, and nongovernmental organizations, originally experienced as "ontological violence," often give rise to new forms of subjectivity and sociality. In a world of polycentric modernities occurring at the same time and in the same places, conflictual, compromised, and innovative relations are actualized and reactualized in the entanglement and the shifting of different ontologies.

In examining (re)actualized relations, this volume asks how and to what extent ontological differences are negotiated, reconfiguring Indigenous (and non-Indigenous) subjectivities and socialities across and between differences (Clammer et al. 2004). The ethnographic analyses in this volume illuminate how contemporary Indigenous peoples come to cosmologically and pragmatically value and manage other ways of being-in-the-world. Entangled religiosity makes itself manifest in multiple contexts and cannot be separated from the gendered political and economic dimensions in which contemporary Indigenous peoples find themselves (this volume: Colpron; Hall). It is indeed hard work to be Indigenous, to maintain relations, to negotiate and manage tensions, improvisations, and regimes of care in an unforgiving globalized world.

As exemplified in most chapters in this volume, contemporary Indigenous conceptions of work and labour remain anchored in dynamic regimes of care and responsibilities towards kin, the land, the ancestors, and future generations (Myers 1986; Povinelli 1993; Dussart and Poirier 2017b). As Australianists, we have both come to understand what the labour of caring implies at the personal and collective levels, as well as all the difficulties that come with managing different ontologies of care, which may at times be entangled. For example, in Françoise Dussart's fieldwork with Warlpiri people in Yuendumu, Central Australia, which she has conducted since 1983, she has examined the struggles many Warlpiri individuals face as they engage with Baptist and Charismatic churches, their customary cosmology (the Dreaming), and the world beyond the borders of their settlement. It is hard work to manage kinship relations and responsibilities vis-à-vis their customary kin, their new Christian families scattered around the world, their ancestors, and the other-than-human realm (Schwarz and Dussart 2010; Dussart 2010; see also, this volume: Laugrand; Vaarzon-Morel). In a personal communication with Dussart in December, 2016, in Yuendumu, a 23-year-old woman reflected on the daily challenges mounted by members of local Charismatic churches against the Baptist Church (which first missionized the Yuendumu Warlpiri people) and the Dreaming:

> They [members of several different Assemblies of God] tell us that
> we need to look after our children and church members all around
> the world, and they think they can stop looking after their own kin,
> their own Dreaming. They should leave the settlement [Yuendumu],
> they cannot stay here if they are not looking after their kin and
> their ancestors. They are selfish [if they say that]...The Bible is for
> everyone, it is for all of us here [as promoted by the local Baptist
> church]. They think they can act like White people, but they are
> not. White people don't own this land!

Indeed, a clear rejection of forms of relatedness—rejecting one's responsibility to ancestors and the land, to one's relatives, and acting White—often drives members of Assemblies of God away from Yuendumu for long periods of time, severing them temporarily from their kin and their emotional, socioeconomic, and political support. Such engagements always remain *in the making* (Dussart 2000; Schwarz and Dussart 2010; Blaser, Feit, and McRae 2004; Austin-Broos and Merlan 2017), and after a few months, most return to Yuendumu to reengage and struggle with different ontologies of care (see, e.g., Laugrand, this volume).

In other cases, as illustrated by Colpron and Rountree in this volume, engagement with shamanic tourism, New Age movements, and other forms of Christian practices has created spaces where individuals negotiate how to provide better care and a better life for their kin and their land. For most Indigenous peoples, their religious affiliations, economic welfare, and political allegiances have long been governed by the principles of kin-relatedness[10] still anchored in their relationship with their customary lands and their ancestors. Allegiances, by their very nature, are to be negotiated and mediated, actualized and reactualized. As the chapters in this volume highlight, Indigenous peoples simultaneously inhabit and act out multiple performative dramas, scripts, and roles from each "tradition" (customary, Christian, and New Age).

Case Studies of Entanglement

The editors and the contributors of this volume have long-term working relationships with the different Indigenous groups presented here. Aside from Caroline Nepton Hotte, who is an Indigenous scholar specializing in contemporary Indigenous arts and media, the editors and the contributors are non-Indigenous anthropologists. As anthropologists, they have been conducting in-depth ethnographic research, some over several decades, abiding by their professional code of ethics. The anthropologists in this volume have been trained in postcolonial anthropology and are thus actively involved at the academic and local levels in collaborative and participatory works and research with

Indigenous organizations, communities, and experts. Over the last decades, they have developed and engaged with various forms and practices of collaborative research with Indigenous communities and organizations. In close partnership and usually at Indigenous people's own request, these endeavours included projects around land claims, local mapping (some digital), website productions for the transmission of local knowledge to younger generations, intergenerational workshops on oral tradition, collaborative museum exhibitions, knowledge repatriation, and the elaboration of protocols to improve the relations between the medical staff and Indigenous patients, among other issues. The outcomes of these works benefited the Indigenous communities and organizations with whom the anthropologists worked and contributed to the strengthening of Indigenous research capacity. In many ways, such complex and entangled relationships may be cautionary tales. Indeed, as anthropologists we can only attempt to unmask colonial and postcolonial legacies.[11]

We have organized this book around three central issues: the notion of the person and the pragmatic dimensions of the indigenization of Christianity (Laugrand; Vaarzon-Morel; Tassinari; Crépeau); the global negotiations of entangled cosmologies (Colpron; Hall; Rountree; Nepton Hotte and Jérôme); and the assertions of Indigenous religiosities and their emplacement within modern settler-states (Pimenova; MacKenzie). This organizational structure is, however, somewhat artificial as all the chapters engage with all of these issues to some extent.

Frédéric Laugrand, Petronella Vaarzon-Morel, Antonella Tassinari, and Robert R. Crépeau offer ethnographic examples of indigenizations of Christianity. They demonstrate the enduring and all-encompassing nature of kin-relatedness and highlight local resistances to the more individualistic notion of the person promoted by Christianity and modernity. Laugrand, in Chapter 2, discusses how Christianity's "*lack of locality*" (Keane 2007, 46; emphasis in the original) allows it to be configured temporally and spatially to confront local experiences of modernity and generate possibilities for social and individual transformation. He also explores how this lack of locality allows for Christianity's rejection when kin and place become too distant physically and socially.

Laugrand sheds light on the limits of the indigenization of Christianity by comparing Inuit responses to Anglican ministry and Catholic priesthood. While Inuit people originally embraced Christianity, they never gave up many of their social values and traditions, among these kin-relatedness. Since the beginning of evangelization, many Inuit individuals have embraced the vocation of Anglican ministry; Catholic priesthood, on the other hand, has not passed the ultimate test of kin-relatedness. There are currently no Inuit Catholic priest or nuns. Based on archival sources and oral testimonies, Laugrand retraces the lives of two Inuit brothers who had chosen, in the middle of last century, to become Catholic priests. During their novitiate, away from their community and isolated, they both renounced their religious vocation and returned home to reengage with their "web of reciprocal kin obligations." Laugrand's case study echoes other ethnographic analyses of the struggles that Christian disciples face in reconfiguring kinship relations and ties to their ancestors and to the land—the loci of their sociospiritual identities. This resonates deeply with how Central Australian Indigenous people incorporated Christianity, as discussed by Vaarzon-Morel.

In Chapter 3, Vaarzon-Morel presents a fine ethnographic example of how the Lander Warlpiri people have absorbed foreign knowledge, practices, and beings (human and other-than-human) that have transformed their traditional lands forever. She illuminates how customary cosmology facilitates or discourages such accommodations. Issues of entanglements with Christian practices and customary cosmology have become key to understanding how agencies of the human and nonhuman worlds are constructed and how such accommodations are lived. The losses of political and economic power in colonial and neocolonial times have been prominent factors for the Lander Warlpiri people's engagement with Christianity. In short, Vaarzon-Morel discusses the materiality of religious activity emphasizing how and why knowledge, humans, objects, and other-than-humans are shared and looked after collectively and individually. Such an Indigenous ontology of care redefines global and local discourses about values and responsibilities in pragmatic ways.

In Chapter 4, Tassinari provides an in-depth analysis of how the Karipuna people from Northern Brazil navigate the discreet fields of indigenized Christianity, customary shamanism, and local politics to negotiate the production and reproduction of the person, of the body, and of alliances with their Indigenous neighbours and with non-Indigenous people. Tassinari argues that for the Karipuna people, "mixing" is valued in positive terms and contrasted with the life of isolation led by animals. Confronted with an ever-changing world, Karipuna people have come to indigenize the production and reproduction of different religious fields of action through dreams, festivals, godparenthood, and marriage alliances. For example, for the Karipuna people, indigenized Christianity makes it possible for "baptized" individuals to intermarry with other "baptized" people downstream. This in turn allows them to control certain residential patterns that are tethered to economic activities and to relationships with invisible shamanic beings and Catholic saints. If Karipuna families wish or need it, these unions can produce new "baptized bodies" without formalized sanction from the Catholic clergy. Human persons are composites of physical traits and religious expertise, both provided by their parents. In a world where the Karipuna people, like the Lander Warlpiri people, establish networks with human and other-than-human beings, the relational aspect of the person thus remains inseparable from the ever-changing outside world. Tassinari's work dialogues with Laugrand's analysis of Inuit production of the person and forms of (inter)subjectivity and sociality. Such practices of recentring power maintain some forms of strategic relationality in times when Indigenous worlds are threatened by exogenous forces.

In Chapter 5, Crépeau, citing Danowski and Viveiros de Castro (2017, 76), reminds us that "periodical apocalypses are the rule in Amerindian mythologies." In our time of turmoil and climate change, narratives of the end of time and the advent of a new era have resurfaced, as exemplified in Crépeau's discussion of the Kaingang people of Southern Brazil. Crépeau, who has worked with the Kaingang people since the 1990s, is in a privileged position to understand how various cosmologies and traditions—shamanic, Catholic, and, more recently, African Brazilian, Evangelical, and Pentecostal—have been entangled and transformed over time. It is in the context of tensions between these various religious allegiances that Crépeau analyzes the end-of-time narratives told by two Kaingang men: a father (a Catholic traditionalist) and his son (a Pentecostal pastor). In the 1990s, the father told a mythical story of the great flood when powerful cultural heroes created a new law—the dual organization of moieties—that instructed people to enact the *Kikikoi*, a second funeral ritual later abandoned under the pressure of the Evangelical Church. In May 2018, the son contributed to the reenactment of the *Kikikoi* after twenty years of censure. Confronted by the ills of modernity—violence, alcohol abuse, breaches in the moieties system, and deforestation—Kaingang people retooled the *Kikikoi* ritual to reestablish harmony in their lives and, more broadly, in the world (see also Vaarzon-Morel, this volume). New cosmological and ritual performative entanglements in the narration of new times to come enable the Kaingang people to project themselves into the future and articulate politics of hope.

Anne-Marie Colpron, Ingrid Hall, Kathryn Rountree, Caroline Nepton Hotte, and Laurent Jérôme analyze how Indigenous peoples manage, articulate, perform, and negotiate connections to the global as they strive to affirm and reproduce their identities. The authors offer examples of foreigners now coming to Indigenous lands with the explicit intention, not to convert them, but to "learn" from their knowledge, cosmologies, and ritual practices.

Based on an in-depth ethnography of the Shipibo-Konibo people of Western Amazonia, Colpron offers a fine analysis of the transformative continuities that shape the practices of female shamans (*onánya*) in view of an increasing demand from a worldwide and much-mediatized shamanic tourism industry. In Chapter 6, Colpron argues that such hypermediatization has revealed how female shamans have risen in number and notoriety. Moving beyond Western preoccupation with "authenticity," Colpron highlights how shamanic power is relational and possesses its own transformative logic. Shipibo-Konibo shamanism thrives on difference and "the embodiment of alterity," whether dealing with entities from the forest, neighbouring ethnic groups, urban *mestizos*, foreign tourists, or novel objects and technologies. Shamanic tourism, we contend along with Colpron, also represents new economic opportunities for these women and their kin. These pragmatic responses and actions participate actively in the reproduction of their world at the cosmological, social, economic, and political levels.

While Colpron addresses local answers to global connections, Hall looks at those ensuing from the global figure of the "ecological Indian" and the international concern for the protection of biodiversity in a few thousands Andean landraces of potatoes. In Chapter 7, Hall offers a thorough ethnography of the festivities around Peru's National Potato Day as staged at the Pisac Potato Park. The Park was created in 1998 on the initiative of a Peruvian NGO and has since acquired national and international recognition. *Papa Watay*—literally "tying down the potato" in Quechua—is the name of a ritual performed by local communities and inscribed in the Andean agricultural and Catholic calendars. Hall's chapter is a significant illustration of the co-presence and entanglements of global and local perspectives: those of visitors from the city and abroad, NGO staff, and community members. For local families and communities involved in the celebrations, a range of practical issues is at stake—among these, an opportunity to transmit local knowledge to the youth and economic opportunities in the forms of prizes for the best performances. Issues of identity politics are also at stake as the local communities use the international presence and interest to champion national political recognition. Furthermore, the staging of the *Papa Watay* in front of an external public is not without tensions and frictions between the varying local religious allegiances and configurations, specifically the "Andean Cosmovision" around Pachamama and the *apu* (spirit beings), the Catholic tradition, and Evangelical churches and converts. Such cosmological and ritual plurality and entanglement have to be negotiated and managed locally while responding to global interest, including ecotourism.

Departing from ethnographic examples of how global connections have intensified the local politics of difference and representation, Rountree discusses how the global is interested in the local. In Chapter 8, Rountree examines contemporary forms of shamanism and argues that it is now difficult to disentangle the "Indigenous" (authentic), "non-Indigenous," "local," and "global" aspects of such beliefs and practices. She highlights in her chapter how, in a world of hyperconnectivity and mobility, religious entanglement is a two-way street in which Indigenous practices from many different places become interwoven with, for example, New Age elements. She illustrates her argument in a lively ethnography of contemporary shamanism in Malta. The Maltese landscape of shamanism seems tethered to the experiential. Shamans can offer *ayahuasca* experiences, healing sweat lodges, and trance-induced ceremonies. Such reembodied practices have restructured relations amongst Indigenous and non-Indigenous people of both Maltese and non-Maltese heritage in the archipelago, thus expanding the sorts of identities an individual shaman can deploy.

In Chapter 9, Nepton Hotte and Jérôme explore social webs and cyberspace as online, global territories that have been appropriated by Indigenous peoples in the (re)affirmation and the (re)configuration of their ontologies, cosmologies, and identities. Through their analysis of online works by two Indigenous women artists and activists, they demonstrate how cyberspace has become a spacetime of Indigenous creative expressions and global connections as well as a means and a channel to express, take part in, and experience decolonization. In the online world, Indigenous artists create a cosmopolitical framework to affirm and renew their identities, to update Indigenous conceptions of the world, and to maintain relations with the broader community of humans and other-than-humans. Here, Nepton Hotte and Jérôme engage with Steven Loft's (2014, xvi) definition of media cosmology as an "Indigenous view of media and its attendant processes that incorporates language, culture, technology, land, spirituality and histories." Their chapter is a potent example of how Indigenous artists and activists appropriate novel technologies to negotiate their place in a globalized world and to reaffirm and revisit their cosmologies.

Ksenia Pimenova and James MacKenzie turn their lenses on how pluralities are managed locally at the ontological and political levels. They also focus on what it means for people to be Indigenous in their interactions and negotiations with national institutions and legal discourses. In Chapter 10, Pimenova offers a rare glimpse of the transcendence of place and how it enables new forms of revitalization. Pimenova's work follows how the local Indigenous population in Southern Siberia (Republic of Altai) is connecting with the remains of a 2500-year-old female mummy exhibited in a local museum. Pimenova helps us understand how the museum space becomes a privileged site where connections with ritual practices of the past and the present are dialoguing with Western scientific analysis of human remains and with national and local politics of recognition. She provides poignant examples of how both visitors and museum staff ritually reconnect with the mummy, called the Altai Princess, through techniques of respect and avoidance. The past and local orders grounded in secular, desecularization, religious, or cultural movements and policies are also reimagined. Pimenova's chapter ultimately sheds light on how such mutable intersections inscribe themselves within global and local cosmological and secular narratives, practices, and techniques of trans-actions and trans-formations.

In the last chapter of this volume, MacKenzie examines how Indigenous people in Guatemala confront modern bureaucracy through ritual and cosmological techniques. He answers Joel Robbins's (2004) call to study how local actors become Christians in service of their own projects. MacKenzie provides examples of how state governance with its bureaucratic apparatus is contested and how successes and failures of changing it rest on actors' cosmologies and ritual performances. He points to the determination of Indigenous people to increase their authority and capacity over their own affairs and futures, to adapt, to change, and to integrate interfering elements of modernity. In other words, MacKenzie shows how shamans and ordinary Indigenous people in Guatemala strive to maintain an ontology of care in the face of relentless assaults on Indigenous ways of life. His examples highlight how institutions of entangled religiosity serve as fields for negotiating power relations between the state and postcolonial subjects.

Conclusion

From precolonial times to engagements with Christianity and New Age movements, modernity, and capitalism, Indigenous cosmologies have provided means to incorporate alterity. As exemplified in this volume, Indigenous cosmologies—platforms of social change and innovations—have remained remarkably flexible and enduring. Such flexibility supports the reinterpretation of core concepts, adaptation of ritual practices, and transformation of notions of person and relationality. They are the keys to the reproduction of Indigenous worlds and identity politics and are thus enduring sites of affirmation and resistance. Indeed, confronted by different sorts of dispossessions and violence—physical, structural, and ontological—contemporary Indigenous peoples, who remain hostages of settler-states and neoliberal corporations, maintain their place and relevance in the world through their local cosmologies. Some may object here and declare that Indigenous people are "losing their culture." Jonathan Lear (2006, 120), reflecting on the Crow Nation's radical and violent encounter with colonialism, offers an answer:

> a world *is not merely the environment in which we move about; it is* that over which we lack omnipotent control, that about which we may be mistaken in significant ways, that which may intrude upon us, that which may outstrip the concepts with which we seek to understand it. *Thus, living within a world has inherent and unavoidable risk.* (emphasis in the original)

According to Lear, among the risks that Indigenous peoples face is the "loss of concepts" (123). We contend that their cosmological openness, their entangled religiosities, and their ability to reframe and reconfigure their cosmologies and rituals allow Indigenous peoples to reproduce their worlds and specific identities within the constraints, appetites, and turmoil of a globalized world.

An exploration of Indigenous contemporary entangled religiosities offers an insight into the interrelationships of local and global processes as they affect the lives of Indigenous peoples worldwide. We hope that the ethnographic examples provided in this volume can contribute to refocusing larger debates in anthropology about personhood and forms of subjectivity, and about ontological, cosmological, and cultural change. As exemplified by our contributors, such plurality and co-existence between various religious allegiances do give way to different situations defined by peaceful co-existence, entangled responsibilities, tensions, and contestations. It is indeed hard work to manage such plurality at the local level. Contemporary frameworks of indigeneity—relationality, caring, autonomy, and alterities—have their roots in precolonial and colonial times. In negotiating these related and distinct ways of being Indigenous, Indigenous peoples make pragmatic decisions about tradition and religiosity to ground themselves in the now and the future. The incorporation of alterity into their world and their cosmologies is a way to affirm and to emplace their specific identity and their own life projects, and a way to connect to new forms of power in a globalized world that undeniably remains hostile to their being-at-home-in-the-world.

Authors' Note

We want first to thank the many Indigenous friends and colleagues who have, for decades, engaged with us and our research in Australia and Canada. We are grateful to Doug Hildebrand for believing in the project and to Mat Buntin for giving us much needed encouragements along the way. The external reviewers' comments allowed us to sharpen our arguments and we are most thankful to them. Our final thanks go to our contributors who have stayed the course and made conceiving and writing this volume so rewarding in such surreal times.

Notes

1. ERSAI has since changed its name to ERCA (Équipe de recherche sur les cosmopolitiques autochtones).
2. *Hyperconnectivity* refers here to the increased mobility of Indigenous people around the world and of non-Indigenous people on Indigenous lands, as well as the cyberspace and social web media.
3. In his work, Boas was concerned with processes of cultural change and creativity and with local forms of historicity.
4. Jonathan Friedman (2002) reminds us not to conflate "modernity" and "contemporaneity." All that is contemporary is not necessarily modern and

"the fact that one desires Western goods does not have anything to do with modernity as such" (299).

5. We acknowledge that most cosmologies around the world value ancestrality and relations with ancestors. Indigenous peoples are surely not an exception in that respect.

6. See also Mark Mosko's (2017) work *Ways of Baloma* and his insightful analysis of how spirit beings, as sentient, dividual persons and powerful and critical agents, participate in virtually all dimensions of Trobriand social lives.

7. Since Mauss's (1938) seminal work, the conception of the person is considered as one of the most fundamental dimensions of local ontologies, cosmologies, and socialities. In this respect, we wish to bring attention here to a current stimulating debate within the discipline of anthropology that deals with the encounter and the entanglement between contrasting conceptions of personhood: the "dividual/multiple/fractal person" and the "individual/ sovereign/autonomous/possessive person," and the transformation of the former within Indigenous (or non-Western) processes of Christianization and modernization. On this debate among Melanesianists, for example, see Mosko (2010), Robbins (2010), and LiPuma (1998).

8. On a similar topic, see also Blaser's (2013) work on "political ontology."

9. In *God is Red*, Vine Deloria Jr. (2003, 84) writes: "The phrase 'all my relatives' is frequently invoked by Indians performing ceremonies and this phrase is used to invite all other forms of life to participate as well as to inform them that the ceremony is being done on their behalf."

10. We are not arguing here that contemporary forms of kin-relatedness are the same as those of the past, but rather that they have evolved and morphed as they engage with the market economy of the poor, different forms of indigenized Christianity and New Age movements, intercultural forms of governance, and demands from state institutions and nongovernmental organizations.

11. Collaborative and participatory works and researches are the outcomes of requests formulated by Indigenous communities and organizations to researchers and anthropologists they trust. This means that Indigenous people participate actively from the start in all the various steps of the project. They are involved all the way through as experts and/or co-researchers and are paid for their work (usually from research grants obtained by the anthropologists or by other local organizations). The outcomes are meant to benefit the communities and the organizations such as the local schools and local media (by designing pedagogical tools for the transmission of traditional knowledge), the local Museum (by documenting archives and artifacts), the community or Nation council (by documenting traditional land rights to present as testimony

to the state in land claims negotiations and processes), or the local clinic (by developing protocols for non-Indigenous medical staff).

References

Abramson, Allen, and Martin Holbraad, eds. 2014. *Framing Cosmologies: The Anthropology of Worlds*. Manchester: Manchester University Press.

Alfred, Taiaiake. 2005. *Wasáse: Indigenous Pathways of Action and Freedom*. Peterborough: Broadview Press.

Asad, Talal. 1996. "Comments on Conversion." In *Conversion to Modernities: The Globalization of Christianity*, edited by Peter van der Veer, 263–74. New York: Routledge.

Austin-Broos, Diane, and Francesca Merlan, eds. 2017. *People and Change in Indigenous Australia.* Honolulu: University of Hawai'i Press.

Barth, Fredrik. 1987. *Cosmologies in the Making: A Generative Approach to Cultural Variation in Inner New-Guinea*. Cambridge: Cambridge University Press.

Bird-David, Nurit. 2017. *Us, Relatives: Scaling and Plural Life in a Forager World*. Oakland: University of California Press.

Blaser, Mario. 2013. "Ontological Conflicts and the Stories of Peoples in Spite of Europe: Toward a Conversation on Political Ontology." *Current Anthropology* 54 (5): 547–68. https://doi.org/10.1086/672270

Blaser, Mario, Ravi De Costa, Deborah McGregor, and Wiliam D. Coleman. 2010. *Indigenous Peoples and Autonomy: Insights for a Global Age*. Vancouver: University of British Columbia Press.

Blaser, Mario, Harvey A. Feit, and Glenn McRae, eds. 2004. *In the Way of Development: Indigenous Peoples, Life Projects and Globalization*. London: Zed Books.

Boellstorff, Tom. 2016. "For Whom the Ontology Turns: Theorizing the Digital Real." *Current Anthropology* 57 (4): 387–407. https://doi.org/10.1086/687362

Bousquet, Marie-Pierre, and Robert Crépeau, eds. 2012. *Dynamiques religieuses des autochtones des Amériques*. Paris: Karthala.

Brock, Peggy, ed. 2005. *Indigenous Peoples and Religious Change*. Leiden: Brill.

Carrithers, Michael, Matei Candea, Karen Sykes, Martin Holbrand, and Soumhya Venkatesan. 2010. "Ontology Is Just Another Word for Culture: Motion Tabled at the 2008 Meeting of the Group for Debates in Anthropological Theory, University of Manchester." *Critique of Anthropology* 30 (2): 152–200. https://doi.org/10.1177/0308275X09364070

Chakrabarty, Dipesh. 2000. *Provincializing Europe: Postcolonial Thought and Historical Difference*. Princeton: Princeton University Press.

Charlesworth, Max, Françoise Dussart, and Howard Morphy, eds. 2005. *Aboriginal Religions in Australia: An Anthology of Recent Writings*. Aldershot: Ashgate.

Clammer, John, Sylvie Poirier, and Eric Schwimmer, eds. 2004. *Figured Worlds: Ontological Obstacles in Intercultural Relations*. Toronto: University of Toronto Press.

Comaroff, Jean, and John Comaroff. 1991. *Christianity, Colonialism, and Consciousness in South Africa*. Vol. 1, *Of Revelation and Revolution,* edited by Jean Comaroff and John Comaroff. Chicago: University of Chicago Press.

Cowan, Jane K., Marie-Benedicte Dembour, and Richard A. Wilson, eds. 2001. *Culture and Rights: Anthropological Perspectives*. Cambridge: Cambridge University Press.

Danowski, Déborah, and Eduardo Viveiros de Castro. 2017. *The Ends of the World*. Cambridge: Polity Press.

de la Cadena, Marisol. 2010. "Indigenous Cosmopolitics in the Andes: Conceptual Reflections beyond 'Politics'." *Cultural Anthropology* 25 (2): 334–70. https://doi.org/10.1111/j.1548-1360.2010.01061.x

de la Cadena, Marisol, and Orin Starn. 2007. "Introduction." In *Indigenous Experience Today,* edited by Marisol de la Cadena and Orin Starn, 1–32. Oxford: Berg Publishers.

Deloria, Vine, Jr. 2003. *God Is Red: A Native View of Religion*. New York: Grosset & Dunlap.

——. 2006. *The World We Used to Live In: Remembering the Powers of the Medicine Men*. Goldon: Fulcrum Publishing.

Dussart, Françoise. 2000. *The Politics of Rituals in an Aboriginal Settlement: Kinship, Gender, and the Currency of Knowledge*. Washington, D.C.: Smithsonian Institution Press.

——. 2010. "'It Is Hard to Be Sick Now': Diabetes and the Reconstruction of Indigenous Sociality." *Anthropologica* 52 (1): 77–87. www.jstor.org/stable/29545996

Dussart, Françoise, and Sylvie Poirier, eds. 2017a. *Entangled Territorialities: Negotiating Indigenous Lands in Australia and Canada*. Toronto: University of Toronto Press.

——. 2017b. "Knowing and Managing the Land: The Conundrum of Coexistence and Entanglement." In *Entangled Territorialities: Negotiating Indigenous Lands in Australia and Canada*, edited by Françoise Dussart and Sylvie Poirier, 3–24. Toronto: University of Toronto Press.

Engelke, Matthew. 2010. "Number and the Imagination of Global Christianity; or, Mediation and Immediacy in the Work of Alain Badiou." *South Atlantic Quarterly* 109 (4): 811–29. https://doi.org/10.1215/00382876-2010-018

Escobar, Arturo. 2018. *Sentir-penser avec la terre: une écologie au-delà de l'Occident.* Paris: Éditions du Seuil.

Friedman, Jonathan. 2002. "Modernity and Other Traditions." In *Critically Modern: Alternatives, Alterities, Anthropologies,* edited by Bruce M. Knauft, 287–313. Bloomington: Indiana University Press.

Goulet, Jean-Guy A. 1998. *Ways of Knowing: Experiences, Knowledge, and Power among the Dene Tha.* Lincoln and London: University of Nebraska Press; Vancouver: University of British Columbia Press.

Hallowell, A. Irving. 1960. "Ojibwa Ontology, Behavior and World View." In *Culture in History: Essays in Honor of Paul Radin,* edited by Stanley Diamond, 19–52. New York: Columbia University Press.

Hann, Chris. 2007. "The Anthropology of Christianity *per se*." *Archives Européenes de Sociologie* 48 (3): 383–410. https://doi.org/10.1017/s0003975607000410

Harvey, Graham, and Amy Whitehead, eds. 2018. *Indigenous Religions: Critical Concepts in Religious Studies,* 4 vols. London: Routledge.

Hefner, Robert W. 1993. "World Building and the Rationality of Conversion." In *Conversion to Christianity: Historical and Anthropological Perspectives on a Great Transformation,* edited by Robert Hefner, 3–44. Berkeley: University of California Press.

Henare, Amiria, Martin Holbraad, and Sari Wastell, eds. 2007. *Thinking Through Things: Theorising Artefacts Ethnographically.* London: Routledge.

Ingold, Tim. 2000. *The Perception of the Environment: Essays in Livelihood, Dwelling and Skill.* London: Routledge.

Jackson, Michael. 1995. *At Home in the World.* Durham: Duke University Press.

Jérôme, Laurent, and Sylvie Poirier. 2018. "Conceptions de la mort et rites funéraires dans les mondes autochtones." *Frontières* 29 (2): 3–7. https://doi.org/10.7202/1044157ar

Keane, Webb. 2007. *Christian Moderns: Freedom and Fetish in the Mission Encounter.* Berkeley: University of California Press.

Latour, Bruno. 1993. *We Have Never Been Modern.* Translated by Catherine Porter. Cambridge: Harvard University Press.

——. 1999. *Politiques de la nature.* Paris: La Découverte.

——. 2009. *Sur le culte moderne des dieux Faitiches.* Paris: La Découverte.

Laugrand, Frédéric. 2013. "Pour en finir avec la spiritualité: l'esprit du corps dans les cosmologies autochtones du Québec." In *Les Autochtones et le Québec: Des Premiers contacts au Plan Nord,* edited by Alain Beaulieu, Stéphan Gervais, and Martin Papillon, 213–32. Montreal: Les Presses de l'Université de Montréal.

Laugrand, Frédéric, and Robert Crépeau. 2015. "Shamanisms, Religious Networks and Empowerment in Indigenous Societies of the Americas." *Anthropologica* 57 (2): 289–98. https://www.jstor.org/stable/26350441

Laugrand, Frédéric, and Denys Delâge. 2008. "Introduction. Traditions et transformations religieuses chez les Amérindiens et les Inuit du Canada." *Recherches Amérindiennes au Québec* 38 (2–3): 3–12. https://doi.org/10.7202/039789ar

Laugrand, Frédéric, and Jarich Oosten. 2010. *Inuit Shamanism and Christianity: Transitions and Transformations in the Twentieth Century*. Montreal: McGill-Queens University Press.

Lear, Jonathan. 2006. *Radical Hope: Ethics in the Face of Cultural Devastation*. Cambridge: Cambridge University Press.

LiPuma, Edward. 1998. "Modernity and Forms of Personhood in Melanesia." In *Bodies and Persons: Comparative Perspectives from Africa and Melanesia*, edited by Michael Lambek and Andrew Strathern, 53–79. Cambridge: Cambridge University Press.

Loft, Steven. 2014. "Introduction: Decolonizing the 'Web'." In *Coded Territories: Tracing Indigenous Pathways in New Media Art*, edited by Steven Loft and Kerry Swanson, xv–xvii. Calgary: University of Calgary Press.

Macdonald, Gaynor. 2008. "Difference or Disappearance: The Politics of Indigenous Inclusion in the Liberal State." *Anthropologica* 50 (2): 341–58. https://www.jstor.org/stable/25605426

Mauss, Marcel. 1938. "Une catégorie de l'esprit humain: la notion de personne celle de 'moi'." *Journal of the Royal Anthropological Institute of Great Britain and Ireland*, 68 (July–December): 263–81. https://doi.org/10.2307/2844128

Merlan, Francesca. 2009. "Indigeneity: Global and Local." *Current Anthropology* 50 (3): 303–33. https://doi.org/10.1086/597667

Morphy, Howard, and Frances Morphy. 2013. "Anthropological Theory and Government Policy in Australia's Northern Territory: The Hegemony of the 'Mainstream'." *American Anthropologist* 115 (2): 174–87. https://doi.org/10.1111/aman.12002

Mosko, Mark S. 2010. "Partible Penitents: Dividual Personhood and Christian Practice in Melanesia and the West." *Journal of the Royal Anthropological Institute* 16: 215–40. https://doi.org/10.1111/j.1467-9655.2010.01618.x

——. 2017. *Ways of Baloma: Rethinking Magic and Kinship from the Trobriands*. Chicago: Hau Books.

Myers, Fred. 1986. *Pintupi Country, Pintupi Self: Sentiment, Place, and Politics among Western Desert Aborigines*. Washington: Smithsonian Institution Press.

Niezen, Ronald. 2000. *Spirit Wars: Native North American Religions in the Age of Nation Building*. Berkeley: University of California Press.

Pasternak, Shiri. 2017. *Grounded Authority: The Algonquins of Barriere Lake against the State*. Minneapolis: University of Minnesota Press.

Poirier, Sylvie. 2004. "La (dé)politisation de la culture." *Anthropologie et sociétés* 28 (1): 7–21. https://doi.org/10.7202/008568ar

———. 2008. "Reflections on Indigenous Cosmopolitics—Poetics." *Anthropologica* 50 (1): 75–85. https://www.jstor.org/stable/25605390

———. 2013. "The Dynamic Reproduction of Hunter-Gatherers' Ontologies and Values." In *A Companion to the Anthropology of Religion*, edited by Janice Boddy and Michael Lambek, 50–68. Oxford: Wiley Blackwell.

———. 2016a. "Cosmologies." In *Anthropen.org*. Paris: Éditions des archives contemporaines. https://doi.org/ 10.17184/eac.anthropen.032

———. 2016b. "Ontologies." In *Anthropen.org*. Paris: Éditions des archives contemporaines. https://doi.org/10.17184/eac.anthropen.035

Povinelli, Elizabeth. 1993. *Labor's Lot: The Power, History and Culture of Aboriginal Action*. Chicago: University of Chicago Press.

Robbins, Joel. 2004. "The Globalization of Pentecostal and Charismatic Christianity." *Annual Review of Anthropology* 33 (1): 117–43. https://doi.org/10.1146/annurev. anthro.32.061002.093421

———. 2007. "Continuity Thinking and the Problem of Christian Culture: Belief, Time, and the Anthropology of Christianity." *Current Anthropology* 48 (1): 5–38. https://doi.org/10.1086/508690

———. 2010. "Melanesia, Christianity and Cultural Change: A Comment on Mosko's 'Partible penitents'." *Journal of the Royal Anthropological Institute* 16 (2): 241–43. https://doi.org/10.1111/j.1467-9655.2010.01619.x

Sahlins, Marshall. 1985. *Islands of History*. Chicago: University of Chicago Press.

———. 1993. "Goodbye to Tristes Tropes: Ethnography in the Context of Modern World History." *The Journal of Modern History* 65 (1): 1–25. https://doi. org/10.1086/244606

———. 1995. *How "Natives" Think About Captain Cook, for Example*. Chicago: University of Chicago Press.

———. 2005. "On the Anthropology of Modernity; or, Some Triumphs of Culture over Despondency Theory." In *Culture and Sustainable Development in the Pacific*, edited by Hooper Antony, 44–61. Canberra: ANU E Press; Canberra: Asia Pacific Press.

Schwarz, Carolyn, and Françoise Dussart. 2010. "Christianity in Aboriginal Australia Revisited." *The Australian Journal of Anthropology* 21 (1): 1–13. https://doi. org/10.1111/j.1757-6547.2010.00064.x

Scott, Colin. 2017. "The Endurance of Relational Ontology: Encounters Between Eeyouch and Sport Hunters." In *Entangled Territorialities: Negotiating Indigenous Lands in Australia and Canada*, edited by Françoise Dussart and Sylvie Poirier, 51–69. Toronto: University of Toronto Press.

Simpson, Leanne Betasamosake, ed. 2008. *Lighting the Eight Fire: The Liberation, Resurgence, and Protection of Indigenous Nations*. Winnipeg: ARP Books.

Starblanket, Gina, and Heidi Kiiwetinepinesiik Stark. 2018. "Towards a Relational Paradigm—Four Points for Consideration: Knowledge, Gender, Land, and Modernity." In *Resurgence and Reconciliation: Indigenous-Settler Relations and Earth Teachings*, edited by Michael Asch, John Borrows, and James Tully, 175–207. Toronto: University of Toronto Press.

Stengers, Isabelle. 2003. *Cosmopolitiques II*. Paris: La Découverte.

Strathern, Marilyn. 1988. *The Gender of the Gift*. Berkeley: University of California Press.

——. 1992. *Reproducing the Future: Anthropology, Kinship, and the New Reproductive Technologies*. New York: Routledge.

Taussig, Michael. 1983. *Devil and Commodity Fetishism in South America*. Chapel Hill: University of North Carolina Press.

Tsing, Anna. 2008. "The Global Situation." *Cultural Anthropology* 15 (3): 327–60. https://doi.org/10.1525/can.2000.15.3.327

——. 2005. *Friction: An Ethnography of Global Connection*. Princeton: Princeton University Press.

Vilaça, Aparecida. 2015. Dividualism and Individualism in Indigenous Christianity: A Debate Seen from Amazonia. *HAU: Journal of Ethnographic Theory* 5 (1): 197–225. https://doi.org/10.14318/hau5.1.010

Viveiros de Castro, Eduardo. 2009. *Métaphysiques cannibales*. Paris: Presses universitaires de France.

Wagner, Roy. 1975. *The Invention of Culture*. Chicago: University of Chicago Press.

Whitehouse, Harvey. 2000. *Arguments and Icons: Divergent Modes of Religiosity*. Oxford: Oxford University Press.

2

EMBRACING CHRISTIANITY, REJECTING WESTERN INDIVIDUALISM?

Inuit Leaders and the Limits of Indigenization

FRÉDÉRIC LAUGRAND

Introduction

The eastern Canadian Arctic has been of particular interest to many scholars who wish to learn more about the conversion of Inuit people to Christianity in the twentieth century (Remie 1983; Trott 1997, 1998; Laugrand 2002; Remie and Oosten 2002; Laugrand and Oosten 2010, 2019). Their primary areas of interest have been the missionary mindset and how Christianity became indigenized. Nonetheless, they have seldom discussed why so many Inuit people were ordained as Anglican ministers and so few as Catholic priests. A secondary area of interest has been the active role of women in the evangelization process (see Laugrand and Oosten 2015), on par with that of men. Although some women were ordained as Anglican ministers, only one became a Grey Nun: Sister Pelagie. Atuat's testimony (Cowan and Innuksuk 1976, 21) shows that Christianity appealed to Inuit women by freeing them from many traditional *pittailiniit* (ritual restrictions). They were numerous among early converts, but in most areas, men received the leading roles as preachers and evangelists and from the outset were recruited as such by the Anglican missionaries. Women also had trouble pursuing a religious vocation because of the sexual division of labour: they had to take care of the children and were far less exposed to outsiders.

Today, the situation is striking. Despite the incorporation of Christianity by the Inuit, no Inuk has ever held a lifelong clerical position in the Catholic Church. Only in the Anglican Church, where marriage is accepted, do many Inuit men and some women enter the ministry and remain active in spreading the gospel their entire lives. Such a contrast raises a big question: To what extent has marriage and the family life it creates been an obstacle to an Inuk entering a religious order and playing a leading role in the Catholic Church? Of course, the rejection of celibacy is not the only factor. On the side of the missionaries, a paternalistic ideology certainly played a role by restricting Inuit initiatives.[1] On the Inuit side, cosmological reasons also explain the very limited interest priesthood generated among the first generations of Christians. Like in other Indigenous societies, as Dussart and Poirier (this volume) recall, the indigenization of Christianity followed pragmatic lines, and conversion was a fragmented and erratic process.

Yet celibacy was soon depicted as an issue. By the 1970s, this obstacle had become serious enough for Catholics to introduce a new leadership model: Inuit catechists could now continue as lay people and marry. Alas, it came too late and created other problems beyond the scope of this paper. Clerical celibacy has often sparked debate among the Inuit and some Catholic missionaries such as Father Lechat (OMI). Louis Tapardjuk (2014, 46), a Catholic and former Igloolik mayor who conducted extensive research with elders, recently explained again the underlying problem:

> Inuit are not in the habit of being alone. It's not their custom to not have a family. Family comes first. You need a wife to look after your needs, such as your kamiit [boots] and everything else. Often Anglican ministers had families, but Roman Catholic priests never. There was no way an Inuk would become a priest unless the Vatican changed its rules and allowed priests to get married.

Tapardjuk is right. In Inuit societies as in other Native societies, being-in-the-world is relational. A person is in continuous relationship with his family, his community, with other human beings and nonhuman beings (Dussart and Poirier, this volume, quoting Blaser et al. 2010). In this chapter, I will argue that Christianity has always been redefined by the groups it spreads into and that certain groups may reject some Christian values as soon as they "break" their social life. Despite their conversion and their general acceptance of the new collective and personal standards of behaviour, Inuit people still reject some Christian values, including one that has always been key to Christianity: extreme individualism. In other words, Inuit people have easily adopted Christian values, but no Inuk has ever felt comfortable with the prospect of entering a Catholic religious order because none has ever been prepared to renounce family life. Similarly, no Inuk is comfortable with *qallunaat* (White people) conceptions of leadership. Like in Brazil (this volume: Crépeau; Tassinari), ancestrality and kinship are sources of power, knowledge, and guidance.

I will first discuss the success of the Anglican Church in training and keeping Inuit ministers, especially when compared to the record of the Catholic Church. I will then present the cases of two men who gave up the priesthood: Anthony Manernaluk and Nick Sikkuaq, brothers who both became Catholic Brothers. They and Sister Pelagie, the only Inuk woman to become a Grey Nun, were the only Inuit individuals to enter a religious order.[2] I conclude that the spread of Catholicism ran into a recurrent, formidable obstacle: the Inuit could easily embrace Christian rituals and cosmology but not celibacy and the idea of living without a family of one's own.

Inuit Lay Ministers and Inuit Reverends

One of the first Anglican missionaries to Inuit communities was Reverend E.J. Peck. In 1876, the Church Missionary Society sent him to Little Whale River on Hudson Bay where he did his best to implement the "Native Church Policy" by recruiting some community leaders and former shamans as Christian pastors. His "Inuit apostles," as he called them, included John Melucto and his son, Moses. Both men helped him learn Inuktitut, translate the scriptures, and spread the gospel. In his notes, Peck referred to John Melucto as "one of the most saintly men I have ever met" (Peck quoted in Laugrand and Oosten 2018, 333). The Anglican archival records say little about the daily lives of these early Indigenous ministers, but Peck noted that they had children and were attached to their families, thereby successfully combining their lay and religious vocations.

In 1894, Reverend Peck founded the first mission post at Uumanarjuaq on Baffin Island and continued to hire Inuit men as ministers. Two famous ones were Peter Tulugarjuaq and Luke Kidlaapik. In an entry in his journal dated November 23, 1903, Peck stated he invited Tulugarjuaq to become the very first Indigenous Christian teacher on Baffin Island. "I spoke to him of the necessity of confessing Christ in every possible way and invited him out of love to Jesus, to become a teacher. To this proposal he readily consented" (quoted in Laugrand, Oosten, and Trudel 2006, 193).[3]

Peter Tulugarjuaq's transition to Christianity may have triggered a series of conversions in Cumberland Sound, especially at Uumanarjuaq. We do not know whether Tulugarjuaq had previously been an *angakkuq* (a shaman). In his journals, Peck avoids any references to shamanism. Nonetheless, Tulugarjuaq was described as a man of power and ability by German explorer B. Hantzsch (1977, 22–30). "One of the most experienced men in those parts..., one of the most intelligent persons of the region." Even if Peck had known about Tulugarjuaq's past as an *angakkuq*, he probably would not have made this detail public. It is likely, then, that shamans played a key role in the conversion process. When the last missionaries left Uumanarjuaq in 1910, the ministry was safely placed in Tulugarjuaq's hands.

In 1911, Rev. Edgar William Tyler Greenshield returned to Uumanarjuaq, and his assessment of the mission was very positive. "On going ashore, I found everything in excellent order, all having been taken care of by Tooloogakjuak."[4] In a letter to Mr. Baring-Gould he stated, "I found the church, house, hospital and store all in perfect order, they having been again taken care of by our Senior Native Teacher, Tulugarjuaq."[5] Tulugarjuaq's life story is interesting. It suggests that

Peck felt free to appoint former shamans as Indigenous leaders and that putting powerful men in such positions helped spread the gospel.

This view is consistent with Inuit oral traditions. Lucaasie Nutaraaluk from Iqaluit, for example, recalled: "My father stopped being an *angakkuq* when he began working for the ministers. It seemed that those who worked for the ministers tended to be leaders" (Oosten, Laugrand, and Rasing 1999, 114).

The 1920s saw Anglicanism spread from South Baffin to North Baffin. During that time, many Inuit people converted by transgressing the old practices and taboos and by performing *siqqitiq* (a conversion ritual). I have shown elsewhere (Laugrand 2002) the degree to which these collective conversions were performed at the initiative of local shamans or leaders, a sign that mission work had become highly indigenized.

The introduction of Christianity also had an influence on Inuit tradition, putting an end to most of the old prohibitions and marking a transition from old ways to new ways. During the *siqqitiq* ceremony in North Baffin, for example, a meeting would be held, and everyone would divide up and eat the heart of an animal, usually a fresh seal. Such eating—previously forbidden, especially for women—thus ritualized the transition.

In the 1940s and 1950s more than a dozen Inuit people were ordained as ministers of the Anglican Church, and none as Catholic priests. One famous Anglican minister was Noah Nasook of North Baffin. He was a well-known religious figure and also an excellent hunter. In 1994, I met his wife Martha Nasook, by that time a widow. She described her husband as a strong Anglican, and was very helpful in explaining how Christianity had spread in the camps. By 1972, the Anglican Church had firmly established itself in North Baffin, creating the Arthur Turner Training School in Pangnirtuuq, where many Inuit people would receive some religious education.

In those days, there were already many Inuit ministers. According to the Anglican Church, the very first Inuit reverend was Armand Tagoona, originally from Naujaat (Repulse Bay). Ordained in 1972, he served many years before returning to Baker Lake, where he opened his own church, the Arctic Christian Fellowship. He raised a family, yet his wife would never join his church, preferring to remain a practising Anglican (Laugrand and Laneuville 2019).

Today, Nunavut has many well-known Inuit Anglican ministers: Jonas Allooloo, Joe Manik, Bobby Patsauq, Eliyah Keenainak, Timothy Kalai, Daniel Aupalu, Moses Killiraq, Iola Metuq, Bobby and Lucassie Nakoolak, Ikey Nashooraituk, Eyetsiak Simigak, Joedee Joedee, Tommy Evic, Caleb Sangoya, Jacobie Iqalukjuak, Loasie Kunilusee, and Peter Ainalik. Some women have also been ordained, such as Jean Simailak in the Kivalliq Region and Leah Qaqqasiq and Loie Mike in South Baffin.

Many Inuit people have been ordained in Nunavik, as well. In Kangirsuk, for example, Inuit ministers have been running the local church since 1972, as shown by the following ministries:

Rev. Isa Koperqualuk, 1972 to 1976
Rev. James Nashak, 1980 to 1982
Rev. Timothy Kalai, 1985 to 1991
Rev. Bobby Nakoolak, 1991 to 1993
Rev. Eyetsiak Simigak, 1995 to 1997
Rev. Iola Metuq, 2000 to 2004

Three Inuit men have even become Anglican bishops: Paul Idlout, the first Inuk to be elected to the episcopacy in the Anglican Church of Canada; Andrew Atagotaaluk, who became the first Inuit Anglican diocesan bishop of the Arctic in 2002; and Benjamin Arreak. The life stories of Idlout and Atagotaaluk in particular show how embedded their religious vocation has been in their family lives.

Bishop Paul Idlout, who retired in 2004 at the age of 69, is presented by his church as a hunter, a translator, and a special constable of the RCMP:

Bishop Idlout was born in 1935, in an era when most Inuit people followed a nomadic lifestyle...

For his first 18 years, he lived on the land with his family and never saw the inside of a school. "I was born near Pond Inlet. In my

early life, I learned the skills of hunting, surviving," he said. He met
his wife, Abigail, in the 1950s. She had gone to school in the south
and coached him in English and writing while he took high school
correspondence courses.

He worked for the Royal Canadian Mounted Police as a trans-
lator and special constable and achieved a measure of anonymous
fame when a 1967 photograph of a group of Inuit individuals
leaving on a hunting trip was used for the engraving on the back of
the Canadian $2 bill.

In 1986, he entered the Arthur Turner Training School to study
for the ministry and was ordained in 1990. He was elected suffragan
(assistant) bishop of the diocese of the Arctic in 1996...

Bishop Idlout and his wife will continue to live in Iqaluit. They
have two daughters and three sons. ("Toronto Archbishop" 2004,
paras. 8–12)

Idlout's case shows how intertwined his religious life was with his
social life and hunting life. For him, these activities could not be separated from each other. As with many Inuit people, Idlout maintained
mutual relationships by hunting and sharing meat, such exchanges
being key to a functioning society. By going out on the land, he kept his
cosmological connections to the deceased and the nonhuman beings
surrounding them.

Attagotaaluk's story, too, shows these kinds of deep connections.
A graduate of the Arthur Turner Training School in Pangnirtuuq,
Attagotaaluk began his first ministry in 1975, when he became the deacon
at St. Jude's Cathedral in Iqaluit. Becoming the assistant minister in
1976 and then the minister in 1977, he was sent to different Anglican
mission posts, including Inukjuak and Pond Inlet. His official
biographical note provides more details:

As well as being a fisher of men and women, he was previously
involved with the federal Department of Fisheries as a guide and
assistant in the beluga survey and polar bear tagging in 1994. A
graduate of the Fisheries Guardian Training course, he also trained

to become a marine surveyor with Transport Canada, where he
later became a ship surveyor in 1998. He was co-ordinator of the
Kativik School Board in 1995, and behavioural facilitator in 1996.
He and his wife, Mary, have six children. ("Bishops Eligible"
2004, under "Andrew Philip Atagotaaluk")

Like Idlout, Attagotaaluk was concurrently a Christian leader, a hunter, a fisherman, an educator, and a father. In the Anglican Church, many Inuit people thus acted as religious leaders without having to change their social lives. They were given high-level responsibilities while remaining involved in their communities and their families as hunters and providers. All of them were parents and as such remained ordinary people.

In the late 1930s, the Roman Catholic missionaries led more and more Inuit people toward religious vocations, hoping not only to show their success but also to inaugurate a new era that would see Catholicism triumph over shamanism and Protestantism, which they considered forms of paganism.[6] The success was short-lived. Inuit people abandoned their shamans and became Christians, but they did not become priests. In the early days, the Oblate missionaries were even considered to be shamans themselves. Their Indigenous helpers were often former shamans, such as Joseph Tuni in Chesterfield Inlet; camp leaders, such as John Ajaruaq; or ordinary hunters. Yet none of these men ever asked to enter a religious order. In fact, not until the early 1960s did the Oblates decide to recruit candidates for the priesthood. Two men, Anthony Manernaluk and Nick Sikkuaq, showed sustained interested in this goal but, as we will see below, their religious careers were brief.[7]

Anthony Manernaluk

Manernaluk was born on April 4, 1937, in the Perry River area and baptized in 1948 by Father Buliard. He was given the name Antoine or Anthony. The family had converted to Catholicism in the late 1940s at the small post of Our Lady of T.S. Rosaire in Garry Lake. The baptism took place in the camp of Kuksut, an *angakkuq* who later opposed

Father Buliard. When Manernaluk's parents died, Father P. Henry, another Oblate missionary, soon adopted him and his brother Nick Sikkuaq, taking the two of them to live in Gjoa Haven on King William Island.

According to the archives, Manernaluk "gave himself" to Father Buliard on May 9, 1953, when he agreed to be the missionary's guide. Father Buliard, who spent about four years with him, reported:

> *With Anthony, my life has changed a bit. It is as if I had a brother with me, and gradually I have asked him to help me, not only for material things but also with respect to human souls...Obviously, I have to feed him, to give him clothing, to provide him with boots, but through his work, he is able as much as any man (except for strength and endurance) to hunt, to fish, to make fishnets, and to help me. So he compensates very well. And in winter, when he will guide me, as he knows very well how to build an igloo and take care of a dog team, we will be able to visit the neighbouring camps and stay there as long as we wish, as no family will be expecting us.[8] (my translation)*

Manernaluk gave Father Buliard a lot of satisfaction. "I consider his presence and his companionship like God's grace. He helps me extensively, and he is very resourceful. He is a truly valuable companion, and I have had nothing to hold against him up to now. He learns very well...He will be my only guide."[9] Father Buliard could indeed use some help. He had poor eyesight and had lost much of his dexterity after an accident in 1939 when he fell through the ice near Naujaat and froze his hands. Unfortunately, in the summer of 1956, Manernaluk became seriously ill and was sent to Churchill, where he was diagnosed with tuberculosis.

According to the archives, Manernaluk stayed at Brandon Sanatorium (Manitoba) from July 10, 1956, to August 30, 1957, during which period Father Buliard had to manage without him. Another young boy, Anthime Simigak, replaced Manernaluk. Then, on October 24, 1956, tragedy struck: Father Buliard disappeared in a blizzard and never came back to his mission.[10] When the Inuit community at Garry Lake heard about Buliard's death they were sad. Pelly (2016, 229) reports Manernaluk's reaction: "When I heard of Father Buliard being lost, I felt I lost a parent" (see also Choque 1985). Manernaluk probably decided to become a priest after Father Buliard's death, while in the hospital.[11]

In March 1958, just after his confirmation, Manernaluk was brought to Gjoa Haven by Bishop Lacroix so he could start his postulancy with Father P. Henry. Some newspapers, including the *Indian Record*, announced this first stage of his religious vocation. Father Henry noted:

> *The time Anthony spent with me should count as his postulate period. He gave entire satisfaction. I think he would be a beautiful addition to the Congregation and to the conversion of his people. He is zealous, but in a bright way, full of patience, of renunciation and humility. If he continues on this track, he will be a priceless companion for any Father, among the Inuit or even elsewhere.[12]*

On September 2, 1958, Manernaluk left Gjoa Haven for the Oblate Noviciate of St. Norbert, Manitoba, where he arrived on September 6, 1958. There he took the habit and became a Brother on December 7, 1958. He took his vows on December 8, 1959. In 1960, he finally received his first obedience for Gjoa Haven with Father P. Henry, Father P. Goussaert, and Father Jérôme Vermeersch. His second vows were taken in Gjoa Haven on December 8, 1960, and his third vows again in Gjoa Haven on December 8, 1961. In the meantime, he had been hired by Father Van de Velde in Pelly Bay where, besides doing manual work, he taught some Inuktitut lessons to Father Jean-Guy Roberge, a new recruit. In late 1961, Manernaluk received his second obedience for Baker Lake with Father Charles Choque as his superior. The Oblates and the Catholic community were quite proud, and between 1960 and 1962 the Oblate press celebrated his progress together with that of his brother Nick Sikkuaq, providing many details about their lives. Manernaluk even appeared on television in Winnipeg, being interviewed with Father Rio and a journalist.[13] At that time Manernaluk was fluent in both English and French and had been successful in his studies. He was also asked to help out by doing some manual and technical work and was thus assigned to such duties as the building of a granary, a garage, and a retirement home.[14]

The journal *L'Apostolat* ran a few excerpts from his letters,which illustrate how much Christianity meant to this Inuk who had adopted the language of the Oblate Fathers. He wrote particularly to Father Thibert, who was providing him with translations of the Roman Missal. Here are a few excerpts written a few years after Father Buliard's death, the first one dated January 1958:[15]

> *I am sending you a small page titled, "Let us pray to God, our Father, for we lack everything." If you think it is appropriate, I believe that it may be useful to my fellow countrymen. My own reflections have induced me to write it, for there is great misery among the Eskimos.*
>
> *Let us pray to receive the life of our soul and our body from the Good Lord. Our Father who is in heaven; You are the Almighty Creator; It is You who has made everything, everywhere on earth: all animals and all people are yours.*
>
> *I want to devote myself completely to You: take me with everything I have. I wish to accomplish your will even if sometimes it seems not to please me, like illness and misery. First I wish to say to You: May Thy Holy Will be done.*

The second excerpt is about the texts Manernaluk was reading and his activities in Baker Lake. The date is March 1958:

> *Thank you for the writings in Eskimo of St. Therese of the Child Jesus, which I have received from you. That life has given me much joy. Just reading that makes us wish to be better.*

The third excerpt is dated May 1958. Manernaluk gives some details about his own religious vocation. He was indeed encouraged to become a priest by his friend, Father Buliard, who told him he could either become a priest or get married and have children. The two options could not be combined.

> *Once the Father whom I accompanied on his voyage, Father Buliard, told me: "Your future is in your own hands; if you wish to become an Oblate Brother, you can do it; on the other side, if you wish to start a family, feel free."*
>
> *Now I have decided to give my life to Jesus: may all my work be for him and for the missionaries who in turn devote their whole life to the Eskimos. I am ready to renounce starting a family or to possess anything personally.*
>
> *In that way I will be free to become a Coadjutor Brother. My greatest wish is to do everything in obedience for the rest of my life.*

The next two excerpts, dated September 1958 and March 1959 respectively, suggest that Manernaluk felt happy with his new life in a new world.

> *It was September 6 when I arrived at the Noviciate of St. Norbert. Since then I have been at work harvesting the potatoes, taking care of the chickens, and assisting at various jobs. Prayer and rosary every day and I am very happy.*

> *Happy Easter, Father! So we are happy! How sad we were this holy week. Good Friday we kept silent all day. Now we can talk and eat meat. We have often meditated on the death of Our Lord and on his cross, and now his resurrection proves his love for us.*

Manernaluk seemed to adapt quite well to his new life at the Noviciate of St. Norbert. Like many Inuit people, he was fascinated by the lives of the Saints. This may be connected to the Catholic tradition of giving converts the names of Saints, a practice that evokes the Inuit tradition of naming newborn children after deceased relatives (Laugrand and Oosten 2010, 126–31). In July and December 1959, he wrote:

I am happy at the Noviciate of St. Norbert; sometimes it is very hot. When working all day I get all sweaty and it gives me a cold. But at the moment I am well and happy...

My sister Alice is still ill. Let us pray that she does not lose courage. She has been ill for ten years, and now she just manages to get by. If she dies, she can go to heaven, but she must use her reason and accept her trial.

In 1960, Manernaluk sent the text of his vows to Father Thibert, who published it in syllabics in an issue of the journal *La Liberté et le patriote* dated February 5, 1960. I found a transcription of this text in roman script with a French translation by Father Thibert in the Archives Deschâtelets:

In the name of Our Lord Jesus Christ...here I, Anthony Manernaluk, vow to God: I renounce having any possessions (poverty); I will not have a wife and I will avoid any fault of the flesh (chastity); I will absolutely obey my superior for a year. Also before God I swear and vow to persevere for a year in the Congregation named: Oblates of Mary Immaculate, who was conceived without original sin. So help me God. So be it.[16]

In 1962, Manernaluk was about to go back north. He was supposed to take his third vows on December 8, 1962, but he suddenly renounced his religious vocation and informed Father Daniélo of his decision.

The Archives Deschâtelets preserve various letters about this about-face. Father Daniélo explained that he had first told him not to worry too much—Manernaluk could remain a Brother and postpone becoming a priest. Clearly, that was not what Manernaluk had in mind. Daniélo reported:

It was yesterday morning. He came to me and asked me to write to you about it; he confessed to me his real thoughts about it. All can be summarized in the following way: "Taqanarmat," it is tiring, I am tired (I translate and interpret "tired of religious life"). I did not ask him directly if, in fact, it is because he wanted to marry that he was now willing to retire from the priesthood. The brothers, who knew him here, three years ago, had found during the summer that he looked less happy than before. And he himself confesses that he thought about quitting the order for about a year or a year and a half, but that he never shared this feeling with anybody.[17]

There is no point in speculating on Manernaluk's decision. In one of his last letters to Father Thibert, Manernaluk likewise stated he was too busy with hunting and everything else and thus very tired. In any case, Father Daniélo clearly did his best to convince him to remain in the order:

In my answer to the priest, I think I only showed him my friendship. First, I told him how much his decision was causing me much suffering; that we, and all of us, had only a good opinion of him so far; that I personally believed so much in the reality of his vocation...In my opinion, but I might be wrong, it is a temptation...I told him that he was the best judge...I asked why he did not mention it before...No clear answer on this. And I asked, "But if you leave, where will you go?" He answered "I don't know"...Finally I told him, "It is the anniversary of Father Joseph Buliard's loss, a Father with whom you have experienced and shared hardship in Garry Lake. Think about the advice that, according to you, he would give you if he were I. And let's pray a novena, to obtain the light we need."[18]

Father Daniélo explained that he spent more than two hours trying to convince Manernaluk. He even consulted Father Beauregard, who told him that Manernaluk had been so perfect in his novitiate that he was probably the best novice he ever had. All these efforts were in vain. Manernaluk brought his letter with his final decision to Father Daniélo, who immediately forwarded it to Father Haramburu, confirming that the Brother was suffering from tiredness and migraines and had not transgressed his vow of chastity.[19]

The Archives Deschâtelets say nothing more about what happened afterwards or about why Manernaluk had really decided to abandon his religious vocation. In his biography of Father Henry, Choque (1985, 205) wondered: "Why, what were the deep-rooted causes of this painful departure? Father Henry blames the profound chasm separating White and Inuit mentalities, different eating habits, customs and climate; the language barrier creating difficulties in communication, discouragement, and in Anthony's case illness."

In a letter to Father Daniélo dated November 6, 1962, Father Haramburu blamed Manernaluk's lack of openness:

He himself confesses that he has been thinking about all this for more than a year, and the reasons he gives show his sensitivity but they are not serious. If only he had shared his thoughts; it would not have been difficult to help him discard them, but I fear that the time spent has now developed in him a stubborn obsession that reason cannot overcome. We face here a major difficulty of primitive temperaments: lack of openness through lack of self-knowledge and expression. [20]

In a letter to Father Daniélo dated November 16, 1962, Father Haramburu accepted that Manernaluk's religious vocation had ended. [21]

Manernaluk emphasized his feelings of tiredness, and when we consider Father Henry's thoughts, as reported by Choque (1985), it seems likely that he felt exhausted trying to live on his own in a *qallunaat* (White) community. He realized he could not go on and opted for a return to Inuit family life. When Jarich Oosten and I met him in Rankin Inlet in 2006, he was earning a living from his art—making knives, ulus, drums, and carvings. He had done underground drilling in the Thompson nickel mine and was involved in some oral tradition research with journalist David Pelly. [22] He preferred not to discuss his past experiences with the Oblates.

Nick Sikkuaq

Born in Gjoa Haven, Nick Sikkuaq (also known as Sikkuark and Sitkoa) was baptized like his brother Manernaluk on April 4, 1948. He was confirmed on April 17, 1960, and soon after decided to become a Brother. In a letter sent from Gjoa Haven dated March 16, 1961, Sikkuaq wrote:

> *Dear Father,*
> *I want to be a Brother Oblate of Mary Immaculate. I want to give*
> *all my life to Jesus. If you accept me I will be very happy. I am the*
> *youngest brother of Brother Anthony. You have seen me many times*
> *at Gjoa-Haven. Please Father, write me and tell me what to do. I am*
> *18 years old now but I do not want to marry. I want to save my soul*
> *and help the others to save theirs. I cannot write longer.*
> *Bless me, Father*
> *Nicolas Sitkoa*[23]

On April 11, 1961, Father Cochard reported that the candidate was to be admitted.[24] In another letter sent the same day to Father Beauregard, Father Cochard stressed the candidate's great qualities, stating that his thinking was well balanced and that he was thorough, intellectually and morally solid, and well instructed in religion, especially on the Eucharist and penance.[25]

On April 24, 1961, Father Henry wrote to Father Beauregard to recommend this exceptional candidate.[26] On the basis of such strong support, Bishop Lacroix accepted Sikkuaq's entry into the Noviciate.[27] Sikkuaq started his postulancy with Father Henry from Gjoa Haven. On May 7, 1961, he arrived in St. Norbert, Manitoba, and received the religious habit from Father Henry on May 21, 1961 (Choque 1985, 222). Sikkuaq took his first vows on May 21, 1962, in the presence of his brother Anthony Manernaluk.[28] In 1962, the Oblates had already recruited Sister Pelagie and were quite proud and excited to present their two candidates. Father Gérald Labossière published an article in *La Vie Indienne* (September 1962) titled "Doublement frères" (Brothers twice over), introducing the two brothers and their project to become priests.[29] In June 1962, an article in the newspaper *La Liberté et le patriote* (June 8, 1962) announced: "A second Canadian Eskimo delivered his vows in St. Norbert." The author evoked "a religious aurora borealis" and linked these first recruits to the progress in Greenland (with Father Fynn Lynge) and Alaska (where some catechists had been appointed by the Jesuits). As Labossière notes in "Doublement frères":

Although the Eskimo people were at the beginning very reluctant in adopting Christianity—the first missionary Bishop Turquetil waited about seven years before making a single conversion—they now give a great hope, and once converted entirely they could certainly become a real asset for the Church, especially since the Eskimo are a rough, brave, joyous, and open people. In addition to the two Oblate Brothers, there is a nun, Sister Pelagie, belonging to the Grey Nuns. Greenland, despite the short history of Catholicism there, has also given a religious person, half-White, half-Eskimo. In Alaska, we have created a special community for the Eskimos and there are 6 of them at the moment. This first blooming is a great comfort for the missionaries of the polar world, a so ungrateful place, and the sign that more will come.[30]

A questionnaire by Father Pierre de Moissac in the Archives Deschâtelets provides not only a better grasp of the Oblate perception of Sikkuaq's personality but also of the way the Oblates worked with him. The final overall assessment concludes on a positive note: "The general impression is very good. We really have no complaints about him. He has made great progress in all respects [and] despite the difficulties of communication I recommend him to your benevolence."[31]

In March 1964, the Holy Rosary Scholasticate provided another assessment of Sikkuaq just before he took his third vows on May 21, 1964:

He is charitable and willing to help others. He is faithful in asking for permissions and obedient to the directions he is given. He is very regular in attendance at the religious exercises of the community. His spirit of faith appears to be sound. His spiritual life in general,

from what is observable appears quite satisfactory. He is a very fine
worker and devoted to his work. He is making progress in learning
the English language. Brother Sikkuark gives away every appear-
ance of being a very obliging, regular and good religious. From what
we have been able to observe during a period of six months, he pres-
ents no problem regarding his advancement to the third temporary
vows.[32]

Another report, however, dated April 4 or May 21, 1965 (both dates
appear on the document), refers to a language problem:

Communication on the spiritual level with Brother Nicholas is prac-
tically impossible because of his limited knowledge of English and of
our complete ignorance of Eskimo. The direction and decision on his
interior spiritual life is in the hands of those Oblate Fathers who can
communicate with him in Eskimo.[33]

The rest of the report was very positive, though also referring to a
health problem: Sikkuaq tired easily.[34]

With this endorsement by the Oblate Provincial Council, Brother
Sikkuaq expressed his willingness to persevere in his religious life,
and the Provincial Council unanimously voted for his admission to the
third temporary vows on May 21, 1965.

However, just before this, on May 19, 1964, Sikkuaq was sent to
the Ottawa General Hospital. A letter from Father McGrath to the
Winnipeg General Hospital on May 20, 1964, suggested that Sikkuaq
was suffering from serious health problems.

After that we lose track of him. We know that he quit the order and
returned to the North, where he would specialize in the arts of carving,
painting, and drawing until his death in 2013. In their assessment, the
Oblates noted his great artistic abilities and creativity. By 1973, at the
request of the Keewatin Region Education Office and the Department
of Education of the Northwest Territories, Sikkuaq had already published
four books with fascinating drawings and stories: *Faces, What Animals*
Think, Nick Sikkuark's Book of Things You Will Never See, and *More*

Stories. These books ably express his desire to share his traditional spiritual knowledge. Later, he made impressive drawings of *qupirruit*, small beings that have strong shamanic connotations. Many of them appear in a book edited by Kardosh (2003) in which Sikkuaq depicted shamans fighting for food, against spirits, or against each other. Sikkuaq often depicted a worm-shaped creature, which already appears in his early drawings and in those of Kardosh (2003, 84–85).

By the mid-1960s, most of the Oblate recruitment strategies had failed. The experiences of Manernaluk and Sikkuaq show how difficult it was for the Oblates to extract people from their extended families and from the North to train them as religious Brothers. The Oblates realized they faced many obstacles when recruiting Inuit individuals for such a life. In the case of Manernaluk, they suspected celibacy might have been the main one. Manernaluk did marry in due time, but he never raised this issue.

To some extent, Manernaluk's, Sikkuaq's, and Pelagie's experiences have much in common. Sikkuaq and Pelagie had trouble understanding and communicating with their fellow Sisters and Brothers. Moreover, they had opted not only for a life of celibacy but also for orders with their own traditions, styles, and rules, which had nothing to do with Inuit traditions. Perceptions of food and the rules of eating in the orders obviously were a far cry from perceptions of country food and rules of food-sharing in the Inuit community. Father Henry was probably right to emphasize cultural differences: "the profound chasm separating White and Inuit mentalities, different eating habits, customs and climate; the language barrier creating difficulties in communication, discouragement..." (Choque 1985, 205). The formal structure and strict hierarchy contrasted sharply with the rather egalitarian organization of Inuit society. Most of the time, Manernaluk and Sikkuaq were the only Inuit people there, a reality that must have strengthened their feelings of loneliness and isolation. I have shown elsewhere (see Laugrand and Oosten 2014) how much it meant to Pelagie to have another Inuk around—like Kukkik, one of her companions—with whom to have fun, speak Inuktitut, do some mischief, and so on. The rules of behaviour, the ways of expressing one's feelings, and so forth were all rooted in *qallunaat* traditions, and in the long run the cultural differences must have put a strain on the Inuit. Such strain could have easily led to the tiredness and migraines that Manernaluk endured. The Oblates and the Grey Nuns knew they were facing a different mentality in Inuit culture but did not work out a clear strategy to deal with this difference and successfully recruit Inuit people for a religious vocation. Caught in a paternalistic ideology, they couldn't imagine the Inuit would manage by themselves and without any guidance. The Arctic was still considered a colony to be developed by *qallunaat*.

Conclusion

Anglican missionaries and Oblate Fathers have strongly impacted Inuit culture. They were successful in converting Inuit people to Christianity, and for a long time they were undisputed authorities in the communities where they had founded their mission posts. Many Inuit people embraced Christianity easily and pragmatically. They were even willing to transgress the shamanic rules by eating the forbidden parts of animals during the *siqqitirniq* rituals (Laugrand 2002). Women were often won over by Christianity because its rules seemed much easier to follow than the many shamanic ritual injunctions. Yet traditions could not be forgotten in a flash, and many social values would remain. Even more importantly, many Inuit people actively resisted certain new values: they never accepted Western individualism, especially in its extreme form of lifelong singlehood. They held strongly to their naming system and with it to the belief that a person has different names, different identities, different positions, and thus connections to many other people, the bottom line being that no one can live without kin. Inuit individuals inherited their strengths and skills from their namesakes, and this practice is still very much alive today. Namesaking provides them with the qualities of their ancestors, enabling them to become stronger and more successful. It also implies social relationships between the dead and the living and supports sharing, which remains key to community survival. The Inuit assume it is impossible to live by and for oneself—that is, to live an atomized life with no web of reciprocal kin obligations. They can therefore become Christians, but only in their own way. As in Brazil (this volume: Crépeau; Tassinari) and in Australia (Vaarzon-Morel, this volume), relationality and caring remain central and Christianity never really managed to erase them.

In their efforts to evangelize Inuit people, Anglicans and Catholics adopted contrasting strategies. Anglicans sought to identify local leaders, former shamans, and camp leaders. They then made them religious leaders within their own communities and allowed them the possibility of having a family. The Oblates, for their part, always felt they had to control the pathways to evangelization. Recruits were extracted from their society and educated in religious institutions in the South. They were not allowed to have a wife or a family, and these prohibitions were too threatening to Inuit relationality, ancestrality, and kinship.

In fact, it wasn't until 1969, a few years after the Second Vatican Council, that the Oblates open a catechist school in Pelly Bay, Nunavut. Created by Bishop Marc Lacroix and initially directed by Father A. Goussaert, the school opened in April and a few families of catechists were registered. These leaders were allowed to marry and have children but were not allowed to perform the Eucharist. Despite this limitation, many couples agreed to enrol. Today, their names are well-known in Nunavut: Walter Porter and his wife, Thomas and Josephina Kubluk, Bartelemi and Sidonie Nirlungayuk, Miriam Aglukka and her husband, Jacki Uyarai and his wife, Charlie Idjuka and his wife, Maurice and Annie Arnatsiaq, Celestin Erkidjuk and his wife, Leonie Qunnut and her husband, and others (Choque 1969; Paradis 1969). The school, however, did not address the issue of clerical celibacy, and no catechist ever decided to become a priest or a nun. In the Canadian Arctic, the Roman Catholic Church, unlike the Anglican Church, is still dependent upon non-Inuit people for its mission activities. Such a contrast seems paradoxical considering that, for a long time, Catholics were more open to Inuit *angakkuuniq* (shamanism) than Anglicans.

Manernaluk's and Sikkuaq's departures from the Catholic Church had nothing to do with lack of faith. The reason had everything to do with a fundamental disruption of social life. They were brothers and were prepared to become Catholic Brothers, thereby expressing their solidarity with and affection for Father Buliard who had converted their families. But they were not willing to do this at any price. One may wonder whether their religious vocation lasted only as long as they felt they could evolve bodily and spiritually, as long as they could retain control over their own lives. This evolution began to go too far when they were sent to the Oblate institutes in the South. Aloneness and the strain of having to function in a *qallunaat* context exhausted them. Their social life had suffered too much disruption, and their fellow nuns and brothers, being non-Inuit, were insufficient compensation. So, they decided to return to their families and communities. Even Sister Pelagie finally came back to her promised husband (Laugrand and Oosten 2014). Clearly, social and cosmological reasons merged and caused them to abandon their vocation, but it did not cause them to abandon their faith, which even later remained very strong.

The Oblates had more success when they began to allow Inuit catechists to marry, thus enabling them to live with their families and remain rooted in the local community while keeping some distance from the *qallunaat*. But these changes came too late and were still in conflict with Inuit models of sociality and leadership. Today, for the Oblates, the issue of bringing Inuit individuals into the Church as leaders remains central and unresolved.

Author's Note

I wish to thank Sylvie Poirier and Françoise Dussart. Their comments helped improve this article. I also express my gratitude to Robert Crépeau and Laurent Jérôme for carrying on the ERCA (Équipe de recherche sur les cosmopolitiques autochtones) project. Thanks also go to the Fonds national de la recherche scientifique (FNRS; F.6002.17) for financial support and to my colleagues at the LAAP (Laboratoire d'anthropologie prospective), Université catholique de Louvain, Belgium.

Notes

1. See, for example, Usher (1971) on this point.
2. I will refer very briefly to Pelagie, as I have discussed her extensively elsewhere (Laugrand and Oosten 2014, 2019). She began her religious vocation in 1946 and, despite leaving the Grey Nuns in the early 1970s, continued to be involved in church activities until she died.

3. ACC, GSA, Edmund James Peck Fonds, M56-1, Peck Journal 1903–1904, 23 November 1903.

4. LAC, An Arctic Diary, Greenshield to his mother and father, 28 August 1911.

5. LAC, G1 C1/0 1991, no. 2, Greenshield to Mr. Baring-Gould, 29 August 1911.

6. Such a strategy was also used in Pelly Bay (Remie and Oosten 2002).

7. In 1964, Father Finn Lynge, an Inuk who had lived in Greenland and Denmark, became the first Inuit Oblate missionary to visit Chesterfield Inlet and Pelly Bay. His religious vocation was similarly short-lived (APN, CPSM, 17–19 August 1964, 280).

8. AD, HH 4230 A62C 120, Frère coadjuteur Oblat esquimau: Le R.F. Anthony Manernaluk, O.M.I.

9. AD, HH 4230 A62C 120, Frère coadjuteur...

10. According to the Archives Deschâtelets, when Manernaluk returned from his convalescence to the Garry Lake mission, Father Ernest Trinel had replaced Buliard after the latter's disappearance. (AD, HH 4865 A62C 29 ex. 1).

11. See AD, HH 4230 A62C 9, Anonymous, "Premières vocations esquimaudes: Anthony Manernaluk," L'Apostolat (February 1960), 18.

12. AD, HH 4230 A62C 120, Frère coadjuteur..., published in The Indian Record no. 21 (April 1958).

13. AD, HH 4230 A62C 120, Frère coadjuteur...

14. AD, HH 4230 A62C 120, Frère coadjuteur...

15. AD, HH 4230 A62C 9, Anonymous, "Premières vocations esquimaudes...," Letters from Manernaluk, 1958–1959. This citation applies to the next six excerpts.

16. AD, HH 4230 A62C 10 ex. 1, originally published in La Liberté et la patriote, vol. 46, no. 43 (5 February 1960).

17. AD, HH 4230 A62C 19, Father E. Daniélo to Father R. Haramburu, 31 October 1962.

18. AD, HH4230 A62C 19, Father E. Daniélo to Father R. Haramburu, 31 October 1962.

19. AD, HH 4230 A62C 15, Father E. Daniélo to Father R. Haramburu, 3 November 1962.

20. AD, HH 4230 A62C 16, Father R. Haramburu to Father E. Daniélo, 6 November 1962.

21. AD, HH 4230 A62C 17, Father R. Haramburu to Father E. Daniélo, 16 November 1962.

22. In 2000, Manernaluk coauthored a text with Nick Sikkuark, Louis Anakanerk, and David Pelly titled "Going home to Kutgajuk" (Pelly et al. 2000).

23. AD, HH 4865 A62 5, letter from Nicolas Sitkoa, 16 March 1961.

24. AD, HH 4865 A62 6, J.M. Cochard to Father A. Lizée, 11 April 1961.

25. AD, HH 4865 A62C 7, Father J.M. Cochard to Father R. Beauregard, 11 April 1961.

26. AD, HH 4865 A62C 9, Father Beauregard to Father Henry, 24 April 1961.

27. AD, HH 4865C A62 8, Mgr Lacroix to Father Beauregard, 15 April 1961.

28. AD, HH 4865C A62C 1 and HH 4865 A62C 1a, Nicholas Sikkuark, 1962.

29. AD, HH 4865C A62C 2, "Doublement frères," Gérald Labossière in *La Vie Indienne* (September 1962).

30. AD, HH 4865C A62C 2, "Doublement frères"...

31. AD, HH 4865 A62C 13, "Frères convers," 10 April 1962.

32. AD, HH 4865 A62C 19 ex. 1, Temporary vows, Missionary Oblates of Mary Immaculate. St. Peter's Province, 30 March 1964.

33. AD, HH 4865 A62CC 20, "Nicholas Sikkuark," 4 April / 21 May 1965.

34. AD, HH 4865 A62C 20, "Nicholas Sikkuark," 4 April / 21 May 1965.

References

Archives

ACC (Anglican Church of Canada)

   GSA (General Synod Archives)

AD (Archives Deschâtelets)

APN (Archives Provinciales de Nicolet)

   CPSM (Chroniques du penionnat Sainte Marie 1955–1968)

LAC (Library and Archives Canada)

Published Works

"Bishops Eligible for Nomination as Primate: Province of Rupert's Land." 2004. *Anglican Journal,* April 1, 2004. https://www.anglicanjournal.com/bishops-eligible-for-nomination-as-primate-province-of-ruperts-land-2200/#sthash.nU5XDyMN.dpuf

Choque, Charles. 1969. "Une école de catéchistes esquimaux." *Eskimo* 79: 12–16.

———. 1985. *Joseph Buliard, pêcheur d'hommes: de la Franche-Comté au Grand Nord canadien (1914–1956)*. Longueil: Le Préambule.

Cowan, Rhoda, and Susan Innuksuk. 1976. *We Don't Live in Snow Houses Now: Reflections of Arctic Bay*. Edmonton: Hurtig Publishers.

Hantzsch, Bernhard. 1977. *My Life With the Eskimos: Baffinland Journeys in the Years 1909 to 1911*. Mawdsley Memoir Series 3. Saskatoon: Saskatoon Institute for Northern Studies.

Kardosh, Robert, ed. 2003. *The Art of Nick Sikkuark: Sculpture and Drawings*. Vancouver: Marion Scott Gallery.

Laugrand, Frédéric. 2002. *Mourir et renaître: la réception du christianisme par les Inuit de l'Arctique de l'Est canadien*. Québec: Presses de l'Université de Laval.

Laugrand, Frédéric, and Pascale Laneuville. 2019. "Armand Tagoona and the Arctic Christian Fellowship: The First Inuit Church in Canada." *Polar Record* 55 (2): 72–81. https://doi.org/10.1017/s0032247419000226

Laugrand, Frédéric, and Jarich Oosten. 2010. *Inuit Shamanism and Christianity: Transitions and Transformations in the Twentieth Century*. Montreal: McGill-Queens University Press.

———. 2014. "The Case of Pelagie Inuk: The Only Inuk Woman to Become a Grey Nun." *Études Inuit Studies* 38 (1–2): 157–76. https://doi.org/10.7202/1028858ar

———. 2015. "Inuit Women in the Process of the Conversion to Christianity in the Canadian Eastern Arctic: 1894–1945." *Polar Record* 51 (5): 513–29. https://doi.org/10.1017/s003224741400062x

———. eds. 2018. *Reverend E.J. Peck and the Inuit, East of Hudson Bay (1876–1919)*. Montreal: Avataq Cultural Institute.

———. 2019. *Inuit, Oblate Missionaries, and Grey Nuns in the Keewatin, 1865–1965*. Montreal: McGill-Queens University Press.

Laugrand, Frédéric, Jarich Oosten, and François Trudel, eds. 2006. *Apostle to the Inuit. The Journals and the Ethnographical Notes of E.J. Peck. The Baffin Years, 1894–1905*. Toronto: University of Toronto Press.

Pelly, David, Nick Sikkuark, Tony Manernaluk, and Louis Anakanerk. 2000. "Going Home to Kutgajuk." *Above and Beyond* (July/August): 34–37. https://www.davidpelly.com/resources/Going-Home-to-Kutgajuk.pdf

Oosten, Jarich, Frédéric Laugrand, and Wim Rasing, eds. 1999. *Perspectives on Traditional Law*. Vol. 2, *Interviewing Inuit Elders*. Iqaluit: Arctic College; Iqaluit: Nortext.

Paradis, Robert. 1969. "L'école des catéchistes esquimaux." *Eskimo* 82: 11–13.

Pelly, David. 2016. *Ukkusiksalik: The People's Story*. Toronto: Dundurn Press.

Remie, Cornelius H.W. 1983. "Culture Change and Religious Continuity Among the Arviligdjuarmiut of Pelly Bay, NWT, 1935–1963." *Études Inuit Studies* 7 (2): 53–77. http://www.jstor.org/stable/42869383

Remie, Cornelius, and Jarich Oosten. 2002. "The Birth of a Catholic Inuit Community: The Transition to Christianity in Pelly Bay, Nunavut, 1935–1950." *Études Inuit Stuides* 26 (1): 109–41. https://doi.org/10.7202/009274ar

Tapardjuk, Louis. 2014. *Fighting for Our Rights: The Life Story of Louis Tapardjuk*. Iqaluit: Nunavut Arctic College; Québec: CIERA.

"Toronto Archbishop, Arctic Suffragan Bishop Will Retire." 2004. *Anglican Journal*, 1 April 2004. https://www.anglicanjournal.com/toronto-archbishop-arctic-suffragan-bishop-will-retire-2206/

Trott, Christopher. 1997. "The Rapture and the Rupture: Religious Change Amongst the Inuit of North Baffin Island." *Études Inuit Studies* 21 (1–2): 209–28. https://www.jstor.org/stable/42869966

——. 1998. "Mission and Opposition in North Baffin Island." *Journal of the Canadian Church Historical Society* 40 (1): 31–55.

Usher, Jean. 1971. "Apostles and Aborigines: The Social Theory of Church Missionary Society." *Social History* 4 (7): 28–52. https://hssh.journals.yorku.ca/index.php/hssh/article/view/40659/36839

3

ENGAGING RELIGIOSITIES

Relationality, Co-existence, and Belonging
among Lander Warlpiri, Central Australia

PETRONELLA VAARZON-MOREL

THROUGHOUT THE WORLD, settler-colonialism has involved massacres and displacement of Indigenous people, the introduction of new species of plants and animals, and environmental degradation (Vaarzon-Morel 2017). Yet in Central Australia, Indigenous people have been able to accommodate both human and other-than-human beings who once were alien but now inhabit their ancestral landscape. Importantly for many people in the region, the cosmological constant remains the land; what has changed since colonization is the beings that inhabit it. Drawing on long-term ethnography among Lander Warlpiri people living at Willowra, my chapter discusses historical factors and entanglements that underlie limits to, and motivations for, co-existence with human and nonhuman Others. In doing so, it addresses how and why people have incorporated Christianity into their lives while continuing to observe practices grounded in traditional Aboriginal cosmology. I contend that underlying this religious plurality is an Indigenous relational ontology (Poirier 2013) that resonates with Christian values of mutuality and care (see also Dussart and Poirier, this volume).

An underlying concern of this chapter is the issue of ontological change. In considering this matter, I track different historical contexts in which Lander Warlpiri have been receptive—or not, as the case may be—to Christianity. In this way, I hope to show how pragmatism, the drive for autonomy, and the values of relatedness and caring, rather than mere beliefs (Dussart and Poirier, this volume) have influenced their choices. In doing so, my chapter attends to modes of person-hood and relationality variously foregrounded during Lander Warlpiri encounters with ancestors, kin, friends, and strangers (human and other-than-human). As Dussart and Poirier (this volume) point out, "In Indigenous conceptions and experiences, relations and relation-ality are...constitutive not only of local forms of sociality, but also of being-in-the-world. They are central to the production of the person." I employ the concept of religiosity, which "acknowledges the open-ness and fluidity of Indigenous perspectives and practices" (Dussart and Poirier, this volume; see also Poirier 2013). In exploring Warlpiri forms of religiosity, my chapter contributes to the literature on Christianity and Indigenous and non-Indigenous relations (see, e.g., McIntosh 1997; Austin-Broos 2009; Schwarz and Dussart 2010). As Fred Myers (2010, 111) points out, the articulations of Christianity in Central Australia "have been more than an abstract embrace of Western modernity" and must be understood in the context of "partic-ular formulations of different communities and traditions" (see also Austin-Broos 1996a).

In what follows, I first situate Lander Warlpiri people in Central Australia and discuss relational aspects of their cosmology through which they accommodated strangers historically. The remainder of the chapter is in three parts, each of which relates to a distinct phase. In the first of these parts, I address the early contact and pastoral periods and paint the background against which Christianity was introduced through missions on settlements in the wider Warlpiri region. The second part explores the rather different trajectory of people's engagement with Christianity at Willowra during the 1970s and '80s, the era of self-determination. The third part focuses on the recent decades and reflects upon Lander Warlpiri people's religiosities as ways of "being at home" (Jackson 1995) in a world experiencing rapid social change.[1]

Background

Willowra is a village located on the Lander River 350 kilometres north-west of Alice Springs in the Southern Tanami Desert. The population is approximately 300 people, of whom about 10 percent are non-Indigenous residents employed in local government offices, the school, clinic, and shop. The Indigenous community is close-knit in that most people belong to groups affiliated with interconnected ancestral estates in the surrounding region or are related through marriage and *Jukurrpa* (the Dreaming) to more distant areas.

Jukurrpa concerns the time of creation of the physical and social world, when ancestral beings travelled across the land bringing plant, animal, and other life forms into existence. In the process, they left behind fragments of their bodies, which metamorphosed to become features of the landscape. Places where ancestral activity occurred are imbued with spiritual power. The journeys of the ancestral beings are referred to in English as Dreaming tracks, and stories about their actions form the basis of Indigenous cosmology and Indigenous Law. Importantly, *Jukurrpa* structures interrelationships among human and other beings who customarily co-inhabit the Lander Warlpiri world.

The pattern of landholding is broadly one in which members of a patrilineal group are *kirda* or "owners" of land (their Country) surrounding sites on sections of Dreaming tracks with which they are spiritually affiliated. Each such group is closely related to spatially proximate groups who share the same Dreaming track and subsection affiliations. Individuals can also be incorporated into groups through associating factors such as totemic conception[2] and long-term resi-dence combined with ritual knowledge. An individual's ideal marriage partner is a person of the same generation level but from the oppo-site patrimoiety. In adulthood, a woman's children act as managers or "bosses" (*kurdungurlu*) for her Country and that of her brothers, and they share responsibility with *kirda* in ritual and land-related contexts. This reciprocal relationship is extended via the classificatory kinship

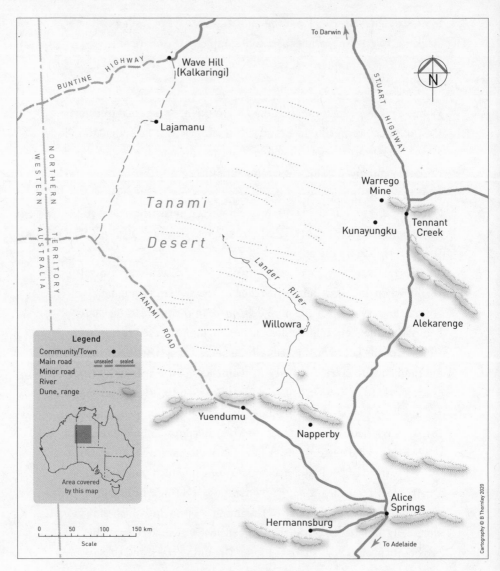

FIGURE 3.1. Map of Willowra and surrounding region.

(Used with permission from Brenda Thornley.)

system to include people other than those related through descent. What I want to emphasize in this discussion of Warlpiri cosmology is that the *kirda-kurdungurlu* relationship involves mutuality, responsibility, and care.

In the past, Indigenous cosmologies were characterized as localized, holistic, and closed as opposed to the universalizing and "open" world religions (see Abramson and Holbraad 2014, 6, 18). For example, Tony Swain (1993) argued that traditional Indigenous religion such as that of Warlpiri was ontologically incommensurable with Christianity. Contending that the religion lacked "social and spatial transcendence" and could not "accommodate outsiders and make a place for strangers" (1), he claimed that the "cosmology is focused on discrete known, observed sites" and "'traditionally' all that was not localized was discarded" (29).

However, in focusing on sites within clan estates, Swain downplayed the value of relationality in Indigenous culture and the fact that people's rights in clan estates derive from an underlying order of Law (Sutton 2003, 130–34). As indicated earlier, sites do not exist on their own but as part of a web of places connected by Dreaming tracks. In addition to kinship and classificatory systems, the latter provide pathways for Indigenous strangers to be incorporated as kinds of relatives during ceremonial encounters (Beckett 1996; see also Austin-Broos 2009). Given that Warlpiri and neighbouring people subscribed to a shared cosmology, how did they respond to the arrival of non-Indigenous strangers with profoundly different religious practices, values, and suppositions? According to Swain's hypothesis, precolonial Indigenous ontology was radically place-based and it was only after colonization that people experienced time. Viewing people as lacking agency and change as externally imposed, his model has been criticized for being essentialist and lacking ethnographic grounding (Austin-Broos 1996a; Morton 1996). It contrasts with more recent studies that attest to hunter-gatherers' openness and flexibility and that explore the nature of the transformations and continuities that result from people's responses to introduced institutionalized religions and the interpenetration of religious forms (Austin-Broos 1996b, 2009; Poirier 2013, 31–32).

Reflecting on this, I consider the changing nature of Lander Warlpiri people's encounters with non-Indigenous outsiders during the first half of the twentieth century and how these outsiders influenced Warlpiri religious trajectories.

Early Interactions with Settlers, the Pastoral Era, and "Mission Time" on Settlements

When I first arrived at Willowra in 1976, many Elders were alive whose childhoods were spent walking their ancestral Countries. While they spoke of good times, they also recalled the violence they endured at the hands of Whitemen who took up grazing licences on their lands during the late 1920s. Their stories reflected a pattern of interaction on the colonial frontier: initially wary, people attempted to establish exchange relations with the strangers once it became evident that they intended to stay. Relationships remained inequitable, however, as the Whitemen chased people away from waterholes and enforced their possession of the land with guns. The situation was brought to a head in 1928 when, in retaliation for attacks on settlers along the Lander, more than sixty people were killed in what has become known as the Coniston Massacre. That no charges were laid against the settlers reflected the politics of settler society at the time. In the words of Warlpiri people, they were "shot like dogs." People continued to be harassed by settlers until the 1940s, when the Northern Territory Native Affairs Branch increased their inspections of pastoral leases and relocated many people to settlements (Vaarzon-Morel 1995). The Yuendumu settlement was established in 1946, followed three years later by Hooker Creek (Lajamanu), then Warrabri (Alekarenge) in 1956. The Australian Baptist Home Mission administered Yuendumu and later established a strong presence at Lajamanu and Alekarenge, introducing Warlpiri to Christianity.

Although the missions did not appropriate land like the pastoralists did, they were nevertheless part of the process of establishing settler sovereignty. That the ontological assumptions of Church institutions spoke to those of the state is evidenced by the Church's mission to "civilize" Indigenous people by making them useful Christian subjects (McDonald 2001, 54, 89). As Carolyn Schwarz and Françoise Dussart

(2010, 3) observe, by the mid-twentieth century, Indigenous "life in the Missions revolved around daily assimilationist routines of labour, schooling and consumption."

However, this was not people's experience at Willowra, where until the 1970s the owners of the pastoral lease resisted the introduction of schools and missions (Henson 1992, 210). As I have discussed elsewhere (Vaarzon-Morel 1995), Willowra was sold in 1948 to the Parkinson family who ran the pastoral lease for twenty years. In contrast to the earlier period, Warlpiri remember the Parkinson era as a peaceful time during which able-bodied people were paid in kind for their labour as stockmen and domestics, and rations were distributed to the elderly. Through such exchanges, people developed relations of mutual dependency with the pastoralist and his family.

As observed elsewhere in Indigenous Australia (Redmond 2005), the Indigenous owner-manager relationship provided a model for such exchanges. Warlpiri also incorporated the Parkinsons into their kinship system as distant kin or "strange relatives" (Redmond 2005, 237). Such relational logic enabled people to sustain their cultural autonomy, which was reinforced by the fact that there was little outside interference in the religious realm.

Developing Christianity at Willowra, 1970s to 1980s

The Arrival of Lutherans and Baptists

While the Baptist Church claimed Warlpiri settlements, Lutheran Protestants expanded their reach from the Hermannsburg Mission on Arrernte land to cattle stations on Anmatyerr land (Henson 1992, 219). However, it was not until the 1970s that Christianity gained a foothold at Willowra. The period coincided with the introduction of the self-determination policy, Western schooling, and the government purchase of Willowra station in 1973 for the resident Indigenous population. As the late M. Nangala told me in 1989, at Willowra "[t]here used to be a missionary come in from Napperby. We had church, but no one was baptized. I was working at the school when the missionary first came here."

Nangala described how the missionary set up a screen in the school yard and invited people to watch "pictures." These were slides that illustrated the story of the fall of man from the Book of Genesis. Uncannily, Nangala related that when a scene that featured the serpent in the Garden of Eden was projected on the screen, a real snake materialized among the viewers on the ground:

> We were watching a picture with a snake, when we saw this snake moving toward us...Some people stayed but most ran away. The missionary said, "Hey, where are they going, they should watch the picture. Why don't you people shake hands with me?" I told them, "Don't shake hands with him, you'll turn into a monster, he's bad,"... and I sent him away.

Ironically, while the Book of Genesis portrays the serpent as a deceptive figure for enticing Eve to eat the forbidden fruit, in Nangala's story it is the missionary who is the trickster. At the time, slides were a novel medium and people interpreted the images through the mimetic lens they employed in ceremonies.[3]

Not long after this event, an Indigenous Lutheran pastor visited Willowra where he camped for a week near the people and, following mission practice, exchanged food with those who prayed with him (Jordan 2003, 54). Today, people recall their bemusement at the strange new ritual (Bowman and Central Land Council 2015, 33). Stories of first encounters with missionaries conform to an epistemological mode that emphasizes continuity in response to revelation through incorporation rather than rupture (Austin-Broos 2009, 91). Divining the significance of marks and happenings in Country is central to this revelatory process of learning (Poirier 2013, 58).

By 1976, when I arrived at Willowra, a Lutheran of Warlpiri Anmatyerr descent named Jakamarra had begun preaching. In addition to Sunday services, he held Christian funerals, which entailed a shift from burial of the deceased on their patrilineal Country to burial in a new "cemetery" at the edge of Willowra. Although the spirits of recently deceased people were said to return to their Country, such funerals provided an opportunity for Jakamarra to proselytize about Christian notions of everlasting life. However, most burials continued to be held on the deceased's Country, and mourning rituals remained focused on the performance of sorrow between different categories of kin as an expression of care and relatedness (Glaskin et al. 2008). As with Indigenous peoples elsewhere,[4] Warlpiri customary mourning practices are complex and involve prohibitions. For example, photographs of the deceased were destroyed along with their possessions. Furthermore, the deceased's name could not be used for years, during which period anyone possessing this name was referred to by the term *kumanjayi*, meaning "no name."

The influence of the Lutheran Church diminished after a Baptist party including Jerry Jangala Patrick[5] and missionary Lothar Jagst made a flying visit to Willowra from Lajamanu in late 1976 in order to bring the Baptist religion. Thereafter, Kumanjayi Japangardi, who was educated and baptized at Yuendumu settlement, ran Sunday services that took place in a central area outside the communal laundry.[6] Typically, the services included gospel singing, Bible readings, and healing prayers for loved ones. Few Elders attended the services, which attracted some younger men from the settlements along with their wives and children. These men had married into Willowra community and, apart from Kumanjayi, were the only people at Willowra who had been baptized.

Exploring Christianity as a System of Exchange

This situation changed during the early 1980s when Christian *purlapas* (public ceremonies) were introduced to Willowra. On one such occasion, people from Yuendumu and Lajamanu who had come to Willowra to attend annual male initiation ceremonies[7] performed a Christian nativity ceremony. According to women who were present, the roles of Joseph, the Wise Men, and shepherds were enacted by senior male dancers; women danced the parts of Mary and the angels, and youths with crosses on their foreheads looked on. Similar *purlapas* were held in years following. They were semiotically syncretic in that they drew upon Warlpiri dance movements, body painting, and ritual paraphernalia but incorporated Christian symbolism (Swain 1988, 457; Jordan 2003). For example, male actors wore crosses on their chests in place of *Jukurrpa* designs and females held their hands in the gesture of prayer as they danced. Illustrating the role of camels and donkeys in the nativity story, the dancers mimicked the animals' movements, just as they depicted totemic animals when enacting *Jukurrpa* stories.[8] It was through such mimetic performance and Bible stories that people came to resignify donkeys and camels as "God's animals"—a point I take up later. Reinforcing this Biblical association, and in continuity with the revelatory mode of learning discussed earlier, are the bodily markings of the donkeys: the contrasting band of fur across their backs is said symbolize the cross of Jesus.[9]

In addition to Christmas *purlapas,* the Baptist Church staged Easter ceremonies which reenacted the Passion of Jesus (Swain 1988, 456–57). These ceremonies were held during conventions that alternated between communities on the Baptist circuit, including Yuendumu, Lajamanu, Wave Hill, and Alekarenge. Easter conventions continue to be held, although the circuit has widened and modes of reenactment have changed. Some time ago, I discussed a photograph of an Easter *purlapa* with Violet Nampijinpa. Taken at Alekarenge in the late 1970s, it pictured a man tied to a cross, his chest decorated with fluff in the pattern of traditional mourning. Reflecting on the image, Nampijinpa remarked that the Easter story was performed like a traditional Warlpiri cere-mony because the "old people didn't understand English. They didn't know how Jesus died on the cross...and they wanted to see the act. Like following Jukurrpa, following the Dreaming of Jesus...They painted their bodies and did that dance, when Jesus died on the cross" (quoted in Bowman and Central Land Council 2015, 58). Although Nampijinpa employs the term *Dreaming* to denote the Easter story, it differs from ancestral narratives in that it is not inscribed in the land.

During the 1970s and 1980s, the Christian *purlapas* involved Elders who rarely attended church but wanted to "master new forms of ritual that might access...[Whitefella] power" (Austin-Broos 2009, 74). As mentioned earlier, mimesis was central to the process; it was employed in novel ways to similar ends in traditional ritual. For example, once during a men's ceremony that I attended, an Elder erected a curtain between two trees to conceal dancers being painted with *Jukurrpa* designs.

When the preparations were complete, the man pulled the curtain to reveal approaching dancers as he called out, "Look, just like video."

Navigating Whitefella Policies, Cosmic Forces, and Discourses of Equality
At the same time, the success of four land claims over Lander Warlpiri territory served to validate the authority of Elders and its cosmological foundation. Conducted under the Aboriginal Land Rights (Northern Territory) Act 1976, the claims provided important opportunities for senior men and women to revisit the Countries of their ancestors while introducing their children and grandchildren to them. Evidence during claim hearings attested to people's spiritual relationships to the land and the nature of relationships between different landed groups.

In the face of change, Elders were determined to maintain cultural and community autonomy. As part of the drive for local management, there was a complementary division of labour with Elders responsible for ceremonial "business" and younger men for secular affairs associated with "Whitefella business" such as council meetings. While gender and age conferred differential social status, the form of relationality was one in which people eschewed other hierarchical social division (Martin 2008, 90). The need to be "level" was an important social dynamic related to the values of reciprocity and respect. The Warlpiri term for respect, *kurnta*, also means embarrassment, shame, and reluctance to interfere in another's business.[10] Evidence from this era suggests that Elders believed the "new government law" of self-determination finally meant respect for their culture, recognition, and equality with Whites.

This was articulated during church services. For example, on one occasion in 1988 I heard preacher Japangardi comment that "White missionaries don't know anything more than the *yapa* [Indigenous] preachers and it isn't any good if they tell *yapa* to go and do this and do that—that's just like stockman times." Other themes concerned young people disrespecting Elders and neglecting responsibilities by "watching too much video" and "doing wrong things" like, for example, "getting drunk, fighting family, and thinking too much about themselves."[11] While "church" provided a venue for reflection on threats to the moral order, concerns also surfaced during Warlpiri ceremonies. For example, while attending an intergenerational initiation ceremony at Kunayungku outstation near Tennant Creek in December 1988, Nungarrayi Martin told me: "We worry for young people and make young men, but they don't worry back."

This ceremony had brought together members of interconnected Warlpiri and Kaytetye Countries stretching from the Lander River to Kunayungku, which is located 300 kilometres to the northeast of Willowra. Two months after the ceremony, when we had returned to Willowra, Kunayungku was the epicentre of three earthquakes. With magnitudes between 6.3 and 6.7, the earthquakes were felt at Willowra where they provoked much speculation, with people attributing causality to cosmological forces unleashed as a result of disjunctive social change and ignorant actions of Whitemen. For example, William Japangardi told me: "Whitemen won't listen but *yapa* know from olden time when things like this start happening, something is wrong, too many changes." He conjectured that the earthquake, which occurred not far from Warrego mine, was caused by Whitemen blasting the land with dynamite and violating the *Warlu* (fire) *Jukurrpa* that runs underground. To illustrate, he drew a diagram in the sand that traced the journey of *Warlu Jukurrpa* from Warrapuntye (on the former Maclaren Creek station) through Warrego up to Lajamanu before travelling back underground along the same route. In doing so, he explained that not only *Jukurrpa* but "olden time people's bodies and our bodies" (that is, a person's life force or spirit, which is consubstantial with their Country) were underground, and that, if disturbed, sickness and ill fortune would befall "everyone."

Immediately following the earthquake, people moved their swags to the church ground near the laundry and prayed for three days and nights. During this period, there was intense discussion of people's situation relative to that of Whites, with individuals pointing to poor housing, lack of money, and ill health as evidence of continuing imbalance (see Swain 1988). Rising material inequality within the Indigenous community was also of concern. Nicolas Peterson (2013a, 172) has observed that the Warlpiri moral economy is "embedded in a universal system of kin classification that requires a flow of goods and services to create and reproduce social relationships." Unequal access to paid jobs in community organizations and traditional owner payments (obtained from mineral exploration activities) gave rise to jealousy and disrupted established processes of redistribution. In response, church leaders invoked the Christian ethos of sharing and care. For example, Rusty Japangardi stated: "Whitefella way is to keep things to themselves and not look after people and share, [but] *yapa* shouldn't worry about money because God loves poor people."

The earthquake also prompted deliberation on the relative status of Indigenous and non-Indigenous people and of Christianity and *Jukurrpa* in God's eyes. For example, William Japangardi declared to his audience (of which I was a part) that the earthquake was something that no one person could understand: "not preachers, not *yapa*, not Whitefellas, not the Queen, not the big bosses in Canberra, and not even the *ngangkayi* [traditional healer]. This is something greater than us all and a warning from Wapirra [God]."[12] To take another example, Richard Jungarrayi told me that the earthquake was proof that *kardiya* (Whitefellas) "didn't know everything" and were "level with *yapa*," and that God was above everyone. He drew parallel lines in the sand to illustrate his belief that just as "Whitefellas have *kardiya* Law and *yapa* Law, *yapa* have *yapa* Law and Whitefella Law."[13] Pitted against explanations offered by Whites, the earthquake was widely regarded as evidence of the power of both *Jukurrpa* and God and a warning that people must observe both ways. Around this time, young people began sharing personal stories that attested to the transformative power of God. Typically, they began their testimonials by describing occasions when they had "done the wrong thing" (e.g., fighting, drinking, or playing cards), then declare that they were now "following" Wapirra. For the most part, the testimonials spoke not to the internal transformations characteristic of Western Christian individualism, but to the need to be more caring kinspersons.[14] Fascinatingly, people's responses to the earthquake resonate with certain themes such as healing (see earlier) and affirmations of normative social and cultural values that are associated with "end-of-time narratives" found among Kaingang in Southern Brazil as described by Crépeau (this volume).

Baptism, Notions of Person, and Causality

A month after the earthquake, a church group from Yuendumu visited Willowra in order to baptize people. Since then, baptisms have occurred sporadically, mostly after summer rain when waterholes in the Lander River fill with water. On this occasion, five women were baptized at Pirdaparnta waterhole in a simple act of immersion performed in the name of the Father, the Son, and the Holy Spirit. That only a small number of people participated was due in part to the fact that many people were at Alekarenge for initiation ceremonies. Commenting on numbers attending and likening some baptisms that he had attended to meaningless "cattle dips," the non-Indigenous pastor who conducted the ritual told me that he only "wanted to baptize people who had really thought about it and were ready to receive the Lord into their lives." On their part, the women wanted to be baptized because they believed God's spirit would make them strong and help them overcome sickness and "troubles" for their families. They reported feeling "lighter" and having a sense of wellbeing after the baptism.

Of the women baptized, four taught at the school and thereafter spent lunch times translating gospel songs from English to Warlpiri. Despite being baptized, they continued to participate in community life and to hold Warlpiri notions of causality and agency. For example, soon after being baptized, Nakamarra felt ill. After visiting the clinic, she decided to visit the *ngangkayi* (traditional healer) because she suspected that her illness was caused by sorcery. According to Nakamarra, the *ngangkayi* massaged her legs with fat and ochre and removed a *yarda,* an ensorcelled object which had been "sung" into her body to make her ill. Nakamarra reported feeling better following her treatment. This incident reveals a dimension of Warlpiri personhood that is at odds with Western Christian notions of the person (see also Laugrand, this volume). While beliefs vary, many Baptists conceptualize bodies as susceptible to supernatural forces, of which only those emanating from God should be entertained. As Knut Rio and Annelin Eriksen (2014, 61) point out, "in the Christian world, agency belongs to an axis between individualized man and God and has no place in the environment outside of this relation." In contrast, Warlpiri not only recognize the interdependence of all manner of entities in their social world (Dussart and Poirier 2017; see also Poirier 2004) but accept that breaches in relationships will have causal effects.[15] As the following anecdote illustrates, this ontology of relatedness extends to nonnative animals such as donkeys who have long lived at Willowra.

During Christmas 1988, some boys stoned five donkeys then locked them in an empty house where the animals died of thirst. Adults expressed disgust at the boys' behaviour, calling them "rubbish kids." Soon, people began to fall ill, and three children with pneumonia were evacuated to Alice Springs hospital. Everyone attributed "the sickness" to the killing of the donkeys, who are regarded as "part of Willowra" and Jesus's animals. The community's association with donkeys dates from the 1940s, when settlers no longer needed the animals for transport and released them to become feral. Subsequently, Willowra people adopted them, travelling with the animals between cattle stations and while hunting, gathering, and visiting Country. While donkey travel ceased in the 1970s, the animals continued living at Willowra. That the deaths of these donkeys were linked to people's illness reflects the Warlpiri ethic of care, which extends to beings with whom they have shared history and undergirds the prohibition against senselessly killing animals for waste. As I have discussed elsewhere, "according to the logic of Warlpiri relational ontology, killing for waste will attract cosmic retribution, with possible punishments including ill health, death, and environmental repercussions such as drought" (Vaarzon-Morel 2017, 200; cf. Crépeau, this volume).

In 1988, Elder Kumanjayi Jungarrayi spoke with me about elders concerns regarding the intersection of "Whiteman's Law" and Christianity with the Warlpiri moral order. Jungarrayi began by reflecting on changes that had occurred in his lifetime: "Aboriginal Law comes from old people, before Whiteman came through this country. I was born under old people; I don't know that new Law that government is trying to change 'em over, belonging to other side." Noting the younger generation was growing up under Two Laws, Indigenous Law and Whiteman's Law, he observed that changing Law was not a simple matter like changing clothes, and that if young people abandoned Warlpiri Law for Whitefella Law they risked losing their moral compass: "Some young people are not carrying on our Law belonging to old people, drink take them bush, and video bin take them bush." [16] Jungarrayi saw Christianity as providing support for Warlpiri Law: "*Yapa* Law, Wapirra give it more power, [but] which way young people going to run—under Wapirra?" Finally, he opined that people were becoming sicker but that "might be all the Christian help us." Illustrating the practical dimension of his engagement with Christianity, Jungarrayi observed, "I only go to Christian when I'm sick."

Lander Warlpiri Religiosities Today

Religious Identifications

In the last section, I showed how Warlpiri engaged with Christianity in order to gain purchase on the Whitefella world and navigate change. Fast forward to the twenty-first century. In this section, I consider people's contemporary religiosities in a time of social upheaval following major shifts in government policy, a burgeoning young demographic versed in new media technologies, and the passing of Elders such as Jungarrayi.

Today, most people at Willowra identify as Baptist, although only a minority attend church. Arguing that Christians "all use one Bible" and "it's one God," people see no problem joining events held by other denominations when visiting family elsewhere. It is thus instructive to consider the Government Census (Australian Bureau of Statistics 2016), which lists the religious affiliations of Willowra community. Out of a population of 301 persons, of which 277 were Indigenous and 24 non-Indigenous, 244 people (99 males and 143 females) identified as Baptist. Among other Christian religions listed, three people identified as Pentecostal (Assembly of God), 11 as Lutheran, and 3 as Christian of no particular denomination. Only 4 people identified with the category "Australian Aboriginal Traditional Religions," and 17 people had no particular religious affiliation.[17]

I want to draw out two points. The first concerns the low number of Indigenous people at Willowra who affiliated with "Traditional Religion." This reflects the fact that, in contrast to "religion," which they associate with Christian faith and a monotheistic God, people tend to think of Indigenous religiosity in terms of "culture," understood as practices, values, and a pluralist cosmology (Martin 2008; Poirier 2013; see also Dussart and Poirier, this volume). Thus, when I discussed the census findings with people in 2018, Napaljarri observed: "*Jukurrpa* is what you are born with. We don't think of it as religion. There are different Dreamings, but all are *Jukurrpa*." In concurrence, Napangardi added: "We thought religion means Christianity, the Church." For most people, *Jukurrpa* is not a matter of individual belief but rather an all-encompassing and emplaced Law that governs relations between human and nonhuman beings. Moreover, *Jukurrpa* does not simply concern the past but is regarded as eternal. Despite a decline in traditional ceremonies, the power of the Dreaming continues to be accessed today during rituals that re-create the activities of ancestral beings.

At the same time, most Indigenous Christians I know position God in an overarching relationship with *Jukurrpa*. As Nampijinpa observed: "God has got the most *Jukurrpa*. He created the world and made all these things." While seemingly hierarchical, the relationship preserves difference. In reconciling Christianity with Warlpiri cosmology, most people do not merge one with the other (Swain 1988, 452).[18] Furthermore, they are not overly concerned with offering coherent explanations of what might strike Westerners as contradictions (Swain 1993, 121, 280).[19] Despite identifying their religion as Christian, however, most people are not "converts" in the classic Paulian sense, which involves rupture (Schwarz and Dussart 2010; see also Dussart and Poirier, this volume). Rather, while people incorporate Christianity into their lives, it coexists with a distinctive Warlpiri cosmology and an ontological framework that is in many ways radically different from—but also folds into—that of the Christian tradition.

Christianity, Materiality, and Modernity

As Jarrett Zigon (2018) observes, Christianity shares certain "proclivities" with other discourses that are part of the Western ontological tradition (e.g., vis-à-vis concepts of individuality, subject-object dichotomies, the economy, and gender relations). Thus, if Warlpiri religiosities now entangle customary and Christian practices, the shaping influences of modernity on people's subjectivities and lives must also be acknowledged (Austin-Broos 1996b).[20] This is illustrated, for example, by the fact that some younger women regard involvement in church as a pathway to achieving greater mobility and gender equality (Burke 2015). The intersection of gender with Christianity is complex and warrants greater attention beyond that which I can give here.

To take a different example, while some burials still occur on the deceased's Country, funeral services have become Christianized. Thus, whereas traditionally the names of deceased could not be spoken, and images and belongings were destroyed, it is now common to have a written order of service that features a photo of the deceased together with lists of their extended family, Bible readings, and gospel songs. Images of the deceased surrounded by angels and other Christian icons are also circulated on mobile phones (Vaarzon-Morel 2014). In continuity with customary mourning practices in which individuals demonstrate shared sorrow and responsibilities, kin now testify during eulogies as to how they looked after and, in turn, were cared for by the deceased. Here we see the materialization of the Christian religious tradition around Warlpiri values of care and relationality.

Indigenous and Non-Indigenous Relations of Care

Looking back over the 2010s, what strikes me is that, while most people's commitment to Christianity has waxed and waned, a small group of people maintains an ongoing relationship to the religion, sustained through intercommunity gatherings and visits to Willowra by non-Indigenous church members. The latter tend to have a cosmopolitan outlook in the sense of being inclusive, tolerant, and understanding of aspects of Warlpiri culture, up to a point. Such relationships have been strengthened since the Federal government's introduction in 2007 of the Northern Territory National Emergency Response, commonly known as the Intervention.[21] Ironically for Warlpiri, the Intervention has served to differentiate between types of non-Indigenous people—those who care (for example, Christians) and those who don't.

The Intervention, coupled with the removal of local councils under the Northern Territory Government (Peterson 2013b), has left a divisive legacy, with people expressing feelings of shame, disempowerment, and anger about the racially discriminatory policy. Many liken the Intervention to "welfare time" under the assimilation policy and feel wounded by the lack of respect accorded them. Moreover, their economic circumstances have worsened as criteria for gaining social security support are so draconian that a large percentage of the community receives no income. As a result, card playing, demand sharing (Peterson 2013a), and other modes of redistribution that encourage reliance on others have increased.

Since the Intervention, and with it the deterioration of economic inputs, church has taken on added importance among some people who have turned to Christianity to maintain a sense of being "at home in the world" (Jackson 1995). The local Baptist Church continues to be run by Warlpiri, with intermittent visits from non-Indigenous preachers who otherwise send memory sticks (USBs) containing Bible readings and sermons. Reading and listening to recordings individually or in groups has replaced earlier mimetic modes of learning about Christianity. Gospel music downloaded from YouTube plays an important role in forging a sense of a Christian community. As Napangardi commented to me in 2018: "When people hear gospel songs and the music flows, they gradually join in and become happy." In addition to local services, people visit other communities for Easter ceremonies and gospel singing. Such occasions provide opportunities for people to catch up with kin, avow their commitment to God, and experience "*communitas.*"

Church also provides a forum for people to form relationships with non-Indigenous Christians who provide support. In contrast to people's frequently oppositional interactions with government staff who tend not to stay long in communities, these relationships are highly valued. Not only do Warlpiri meet Baptist friends at conventions in cities, but volunteers from Melbourne sometimes visit Willowra when, in addition to participating in church services and bush-food trips, they collect firewood for Elders and carry out practical projects such as building churches. Despite missionaries not living at Willowra, in discussions with me, people have highlighted the mutuality and caring nature of their relationships with these "strange relatives," contrasting them with government staff who are perceived to have "no feeling for Aboriginal people."

The last decade has been a period of rapid change. Moreover, the social cohesion of earlier times has given way to periods of heightened conflict fueled by sorcery accusations. Christianity has helped fill the breach. As one person told me, "churches are very important for the community. They care and make peace for people who are hating one another." A practical example of such care is the nailing of signs with the word *Jesus* to trees and fences. The idea, explained Napangardi, is that "people see them and feel the presence of Jesus and don't fight." At the same time, people call on spirits of the "old people" to look after them.

Making people happy by fostering relationships of mutuality and care are enduring themes in local Christian discourse. Whereas the focus of people's engagement with Christianity twenty years ago was on intercultural relations, it has now shifted to intracultural relations. For example, in 2018 Japaljarri, a local preacher, told me that during church, he "always pray[s] for Black and White to make us one, one peace, one country, one Lander Warlpiri family." Revealing the extent to which God is an actor in his world—a world that entwines both autochthonous and introduced human and nonhuman beings— he continued:

> This place had a lot of problems—they used to fight nearly every day and night. God helped us stop fighting. I went to church and put on music loudly and prayed for people to come, and they came and shook hands and said sorry. That trouble is finished now...Now everyone is going hunting like friends. Yesterday two groups got together—we told them to forget these troubles and be friends, one

big family for God. That way people can go to funerals, football,
and camp together at business [initiation ceremonies] as one. When
everyone was fighting, this place got dry; donkeys bin die and
people got sick. But when we went to church and said sorry to God,
we got a lot of rain and everything bin grow. The Lander River
flowed—a miracle from God. He blessed this country and people.
I always tell people, "Please, no more fighting—we got to be
strong people."

Japaljarri's emphasis on the need to care for relatives contrasts with that of non-Indigenous Baptists who prioritize an individual's relationship with God and membership in His family. Indeed, they may regard Warlpiri forms of relationality as problematic. Thus, when conflict erupted between family groups at a nearby settlement, the church arranged for a busload of people to travel from Willowra to Adelaide (cf. Hinkson 2018). While this intervention was meant to protect people from the pressure of relatives, it did so by removing them from the community and preaching about notions of individual responsibility and rights that derive from the Western ontological tradition (Zigon 2018, 130–31). Whereas in Japaljarri's world causality is conceptually linked with social rupture, in the Western Christian world causality is linked to sin and the individual.

Warlpiri people are aware that some of their practices such as card playing, demand sharing, and sorcery remain points of contention with non-Indigenous preachers, who espouse the virtues of possessive individualism and non-reliance ("not bludging") on kin. Recently, Nancy Nampijinpa told me that these proselytizers refer to sorcery as cursing. However, she pointed out that for Warlpiri people a curse is not something the individual can settle with God. Instead, the person who is responsible for the curse must heal the afflicted. Explaining that you cannot confront the sorcerer directly, she said, "Warlpiri might dream that someone's *Jukurrpa*—like a snake—is inside making them sick. Or the person that made them sick will appear in their dream. On waking, they'll talk to the family of that person and ask them to come and massage them."

As indicated earlier, sorcery, like revenge "payback," involves recip-rocation and is a negative dimension of Warlpiri relational ontology. As Martin (2008, 95) points out, sorcery accusations are also "a means by which causality is both externalized and personalized, by which social conformity is maintained, and by which relations between dominant and marginal individuals and groups are sustained and reproduced." Sorcery practices reflect Warlpiri concepts of person, not as bounded individuals, but as socially porous beings whose spirits and bodies are constituted interrelationally. In this scenario, the Holy Spirit is yet another—albeit powerful and diffuse—transformative force. As Nampijinpa explained to me in 2018: "As Baptists, we pray for the healing power of the Holy Spirit to come down on us. This healing power makes our *pirlirrpa* and body strong." *Pirlirrpa* is the Warlpiri term for "life force" or "spirit," which is located in the body near the kidneys. Here we see how the work of the Holy Spirit on the body folds into Warlpiri notions of the person.

Spirits, Agency, and Land

Given that, in theory, Western Christianity "cancels out the possibility of spirits, animals or land to have agency" (Rio and Erikson 2014, 61), how are people's engagements with Christianity and Warlpiri "culture" figured on the land? Over many years, I have accompanied families on visits to their Countries, while Elders teach younger people about asso-ciated *Jukurrpa* stories, songs, and ceremony. For example, spirits only reveal resources to familial people. Hence, when approaching sacred sites, *kirda* and *kurdungurlu* ritually announce their identity to *milarlapa,* lest these ancestral spirits mistake them for strangers and cause them to become ill. Elders also point out sacred trees that embody spirits of people's deceased relatives. While views vary, most people today believe that when they die, part of their spirit will go to heaven and part to their Country (Swain 1993, 119). Although Christianity is, unlike *Jukurrpa,* not inscribed in the land, it nevertheless pervades people's world, and while people interact with ancestral spirits, they may also call on God for help. For example, my female Warlpiri friends sometimes call on God to prevent the tires on our vehicle from getting punctures. On one occasion, when bogged in sand, my companion knelt and prayed to God, imploring him to give us the strength to dig out the vehicle. Another person instructed me to pray with her so that God would reveal the remote sacred sites that we were attempting to locate. The cultural logic underlying such appeals to God is not dissimilar to that invoked when addressing ancestral spirits: both involve recognition, respect, and mutuality. Moreover, the way people strengthen their relationships with God through appeals for help resonates with the way people incorporate strangers as relatives through the owner-manager framework (Redmond 2005). These examples further illustrate the pragmatic dimension of people's engagement with Christianity.

Conclusion

In this chapter, I sketched phases in Willowra people's history since colonization and explored limits to, and motivations for, their co-existence with Others, both human and nonhuman. In doing so, I have illuminated the nature of Warlpiri values of relatedness, responsibility, respect, and care and have shown how people's engagements with Christianity reflect wider social transformations. Although today most Willowra people identify their "religion" as Baptist, they do not oppose Christianity to Warlpiri Law and cosmology. Rather, underlying this religious plurality is an Indigenous relational ontology that resonates with Christian notions of mutuality and care.

The first part of my chapter discussed the period when settlers established cattle stations on Lander Warlpiri country. Despite changes in their subsistence economy, Willowra people retained an autonomous ritual life. The second part of the chapter addressed the self-determination and land-rights era, when people began engaging with a newly Indigenizing Christianity as a way of exploring moral alignments between Whitefella Law and Warlpiri Law. In the contemporary period, with Elders having passed away, changes such as the Intervention have occurred, and social cohesion has, at times, given way to increased inter-Indigenous conflict. Although only a minority of people regularly participate in Christian gatherings, attendance has risen during periods of community strife and hardship, when people enlist God's help in sustaining peaceful and caring relationships. Through such examples of Willowra people's religiosities, I have shown how pragmatics and the values of cultural autonomy and relatedness have influenced their choices through time.

Author's Note

I would like to thank Françoise Dussart and Sylvie Poirier for their invitation to participate in their panel at the 34th Conference of the International Society for the Sociology of Religion in Lausanne, Switzerland, at which I presented a version of this chapter. It has benefited greatly from their comments. I also thank Jim Wafer and Marcelis Avery for helpful suggestions. As ever, I am indebted to my Warlpiri friends who have shared their stories and experiences with me over many years.

Notes

1. I have undertaken ethnographic field work with Lander Warlpiri and Anmatyerr people at Willowra for more than four decades. I first lived in the community from 1976 to 1977 as a schoolteacher, then from 1987 to 1989 when I conducted anthropological research for a PHD. During the years between 1979 and 1991, I researched and coauthored four major anthropological reports for Warlpiri and Anmatyerr people's claims to their traditional lands. Since then, I have continued to collaborate with Willowra people on various social justice, archival repatriation, and livelihood projects, including (from 2014 to the present) the Lander Warlpiri Cultural Mapping project. The personal communications cited in this chapter have been collected during these periods.

2. This involves animation of the person by a *Jukurrpa* spirit. Upon birth, the child is affiliated with the place at which totemic conception occurred.

3. That is, copies were thought to hold the power of the original (Taussig 1993, xiii; see also Deger 2006, 88–89).

4. For a fascinating discussion of taboos and beliefs held by Altaian people in Russia, see Pimenova (this volume).

5. Jangala was instrumental in translating the Bible into Warlpiri.

6. During the 1970s, the Baptists attempted to build more equitable relationships by encouraging local ownership and syncretic innovations (Jordan 2003).

7. During initiations, young boys are ritually transformed into men (Meggitt 1974).

8. Elsewhere, nativity plays sometimes featured real camels and donkeys.

9. Coincidentally, the English term *bray*, which refers to a donkey cry, sounds the same as *pray* to Warlpiri speakers.

10. See Myers's (1986) discussion on a similar Pintupi concept.
11. See Crépeau (this volume) for a discussion of similar issues raised by Kaingang Pentecostals in Southern Brazil.
12. *Wapirra* is the kin term for "father."
13. See Austin-Broos (1996) for a discussion of differing meanings of the Two Laws among Arrernte and other Indigenous Australian communities.
14. See Laugrand (this volume) on the importance of care in kin relations among Inuit people.
15. This illustrates the value accorded to relationality and the fact that for many Indigenous peoples "being well is therefore relational" (Blaser et al. quoted in Dussart and Poirier, this volume).
16. Here, "take them bush" is used metaphorically to mean something that makes a person lose their way or become wayward.
17. I estimate that half of these were non-Indigenous.
18. Similarly, Eickelkamp (2017, 237) notes that Anangu in the Western Desert "tend to keep apart...the two great stories in their lives."
19. Tassinari (this volume) similarly notes that Karipuna people of Northern Brazil are not concerned with providing an "integrated cosmological explanation."
20. For other examples of the effects of modernization on Indigenous peoples' subjectivities, see Pimenova (this volume) and Hall (this volume).
21. While the rationale for the Intervention was to address allegations of child sexual abuse and neglect in Indigenous communities, the government also aimed to "normalize" the Indigenous population (Altman and Hinkson 2010). Ultimately, allegations of widespread sexual abuse proved unfounded. Still, the Intervention continues, albeit with a new emphasis on consultation.

References

Abramson, Allen, and Martin Holbraad. 2014. "Introduction: The Cosmological Frame in Anthropology." In *Framing Cosmologies: The Anthropology of Worlds*, edited by Allen Abramson and Martin Holbraad, 55–76. Manchester: Manchester University Press.

Altman, Jon C., and Melinda Hinkson, eds. 2010. *Culture Crisis: Anthropology and Politics in Aboriginal Australia.* Sydney: University of New South Wales Press.

Austin-Broos, Diane J. 1996a. "What's in a Time, or a Place? Reflections on Swain's Hypothesis." *Social Analysis: The International Journal of Anthropology* 4 (September): 3–10. https://www.jstor.org/stable/23171693

——. 1996b. "'Two laws', Ontologies, Histories: Ways of Being Aranda Today." *Australian Journal of Anthropology* 7 (1): 1–20. https://doi.org/10.1111/j.1835-9310.1996.tb00334.x

———. 2009. *Arrernte Present, Arrernte Past: Invasion, Violence, and Imagination in Indigenous Central Australia.* Chicago: University of Chicago Press.

Australian Bureau of Statistics. 2016. "Table G14 Religious Affiliation by Sex." *Census of Population and Housing, Willowra (L) (UCL722036) 13.7 sq km.* https://quickstats.censusdata.abs.gov.au/census_services/getproduct/census/2016/communityprofile/UCL722036?opendocument

Beckett, Jeremy. 1996. "A Comment on Tony Swain's *A Place for Strangers*: Towards a History of Aboriginal Being." *Social Analysis: The International Journal of Anthropology* 40 (September): 11–19. https://www.jstor.org/stable/23171694

Bowman, Marg, and Central Land Council. 2015. *Every Hill Got a Story: We Grew Up in Country.* Richmond: Hardie Grant Books.

Burke, Paul. 2015. "Rupture and Readjustment of Tradition: Personal Autonomy in the Feminised Warlpiri Diaspora in Australia." In *Strings of Connectedness: Essays in Honour of Ian Keen*, edited by P.G. Toner, 215–34. Canberra: ANU Press.

Deger, Jennifer. 2006. *Shimmering Screens: Making Media in an Aboriginal. Community.* Minneapolis: University of Minnesota Press.

Dussart, Françoise, and Sylvie Poirier. 2017. "Knowing and Managing the Land: The Conundrum of Coexistence and Entanglement." In *Entangled Territorialities: Negotiating Indigenous Lands in Australia and Canada*, edited by Françoise Dussart and Sylvie Poirier, 3–24. Toronto: University of Toronto Press.

Eickelkamp, Ute. 2017. Finding Spirit: Ontological Monism in an Australian Aboriginal Desert World Today. *HAU Journal of Ethnographic Theory* 7 (1): 235–64. https://doi.org/10.14318/hau7.1.019

Glaskin, Katie, Myrna Tonkinson, Yasmine Musharbash, and Victoria Burbank, eds. 2008. *Mortality, Mourning and Mortuary Practices in Indigenous Australia.* Farnham: Ashgate.

Henson, Barbara. 1992. *A Straight-Out Man: F.W. Albrecht and Central Australian Aborigines.* Carlton: Melbourne University Press.

Hinkson, Melinda. 2018. "Turbulent Dislocations in Central Australia: Exile, Place Making, and the Promises of Elsewhere." *American Ethnologist* 45 (4): 521–32. https://doi.org/10.1111/amet.12706

Jackson, Michael. 1995. *At Home in the World.* Durham: Duke University Press.

Jordan, Ivan. 2003. *Their Way: Indigenous Christianity Amongst the Warlpiri People.* Darwin: Charles Darwin University.

Martin, David. 2008. "Aboriginal Sorcery and Healing, and the Alchemy of Aboriginal Policy Making." *Journal of the Anthropological Society of South Australia* 33: 75–128.

McDonald, Heather. 2001. *Blood, Bones and Spirit: Aboriginal Christianity in an East Kimberley Town.* Melbourne University Press.

McIntosh, Ian. 1997. "Anthropology, Self-Determination and Aboriginal Belief in the Christian God." *Oceania* 67 (4): 273–88. Published online 2015. https://doi.org/10.1002/j.1834-4461.1997.tb02621.x

Meggitt, M.J. 1974. *Desert People: A Study of the Walbiri Aborigines of Central Australia.* Sydney: Angus and Robertson.

Morton, John.1996. "A Place for Strangers and a Stranger Out of Place: Towards a History of Tony Swain's Aboriginal Being." *Social Analysis: The International Journal of Anthropology* 40 (September): 43–50. https://www.jstor.org/stable/23171696

Myers, Fred. 1986. *Pintupi Country, Pintupi Self: Sentiment, Place, and Politics among Western Desert Aborigines.* Smithsonian Institution Press, Washington D.C.

———. 2010. "All around Australia and Overseas: Christianity and Indigenous Identities in Central Australia 1988." *The Australian Journal of Anthropology* 21 (1): 110–28.

Peterson, Nicolas. 2013a. "On the Persistence of Sharing: Personhood, Asymmetrical Reciprocity, and Demand Sharing in the Indigenous Australian Domestic Moral Economy." *Australian Journal of Anthropology* 24 (2): 166–76. https://doi.org/10.1111/taja.12036

———. 2013b. "Community Development, Civil Society and Local Government in the Future of Remote Northern Territory Growth Towns." *The Asia Pacific Journal of Anthropology* 14 (4): 339–52. https://doi.org/10.1080/14442213.2013.804868

Poirier, Sylvie. 2004. "Ontology, Ancestral Order and Agencies among the Kukatja (Australian Western Desert)." In *Figured Worlds: Ontological Obstacles in Intercultural Relations*, edited by John Clammer, Sylvie Poirier, and Eric Schwimmer, 58–82. Toronto: University of Toronto Press.

———. 2013. "The Dynamic Reproduction of Hunter-Gatherers' Ontologies and Values." In *A Companion to the Anthropology of Religion*, edited by Janice Boddy and Michael Lambek, 50–68. Hoboken: John Wiley & Sons, Inc.

Redmond, Anthony. 2005. "Strange Relatives: Mutualities and Dependencies between Aborigines and Pastoralists in the Northern Kimberley." *Oceania* 75 (3): 234–46. https://doi.org/10.1002/j.1834-4461.2005.tb02883.x

Rio, Knut, and Annelin Eriksen. 2014. "A New Man: The Cosmological Horizons of Development, Curses, and Personhood in Vanuatu." In *Framing Cosmologies: The Anthropology of Worlds*, edited by Allen Abramson and Martin Holbraad, 55–76. Manchester: Manchester University Press.

Schwarz, Carolyn, and Françoise Dussart. 2010. "Christianity in Aboriginal Australia Revisited." *The Australian Journal of Anthropology* 21 (1): 1–13. https://doi.org/10.1111/j.1757-6547.2010.00064.x

Sutton, Peter. 2003. *Native Title in Australia.* New York: Cambridge University Press.

Swain, Tony. 1988. "The Ghost of Space: Reflections of Warlpiri Christian Iconography and Ritual." In *Aboriginal Australians and Christian Missions*, edited by Tony Swain and Deborah Bird Rose, 452–69. Bedford Park: Australian Association for the Study of Religions.

———. 1993. *A Place for Strangers: Towards a History of Australian Aboriginal Being.* Cambridge: Cambridge University Press.

Taussig, Michael. 1993. *Mimesis and Alterity*. New York: Routledge.

Vaarzon-Morel, Petronella, ed. 1995. *Warlpiri Karnta Karnta-Kurlangu Yimi; Warlpiri Women's Voices: Our Lives, Our History*. Alice Springs: IAD Press.

———. 2014. "Pointing the Phone: Transforming Technologies and Social Relations among Warlpiri." *The Australian Journal of Anthropology* 25 (2): 239–55. https://doi.org/10.1111/taja.12091

———. 2017. "Alien Relations: Ecological and Ontological Dilemmas Posed for Indigenous Australians in the Management of 'Feral' Camels on Their Lands." In *Entangled Territorialities: Negotiating Indigenous Lands in Australia and Canada*, edited by Françoise Dussart and Sylvie Poirier, 186–211. Toronto: University of Toronto Press.

Zigon, Jarrett. 2018. *Disappointment: Toward a Critical Hermeneutics of Worldbuilding.* New York: Fordham University Press.

4

MAKING PEOPLE

*Manipulating Alterity in the Production of the Person
among the Karipuna People of Northern Brazil*

ANTONELLA TASSINARI

Introduction

This chapter analyzes some aspects related to the production of the
person among the Karipuna people, a process that articulates Catholic
and shamanic practices and beliefs.[1] A focus on the production of proper
and healthy bodies allows a better understanding of how the Karipuna
people pragmatically combine these different traditions, in the sense of
"entangled religiosities" that are "always *in the making,*" as proposed
by Françoise Dussart and Sylvie Poirier (this volume). Such an entanglement involves daily practices, techniques, and knowledge about
pregnancy, childbirth, and baby care rather than a theoretical and
specialized corpus of abstract knowledge.

The focus on corporeity as a major symbolic idiom has been identified in Lowland South American ethnology since the 1970s as a common
feature of Indigenous societies (Seeger, de Matta, and Viveiros de Castro
1979). Researchers worked with the concept of person, proposed by
Marcel Mauss (1936), as a category of collective thought, and pointed
to some theoretical consequences of this choice of focus for a better
understanding of Lowland South American societies. They defended a
preference for this notion of the person over the idea of the individual,

which does not coincide with native categories. They also highlighted the prevalence of the symbolic idioms that focus on the person rather than on kinship groups established through filiation or alliance and argued mainly for the centrality of corporeity in the production of the person.

Anchored in debates of the 42nd and 43rd International Congress of Americanists held in Paris in 1976 and Rio de Janeiro in 1978, the notion of the person became understood as a central category of social thought used by Indigenous people of Lowland South America to reflect on social life (Seeger, de Matta, and Viveiros de Castro 1979).[2] It is interesting to note here that the movement against the materialistic explanations used by Africanists led Americanist scholars to another kind of materialism— not that of "corporate groups," but that of "corporeity." Corporeity is understood here as processes of fabrication, ornamentation, transformation, and destruction of bodies, which are crucial strategies for the production of persons. Corporeity also roughly relates to the mythology, social organization, and ritual life of these societies.

Renate Viertler (1979), writing about the Bororo people, shows, for example, how ideas about pregnancy, childbirth, growing up, growing old, and death are related to naming, ritual paraphernalia, hunting, gender dichotomies, and prestige hierarchies. Eduardo Viveiros de Castro (1979), when examining the Yawalapiti people, emphasizes their belief that the human body must be constantly fabricated, first by its production in the mother's womb through multiple sexual intercourses, and later by processes of manipulating the body by balancing its external contacts with corporal fluids, vegetal oils and dyes, foods and beverages, and tobacco and smoke. Following these researchers, I argue in this chapter that the term *corporeity* refers to an effort by Indigenous peoples of Lowland South America to produce healthy and proper bodies and that such production represents sociological and cosmological processes of great interest.

Karipuna Families

Karipuna families live in the Uaçá Basin in Northern Brazil, mostly in fourteen villages along the Curipi River. There are two other Karipuna villages on the Juminã and Oiapoque Rivers, and three others alongside federal highway BR156. The Brazilian 2010 demographic census (Censo Brasil 2012) recorded the Karipuna population at 2297 persons. Their territory was formally demarcated as an Indigenous Land in 1992. They live there with three other Indigenous peoples: the Palikur, Galibi-Marworno, and Galibi-Kaliña. Most of 518,454 hectares are floodplains; villages are built on islands of permanently dry lands or forest ground. Some Karipuna families live outside this territory, mainly in the neighbouring cities of Oiapoque or Saint Georges (in French Guiana), and even in the more distant and larger cities of Macapá and Cayene.

While most Indigenous lands in Brazil have been destroyed, Karipuna territory has, fortunately, been well preserved. Hunting and fishing remain important subsistence activities. Karipuna people also produce manioc flour for themselves as well as for sale. They plant various species of manioc, as well as a large variety of sweet potatoes, bananas, pineapples, and other local fruits, which they sell from time to time at the Oiapoque city market. The gathering of forest products—mainly açaí and a variety of palm nuts—is also an important source of income. In recent decades, most Karipuna people have become public servants in schools or health clinics.

Historically, the Karipuna people were probably descendants of families who were dispossessed, displaced, and forced to live on Catholic missions during the seventeenth and eighteenth centuries. Some authors (Coudreau 1893; Arnaud 1969) have claimed that they were refugees from the Cabanagem.[3] Based on historical and genealogical data, I understand that they have heterogeneous origins with both foreign and local ancestors (Tassinari 2003). Some of their ancestors were probably Indigenous people living on Portuguese Jesuit missions in the Lower Amazon during the eighteenth century, where Nheengatu was used as a vernacular language.[4] After these missions were closed and the Jesuits expelled from Brazil in the late eighteenth century, the families returned to their former lands in the Uaçá Basin and established villages on the Curipi and Uaçá Rivers.

Karipuna people explain that their common identity as "baptized" facilitates intermarriages among families and cements connections with other ancestors from the Lower Oiapoque River and the Uaçá Basin—this despite their different linguistic backgrounds and origins. Meanwhile, other alliances have been avoided with "nonbaptized" local peoples such as the Aruak, Arakare, Urukuyan, and Palikur peoples (Tassinari 2011). Catholic practices were common during the nineteenth century through the Karipuna people's own initiative, although they did not abandon shamanic beliefs and rituals. They would baptize their children on their own during their festivals, ask missionaries to conduct baptisms during their occasional visits to the villages, or travel to prisons in Guiana and ask prison chaplains to perform baptisms and marriages. Festivals for Catholic saints were commonly performed by Karipuna communities, with Catholic prayers and hymns in Latin that are still chanted in their villages. Meanwhile, shamanism continued to be a potent source of knowledge and power used to access a myriad of *karuãna*: beings from "other worlds" (*uot tã*), the "deep forest" (*fõ dãbua*), the "deep waters" (*fõ djilo*), or stellar constellations.

The hypothesis that the Karipuna families have a heterogeneous origin is important to explain a pattern of marriage choices that they have maintained for a long time. Among the Karipuna people, marriage choices are based on two principles: a valorization of "mixing blood" and an effort to "not let the blood spread," as they say (Tassinari 2003). The first principle produces an exogamous movement and a valorization of marriages with nonrelated (or not-yet-related) families such as Karipuna from other villages, Galibi-Marworno, or other Indigenous neighbours, and even non-Indigenous people. The second principle stimulates endogamous alliances, which may include very close choices such as parallel cousins and avuncular marriages. A pattern emerges here where a first exogamous alliance may mix nonrelated families, generating a subsequent movement to repeat alliances among these families.

In my analysis of Karipuna marriage choices along five generations (Tassinari 2003), I argued that the Karipuna people systematically try to balance properly distant exogamous and closed endogamous alliances. Such a balance also determines the variety and composition of villages. Some small ones are composed of extended families whose sons and daughters intermarry. In these cases, after the repetition of endogamous alliances, we usually see efforts to balance these closed alliances with the further choice of nonrelated spouses. Foreign or nonrelated spouses are, in general, highly esteemed, because they provide Karipuna families with important, previously unknown knowledge about, for example, midwifery, gold-digging techniques, and cattle farming. In larger villages, these endogamous nexuses of families compose roughly disconnected neighbourhoods. One of these groups may occasionally decide to open another village in order to, as they say, live peacefully in familial comfort.

Lux Vidal (1999) has approached the subject of closure and opening, which she understands as complementary opposites, based on the analysis of some graphic motifs repeatedly applied to objects of ordinary or ritual use, revealing that these patterns have a major cosmological and sociological significance among Indigenous peoples from the Uaçá Basin. My point is that this balance between closure and opening, present in Karipuna marriage choices and residential patterns, is also evident in the relations they maintain with the shamanic beings (*karuãna*; also called *invisíveis* in Portuguese),[5] as well as Catholic saints. As Dussart and Poirier (this volume) observe, "In Indigenous conceptions and experiences, relations and relationality are thus constitutive not only of local forms of sociality, but also of being-in-the-world," hence articulating kinship and the production of the person.

In the first decades of the twentieth century, another movement towards openness occurred, this time involving schooling. The Brazilian government offered schooling to the region's Indigenous people to "civilize" them, eliminate their French Guianese creole, and assure the Brazilian possession of their lands after the resolution of a long territorial dispute with France. I see Karipuna people's interest in schooling as similar to their efforts to attract other potential and dangerous sources of power, which were well described by Peter Gow (1991) among native Peruvian communities. Although schooling will not be analyzed in this chapter,[6] it helps explain some aspects of this process, which is very similar to their efforts to interact with both Catholic and shamanic beings.

Through schooling, a new identity feature has emerged among Karipuna families: that of "civilized" or "schooled" people, in contrast with their Palikur neighbours on the Urukaua River who refused schooling until the 1950s. The Karipuna people's first school was organized in 1934 in the Espírito Santo Village in the Chief's house. The first teacher, Verônica Leal, a 14-year-old woman from Belém, Pará, was considered to be a relative of the village leader because they both recalled an ancestor of similar description who they understood to be the same person. The families became engaged in the schooling project led by Leal and remembered her name with kindness and respect (Tassinari 2001) despite her rigid methods and refusal to allow them to speak in their language. Daily school activities promoted national symbols and values (the national anthem, flag ceremonies, and civic holidays), and mandatory use of the Portuguese language. At school, they did more than just learn school subjects (reading and writing in Portuguese, basic math, and soccer, etc.); they were also able to engage in more equal socioeconomic and political relations with non-Indigenous peoples, and to exchange mutual invitations to festivals.

We can see that the school, its activities, and the teacher were immersed in Karipuna daily life, according to the conventional local pattern of attracting "foreign" partners into the local kinship network. A similar situation is presented by Vaarzon-Morel (this volume) about the Warlpiri in Australia, who "also incorporated the Parkinsons [landowners] into their kinship system." The next sections will analyze processes of "making people," among the Karipuna. It will focus on the strategies Karipuna people use to attract beings from Catholicism and shamanism that, as previously mentioned, allow them to relate with different kinds of alterity. I will focus on the production of proper and healthy bodies in order to reveal the combination and articulation of these different strategies—traditions and practices that they call *no sixtem* (our system; see below)—which occurs in ordinary life through practices and knowledge about pregnancy, childbirth, health, wealth, sickness, and death rather than in a theoretical corpus of abstract knowledge.

Shamanism and Alliances with the *Karuãna*

When I initiated fieldwork in Karipuna villages in the 1990s, women would tell me about their experiences with pregnancy, some of them related to a *karuãna* agency. They explained that pregnancy may result from a woman taking a bath in the river during her period. Her menstrual blood in the river water may attract a *karuãna* as a kind of sexual partner, and she may become pregnant by him. To be completed, this conception by an invisible being also depends on human sexual intercourse. The pregnancy might be considered normal until the pregnant woman begins to dream of her *karuãna* partner in truly distressing nightmares, which can progressively become pleasant if the pregnant woman can overcome her fear of this strange being and begin to enjoy a relationship with him. To help in this process, some women call a shaman to control the *karuãna* lover and prevent him from taking his child to his world (*uot tã*, the deep worlds), which would mean the death of the newborn.

These frightening *karuãna* appearances are associated with animal features such as the black hair of a monkey, the skin of an anaconda, or the eyes of a dolphin, which are recognized when the newborn's body is examined. Some of the babies would be considered by Western medicine to be cases of fetal malformation and die within hours or days after birth. Others would be considered to have disabilities or simply to have unusual behaviour. One boy, for instance, did not walk until three years of age, instead crawling on the floor; he was considered to be the son of an anaconda. In all these cases, the child is considered to be a "shaman from birth," and a potentially powerful shaman at that.

The Karipuna people use the Portuguese word *gente* or the French Guianese creole word *mun* to refer to "people," including people from Uaçá, people from Oiapoque, and people from the deep worlds: *fõ dãbua* (deep forest) and *fõ djilo* (deep waters). These invisible beings live in the *tã dji fõ* (time of deep worlds)—worlds that are parallel to our own. As in other descriptions of ontologies in this part of the world (see, e.g., Lima 1996), these invisible beings share a common humanity with people from our world and are believed to have a similar way of life in that they have families, homes, villages, and *turé* (shamanic festivals) in their respective worlds. They are, however, different from human beings, and this difference is grounded in their corporeity. Particularly in reference to the Karipuna and Galibi-Marworno peoples, Ugo Andrade (2011) argues that the *karuãna* can be defined through their process of "appearance," which he describes as a movement of becoming visible alongside a relationship with people from our world (*no tã*). For Andrade, their ontology does not define beings by their previous essential qualities but by their changeable conditions of appearance in this world—along, in Andrade's words, their "horizons of a relationship" with specific people. The *karuãna* may be frightening or distressing to one person, but attractive and charming to another; they can cause sickness here but restore health there. This ontology can exemplify what Dussart and Poirier (this volume) point out about relational ontologies, including those presented in this volume, which emphasize relatedness more than essential qualities of the beings.

To appear in our world, the *karuãna* must wear the cloak of an animal to be seen by or to contact people. A hunter in the forest might occasionally meet a *karuãna* in the appearance of a monkey; someone fishing may see them as anacondas in a river; a woman, as mentioned, may contact them while bathing in a river. These unexpected, uncontrolled relations may lead some people to sickness, madness, or even death. Others may feel attracted by these *karuãna* and begin a process of corporal metamorphosis. A hunter may get lost in the forest and come to live with monkeys in their *fõ dãbua* village; a fisherman may progressively change his skin and definitively plunge into the *fõ djilo* world as an anaconda; a woman may become pregnant with a *karuãna*'s child.

If well controlled, a proper relation with a *karuãna* may become a shamanic apprenticeship. These invisible beings are masters who can teach shamanic knowledge in the form of songs, artifacts, visual motifs and health treatments. First contact with them usually occurs in a dream.

Such initial dreams are always frightening and dangerous, resulting in physical and mental disturbances. To restore their health, the person contacted must ask an experienced shaman for help. The shaman may ask the *karuãna* to stop making contact or may teach the person contacted by the *karuãna* how to properly establish contact back—the first step in shamanic initiation. The healing process, therefore, may also be a shamanic apprenticeship. The novice will then mainly learn dreaming techniques: how to sleep and open the eyes to *uot tã*, how to contact and attract the invisibles through dreams, how to choose a *karuãna* to become one's master, and how to learn songs and decorative motifs from them.

In the same way, a woman who becomes pregnant from a *karuãna* may begin a shamanic apprenticeship with this *karuãna*, with the help of a shaman. It is thus common for Karipuna women to be shamans. These women shamans develop a life with two families: one in our world, lived during the day, and another in the *uot tã*, visited through dreams while asleep at night. This connection of affinity with the *karuãna* also points to the centrality and extension of affinity for producing people, involving not only human spouses but also relationships with invisible beings.

Other possibilities for controlled encounters with *karuãna* may occur during the *turé* shamanic festivals or during shamanic healing sessions called *xitoto*. *Turé* festivals are usually organized by a shaman in November, at the end of the dry season, during the full moon. The *karuãna* are attracted to dance and drink with people through the song of *turé* clarinets and maracas and the offer of a brewed cassava beverage. The dance space is marked and decorated with benches and embellished with visual motifs that the shaman had learned in previous dreams. *Xitoto* are private healing ceremonies that can occur either in the shaman's or in the ill person's house. A tent made of mosquito netting is prepared. Inside the tent, the shaman sings with maracas and smokes cigars made with tauari fiber (from the *Couratari guianensis* tree) to call out their *karuãna* masters. These are the rare moments when people can experience a controlled relation with the *karuãna*, guided by an experienced shaman whom they trust.

Catholicism and Alliances with Saints and through Godparenthood

The Karipuna people consider Catholicism to be their religion and to be as genuine and rooted in their experience as shamanism.[7] Similar to other contexts described in this volume (Crépeau, Laugrand, Vaarzon-Morel), the explicit assertion of Christian faith does not deny shamanic practices. Catholic techniques and beliefs are therefore as important to a proper production of the person as shamanic ones. As I have mentioned above, baptism is an important feature of their identity. For babies, it is considered important not only to give them strength and protection against disease, but also to enlarge the network of people protecting them through the role of godparents. Through baptism, they may rebuild kinship relations by inviting an already related person—usually a sibling or an uncle—to be the godparent, thus reinforcing existing links. They may also create a new bond with someone who is not yet a relative: a neighbour, a non-Indigenous teacher, or a nurse from the town. As Vaarzon-Morel (this volume) observes about the Warlpiri people of Australia in relation with the Baptist faith, the baptism is also used as a way to make people strong and build relations with non-Indigenous families within the local Baptist community.

The baptism ritual can be performed by a priest visiting the villages but is more frequently conducted by the Karipuna people themselves during a festival for a saint. They prepare a bonfire and godparents dance around it together, performing their alliance. The links of cooperation and mutual aid among families that are created through baptism are crucial strategies for forming alliances beyond marriage. In the same way, asking someone to become a child's godfather or godmother allows the creation of consanguinity without descent. By baptizing their children, the Karipuna people can build relatedness to accommodate foreign people or families in the village or to join with people from the villages who are living in nearby towns.

These kinds of mutual aid networks are mainly reinforced through the festivals to the saints, which are organized by each village to honour a patron saint. Each large village has its patron saint, following a model initiated in the Espírito Santo Village through the Chief, Captain Teodoro, who also housed the first Karipuna school. As I mentioned earlier, the teacher Verônica Leal became integrated in the community through the memory of a common ancestor; more than this, she also became the godmother of several children.

The *Festa do Divino* (Holy Spirit Festival) is also known as the Big Karipuna Festival. For two weeks each May, the Karipuna community (*lasosiete Karipun*), as they call themselves, congregates. This community consists of families living in all the Karipuna villages and in the neighbouring towns. The same way that the Holy Spirit is considered the patron saint for the entire Karipuna community, each village chooses its own patron saint to be honoured at community festivals. Devotion to the saints also involves a sense of belonging to a village, which is associated with the figure of its Chief. Being a devotee to a particular saint, being part of a community, and following the leader are three forms of positioning oneself within the Karipuna community networks. Therefore, to propose a patron saint for a village and to promote a festival for the saint are both political acts.

These feasts are moments to thank the saints for blessings granted and to ask for future ones. Karipuna families usually make promises to saints, asking for blessings related healing of persistent sickness, conceiving a baby, or building a house, for example. During these festivals, saints receive food, beverages, or even candles in accordance with the blessings received and whatever the donors can afford. What I wish to stress here is that the same kind of mutual aid networks that families create through baptism are extended to the Catholic saints; the saints are directly involved in the aforementioned webs of support. A similar strategy is used to attract people from other worlds, as they do with the *karuãna* shaman masters.

However, there are differences between the possibility of contact with the Catholic saints and with the *karuãna*. The Karipuna people cannot contact the Catholic saints by dancing or drinking with them, as they do with the *karuãna*. They can only try to please the saints with the festivals, raising flags to them and singing religious hymns in the saints' own language, Latin. A traditional prayer, the Litany of the Blessed Virgin Mary, has been transmitted orally for generations. It is recited during the Festival of the Holy Spirit and at funeral ceremonies.

Unlike the *karuãna*, the Catholic saints do not appear to Karipuna individuals, though it is possible to observe some signs of their blessings: the wealth of a family or the birth of a healthy baby, for example. Unfortunate situations such as a house fire, an illness, or the death of a relative are, conversely, signs of saints' anger or disapproval. In contrast to Kaingang cosmology described by Robert Crépeau (2002, this volume), Catholic saints do not appear in shamanic contexts. These are different features of what they both call "our system," *Kaingang Jykré* to the Kaingang, *no sixtem* to the Karipuna: their own ways of entangled religiosities.

No Sixtem

Beyond shamanic and Catholic practices and beliefs, there are a myriad of techniques and knowledge that are roughly related to one or another tradition, but equally important to the production of a healthy and proper person. As already mentioned, the Karipuna people describe this ensemble as *no sixtem*. I argue that the elements of this system are not connected in an abstract and articulated theory but are entangled in ordinary life in order to "make people" through spiritual and physical labour. As an ultimate and encompassing explanation, the Karipuna people say that "all power comes from God." This means that the power of shamans, of all kinds of invisibles, of beings with spirits, of the saints, of the souls of the dead, of the forces in the environment—all comes from God. Although this may at first look like a "monotheist religion," when we consider the emphasis on the multiplicity of beings a person can pragmatically relate to, it is in fact an example of an "entangled religiosity" (see Dussart and Poirier, this volume).

During my research, I found it unfruitful to look for an integrated cosmological explanation that connects this myriad of invisible people and powerful forces. I recognized that commonly held beliefs and daily practices linked to the Catholic saints and *karuãna* complement each other as explanatory resources but do not merge into a single, embracing theory of the world.[8]

Among the Karipuna people, saints and *karuãna* belong to different domains; they are evoked and celebrated on different occasions, and they are related to very specific explanatory theories, lines of reasoning, attitudes, and practices. In daily life, these domains are used for the same purposes, such as explanations for accidents, diseases and their cures, success in pregnancy and childbirth, and abundant harvests. Thus, I analyze the importance of focusing on daily life and the production of the person to understand how these traditions are pragmatically entangled. My purpose in this last section is to describe the complex of traditions, practices, and knowledge that they call *no sixtem* in relation to the production of proper and healthy bodies, with a focus on childhood.[9]

According to Camila Codonho (2013), who conducted research on childhood among the Galibi-Marworno people, children are considered active beings from the time of their gestation and birth. This is also true for Karipuna childhood. A fetus is considered to be the product of the mixing of the father's and mother's blood and it is formed by the foods eaten by the pregnant woman along with the retained menstrual blood. Its *nam* (the vital principle; also translated as "soul")[10] accesses the fetus's body beginning in the fourth month of pregnancy when the eyes are formed. A *nam*, which develops with the baby's body, is considered to be the force that leads to birth, ultimately giving the child the energy to leave the womb.

Based on this principle, midwives use techniques called *hale van* (pulling the belly) to feel the growth of the baby in the womb by massaging the mother's belly after the third or fourth month of gestation. In these sessions, the midwives say they can feel the baby's body and interact with it, encouraging the correct position in the birth path. They say that the baby becomes calm after the massage and this is important for having a good pregnancy and birth. During childbirth, the midwives also prepare a mild pepper tea for the pregnant woman to drink in order to give the baby strength enough to be born.

Care for the newborn involves a set of techniques that are roughly articulated by shamanism, popular Catholicism, and other forms of knowledge. Their basic purpose is to keep the *nam* in the baby's body; during the postpartum quarantine in particular, but also in early childhood, the link of *nam* to body is not yet strong. Earlier, I discussed the importance of baptism for giving a baby strength and protection against disease. Most infant sicknesses are believed to be caused by the agency of invisibles—a *vã ãthavé* (crosswind), a *txi vã* (light wind), or a *mitã lakãsiél* (half-rainbow), for example. Treatments for such illnesses are performed several times a day. The treatment technique involves whispering some prayers near the ill person and gently blowing on their body to remove the sickness. The blowings are prayers in the form of songs, usually in French Guianese creole, that evoke the individuals, animals, or climatic phenomena involved in the infirmity. If the disease is caused by unfaithful sexual intercourse during the postpartum quarantine, for example, the name of the lover must be mentioned in the prayer. There are blowings to improve children as they grow to favour the development of certain qualities; there are blowings to help children talk, to grow up healthy, and to be intelligent. The whispered prayer usually refers to the desirable qualities of certain animals, such as a talkative bird or an animal known to be active or clever.

Other techniques more closely related to popular Catholicism are also used to protect children, mainly newborns, for instance by helping them sleep or breastfeed well, or to heal them from diseases such as erysipelas and the *olho gordo* (an expression that literally means "fat eye," and is used to describe a sickness caused by envy). These techniques are known to certain women called *rezadeiras* who specialize in giving blessings and usually also know about medicinal herbs. Unlike blowings, these prayers (*rezas*, in Portuguese) usually refer to Catholic saints or to the power of God. They are only mentally repeated, not spoken or whispered by the *rezadeiras*, though the latter may use a twig or knife to softly touch the diseased part of the body to remove or metaphorically cut out the illness. Similar to a blowing, the treatment must be done three or more times a day. The *rezadeiras* also make small cloth bags that are placed on the necks of young children who get sick easily. Called *bhebs*, these sachets contain herbs and folded papers with written prayers, usually addressed to God or the saints.

Food restrictions during pregnancy and later during the postpartum quarantine are also important strategies for "making people" and must be observed by the mother. In general, the restrictions are related to the corporal qualities of certain animals that must not be eaten. During pregnancy, these corporal qualities are associated with dangers for gestation or birth. Tapir and other large or burly animals, for example, are considered dangerous for a pregnant woman to eat because they are associated with exceptional, undesirable growth of the fetus. The slippery quality of an eel is also considered dangerous because it can cause a baby to slip from the womb before the proper time of birth. In the same way, animals who live in burrows, such as armadillos, may cause a baby to remain too long in the womb. These associations seem to be naïve if merely understood as symbolic associations, but they are not. It is important to focus on corporeity to understand the relations between the corporal qualities of the ingested animal, the pregnant woman, and the fetus.

The mother's food restrictions during quarantine are in place to heal her *mamãpitxi* (motherbody). *Mamãpitxi* is usually translated as "the womb," but the local significance exceeds the idea of this physical organ. It is defined as both the location in which the fetus grows and the woman's essence. It is properly located near the belly button, where it pulses when it is healthy. During childbirth or heavy activities, a woman may have a motherbody displacement, which produces discomfort, pain, and even infertility if not properly healed.

Although the diet during the pregnancy and quarantine must only be followed by the mother, both parents must respect some work restrictions and sexual interdictions. The father must not go hunting or perform difficult jobs because the spell of the hunted animal or of hard work can reach the newborn and make it sick. The corporal disposition of the parents and hunted animals can affect the newborn. In general, the couple must be watched by someone, usually the wife's mother, to ensure that they properly follow all of the quarantine restrictions. This shows the importance of the network of cooperation mentioned above.

Such networks are at work in the closely related women who help each other during pregnancy and in child care. These women are usually together during the "pulling the belly" sessions mentioned above, when a midwife and the pregnant woman's relatives, such as her mother and sisters, reinforce crucial links of mutual aid, encouragement, and familial memory by practising techniques of manipulating the body. Some massage techniques for the babies are also important moments when mother, baby, and some invisible forces of growth bond together.

The purpose of one such technique, known as *aple laxé* (calling the flesh), is to produce a healthy and strong body by having a mother massage her baby a few times a day, usually around bath time. With her hands around the baby's arms and legs, the mother places gentle pressure on the muscles and carefully manipulates them. She manipulates the buttocks, back, head, and face to model the body according to their standard of beauty. While they massage the baby, they make a constant sound by popping the tongue on the roof of the mouth to "call the flesh" and fatten the baby (Tassinari 2013). The *aple laxé* technique is considered to be as important as food for "creating the body."

Among the Karipuna strategies for "make people" by producing healthy and proper bodies, we have discussed the special diets and precautions taken by the parents during pregnancy and the postpartum quarantine, the *hale van* massage performed by the midwives during pregnancy, the midwives' knowledge about birth and postpartum, the *aple laxé* massages given to babies by their mothers, and the techniques for growing up properly. To these, we could add: the miniature tools and dull knives used for training small children; the encouragement to leave children free in the village to observe, experiment, imitate, and learn through their own efforts; and the immediate response of adults to children's attempts at imitation in order to show them the correct ways.

These strategies are articulated with shamanism and Catholicism in two different manners. The first, which was described in the previous sections, is related to kinship: the creation of alliances, filiation, or apprenticeship ties that connect people and families with shamanic and Catholic beings. The second, discussed in this section, is related to a repertoire of practices and beliefs that the Karipuna people define as *no sixtem*. In this system, both shamanism and Catholicism are used, but not mixed. To better explain how these different domains can be articulated in practice yet separated as explanatory theories or lines of reasoning about some facts, this section concludes with two examples.

A young woman from the village of Manga was pregnant with her second child. Her first baby had died shortly after birth due to fetal malformation. At that time, a shaman diagnosed her baby as the son of an invisible and she recalled repeated dreams she had during the pregnancy. She dreamed that a monkey was looking at her near the stream where she used to wash clothes and concluded that her first baby was his son. To avoid the same problem in the second pregnancy, she stopped washing clothes in that stream, consulted an obstetrician in the town of Oiapoque, asked for help from a shaman she trusted, and made a promise to Our Lady of Guadalupe (who was in the process of being chosen as the patron saint of the village of Manga). Neither the shaman nor the doctor provided comfort for her affliction: the doctor did not require medical exams to check the health of the fetus, and the shaman just explained that if it is the son of a *karuãna*, it is already done and we cannot change it. Consequently, she found support in her faith in Our Lady of Guadalupe. Since she could not afford to be a *festeira* (i.e., one who donates food and supplies for a festival, in this case for Our Lady of Guadalupe), she promised to take care of the chapel by keeping it clean and decorated with flowers.

Fortunately, the woman's second birth occurred normally, and the baby was healthy. This was considered one of the first miracles of Our Lady of Guadalupe in the village and influenced her selection as patron saint of Manga. Using this example, we can say that the invisible monkey, Our Lady of Guadalupe, and even the obstetrician could not have had any possible encounters or relations. They belong to different domains. The dreams about the stream, the chapel, and the hospital in town are accessed through different and specific ways: a shamanic intervention, a promise, and the state health system. They are related to distinct explanatory lines of reasoning. The next example is even more elucidative on this subject.

Another woman from the same village was pregnant with her seventh baby. She was worried about having sores during breast-feeding, as she did with her other children, and she decided to make a promise to Saint Antonio. At that time, before Guadalupe was chosen, Antonio was the patron saint of Manga and this woman promised to be the *festeira* that year. She was a shaman and went to heal some patients in French Guiana to earn money to meet the expensive costs of the festival. When she was nine months pregnant and on the journey home, her family's boat crashed into another vessel and sunk with all the supplies she had purchased for the feast. Even worse, although she was able to save herself and her two children, her husband unfortunately drowned. A week later, although she was quite worried about her situation as a widow and the destiny of her husband's soul (*nam*), she gave birth to a healthy child.

To explain the accident and the destiny of the husband's soul, two lines of reasoning began to gain force. The first was delineated during the funeral when people began to mention a miracle: a woman, nine months pregnant, remained safe from rough waters with two children in her arms. The talk emphasized that the husband had died while he was working for the Festival to Saint Antonio and that his soul was going to live in an eternal feast. Despite her efforts to cancel her obligations as *festeira*, the village leader considered she had made a promise to the Saint that could not be broken because this would endanger the entire community.

Another explanation was developed by the widow herself, based on her dreams. Since she was in quarantine after childbirth, she could not dream about her *karuãna,* but she had repeated dreams about her husband, revealing that he had been a victim of sorcery that had actually been aimed at her. Distressed, she recalled that she had made a few *bhebs* to protect the family during the boat trip, and the husband was the only one who had not placed a *bheb* on his neck. Worried about the destiny of her husband's soul, she asked an expert to pray several litanies in his honour. She also asked a shaman who was considered powerful to make an invisible fence surrounding her house to keep her husband's soul away. Perhaps it was a miracle or sorcery, perhaps a miracle and sorcery; in any case, the solution to her distress arrived sometime later, when she met a new *karuãna* in her dreams who protected and comforted her.

Once again, saints and *karuãna* were sought out for help for the same reason. The shaman made a promise to Saint Antonio and worked with the *karuãna* with the same goal: to avoid breast sores. To keep the husband's soul away, she turned to Catholic prayer and shamanic deeds. But Saint Antonio, the husband's soul, and the *karuãna* did not encounter each other or participate together in a common domain, beyond the explanation that they are all under the power of God.

These examples seem to elucidate how the Karipuna people appeal to shamanic and Catholic practices and explanations in daily life without merging them into syncretic practices or into a single explanatory line. Behind the generic idea embracing all beings in "our system" that "all power comes from God," there are ordinary practices and knowledge that produce the person.

Conclusion

This chapter sought to show how a focus on the production of the person offers an understanding of Karipuna modes of manipulating alterity that involve outside partners or families as well as Catholic and shamanic beings. Although this production of the person occurs throughout the person's life, the chapter focused on practices and beliefs related to gestation and early childhood that are used to create healthy and proper bodies.

The chapter described two pragmatic ways the Karipuna people approach these heterogeneous domains of beings. The first may be understood as sociological and reflects Dussart's and Poirier's point in this volume about Indigenous cosmologies and their relation to kinship. The principles the Karipuna people use to produce relatedness with different kinds of people can embrace not only Karipuna families, other Indigenous peoples, and non-Indigenous people, but also the shamanic invisible beings and Catholic saints. By attracting alterity to community and associated reciprocity connections, they seek to produce a person within an ideal balance between sameness and otherness. In this way, shamans can have a *karuãna* as a spouse and have families in the deep worlds, unrelated families can become partners through their children's baptism, and an unknown saint can become the patron saint of a village and part of a community reciprocity network. As such, a person is produced inside a network of relatedness that embraces both saints and *karuãna*.

As discussed above, alterity is valued as a source of power and knowledge, and is both appreciated and feared. This is a common feature of

Lowland South American Indigenous peoples, as Joanna Overing (1983, 333; formerly Overing Kaplan) indicated in a comparative approach to three Indigenous contexts in Central Brazil, Northwest Amazonia, and the Guianas:

> In brief, social existence is identified with both difference and danger, and inversely, asocial existence (e.g. the afterworld) with identity and safety. It is for this reason that Amerindians place such considerable emphasis in social life upon the proper mixing of elements and forces, which must of necessity be different each from the next for society to exist: it is only through such "proper" mixing that safety can be achieved in society and danger averted.

What is peculiar among the Karipuna people is the scope of exogamic practices, involving alliances with non-Indigenous people and shamanic beings as well as relations managed with and through Catholic saints. Alliances with non-Indigenous people have been appreciated for providing access to various forms of knowledge: schooling, midwifery, techniques for panning gold, and cattle breeding are some examples of expertise that have come from the outside. These alliances can be compared to those performed by shamans in contact with *karuãna* who give them access to shamanic knowledge that is also considered exogenous. The same is true of the Catholic saints who are attracted by the families to be patrons of a village. They are included in local reciprocity networks in which they exchange graces and blessings during the festivals where people re-create these networks through godparenthood ties.

The other way the Karipuna people have approached these different domains of beings is related to corporeity. Although dependent on the group of relatedness produced through the strategies mentioned above, corporeity is associated with techniques, practices, and forms of knowledge related to the body and its affections and forces. These practices can be roughly associated with shamanic and Catholic beings in the sense that the expertise of blowing and blessing can dialogue with these repertoires and combine with beliefs about the environment—animal behaviour, atmospheric phenomena, and corporal forces and dispositions.

These practices are deeply rooted in corporal experiences that are managed by a group of relatives so a child can be given proper foods and beverages, receive healing songs and blessings made by experts in different therapies, and be massaged by the pregnant mother's midwife or the mother herself. Alterity is manipulated through the body to produce the person. In other words, if we look for the entanglement between Catholic and shamanic domains among the Karipuna people, we find it only in the production of the body and the person.

Author's Note

I would like to thank Sylvie Poirier and Françoise Dussart for their accurate and useful suggestions that greatly helped to improve the chapter. My sincere gratitude to Lux Vidal for her continuous research partnership since her supervision of my PHD thesis. This research was supported by Conselho Nacional de Desenvolvimento Científico e Tecnológico, Brazil (CNPq; process no. 308259/2018-1) and Instituto Nacional de Ciência e Tecnologia Brasil Plural (IBP).

Notes

1. I conducted fieldwork in Karipuna villages between 1990 and 1998 for a total of six months. I focused on cosmology and ritual life, history, schooling, and educational practices to produce my PHD thesis (Tassinari 1998). I maintained contact with Karipuna families during further fieldwork I conducted in Galibi-Marworno villages in 2001, 2006, and 2010. In 2013 and 2016, I returned to Karipuna villages for a month to research midwifery and propose an ethnographic blog to make research data available to them (www.memoriasoiapoque.wordpress.com). This chapter presents data from this long-term investigation.

2. Seeger, de Matta, and Viveiros de Castro (1979), following the movement proposed by Joanna Overing Kaplan (1977, 9), looked for categories that could be meaningful to South American societies: "Our analytical problem is that of phrasing order when we know order is there but have no language through which to express it." The panel "Social Time and Social Space in Lowland South American Societies," held at the 42nd International Congress of Americanists, congregated almost thirty researchers who discussed more accurate categories for understanding these peoples. Different from the language of "descent," "filiation," or "corporate groups" used to describe social structures of African societies, Overing Kaplan suggested categories such as social time or social

space to better capture social organizational features of South American societies.

3. The Cabanagem was popular nineteenth-century revolutionary movement led by enslaved Indigenous and Black peoples who spoke the Nheengatu language in Pará State, Lower Amazon.

4. While some Elders remember words from the Nheengatu language, the Karipuna people nowadays speak a variation of French Guianese creole and Portuguese. The idiom was phonetically transcribed by linguists during the 1980s and is now used in bilingual schools.

5. *Invisível* (invisible) is a local term used to talk about shamanic beings. I prefer to use this term and not *nonhumans* because, for the Karipuna people, they are considered "people" in their own worlds and therefore they cannot be properly called nonhumans. This point will be developed in the next section.

6. This analysis can be found in Tassinari (2001) and Tassinari and Cohn (2009).

7. Nowadays, Protestant churches have a considerable number of followers in Karipuna villages, but I have not yet been able to analyze their role in the production of the person.

8. This is not so for the Kaingang people of southern Brazil (see Crépeau 2002, this volume) for whom some Catholic figures popular in the region, such as São João Maria, have been integrated into their shamanism and can become the masters (*jagre*) of the shamans.

9. In a previous paper (Tassinari 1999), I analyzed this intertwining of Catholicism and shamanism with a focus on feasts and healing rituals.

10. Although it is common to translate the local term *nam* with the Portuguese word *alma* (soul), the word does not have the same meaning as *soul* in the Judeo-Christian tradition. Some species of plants or trees, for example, are also said to have a *nam*.

References

Andrade, Ugo. 2011. "A physis e o pensamento ameríndio." *Avá: Revista de antropología* 19: 79–105. http://www.redalyc.org/articulo.oa?id=169029211004

Censo Brasil. 2012. "Demográfico 2010." *Características gerais da população, religião e pessoas com deficiência*. Rio de Janeiro: IBGE. https://biblioteca.ibge.gov.br/visualizacao/periodicos/94/cd_2010_religiao_deficiencia.pdf

Codonho, Camila. 2013. "Cosmologia e infância Galibi-Marworno: aprendendo, ensinando, protagonizando." In *Educação indígena,* edited by Antonella Tassinari, Beleni Grando, and Marcos Alexandre Albuquerque, 53–76. Florianópolis: EDUFSC.

Arnaud, Expedito. 1969. "Os Índios da região do Uaçá (Oiapoque) e a proteção oficial brasileira." *Boletim do Museu Paraense Emílio Goeldi, serie antropologia* 40: 1–43.

Coudreau, Henri. 1893. *Chez nos Indiens: quatre années dans la Guyane Française (1887–1891)*. Paris: Librairie Hachette et Cie.

Crépeau, Robert. 2002. "A prática do xamanismo entre os Kaingang do Brasil meridional: uma breve comparação com o xamanismo Bororo." *Horizontes Antropológicos* 8 (18): 113–29. http://dx.doi.org/10.1590/S0104-71832002000200005

Gow, Peter. 1991. *Of Mixed Blood: Kinship and History in Western Amazonian Cultures*. Oxford: Oxford University Press; New York: Clarendon Press.

Lima, Tânia Stolze. 1996. "O dois e seu múltiplo: reflexões sobre o perspectivismo em uma cosmologia tupi." *Mana* 2 (2): 21–47. http://dx.doi.org/10.1590/S0104-93131996000200002

Mauss, Marcel. 1936. "Les techniques du corps." *Journal de psychologie* 32: 3–4.

Overing, Joanna. 1983. "Elementary Structures of Reciprocity: A Comparative Note on Guianese, Central Brazilian, and North-West Amazon Socio-Political Thought in Themes in Political Organization: The Caribs and Their Neighbours." *Antropológica* 59–62: 331–48.

Overing Kaplan, Joanna, ed. 1977. *Social Time and Social Space in Lowland South American Societies*. Vol. 2, *Actes du XLIIe Congrès international des américanistes*. Paris: Congrès international des américanistes.

Seeger, Antony, Roberto da Matta, and Eduardo Viveiros de Castro. 1979. "A construção da pessoa nas sociedades indígenas brasileiras." *Boletim do Museu Nacional* (32): 2–19.

Tassinari, Antonella. 1998. "Contribuição à história e à etnografia da região do Baixo Oiapoque: a composição das famílias Karipuna e a estruturação das redes de troca." PHD thesis, Universidade de São Paulo. Repositório Institucional UFSC. https://repositorio.ufsc.br/xmlui/handle/123456789/158197

——. 1999. "Catolicismo e xamanismo entre as famílias karipunas do Rio Curipi." In *Transformando os deuses*, edited by Robin Wright, 447–78. Campinas: Editora da UNICAMP.

——. 2001. "Da civilização à tradição: os projetos de escola entre os Índios do Uaçá." In *Antropologia, história e educação: a questão indígena e a escola*, edited by Aracy Lopes da Silva and Mariana Ferreira, 157–95. São Paulo: MARI; FAPESP; Global Editora.

——. 2003. *No bom da festa: o processo de construção cultural das famílias karipuna do Amapá*. São Paulo: EDUSP.

———. 2011. "Organização social e história Galibi-Marworno." In "XXXII Convegno internazionale di americanistica." Special issue, *Quaderni di THULE—Rivista italiana di studi americanistici* X: 1173–81.

———, producer. 2013. *Creating the Body in Kumarumã*. Video with English subtitles, 18:22. https://vimeo.com/70519902

Tassinari, Antonella, and Clarice Cohn. 2009. "Opening to the Other: Schooling among the Karipuna and Mebengokré-Xikrin of Brazil." *Anthropology & Education Quarterly* 40 (2): 150–69. https://doi.org/10.1111/ j.1548-1492.2009.01033.x

Vidal, Lux. 1999. "O modelo e a marca ou o estilo dos misturados: cosmologia, história e estética entre os povos indígenas do Uaçá." *Revista de antropologia* 42 (1–2): 29–45. https://doi.org/10.1590/S0034-77011999000100003

Viertler, Renate. 1979. "A noção de pessoa entre os Bororo." *Boletim do Museu Nacional* 32: 20–30.

Viveiros de Castro, Eduardo. 1979. "A fabricação da pessoa na sociedade Xinguana." *Boletim do Museu Nacional* 32: 40–49.

5

DISCOURSES ON THE ADVENT OF NEW TIMES AMONG THE KAINGANG PEOPLE OF SOUTHERN BRAZIL

ROBERT R. CRÉPEAU

Unlike us, the white people are not afraid to be crushed by the falling Sky. But one day they may fear that as much as we do! (Kopenawa and Albert 2013, 410)

FROM THE PUBLICATION, at the beginning of the twentieth century, of the first versions of the Great Flood narrative (Borba 1908; Schaden 1953, [1945] 1988) to recent testimonies collected in the field (L. Almeida 2004; Crépeau 2008; Rosa 2005), narratives based on the end of time occupy an important place in the way the Kaingang people of Southern Brazil think of themselves in their communities, in Brazilian society, and, more generally, in the cosmos. These narratives are closely linked to a context of religious plurality influenced by the Catholicism of the colonizers and, in recent decades, by the various Evangelical denominations to which many among the Kaingang people adhere. As Françoise Dussart and Sylvie Poirier (this volume) point out, religious plurality is an intrinsic dimension of the Indigenous worlds and is a source of tensions, challenges, and entangled responsibilities. This chapter analyzes the actuality—and thus the constant actualization—of these important narratives that predict the end of an era and the advent of a better world. Several contrasting perspectives will be presented and compared in order to identify current ideological and practical trends concerning the future, which, in the minds of many, remains uncertain.

As Déborah Danowski and Eduardo Viveiros de Castro (2017, 76) note, "periodical apocalypses are the rule in Amerindian mythologies." Indeed, the beginning of time often coincides with the end of an era after its destruction by fire, by water (flood), or by other means. These events lead to the end of a previous humanity that is survived only by a handful of humans or, in the worst cases, a couple or even a single individual. In these narratives, the survivors are prototypical characters, cultural heroes, or tricksters. As I will argue below, these cultural heroes re-create the world through the (re)institution of social life and its rules and norms.

In light of the most recent studies on climate change and the depletion of the planet's resources, and more recently with the global crisis brought on by the COVID-19 pandemic, end-of-world narratives seem more than plausible, real possibilities in the Anthropocene era—a new geological period defined by the concrete and direct impact of human activities on the global climate and the general ecosystem of the Earth. As Danowski and Viveiros de Castro (2017, 95) point out, the emergence of a contemporary eschatology is becoming increasingly clear for some part of the Western population, at least among "those who have realized that, this time, things will turn out bad for everyone, everywhere." Indigenous societies are a "figuration of the future, not a remnant of the past" (123) and have much to teach us as true "end-of-the-world experts...now that we are on the verge of a process in which the planet as a whole will become something like sixteenth-century America: a world invaded, wrecked, and razed by barbarian foreigners" (108).

A vast literature is dedicated to the study of end-of-time narratives in anthropology and other disciplines such as classical studies, history of religions, and religious studies. Flood stories are first on this list, followed by the destruction of the world by a universal fire and a large number of other motifs (see, e.g., Bornet et al. 2012; Dundes 1988; Monnier 1999; Sergent 2012; Sullivan 1988). For instance, André Thevet ([1575] 1953, 39–40) published a narrative collected from the Tupinambas people of Brazil in which the world was destroyed by fire followed by a flood. The only survivor was a man, Irin-Magé, from whom, according to the Tupinambas people, humans descended. Before him, Jean de Léry ([1557] 1957, 346–47) claimed of the same Tupinambas people that they do not know the true Christian God and wondered, "[W]here can these savages come from?" (my translation).[1] Responding to his own question, he says he is "quite certain that they came out of one of the three sons of Noah," but speculated about which one of the three. Léry ultimately concludes that they were possibly descendants of Cham.

Emergent comparative anthropology has emphasized the religious dimension of these phenomena (particularly through the work of Edward Burnett Tylor [1874] and James George Frazer [1890]) to the detriment of comparative law (Descola 2019). Instead of offering literal, realistic, or referential readings that refer to "historical facts" associated with a more or less distant past, comparative anthropology has proposed a symbolic, archetypical, or inferential reading of these narratives based on general hypotheses of psychological, psychoanalytic, or sociological natures. The legal dimensions of these narratives have been neglected in the past with the notable exception of Hans Kelsen (1881–1973), who is regarded by many to be one of the greatest theorists of law of the twentieth century. Kelsen adopted a point of view that partly escapes the perspectives of early comparative anthropology when he used the flood stories as an illustration of his principle of retribution,[2] which led him to consider the legal dimension of these narratives (Kelsen [1946] 2011, 170). By affirming that "every social order is virtually a moral order," Kelsen (1936, 55) contradicts Tylor (1874) who conceived "primitive religions" as "morally indifferent" (Larsen 2013). Although reductionist,[3] Kelsen's proposal is nonetheless a critical reading of the approaches advocated at the time, which, he thought, were at odds with the Indigenous perspective: "The social order has from the very beginning the character of a legal order" (Kelsen 1936, 7).

More recently, Alain Monnier (1999) provided a comparative analysis of stories of devastating floods and other disasters from the

Amazon and New Guinea.[4] He adopted a resolutely sociological perspective insisting that these types of narrative are the foundations of the order of the world and of things—that is, the foundations of the current structure of society. Monnier is one of the few authors who clearly articulates how the catastrophic destruction of an earlier world transforms mere oppositions into a system of complementarities. Thus, about the Kamoro people of Irian Jaya following the flood caused by the rupture of reciprocity between upstream and downstream peoples, Monnier writes: "What was at the beginning only an opposition from upstream and downstream...is amplified to form a system of orientation" (34). We thus move from the implicit to the explicit or the indeterminate to the determinate: "It is in fact the rupture that creates the rule: what was latent becomes the law, as a result of a first discontinuity" (35). In other words, the story refers to an initial prelegal (or prenormative) situation that the disaster eventually transforms into a system of explicit laws and rules governing the cosmos and the current society instituted by the survivors. From such a perspective, it is possible to argue that end-of-world narratives, rather than outlining an essentially magical-religious or theological conception of a society's founding constitution or initial moment, instead introduce a temporality: the constitutive spiral movement of society on itself. Indeed, the validity of the legal order is something "essentially" temporal in the sense that "it necessarily emerges from a past...and necessarily projects itself towards a future" (Kojève 1981, 43).

Flood narratives among the Kaingang people describe this sociological totality formed by the survivors and their descendants as a zero order[5] of sociality that is strictly speaking neither a beginning nor an initial moment of rupture. In reality, it is not in the disaster itself that the basis for the validity of the social system or the legal order must be found, but in the dynamic process that develops subsequently (see, e.g., Accetti 2016, 193). In the case of the flood, this process is constituted by the institution of the system of reciprocity between moieties by the survivors in order to organize social life and by the realization of the *Kikikoi,* the great second funeral ritual, for the victims of the flood

(Crépeau 2008; Crépeau and Rosa 2018). It could therefore be argued that devastating floods and other catastrophe narratives create the contexts in which survivors literally institute the norms currently in force—the *Kaingang Jykré*, an expression that could be translated as the Kaingang system, culture, or law.

Ethnographic Background on the Kaingang People

The Kaingang people are the largest group of the Gê linguistic and cultural family of Brazil with approximately 45,000 persons living mainly on reservations located in the southern Brazilian states of São Paulo, Paraná, Santa Catarina, and Rio Grande do Sul.[6] In contrast to other Gê and Bororo societies (Crocker 1969, 1985; Maybury-Lewis 1967; Nimuendajú 1939, 1946; Turner 1979), the Kaingang people are not, historically at least, known to have built circular or semicircular villages that directly express and represent their social organization and cosmology. The Kaingang dual organization consists of moieties called *kamẽ* and *kanhru*, which are conceived as asymmetric and complementary. *Kamẽ* moiety is first and masculine, and is associated with the sun, the east, political power, and shamanism. In contrast, *kanhru* moiety is second and feminine, and is associated with the moon, the west, and the organization of the second funeral ritual. Each moiety has a section or submoiety: *votôro* is associated with *kanhru* while *veineky* is associated with *kamẽ*. Moiety and section membership are patrilineal but can in special cases also be acquired by nomination. The Kaingang people describe the rule of exogamy by saying that one should ideally marry a person of a different facial painting, meaning a person of a different moiety or section. In formalized contexts such as myth and ritual, social relations are described or actualized as being mainly dyadic, using the *kamẽ-veineky* / *kanhru-votôro* moiety contrast. Spatial relations are described according to two triadic schemes: horizontally by using the "house, clean space, forest" domains, or vertically by using "high, middle, low" contrasts.

Religious Plurality

The first direct contact of the Kaingang people with Christianity probably dates back to the early seventeenth century. Wilmar D'Angelis and
Juracilda Veiga (1993, 11) indicate that from 1609 to 1629, during the
so-called Jesuit Reductions of Guairá in the present Brazilian state of
Paraná, the Jesuits led a mission with the Gualachos (possibly of the
Gê-Kaingang) and another with the Coroados (a term still used as self-
denomination designating the Kaingang people by some Elders I met
in the 1990s). The first reduction was Conceição de Nossa Senhora
dos Gualachos in the Piquiri River region; the second was Encarnação
on the banks of the Tibagi River. In 1631, these reductions were
destroyed by the Bandeirantes, causing the dispersion of the population and ending the Jesuit enterprise in the state of Paraná (Mota 1994,
69–70). The Jesuits moved their missions to Paraguay, as well as to
the province of Misiones in Argentina and the State of Rio Grande do
Sul in Brazil. The geographical proximity of these missions from the
historical (and present) territory of the Kaingang people implies their
participation in the Jesuit sphere of influence, which, I believe, remains
underestimated. Kaingang cosmology includes narratives that refer to
the ontologies of different traditions, including popular Catholicism
and, more recently, African Brazilian religions and Evangelical
Protestantism.

According to Romulo Machado de Almeida and Rogério Jerônimo
Barbosa (2019, 265), the decline of Catholicism in recent decades in
Brazil has been mainly in favour of Evangelical denominations and
more particularly Pentecostals. Indeed, Catholicism is facing a major
offensive from various Evangelical and Pentecostal churches. This
offensive, which began around 1950 with the arrival of Protestantism
in southern Brazil, was perceived by the Elders I met in the 1990s as
an important destabilizing factor of Kaingang culture dominated until
then by popular Catholicism. Ledson Kurtz de Almeida (2004, 289) and
Marie-Charlotte Pelletier-De Koninck (2016) indicate that Evangelical
and Pentecostal churches have destabilized the Kaingang context so
much that Catholic traditionalists now form a minority group that
is trying to resist and adjust to the growing influence of the *crentes*

(believers). The situation of the Kaingang people is not an isolated case, but rather illustrates an important religious transition that has accelerated significantly over the past twenty years in Brazil: "Diversity and competition among alternative faiths, circulation of followers, and the non-institutionalization of practices and beliefs are some of the dimensions of the religious transition in Brazil in recent decades" (R. Almeida and Barbosa 2019, 280). Hence, the administrative headquarters of Terra Indígena Xapecó alone counts a dozen denominations, eight of which are run by Kaingang pastors. Each church has its own doctrine, which is expressed in practice through values, rules, and customs that vary according to each church's conservative or liberal application of Kaingang traditions (Pelletier-De Koninck 2016, 59). As a result, the celebration of the *Kikikoi*, a second funeral ritual still considered by many to be the most important aspect of Kaingang traditions and cosmology, has been the subject of intense discussion in the last decades, particularly regarding the ritual consumption of honey beer it implies (Crépeau and Rosa 2018). Its performance in May 2018 at the Terra Indígena Xapecó was significant since it involved, for the first time in Kaingang history, the participation of ritual singers converted to Pentecostalism. This performance has been the subject of important adjustments considering the local political dynamics and religious sensitivities.

Indeed, one of the main motivations of conversion to Pentecostalism among the Kaingang people is the negative impact of alcohol consumption and its social and familial consequences from the point of view of the converts (L. Almeida 2004). Alcoholism is considered as a disease that "afflicts not only individuals, but also the entire community" (Pelletier-De Koninck 2016, 93; see also Langdon 2005; Oliveira 1996). Therefore "the evangelization efforts of the *crentes* are largely aimed at reducing the rate of alcoholism on the reservation in order to save the souls of the unfortunate, but also for the sake of social healing." The establishment of rules and standards of behaviour by Pentecostal churches also target interpersonal conflicts, marital violence, and the economic wellbeing of individuals and families. Referring to the end of time or to the advent of a new time, most pastors specifically mention alcohol and drug abuses, interpersonal conflicts, domestic violence, and murder of close relatives as symptoms and signs of the social chaos from which the *crentes* must extricate themselves to be saved.

The End of an Era According to the Pentecostal Pastor Lucio Fernandes

Since 1999, Lucio Fernandes has been the Kaingang pastor of the Rei da Gloria Pentecostal church, one of the many Pentecostal churches located in the heart of the administrative centre of Terra Indígena Xapecó. In 2008, I conducted an interview with him in Terra Indígena Xapecó. When asked about the story of the flood—the great inundation that his father, Vicente Fokâe Fernandes, narrated in the 1990s (see "Great Flood," below in this chapter; see also Crépeau 2008)— Lucio Fernandes stated that the story of his father is identical to the Biblical book of Genesis: "It was while reading the Bible that I realized that the story my father told when I was young about the flood was true. It is following the flood that a new Kaingang humanity emerged from the earth and that the animals taught them the songs and dances of *Kikikoi* ritual. Following the flood, humanity began to rebuild everything again."

Fernandes fully recognizes the role of the animals mentioned in his father's story although he does not find any mention of them in the biblical text. According to Fernandes, God caused the flood because humans were misbehaving at the time—abusing alcohol, fornicating, murdering close relatives, and engaging in other types of violence in the world. "Today, for example, Catholics have their own church, but they do not attend it and do not make the effort to pray. They only want to do better, while some prostitute themselves, abuse alcohol or kill each other instead of thanking God for existing. When a misfortune happens to them, it is the will of God that is expressed since nothing happens without God's permission."

According to Fernandes, the Bible predicts the end of the world, but he notes that he is not able to predict when exactly the end will come since even the angels and Jesus do not know. Only God knows. Although Fernandes is sure the world will end, he doesn't want to try to predict it himself. He mentioned in passing one Brazilian pastor who predicted that the world would end in 1999. When it did not happen, he ran away before being killed by angry followers!

According to Fernandes, there are many signs of the end of time around us: murders of parents, prostitution, drugs and alcohol consumption, and absence of respect for God (mainly by the Catholics who are not regularly going to church or praying to God). Our times are like the past and Noah and the ark are now present through the figures of the pastor and the church. The church is the ark and the pastor is the Noah of present time. People are invited to join Fernandes's church to be saved: "The ark today is in fact the church and the pastors are Noahs who announce salvation through the change of life: If someone was fighting with his family or abusing alcohol, he goes to church and no longer fights. He has a more dignified life as well as his family and his children by no longer spending his money on drinks. The church is the boat that will save the world."

The Great Flood

In the mid-1990s, I discussed at length the story of the great flood with Pastor Fernandes's father Vicente Fokâe Fernandes,[7] an influential Elder, who was in charge of organizing the celebration of the *Kikikoi*. Fokâe and his wife Rivaldina Luiz Niwẽ were important cultural and ritual leaders. Fokâe had inherited his responsibilities from his paternal uncle Manoel Gaspar Kaitkâg; he was surrounded by several Elders who were fighting for the respect of territorial rights and the transmission of Kaingang traditions and culture (Crépeau and Rosa 2018). Like most members of his generation, Fokâe was concerned about the rise of Protestantism, which he considered a threat to Kaingang culture and values. Fokâe, who was a very talented and dedicated storyteller, narrated his own version of the great flood to several researchers (e.g., L. Almeida 2004; D'Angelis and Veiga 1993; Oliveira 1996) and to me (Crépeau 1994, 2008).

On the very first day we met in 1994, on the eve of the celebration of the *Kikikoi*, Fokâe gave me a tour of the large wooden Catholic church of the *sede* (administrative centre) of Terra Indígena Xapecó. He described himself explicitly as a Catholic: "The Catholic religion and our religion is one and the same religion." I learned afterwards that he meant by this that most Elders of his generation were devoted Catholics and considered themselves Kaingang through the perpetuation of the traditional dual social organization or moieties system, the naming and kinship practices, and the ritual practices, especially the *Kikikoi*. Fokâe often referred to *"nosso sistema"* (our system), stressing the differences between Kaingang cosmology and the colonial one associated with Brazilian society.

According to Fokâe's narrative, when the world was destroyed by the great flood, it became possible for their *kamẽ* ancestors who survived to restructure the present world by instituting the divisions of the moieties system. The following is a short version of Fokâe's flood story:

> *The flood was announced by God: "The day this woman washes the oven in the river, there will be a very great flood." Joseph, the father of Jesus Christ, then built a boat where he gathered a couple of each animal and a human couple, a* kanhru *woman and her husband, a* kamẽ. *The water rose for a full day. It then began to decrease and withdrew in three days. There were no more people or animals on the earth.*
>
> *Woodpecker, who is* kamẽ, *stole the fire and gave it to the* kamẽ *and the* kanhru. *The animals then organized a celebration, called* Kikikoi, *for those who perished. The first who came to his fire was* yamuyé yãgrè, *the cayman, because the* kamẽ *always comes first to their fire. Then the* kañer *monkey who is* kanhru *went to his fire... The Kaingang people learned the songs and dances of the* Kikikoi *from these animals.*

Kikikoi literally means "to eat the honey beer together." This second funeral ritual is celebrated approximately one year after the first funeral of the deceased. Family members must formally ask a ritual singer of the opposite moiety or the ritual organizer to perform the ritual. The ritual is organized and performed only if demands originate from at least one family from each moiety or section since it cannot be performed for only one moiety. *Kikikoi* usually takes place after harvest, somewhere between April and May. It is consequently a period during which maize, black beans, and other agricultural products become more abundant. It is also the period during which Araucaria pine trees (*Araucaria angustifolia*) produce their fruit, called *pinhão*, which were a very important source of food for the Kaingang people before massive deforestation. In the past, they were also an important food source for rodents and monkeys, who were consequently easily and abundantly captured by hunters.[8] The central symbol of the *Kikikoi* is in fact an Araucaria pine tree, considered *kamē*, which is sacrificed ritually and transformed into a five-metre trough in which honey beer is prepared. The pine trunk is treated as a deceased person and occupies the centre of the western pole of the ritual space-axis, the other pole being the cemetery.

Although I will not describe the ritual in detail, it is important to underline one of its fundamental aspects: the obligatory complementarity of moieties for its successful enactment. This essential complementarity is reiterated by the ritual performance, which literally and explicitly enacts the ideal of reciprocal exchange of services between moieties. When the Kaingang people describe the *Kikikoi* as "beautiful," particularly its final dance, they are referring to the fact that the ritual implies the coordinated reciprocal participation of people from each moiety and section—in short, the union of the community. According to them, the *kamē* moiety is always first and constitutes a logical encompassing totality, which they used as a standard, starting point, or zero order of sociological and cosmological institution (Crépeau and Rosa 2018).

A second flood narrative by João Xê Coelho of Terra Indígena Palmas, located in the state of Paraná, describes explicitly how a primordial couple instituted Kaingang dual social organization. It was collected in 1947 and published by Egon Schaden (1953) in Terra Indígena Palmas, which is linked to Terra Indígena Xapecó through kinship and ritual partnership. Indeed, the two communities jointly organized all *Kikikoi* celebrations during the second half of the twentieth century. Coelho's flood narrative is as follows:

> *Numerous Indians died following a flood, which took place in this area. The only survivors were a couple, a brother and his sister, both*

still very young. They were members of the Kamẽ *group. The couple
swam toward a very high mountain named* Krim-Takré. *They went
to the summit and climbed into the branches of the trees. When the
water withdrew, they went back to earth. They married, the brother
and the sister, and the Indians reproduced themselves. They made
fire because they had knowledge of the rope used to make fire. They
had numerous children.*

*Before they died, the couple re-established the division in two
groups: the* kamẽ *are stronger and the* kanhru *are weaker. They
divided us to organize the marriages between them. After they
multiplied themselves, the Indians also re-established the division
between* votôro *and* veineky. *The* votôro *have the strength of the*
kanhru *and the* veineky *the strength of the* kamẽ. *(quoted in
Schaden, 1953, 140–41)*

This narrative more precisely describes the institution of postdilu-
vium social order and the rules or laws (the latter term being used by
most Elders) of the Kaingang dual social system. The initial logical unit
of this new social order is constituted by a primordial couple who survived
the great flood. They constitute the zero order of alliance. Since the
brother and sister survivors are of the same *kamẽ* moiety, their children
are also *kamẽ* following the rule of patrilineal affiliation to moiety and
section. Interestingly, the normative frame of João Xê Coelho's narrative is not an implicit principle such as exchange or reciprocity but
rather a triangular configuration of social relations constituted by two
individuals of the same moiety (the primordial couple) and a third term:
Kaingang society and the rules that their children will have to follow in
the future.

In a long conversation in 1995, Fokâe commented at length on the
story of the flood by first borrowing elements from the biblical account
of the Old Testament. He noted that "the great flood occurred because
the people were against God." He expanded on this by describing a
dialogue between God and his son Jesus, the latter questioning his father
on the reasons for the flood and the death of so many innocent people:

"Father, why was there this flood? Then the father replied: 'So that a new world, the new world, may come.' 'Why, father?'...'They were doing more than God, they respected no one.'" Fokâe continued, referring to the fact that there were only five years left before the year 2000 and that the next millennium was approaching. According to the prophecies of São João Maria[9] and the secret teachings of the *kujà* (shamans), a new world should emerge, different from the current postdiluvian world and in which "only those who have committed sin shall pay." Fokâe suggested by this last formula, which he used frequently when he spoke of the future, that the flood triggered by God had been unjust since many innocent people had perished and that in the future, only those who are at fault should disappear.[10] Fokâe elaborated, stating that the failure of many of his contemporaries to respect the rules of community life was the cause of what was soon to happen. His description largely overlaps with that of his son Lucio Fernandes (see "End of an Era," above in this chapter). Indeed, Fokâe referred to the fact that the people had abandoned the precepts of the Catholic religion and, even more importantly, of common life: "The people no longer believe...The people do so many things that are not necessary, killing each other, killing their own brother, killing their own mother, killing their own father...The father, the mother kills the son, the son... and so on." Fokâe explained this context by the fact that the people have abandoned God's laws to respect the lives of others, including animals: "We must respect the nature that God has left us." He then broadened his discourse to include land rights and claims. He borrowed from the theology of liberation to which he was exposed by CIMI (Conselho Indigenista Missionário)[11] agents, with whom he has worked closely in the 1970s and 1980s. Considering everyone should have a right to a piece of land, he denounced the capitalists who deny the poor that right for their own benefit. He denounced the political system within which the Kaingang people cannot protect their rights: "We have already been deceived a lot. That's why we fight to defend our rights, our powers, our customs. We have our tradition, the *Kikikoi*, our custom, which is expressed in the way we plant, our culture, our language, our naming system." Unlike his son, Fokâe included territorial rights and cultural difference in his commentary on the story of the flood.

He then shared with me a story that he said was very important for me to know. He affirmed that he had been informed of it the previous month:

> It is the story of a very sick young boy who is brought to the doctors and the healers without success. His mother and father were stubborn and obstinate, as they refused to give their child a Kaingang name. At one point, God called the child to himself and said to him: "Why do you live like this? Why didn't your father and your mother want to give you an Indigenous name? Go back to where you came from and require your parents to give you an Indigenous name." The boy lived again and told his parents about his journey: "I came back because you refused to give me an Indigenous name. God has given us this law, these names in our own language." Finally, after receiving a Kaingang name, the child grew and lived normally.

The importance of this story, used by Fokâe as a complement to his commentary on the story of the flood, lies in the fact that the boy who returns from his encounter with God carries a lesson and teaching about the fading Kaingang naming system, which Fokâe calls a law. Indeed, God appears in this narrative as a legislator willing to enforce and protect the naming system. Fokâe emphasized that receiving an "Indigenous name" is a true baptism and that an Indigenous person cannot live without such a name. Much more, the sole use of Portuguese names constitutes an unnatural change. At the time of our conversation, this was an unequivocal criticism of the current confusion about the use of Kaingang names, which many parents considered to be things of the past and unnecessary for their children's future.[12]

The Harvard Central Brazil Project directed by David Maybury-Lewis (1979) in the 1960s and 1970s focused on kinship and moiety systems of several Gê societies. One of the main conclusions of this large comparative project was that the naming system or more precisely, the act of naming takes precedence over the rules of descent and filiation among Gê societies: "We saw that naming was as effective a means of setting up social categories, organizing groups, and allocating new people to them as descent and filiation. In fact, the Central Brazilian peoples used naming and filiation through kinship as alternative principles of social organization" (Maybury-Lewis 1979, 311). That is precisely the point of João Xê Coelho's narrative discussed above. The reinstitution of moieties and sections through nomination by the primordial *kamẽ* brother and sister couple makes explicit the centrality of naming in this patrilinear society: name-giving can determine a moiety membership contrary to descent in certain circumstances.[13] Indeed, each moiety is the fiduciary of a stock of names that constitute its ancestral patrimony. The act of naming implies the transmission of the strength and qualities of an ancestor to a newborn child and thus links the past and the future of Kaingang society.[14]

Reciprocity and solidarity between partners of opposite moieties were the core values of the Kaingang social system in the past (Crépeau 1997). As Schaden ([1945] 1988, 112) wrote: "The division of the Kaingang society into exogamic moieties and the reciprocal position of these factions is, so to speak, the basic problem of the tribal myth." Kaingang anthropologist Adriana Biazi (2017, 59) of Terra Indígena Xapecó sums up this conception:

> *This division influenced the traditional Kaingang marriage. The Kamẽ can only marry Kanhru and vice versa...Those who belonged to the same moiety considered themselves as brothers, thus this prohibition. By marrying the opposite moiety,* the cosmic balance of the moieties is maintained. *The kófa [Elders] say that if one married someone belonging to the same moiety, the marriage will fail. Since the characteristics and personality of the spouses are the same, they will not complement, get along and understand each other.* (emphasis added)

Recently, Jorge Kagnãg Garcia, an influential Elder of Terra Indígena Nonoai, located in the state of Rio Grande do Sul, used the term *law* while referring to this system: "Our most important belief is about the moieties *kamẽ-kanhru* and the exogamic rules that preside their relationships. It is our law" (pers. comm. with Rogério da Rosa, October 2018). Indeed, one of the main motivations of the *Kikikoi* organizers of 2018 was to maintain the moiety system, which is fading out of memory and practice. The Catholic and Pentecostal ritual organizers and singers emphasized the importance of teaching and transmitting Kaingang culture and values as distinct from religion. In a context of religious and political plurality, the affirmation of the culture and rights of the Kaingang people through the realization of the ritual makes explicit the vivacity, strength, and unity of *Kaingang Jykré*. As Dussart and Poirier (this volume) write, this ritual performance constitutes a process through which the Kaingang people "rethink their entangled cosmologies and pragmatically engage in the definition of their own contemporaneity."

Conclusion

In 1998, Fokâe predicted that in a near future all Brazilian cities would wake up one morning covered by forest. This would be the end of time for the Brazilian conquerors, the end of sufferings for the Kaingang people and the Indigenous peoples of Brazil, and the beginning of a new era. As Fokâe used to say: "*Vai pagar quem deve*" (only those who committed sins will pay). In this context, only Brazilian people will suffer losses, rather than the Indigenous people who are native to the forest.

The forest was still conceived as the location of power par excellence by Fokâe's and Jorge Kagnãg Garcia's generation—that is, for those who were born in the forest in the 1920s or 1930s, grew up, and lived there for part of their life. As Jorge Kagnãg Garcia expresses it: "I grew up in the forest where I acquired my knowledge. I only learned in the forest with birds and animals. We are the owners of the forest and we were owners long before Brazil was invaded" (pers. comm. with Rogério da Rosa, October 2018). Attachment to this ancestral territory was all the more fundamental since it is understood in narratives and testimonies to be the source of collective and individual power through partnership with nonhumans.[15] Hence, ancestrality is "a paramount source of knowledge, power, inspiration, and guidance" that "binds together land, kinship, and spirit realm," as Dussart and Poirier (this volume) aptly argue.

Indeed, if we want to make explicit contemporary Kaingang sociological logic, the term *partner* should be at the centre. The *jamré* (members of the opposite moiety, brothers- and sisters-in-law) are partners in the full sense of the term: parts of a whole, they form an essential complementarity that extends cosmologically to the stars, animals, and other nonhuman beings (Fernandes and Piovezena 2015, 119–20). For example, the bond formed by the master entities with whom Kaingang humanity must collaborate—the masters of animals, fish, forest, and so on—are prototypical entities that play the role of third parties included in any implicit interaction involving predation and appropriation of a nonhuman by a human. In other words, in this legal system, still very much alive and explicitly opposed to the Brazilian one, the law of the strongest is replaced by rules prohibiting the strictly technical and strategical individual appropriation of resources (e.g., land, animal, plant). What makes an act of predation and appropriation legitimate in this framework is based on a fundamental cosmological partnership between humans and nonhumans. By their specific identity and position, master entities introduce a metarelational level into the chain of beings, which is superimposed on that of the human interpersonal relations (Crépeau 2015; Rosa and Crépeau 2019).

Nowadays, for Catholics, Evangelicals, and others, the motif of the end of time appears as the expression of a possible future and the advent of a better world through the institution of a new partnership between humans and nonhumans. Those who survive the destruction or the transformation of the previous world are those who will participate in the construction of a better future world as full and powerful partners: "To speak of the end of the world is to speak of the need to imagine, rather than a new world to replace our present one, a new people, the people that is missing" (Danowski and Viveiros de Castro 2017, 123).

Author's Note

This chapter is a substantially revised version of a paper presented in July 2017 as part of a conference session organized by Françoise Dussart and Sylvie Poirier: "Indigenous Contemporary Religiosities: Between Solidarity, Contestation, Convergence and Renewal" at the 34th Conference of the International Society for the Sociology of Religion in Lausanne, Switzerland. I would like to thank the organizers Sylvie Poirier and Françoise Dussart for their invitation to participate in this rich and stimulating meeting, and for their careful reading of and judicious comments on preliminary versions of this chapter. I would also like to express my deepest gratitude to the Kaingang people of the Terra Indígena Xapecó who have always guided me with generosity and patience. Finally, my thanks go to the Fonds de recherche du Québec sur la société et la culture (FRQSC) and the Social Sciences and Humanities Research Council of Canada (SSHRC) for their financial support.

Notes

1. All translations in this chapter are mine, unless otherwise indicated.
2. As Kelsen ([1946] 2011, 60) explains, "[t]he idea of an equivalence between the wrong sustained and the wrong to be inflicted is characteristic of the principle of retribution. This makes retribution appear a kind of exchange, although it is more correct to consider exchange a special kind of retribution...Retribution does not only mean punishment but also reward."
3. Marcel Mauss (quoted in Kelsen 1936, 81) criticized Kelsen's use of the term *primitive* as an unacceptable generalization, while Gurvitch (quoted in Kelsen 1936, 81–82) questioned the links between Kelsen's sociological study on the notion of the soul and his earlier work on pure legal theory. Gurvitch believed, based on the work of Lévy-Bruhl, that "primitives" possessed not legal but mystical thought. According to Gurvitch, Kelsen reduces the moral and religious beliefs of the "uncivilized" to legal beliefs, while "the differentiation of legal beliefs presupposes a certain development of rationalism that is characteristic of advanced civilizations" (quoted in Kelsen 1936, 82).
4. Monnier (1999, 26) lists the disasters described in the stories he analyzes: "flood, fire, earthquake, stones, rocks, volcano, ash, mud, drought, engulfment in the earth, crushing of the earth by the sky, wind, darkness, blood, epidemic, monster animal...animal revolt...object revolt."
5. I borrow this concept from Gauthier's (2002, 198) logic of zero order or propositional logic.
6. Our data were collected between 1993 and 2018 in collaboration with the Kaingang people of Terra Indígena Xapecó reservation located in Santa Catarina State in Southern Brazil. The fieldwork has been realized in collaboration with

Professor Silvio Coelho dos Santos of the Universidade Federal de Santa Catarina in Florianópolis.

7.   Vicente Fokâe Fernandes passed away on February 25, 2006. I will hereafter refer to him by his Kaingang name: Fokâe.

8.   Interestingly, Santos (1987, 28) mentions that the Kaingang people historically competed with the Xokleng, their immediate Gê neighbors, for the control of these rich pine forests. It's probably no coincidence that the *Kikikoi*, a moment of great social solidarity among the Kaingang people, coincided with this time of the year.

9.   Although São João Maria de Agostinho was never canonized, he is considered one of the most important saints of regional popular Catholicism in southern Brazil. The researchers know him as a historical figure: Giovanni Maria de Agostini (Crépeau and Désilets 2010).

10. Deuteronomy (New International Version, 24:16) enunciates this law as follows: "Parents are not to be put to death for their children, nor children put to death for their parents; *each will die for their own sin*" (emphasis added).

11. The CIMI is an organization, created in 1972, linked to the National Conference of Bishops of Brazil and responsible for the support given by the Catholic Church to the Indigenous peoples of Brazil.

12. This recalls Petronella Vaarzon-Morel's contribution to this volume about Warlpiri cosmology, in which Christianity is also conceived as providing support for the ancestral law, the *Jukurrpa*.

13. For instance, in the context of a disease endangering the survival of a child, assigning the child to the other moiety by giving them a new name protects them from the harassment of a *veinkupri* (spirit of a deceased person) of their birth moiety.

14. Frédéric Laugrand (this volume) makes a similar point regarding the enduring centrality of Inuit naming systems.

15. See Helm (2018, 60–61), who records the testimony of Balbina da Luz Abreu Souza on this subject.

References

Accetti, Carlo Invernizzi. 2016. "L'idée d'ordre dynamique et la théorie de la *grundnorm*: une interprétation du fondement de la validité du droit chez Hans Kelsen." *Droit et sociétés* (1) 92: 181–99. https://doi.org/10.3917/drs.092.0181

Almeida, Ledson Kurtz de. 2004. "Análise antropológica das igrejas cristãs entre os Kaingang baseada na etnografia, na cosmologia e dualismo." PHD dissertation, Programa de Pós-Graduação em Antropologia Social, Universidade Federal de Santa Catarina.

Almeida, Romulo Machado de, and Rogério Jerônimo Barbosa. 2019. "Religious Transition in Brazil." In *Path of Inequality in Brazil: A Half-Century of Changes*, edited by Marta Arreche Cham, 257–84, Springer.

Biazi, Adriana Aparecida Belino Padilha de. 2017. "Espiritualidade e conhecimentos da mata na formação dos especialistas de curas Kaingang da Terra Indígena Xapecó/SC." Master's thesis, Programa de Pós-Graduação em Antropologia Social, Universidade Federal de Santa Catarina.

Borba, Telêmaco. 1908. *Actualidade indígena.* Curitiba: Impressora Paranaense.

Bornet, Philippe, Claire Clivaz, Nicole Durisch Gauthier, Philippe Hertig, and Nicolas Meylan, eds. 2012. *La fin du monde: analyses plurielles d'un motif religieux, scientifique et culturel.* Genève: Éditions Labor et Fides.

Crépeau, Robert R. 1994. "Mythe et rituel chez les Indiens kaingang du Brésil méridional." *Religiologiques* (10): 143–57. http://www.religiologiques.uqam.ca/no10/crepe.pdf

———. 1997. "Les Kaingang dans le contexte des études gé et bororo." *Anthropologies et sociétés* 21 (2–3): 45–66.

———. 2008. "Le rite comme contexte de la mémoire des origines." *Archives des sciences sociales des religions* 141: 57–73. https://doi.org/10.4000/assr.12552

———. 2015. "'Les animaux obéissent aussi à la religion': paradoxes du chamanisme kaingang (Brésil) en contexte pluraliste." *Anthropologie et sociétés* 39 (1–2): 229–49. https://doi.org/10.7202/1030847ar

Crépeau, Robert R., and Maude Désilets. 2010. "La figure de l'étranger chez les Kaingang du Brésil meridional." *Recherches amérindiennes au Québec* 40 (1–2): 75–81. Published online 2012. https://doi.org/10.7202/1007499ar

Crépeau, Robert R., and Rogério R.G. da Rosa. 2018. "Actualité et transformations de la fête des morts chez les Kaingang du Brésil méridional." *Frontières* 29 (2): 16–25. https://doi.org/10.7202/1044159ar

Crocker, J. Christopher. 1969. "Reciprocity and Hierarchy Among the Eastern Bororo." *Man* 4 (1): 44–58. https://doi.org/10.2307/2799263

———. 1985. *Vital Souls: Bororo Cosmology, Natural Symbolism, and Shamanism.* Tucson: The University of Arizona Press.

D'Angelis, Wilmar R., and Juracilda Veiga. 1993. "Em que crêem os Kaingang? Religião, dominação e identidade." In *O peso da cruz: conquista e religião*, edited by A. Tedesco et al., 43–56. Chapecó: Secretariado Diocesano de Pastoral.

Danowski, Déborah, and Eduardo Viveiros de Castro. 2017. *The Ends of the World.* Cambridge: Polity Press.

Descola, Philippe. 2019. "Qu'est-ce que comparer?" Course at the Collège de France, February 13, 2019. https://www.college-de-france.fr/site/philippe-descola/course-2019-02-13-14h00.htm. Accessed March 23, 2019.

Dundes, Alan. ed. 1988. *The Flood Myth*. Berkeley: University of California Press.

Fernandes, Ricardo Cid, and Leonel Piovezana. 2015. "The Kaingang Perspectives on Land and Environmental Rights in the South of Brazil." *Ambiente & sociedade* 18 (2): 111–28. https://doi.org/10.1590/1809-4422asocex07v1822015en

Frazer, James George. (1890) 2012. *The Golden Bough: A Study in Magic and Religion*. Cambridge: Cambridge University Press.

Gauthier, Yvon. 2002. *Internal Logic: Foundations of Mathematics from Kronecker to Hilbert*. Dordrecht: Kluwer.

Helm, Cecília Maria Vieira. 2018. *A contribuição dos laudos periciais antropológicos para a investigação da antiguidade da ocupação de terras indígenas no Paraná*. Curitiba: Edição do Autor.

Kelsen, Hans. 1936. "L'âme et le droit: rapport de Hans Kelsen (followed by a 'Discussion' with M. Mauss, A. Lévi, H. Hubert, A. Koulicher, G. Gurvitch, M.G. Tassitch)." *Annuaire de l'Institut international de philosophie du droit et de sociologie juridique* 2, 60–82.

———. (1946) 2011. *Society and Nature: A Sociological Inquiry*. Oxford: Routledge.

Kojève, Alexander. 1981. *Esquisse d'une phénoménologie du droit*. Paris: Éditions Gallimard.

Kopenawa, Davi, and Bruce Albert. 2013. *The Falling Sky: Words of a Yanomami Shaman*. Cambridge: Harvard University Press.

Langdon, E. Jean. 2005. "L'abus d'alcool chez les peuples indigènes du Brésil: une évaluation comparative." *Drogues, santé et société* 4 (1): 15–52. https://doi.org/10.7202/011328ar

Larsen, Timothy. 2013. "E.B. Tylor, Religion and Anthropology." *The British Journal for the History of Science* 46 (3): 467–85. https://www.jstor.org/stable/43820407

Léry, Jean de. (1557) 1957. *Journal de bord de Jean de Léry en la terre de Brésil 1557*. Presented and annotated by M.-R. Mayeux. Paris: Éditions de Paris.

Maybury-Lewis, David. 1967. *The Akwe-Shavante Society*. Oxford: Clarendon Press.

———. 1979. "Conclusion: Kinship, Ideology, and Culture." In *Dialectical Societies: The Gê and Bororo of Central Brazil*, edited by David Maybury-Lewis, 301–12. Cambridge: Harvard University Press.

Monnier, Alain. 1999. *Déluges et autres catastrophes: mythes d'Amazonie et de Nouvelle-Guinée*. Genève: Éditions Slatkine.

Mota, Lúcio Tadeu. 1994. *As guerras dos Índios kaingang: a história épica dos índios Kaingang no Paraná (1769–1924)*. Maringá: Editora da Universidade Estadual de Maringá.

Nimuendajú, Curt. 1939. *The Apinayé*. Washington: The Catholic University of America Press.

———. 1946. *The Eastern Timbira*. Vol. 41, *University of California Publications in American Archaeology and Ethnology*. Berkeley: University of California Press.

Oliveira, Maria Conceição de. 1996. *Os especialistas Kaingang e os seres da natureza: curadores da aldeia Xapecó-Oeste de Santa Catarina*. Florianópolis: FCC edições.

Pelletier-De Koninck, M.-C. 2016. "Le pentecôtisme sous l'œil des femmes kaingang: adaptations et transformations suite à la conversion." Master's thesis, Université de Montréal. Papyrus: Institutional Repository. http://hdl.handle.net/1866/18409

Rosa, Rogério R.G., da. 2005. "'Os kujà são diferentes': um estudo etnológico do complexo xamânico dos Kaingang da terra indígena Votouro." PHD dissertation, Programa de Pós-Graduação em Antropologia Social, Universidade Federal do Rio Grande do Sul.

Rosa, Rogério R.G., da, and Robert Crépeau. 2019. "Puissance et connaissance animales chez les Kaingang du Brésil méridional." *Anthropologica* 62 (1): 60–9. https://doi.org/10.3138/anth.2018-0105.r1

Santos, Sílvio Coelho, dos. 1987. *Índios e brancos no sul do Brasil: a dramatica experencia dos Xokleng*. Brasil: Movimento.

Schaden, Egon. 1953. "A origem dos homens, o dilúvio e outros mitos kaingang." *Revista de antropologia* 1 (2): 139–41. https://www.jstor.org/stable/41615531

———. (1945) 1988. *A mitologia heróica de tribos indígenas do Brasil: ensaio etnossociológico*. 3rd ed. São Paulo: Editora da Universidade de São Paulo.

Sergent, Bernard. 2012. *La fin du monde: treize légendes, des déluges mésopotamiens au mythe maya*. Paris: Librio.

Sullivan, L.E. 1988: *Icanchu's Drum: An Orientation to Meaning in South American Religions*. New York: Macmillan Publishing Company.

Thevet, André. (1575) 1953. *Le Brésil et les Brésiliens*. Vol. 1, *Les Français en Amérique pendant la deuxième moitié du XVIe siècle*, edited by Suzanne Lussagnet. Paris: Presses universitaires de France.

Turner, Terence. 1979. "The Gê and Bororo Societies as Dialectical Systems: A General Model." In *Dialectical Societies: The Gê and Bororo of Central Brazil*, edited by David Maybury-Lewis, 147–78. Cambridge: Harvard University Press.

Tylor, Edward B. 1874. *Primitive Culture: Researches into the Development of Mythology, Philosophy, Religion, Language, Art and Custom*. New York: Henry Holt and Company.

6

FROM UNKNOWN TO HYPERMEDIATIZED

Shipibo-Konibo Female Shamans in Western Amazonia

ANNE-MARIE COLPRON

Introduction

Although Shipibo-Konibo shamanism has been well documented in
the ethnological literature, there is little documentation about female
shamans. Many scholars believed that only men engaged in shamanic
practice (Heise, Landeo, and Bant 1999), while others made veiled or
contradictory references to female practices (Cardenas 1989; Roe 1988;
Morin 1998). Such empirical vagueness convinced me to carry out field
research on Shipibo-Konibo female shamans in Western Amazonia
between 2000 and 2001 for my doctoral thesis (Colpron 2004).

The lack of information at the time reflected the difficulty of
encountering female shamans in the field. During my first stay in the
community of San Francisco in 1996 when I was pursuing my MA,
I worked with a shaman named Lucio. As a novice ethnographer, I
asked him a series of questions in Spanish. To the question "Are there
any Shipibo-Konibo female shamans?" Lucio replied with a simple
"No."[1] I would have stopped at this answer had a misunderstanding—
which I shall explain below—not piqued my curiosity. When I asked
my Shipibo-Konibo friends whether they knew any female shamans,
my question always seemed to provoke a certain perplexity and lead to
evasive responses: someone had heard second-hand information about

a woman, or a female relative had practised shamanism in the past, and so on.

It was not easy to contact female shamans for my doctoral project. I travelled far and wide through Shipibo-Konibo territory, guided by hearsay, visiting one community after another. Gradually, I began to meet female shamans—in the end, over a dozen of them (Colpron 2004, 2005). At the time, I presumed that several others must not have been identified due to the difficulty in tracking them down.

The difficulty back then contrasts radically with the situation today. Now it is possible to find these specialists from the comfort of your home: Just sit at a computer and search the web using the key words *female Shipibo shaman* and you will be rewarded with a wide range of photographs, videos, and news about them. The clips of female shamans chanting *ikaros*[2] abound on YouTube, and some female specialists can be found in a few clicks on Facebook. Just a few minutes of browsing are needed to locate an impressive number of Shipibo-Konibo female shamans. Additionally, their practices are greatly advertised in centres catering to tourists interested in taking *ayahuasca*.[3] The website of one *ayahuasca* retreat, close to the town of Iquitos, shows ten Shipibo-Konibo female shamans; dozens of such centres exist in the area. In a 15-year period, the change in the visibility of female shamans has been dramatic.

This turnaround results, of course, from various factors that can be attributed to globalization, in particular the increasing number of foreigners interested in shamanic practices (e.g., tourists, anthropologists, and representatives of NGOs travelling in the region) and the development of computer-based communication technologies (e.g., the internet and smartphones). In this chapter, I do not document the way in which contact with foreigners and new technologies have led to the emergence of Shipibo-Konibo female shamans; rather, I highlight how the contemporary appropriations of these women are linked to the practices of the past. In other words, I am interested in how their "audacious innovations" (Gow 2001) fit into their own shamanic logic as "transformative continuities" (Laugrand and Crépeau 2015). In earlier works, I have detailed their shamanic practices (see, e.g.,

Colpron 2004, 2005, 2006); here I revisit some of this data in light of the current context.

Because female shamans were largely unknown only a decade and a half ago, their sudden growth in both numbers and visibility (the latter resulting especially from their presence in shamanic tourism) has generated a new literature that analyzes their *very existence* (and not just their visibility) as a novelty imputable to the impact of globalization.[4] Recognized for their ability to sell craftwork to foreigners, some Shipibo-Konibo women have supposedly seized the opportunity to extend their skills to the transactions involved in shamanic tourism by improvising as "shamans."[5] Without denying this eventuality, such an argument tethers the increase of female shamans to globalization and engenders a more or less implicit discourse on the "authenticity" of their practices: Since they work with tourists, are they really shamans? Did a traditional female shamanism ever exist?[6] This new literature shows that the hypervisibility of female shamans has failed to change the discourses about them, which continue to either deny or doubt their existence.[7]

It is important to stress, therefore, that the presence of Shipibo-Konibo female shamans is not a novelty bound only to globalization. If I highlight their earlier presence, it is not to defend a supposed traditional female shamanic practice reflecting an unchanged past.[8] Whether practised by men or women, Shipibo-Konibo shamanism has little to do with the Western ideal of authenticity.[9] Indeed, the singularity of this practice is to create bridges between different worlds and temporalities, constructing itself through these relations with others, whether forest entities, neighbouring ethnic groups, *mestizos*[10] from the towns, or foreign tourists. Shipibo-Konibo shamanic practices do not precede the relationships that forge them; they are, rather, constituted by these relations of difference. The fact that relationality comes first allows us to better understand the openness and inclusiveness of shamanism as a "process always *in the making*" (Dussart and Poirier, this volume).[11] Female shamans participate in the dynamism inherent to shamanism. Whether they were initiated before the intensification of tourism (as in Justina's case below) or with the aim of working with tourists (Elisa's case below), their audacious innovations remain in line with a shamanic ontology of transformation and the incorporation of alterity.

Shamanic tourism has certainly had an impact on the visibility and the growth of Shipibo-Konibo female and male shamanism. One only has to note the number of women working in the tourist retreats to be persuaded of this increase. However, highlighting the presence of female shamans before the increase of shamanic tourism provides a more complex picture of their practice: neither a contemporary invention nor an archaic and immutable vestige, but a practice in movement that—through its investment in shamanic tourism—also projects itself into the future. Furthermore, when a temporal dimension is added to this contemporary shamanism and the past practices of these women are considered, new questions emerge. Since not all cases of female shamanism can be reduced to the current conjunctures of globalization, and since some women practice shamanism in their own community, how can we understand the discourses denying their existence or hesitating about their presence? The case studies presented below allow us to consider this question and broaden our understanding of Shipibo-Konibo shamanism.

A Significant Misunderstanding and Uncertain Documents: Beginning Research

In my naïveté as a novice ethnographer, I thought I had explained clearly to Lucio the academic objectives of my research. It took me some time to realize that Lucio had interpreted my interest in his shamanic practice differently: my insistence on questioning him meant that I myself wanted to become a shaman. I finally understood the equivocation one day when, overwhelmed by all my questions, Lucio said to me: "It's pointless asking me so much, drink *ayahuasca*, it's the one that gives the answers." He added that only women who devoted themselves seriously to the task become very powerful shamans. This statement surprised me: How could Lucio have replied "no" to my question about the existence of female shamans and, at the same time, acknowledge their power?[12] I remained without a clear answer, because Lucio had decided that only *ayahuasca*, not he, would provide answers to my questions.

In the ethnological literature of the time, the only two explicit references to Shipibo-Konibo female shamans failed to shed much light on the topic. Peter Roe (1988, 128) records the myth of "Wasëmea, the rare female *meráya*." This Shipibo-Konibo term *meráya* translates as "they who meet" and refers to expert shamans who can mediate without drinking *ayahuasca*. This title distinguishes renowned practitioners from common shamans, designated *onánya* (they who know), who mediate with the help of *ayahuasca*. According to Roe, women can become *onánya* when they enter menopause and transform into "honorary males." Wasëmea's rarity had been to access the essentially male social role of *meráya*, an influential position, unusual for a woman and contested by men who stigmatized her as a sorcerer (*yobé*).

The second reference is provided by Françoise Morin (1998) who noted, through the genealogy of an influential shaman, the presence of female shamans, including—contrary to Roe's (1988) assertion—two notable *meráya*. In a footnote, Morin quotes the shaman's observation that there used to be one female *onánya* for every five male peers. Morin states, however, that today shamanism is "almost exclusively practiced by men" and that herbalist women (*raómis*) only assist their shaman husbands.

This sparse and divergent data on the subject of female shamans echoes the apparent contradictions highlighted earlier in my work with Lucio: no female shamans or very powerful female shamans; a negligible number of them or numerous in the past; women about whom, in the end, we know very little. Recent literature reifies their elusiveness insofar as it portrays female shamans only in the context of shamanic tourism. This portrayal, in effect, tags the women's shamanic practices as "inauthentic" and the women themselves as "not real shamans." The data presented here shed fresh light on this phenomenon.

An Overview of Female *Onánya* in 2000–2001

As mentioned earlier, during my first fieldtrip in 2000 I encountered a dozen female shamans and collected first-hand data on their stories and practices. In the following paragraphs, I provide an overview of my findings.[13]

The first two *onánya* I met, Maria (from Paoyan) and Juana (from Santa-Ana), were elderly grandmothers who mostly practised cures on their grandchildren and were not particularly influential characters in their community. They seemed to confirm Roe's (1988) hypothesis that female shamans are menopausal neophytes. However, two women of about forty years of age whom I met subsequently, Justina (from Vencedor) and Emilia (from Konshanmay), had been initiated in their twenties and had young children, combining maternity with shamanic practices. They were highly respected in their community and performed the same political-economic tasks as their male peers, negotiating with the masters of game and practising cures with the aid of offensive/defensive methods. These contemporary Wasëmeas did not seem to bother their male entourage.

Limiting my study to the first or second set of cases would have had a pronounced impact on my research findings. This methodological consideration is far from trivial: encountering a dozen female shamans prevented me from overgeneralizing. Age, background, and notoriety vary similarly for both female and male shamans. Furthermore, although a few had been initiated after menopause, most had begun their apprenticeship at puberty, some (Maria, Rosa, and Manuela) before marriage, several when they were in their twenties, and others as young children. None of them considered their offspring to be obstacles to apprenticeship since their children could be cared for by close relatives. Five of these women (Justina, Emilia, Rosa, Isabel, and Angela) were very active, treating people through the mediation of *ayahuasca* at least three times a week, and tackling very serious cases such as patients affected by pathogenic darts (*chonteado*).

All of the women I met have at least one close *onánya* relative, whether it be their father, their maternal or paternal uncle, their mother (Herminia, Manuela, and Elisa), or their husband. Husbands are not necessarily the source of these women's knowledge: although some initiated their wives (four cases), other women had learned before meeting their husbands (five cases) and some encouraged the shamanic practice of their spouses (Justina and Emilia). Forming a shamanic couple seems to facilitate the practice of shamanism, especially since it is easier to respect the recurring periods of seclusion and abstinence. In addition, the majority of the *onánya* prefer practising the rituals in a group since treatments and defences are more effective when performed collectively. Close *onánya* relatives tend, therefore, to join forces. Two women (Isabel, Elisa) did not acquire their knowledge from relatives, which is exceptional since suspicion governs most relations involving *onánya*. Isabel was initiated by a *mestizo* master; Elisa's case will be discussed at length below.

The origin of the shamanic vocation has no single explanation. What was most commonly mentioned as a motivation to become a shaman was healing younger relatives. Many women also referred to a major illness that they experienced during their childhood and a treatment they received with a powerful plant or animal substance (*ráo*), which predisposed them to their shamanic activities. Others mentioned childhood recollections of shamanic songs performed by their *onánya* relatives and the eagerness to revive their memory by engaging in the same practices. The desire for revenge was also reported, as well as the wish to earn a living, particularly by working with *mestizos* (at this point, no one talked about tourists).

Many *onánya* women emerge from my work on genealogies (the mothers of Herminia and Elisa, the maternal aunt of Elisa, the paternal aunts of Herminia and Aurora, the sister and sister-in-law of Maria, the wife of Justina's maternal uncle) and some from local conversations, notably the deceased *meráya* Wasëmea (cited by Roe 1988) and Camila (a relative of Lucio). Camila solidified her reputation after a tip to Cuzco where it was said she acquired Inca: shamanic auxiliaries (mythic heroes). Indeed, as it will be discussed, an exogenous source to shamanic knowledge is valued and sought after (either from neighbouring ethnic groups, *mestizos,* or others). Some *onánya* women identify as Catholic, others as Evangelist, and no one seems to find it contradictory that these religions disapprove of their practices (Colpron 2012).

This brief overview outlines the diversity of female shamans I encountered in the field between 2000 and 2001. While they were difficult to find, they were there, and genealogies highlight their presence across generations. Thus, the estimate quoted by Morin (1998)—namely that there used to be one female *onánya* for every five male peers—does not seem exaggerated.

The Shamanic Beginnings of Two Women

Among the *onánya* women I met between 2000 and 2001, several are now involved in shamanic tourism, namely Manuela, Elisa, and Justina. Manuela descends from renowned shamanic families. She was initiated at a very young age by her father Manuel Mahua and continued to learn in adulthood from her mother Maria Awanari. Although Manuela has worked in *ayahuasca* retreats since 2009, her shamanic past precedes her investment in tourism. The same is true for various other female *onánya* who appear on the retreat websites: many of them come from important shamanic families and their biographies show that I missed them during my 2000–2001 field research. These women—more numerous than in my previous estimates—would have already been active but not publicized.

I focus here on the cases of Elisa and Justina, women now present on the internet and for whom shamanic tourism has become central. These women's profiles contrasted in several ways in 2000 and 2001. Elisa came from the large community of San Francisco, situated close to the town of Pucallpa, and earned a living at the time from selling craftwork to tourists. Justina resided in Vencedor, a community on the smaller Pisqui river, less accessible to the *gringos* (at that time, few ventured there). She lived on hunting, fishing, and horticulture. The way of life of these women, as well as their relations with foreigners, was then very different.

Elisa was not practising shamanism in 1996 when I first met her. Her initiation only began in the 2000s after deciding that she wanted to practise shamanic tourism, then in high demand in San Francisco. During the same period, Justina had been practising shamanism in her community for about fifteen years. Highly reputed and active, she carried out mediations with forest entities, including masters of game, and intervened in diverse domains such as hunting. In order to compare their respective paths, I describe in detail the beginnings of their becoming *onánya*.

Elisa

Elisa and her husband Alberto accompanied my first research trips and introduced me to relatives living in communities far from San Francisco, thus facilitating my welcome in a context where rumours of *pishtako* (an anthropophagic killer) circulated.[14] Living and mixing with their networks of allies allowed me to experience the tensions prevalent between *onánya*. Arriving at the home of Alberto's paternal uncle, for example, I discovered with some disappointment that this *onánya* abhorred the female shaman with whom I wished to work, labelling her a *yobé*. My friends complied with their relative's remarks and insisted on leaving the community. They constantly warned me against the dangers of working with several *onánya*. This could be explained by the criteria of kinship and locality, which determine who is a shaman (a relative who works in our interest) and who is a sorcerer (a stranger who favours the interests of someone else at our expense). Since most female *onánya* are, for them, strangers, they are suspicious and tend to stigmatize them as sorcerers.

In this atmosphere of distrust, it was highly surprising that Elisa developed an affinity with Justina who was not kin. Indeed, during my second trip to Vencedor, Elisa decided to accompany me without her husband so she could learn from this reputed *onánya*. I thus was able to follow Elisa's shamanic initiation closely: for more than a month, and under the care of Justina, she fasted, practised sexual abstinence, and ingested *ayahuasca* mixed with powerful plants (*ráo*), an experience she would repeat in 2001. It was in this specific context of initiation that I learned about an unknown facet of Elisa's life: her late mother, Anita, had been an *onánya*. This left me bewildered since Elisa knew of my interest in female shamans. Why, then, had she not mentioned her mother's practices? Once more, I was quite puzzled, and once more the misunderstanding pointed out something important: information that seemed essential to my research was not provided in response to my abstract questions (e.g., Do female shamans exist?) but rather in specific contexts of lived relations.

Elisa accounted for her shamanic initiation through her family. As the main source of her motivation, she evoked the memory of her mother, who was killed by her shamanic practices; her own apprenticeship allowed her to rekindle her mother's memory and life course. She also mentioned her desire to look after her young children, but never explicitly articulated her wish to work with tourists.

Justina

In 2000 and 2001, Justina treated many people on a daily basis, mostly her relatives but also Shipibo-Konibo people from neighbouring communities and sometimes *mestizos.* Her reputation extended beyond the confines of her community. She often took *ayahuasca* with her husband César and sometimes with her brother Armando, but she was clearly the one who presided over the rituals.

Over the course of our conversations, Justina related different events that led her to become an *onánya.* When she was a child, two of her siblings died and her father took her to the forest for a month of seclusion to strengthen her. He bathed her with the leaves of the *níwe ráo* tree[15] and gave her a decoction of the root of the *sanánco* tree (*Tabernaemontana sananho*)—renowned for its strength. He also told her to observe dietary and behavioural restrictions (*samá cóshi*). This episode would be decisive for her subsequent initiation.

Justina also mentioned a serious illness caused by her first husband following their separation when she was a very young mother. Her husband had taken revenge through a *yobé.* Very ill, Justina consulted the *onánya* Guillermo from Santa-Maria—her mother's cousin who was married to a female shaman, Giorgina. Justina was treated with a beverage made from the seeds of the *camalonga* tree (*Strychnos* sp.), followed by a new period of seclusion and abstinences. Her uncle then noted her "force" (*cóshi níwe*), the result of the treatment administered by her father in her childhood. Furthermore, after drinking *ayahuasca*, he realized that Justina is a "spirit child" (*yoshín báke*) with a master of the forest (*Cháikoni*) as a pater. Thus predisposed to shamanism, Justina followed

FIGURE 6.1. Justina and Elisa in Vencedor (Pisqui River).

(Photograph by Anne-Marie Colpron, 2001.)

a year-long initiation with Guillermo and Giorgina. Her main reasons for becoming an *onánya* were a desire to take revenge on her former husband and to care for her children.

At the end of her apprenticeship, her attempts to treat Vencedor people with *ayahuasca* had provoked mockery since nobody had witnessed her initiation. Even so, Justina continued, encouraged by her *onánya* brother and later by her new husband, César. Although he had not practised shamanism previously, César invested in it with her and his brother-in-law, and together they consolidated their reputation.

For over fifteen years, Justina practised as an *onánya* for her kin before getting involved in shamanic tourism. As I have shown, her initial apprenticeship took place in the context of local social relations, with objectives quite different from those pursued today. Elisa, for her part, became initiated in order to work with tourists, although her mother's vocation and her thirst for knowledge rendered her motives more complex. My ethnographic field research had led to Justina and Elisa encounter, which proved decisive for their subsequent investment in shamanic tourism. Justina took Elisa under her wing to initiate her into shamanism; Elisa introduced Justina to shamanic tourism.

Female Shamans: An Intrinsic Aspect of the Shamanic Institution

Justina and Elisa underwent a proper shamanic initiation, manipulating powerful plants and following periods of seclusion and abstinences. In the following paragraphs, I describe this process in detail, showing how becoming a shaman, for a woman, is considered a plausible avenue within the Shipibo-Konibo shamanic institution. I also present the case of "spirit children" (*yoshín báke*): girls who are born with a predisposition for shamanism. My research points to a shamanic practice that does not a priori discriminate between the sexes.

Shamanic Becoming:
The Importance of the *Ráo* and the "Spirit Children"

The life stories of the *onánya*—both those gathered in the field and on the internet—underline the importance of the *ráo* for shamanic initiation. Commonly translated as "medicinal plants," this term also refers to poisons and charms, certain animal parts, and objects that manifest a power or exert an influence. The faculties of the *ráo* are reflected in their form, smell, consistency, and other peculiarities. Thus, a fragrant liana will communicate its ability to charm; a medicinal plant its capacity to heal; a large, robust, and thorny tree its sturdiness and its pathogenic darts used for offensive/defensive shamanism. Likewise, the phlegm of the woodpecker facilitates treatments by suction, jaguar fat induces strength and courage, the mucus of the harpy eagle develops sight, and so on (Colpron 2004).

The utilization of *ráo* is not restricted to shamans.[16] Since they are the origin of knowledge and strengthen the body, their use is widespread and prescribed from early infancy, as illustrated by Justina's life story. At a very young age, she followed commensal practices with large trees (e.g., immersion in the forest, baths, ingestions, fasts) to incorporate their power and share their qualities consubstantially, becoming solid like their trunk and fragrant like their leaves. The body of children is said to be permeable and malleable. As a consequence, the properties of the *ráo* are assimilated in an effective and durable manner, but only if the prescribed restrictions are followed. Otherwise, the child falls ill or acquires undesirable attributes—rather than strong, they become feisty and violent. The olfactive aspect is crucial here: foods or activities that alter the smell of the *ráo* must be avoided. On this point, the virgin child has an advantage over the adult initiate who will eventually resume their sexual activities, the odour of which compromises the scented powers of the plants. A *ráo* administered in childhood may follow a certain sexual division of labour (such as developing the sight of the future hunter or craftswoman), but the acquired faculty—in this case vision—will subsequently be useful in shamanic practice whatever the child's gender.

Justina's life story shows how someone who received an adequate treatment with *ráo* in their childhood can be encouraged to become a shaman regardless of their gender. Having an *onánya* parent also helps one grow into a shaman, as shown in Elisa's case. Although initiated in adulthood, the memory of her late *onánya* mother is still very much present. It has repeatedly been explained to me that the children of *onánya* possess the force of the *ráo* mastered by their parents. In fact, very young children are said to share the same body as their genitors, underlined by the practices of the couvade,[17] where what one person eats or does affects the others. It is therefore easier for the child of an *onánya* to become a shaman, because the *ráo* "already know" them. Elisa thus justifies becoming a shaman through this kind of embodied memory of her *onánya* mother.

In addition, certain children—called "spirit children" (*yoshín báke*)— are born with an even more pronounced predisposition for shamanism. These children are conceived during erotic dreams, which translate as promiscuous relations with forest entities.[18] Multiple paternity is recognized among the Shipibo-Konibo: various paters may be declared as a child's genitors and the contributors surpass the human sphere. This is the case of Justina who has a human and a *Cháikoni* pater. According to the mythical narratives, the *Cháikoni* personify the ancestors who remained faithful to the precepts of the Inca, the civilizing hero. Now living hidden in the forest, they flee from the presence (and smell) of the Shipibo-Konibo people and only visit the *onánya* whose body has the pleasing aroma of the *ráo*. The *Cháikoni* are also considered the masters of certain trees, notably the *níwe ráo* administered to Justina in her infancy.

The *Cháikoni* embody an ideal form of humanity that surpasses the Shipibo-Konibo in all aspects: strength, speed, hunting ability, and shamanic power. Likening her to the *Cháikoni*, Justina's kin emphasized her particular physique (dark skin, small size) and her uncommon abilities (strength, agility, and charm), as well as her character (mischievous and mirthful). *Yoshín báke* are known for reaching the most advanced states of shamanic power: mediating without the use of *ayahuasca*. Shipibo-Konibo shamanic institution thus acknowledges that some girls are born with a particular filiation that predisposes them to the great powers of *meráya*.[19]

Shamanic Becoming: The Embodiment of Alterity

Justina and Elisa's life stories foreground both episodes from their childhood in which they directly or indirectly incorporated *ráo* and factors that precede their birth and exceed their person, especially their particular parentage (Elisa's *onánya* mother and Justina's *Cháikoni* father). Consequently, the principles at work that favour women to become shamans are not tethered to gender identity but rather to *the potential to become other* and the embodiment, to varying degrees, of alterity. This embodiment may be enabled by the manipulation of *ráo*, but may also precede the person born with a predisposition inherited from *onánya* parents who have enhanced the body of their offspring by using *ráo*, or from *Cháikoni* parents, themselves masters of *ráo*. Although certain parentages favour becoming a shaman, the period of apprenticeship should nonetheless be reiterated in order to reactivate the relations with the masters of *ráo*. Shamanic powers are thus *relational* since they derive from the incessant relations with "other" entities from which the *onánya* learn.

Over time, Justina multiplied her periods of seclusion and apprenticeship with *ráo*. She likens her accumulated knowledge to a huge closet: when taking *ayahuasca*, she literally clothes herself in her powers; when they become worn out, she must renew them (Colpron 2012). In fact, the *ráo* masters communicate their powers to initiates in the form of adornments: clothes, crowns, rings, and weapons slung over the shoulder.[20] Through this process, the *onánya* become decorated like the masters, themselves transforming into *ráo*, literally incorporating their perspectives (Viveiros de Castro 2004)—for example, the flowers, branches, and thorns become crowns, shields, and weapons necessary for the shamanic mediations.

These mediations form part of the offensive/defensive shamanism prevailing throughout the Amazonian region where healing rituals involve diverse forms of combat. In the shamanic ontology where everything can become a potential subject, an ill person is the manifestation of the action of a troublemaker. Thus, the question asked is not so much "What caused the illness?" but "*Who* caused the illness?" To outwit their adversaries, the *onánya* accumulate a diverse range of knowledge and focus their interest on exogenous influences unknown to their rivals, the ignorance of one becoming the strength of the other. Since the aim is to diversify one's powers, one cannot claim a *single* legitimate and authentic Shipibo-Konibo shamanic knowledge, but rather *diverse kinds* of knowledge that get enriched during the shaman's contacts and encounters.

Since the *onánya* seek to encounter various agents of alterity in order to incorporate their knowledge, working with tourists is an appealing opportunity, especially as they generate significant economic revenues and value their shamanic knowhow. Tourists come from a variety of places, but according to the *onánya*, they share a habitus of urban comfort and, consequently, possess a soft and malleable body similar to that of Shipibo-Konibo children. This permeability facilitates the absorption of knowledge and thought (*shinán*) through the intermediation of *ayahuasca*. Furthermore, just as the *ráo* are the vectors of knowledge of the masters of the forest—knowledge they wear like clothing—the machines and technological gadgets of the tourists are in metonymic relation with their owners and allow the embodiment of their powers, which take the form of peculiar accessories useful in shamanic combats.

For the shamans, these new appropriations from tourists do not eclipse the previous ones, but add to them, following similar bodily practices. Especially since initiation with *ráo* from the forest is a necessary first step to further consider subsequent exogenous apprenticeships. Justina absorbed the powers of the *ráo*, the accumulation of which gradually transformed her body into as a cluster of formidable predators. Similarly, *ráo* from the Andes, with powerful masters, adorned her in their image and enabled an Inca-becoming. She has also integrated the power of manufactured products transmitted by *mestizos*, like the energy from batteries or the attraction of magnets, adding them to her *ayahuasca* preparations (Colpron 2013). More recently, she has handled the touch pads and laptops of tourists, which enabled her to incorporate a cutting-edge digital shamanic arsenal. She has transformed her body into a sophisticated machinery, then, with cyborg adornments and shields that defy our futuristic fantasies.

More than a bricolage of symbols or representations, more than mimesis, what is at stake here are the possibilities for *becoming other*—masters of the forest, Inca, *mestizo,* or *gringo*—afforded by concrete bodily practices. These embodiments are *powers* in themselves. Shamanism depends upon these relationships of alterity; openness to the outside is the foundation of the whole practice. Even the *Cháikoni,* mythical ancestors, are considered to be Others with whom the shaman seeks alliances. This explains their "constant actualization" (Crépeau, this volume): the masters of the forest precede and encompass all relationships of otherness,[21] allowing the later mediations with strangers. Seen in this light, relations with tourists are not such a novelty. Rather, they form part of a long history of contacts with Others: foreigners whose powers are incorporated according to the same procedures as those of initiation with the masters of the forest. Hence the transformative continuities at play: although Shipibo-Konibo shamanism is, by definition, in movement—feeding on difference and accumulating exogenous knowhow—there remains a continuity in the way in which these appropriations are effected, which involves various and specific bodily practices and a process of *becoming other* that all follow a specific logic in which the *ráo* of the forest (including *ayahuasca*) still possess a primordial role.

Conclusion

The turnaround in the visibility of Shipibo-Konibo female shamans has been very rapid. In just a few years, it became much more common to hear about them. In 2006, I heard a young Shipibo-Konibo man proudly announce to a tourist: "We have female shamans," as if it were a mark of cultural identity.[22] Despite this new visibility, the scholarly literature still evokes an essentially male shamanism, hesitating to call these women shamans and linking their practices solely to tourism, making them, by definition, inauthentic (Herbert 2010; Brabec de Mori 2014).[23]

Frequent contact with foreigners and the appropriation of new technologies are now part of Shipibo-Konibo lived experience, both near urban centres and in more remote communities. Whether they are representatives of NGOs, anthropologists, tourists, or other travellers, these foreigners increasingly visit the region, staying for both short and long periods. Their presence is sometimes feared (e.g., *pishtako* rumours), sometimes welcomed, allowing economic opportunities (e.g., the sale of craftwork, shamanic tourism) and the creation of bonds. These bonds can translate into friendships, marriages, or initiations into shamanism. Considering the diversity and complexity of social interactions in the region, the shamanism practised by women cannot be reduced to a mere synopsis without running the risk of a caricatural and thus incomplete understanding.

The examples of Justina and Elisa presented in this chapter are not intended to be *representative* of the shamanic practices performed by Shipibo-Konibo women. Rather, they highlight some of what is *possible* and provide a more complex picture of female shamanism. In one case, a reputed *onánya* practised shamanism for fifteen years within her community before getting involved in shamanic tourism; in the other, a woman who made a living from tourism became a shaman following the usual initiatory steps; her decision was motivated by economic reasons, but also by personal ones, her own mother having been an *onánya*. These life stories highlight the fact that shamanism practised by women cannot simply be explained by the novelties of tourism and globalization, nor bound to the naïve idea of an "authentic" shamanism. Rather, they foreground the *continuities* that exist between new and past practices: although these women now work with tourists and their practices are transformed by these novel relations, these transformations nonetheless follow the logic of embodying alterity intrinsic to Shipibo-Konibo shamanism.

The idea of an authentic or more representative Shipibo-Konibo shamanism does not make sense when we recognize that this practice is based on both the *relations* that the *onánya* enter into with Others with the aim of embodying their attributes, whether these are beings of the forest, *Incas*, *mestizos,* or *gringos*; and the *experience* of the *onánya,* whose knowledge/powers vary according to the apprenticeships undertaken. Such diversity is encouraged by an inherently offensive/ defensive shamanism. Since Shipibo-Konibo shamanism is *relational* by definition, we cannot exclude a priori the practices involving new social actors—in this case, tourists—as inauthentic by definition. To pose the question in these terms is to appeal to Western ideals of purity and authenticity and to essentialize a practice founded on relations of alterity (Vilaça 2000; Chaumeil 2009).

Through their apprenticeships, female *onánya* become the composite of their relations, and these relations now include foreigners. Since the start of the 2000s, Elisa has been drinking *ayahuasca* with tourists. This does not mean that she is not building knowledge, but that she does so in relations with foreigners. In a shamanic ontology of transformation where becoming precedes form, nothing is determined in advance: it is the relations and practices of incorporating alterity that make it possible to say that a person "knows." This translates into *the effectiveness of the practice*, no matter the origins of the knowledge or the practitioner's gender. Rather than relying on the logic of *being* (the biological, individual man or woman), it is a question of *becoming other*, going beyond the self. Moreover, the reasons invoked by Justina and Elisa to legitimize their shamanic practice exceed their gendered personhood. Instead, they refer to past experiences of incorporating alterity, whether through a particular parentage (*onánya* or *Cháikoni*) or the utilization of *ráo*. *Ráo* and *Cháikoni* refer here to the powers of the forest and are always essential to shamanic initiation. Justina and Elisa do not therefore abandon the knowledge of the forest for the knowledge offered by the tourists: much the opposite, since the former is the prerequisite for their subsequent appropriations. As Robert Crépeau (this volume) points out (referring to another Amazonian context), the forest is still conceived "as the location of power par excellence."

Finally, the case studies of Justina and Elisa allow us to return to the equivocation introduced at the beginning of this chapter: How are we to understand the negations, hesitations, and contradictions in relation to direct questions asked locally about female shamans? It seems problematic to look a priori for a correspondence between fixed and preestablished categories—women and shamans—when the question here is one of becoming, experience, and kinship relations. Compared to my initial abstract questions, when I asked Lucio about his niece Elisa or Armando about his sister Justina, the contrast in responses was striking: these men described their close relations with a female relative. Elisa and Justina have been initiated in the prescribed way; they have demonstrated the effectiveness of their practices; they thus know and are called *onánya*. These explanations come a posteriori to account for an effective shamanic practice. However, someone whom they have not treated and, above all, who has no kinship relation with them may equally say that they are not really shamans or even that they are *yobé*. A woman—just like a man, as it happens—is not *onánya* in any absolute sense: she is so for a kin group who she treats successfully, reaffirming her efficacy day after day. Consequently, an *onánya* who works exclusively for tourists, without sharing the fruit of her labour with her family, could eventually be stigmatized as a *yobé*.[24]

New research will further explore the implications of shamanic tourism for kinship relations, especially the rivalries and jealousies that can arise from economic transactions with tourists. Nevertheless, to close this chapter, I wish to underline how Justina and Elisa managed to forge paths and assert their shamanic practices with foreigners, thereby creating a network of allies and a far-from-negligible visibility in a context of colonial politics, the spread of Evangelical Christianity, and the hegemony of Western thought. These women's practices challenge our Western "ethos of exclusiveness" where a so-called authentic shamanism could never be linked with tourism; they invite us to think differently through an "ethos of inclusiveness" (Poirier 2008), where webs of relationality bring together in a peculiar shamanic way masters of the forest and foreign tourists. Through their contemporary practices, which involve the new actors present in their region, these women show that they are not stuck in a bygone era—a supposed dying tradition—but project themselves well into the future while actualizing past shamanic practices.[25] Indeed, Shipibo-Konibo shamanism has a long history of contact with "foreigners," redefining itself constantly in relation to such Others. By recognizing this inherent transformative logic at the heart of Shipibo-Konibo shamanism, we are able to look afresh at the female *onánya* who work with tourists.

Author's Note

A previous version of this chapter was presented at the joint American Anthropological Association and Canadian Anthropology Society meeting in Vancouver in 2019. I thank Elisa and Justina for sharing their knowledge with me. I also thank Sylvie Poirier and Françoise Dussart for their detailed comments and suggestions. Field research among the Shipibo-Konibo people was funded by the Fonds de recherche du Québec sur la société et la culture (FRQSC). This chapter was translated from French by David Rodgers.

Notes

1. Ethnologists who conducted research in this community at the end of the 1990s also received a negative reply to this question (Gonzáles 2002).
2. A regional name for shamanic songs.
3. A beverage composed of the *ayahuasca* vine (*Banisteriopsis caapi*) and leaves from the chacruna shrub (*Psychotria viridis*) that elicits hallucinogenic effects. *Ayahuasca* tourism began in the 1960s and 1970s, but intensified at the start of the 2000s.
4. On this topic, see Brabec de Mori (2014), Brabec de Mori and Silvano de Brabec (2009), and Herbert (2010).
5. Sexual abuse of tourists by male shamans made international headlines and created a demand for female shamans in shamanic tourism (Morin 2015).
6. Herbert (2010) also asks: "Is there something like a traditional female ayahuasca healer?...Are the women discussed in this article indeed shamans?"
7. Discussing this topic, Brabec de Mori (2014, 212) comments on a film made by North Americans on "female Shipibo *ayahuasca* drinkers": "usually, among

both Shipibo people and researchers, 'ayahuasca shamanism' is considered a male profession. This project, involving only women shamans, therefore occupies a niche in ethnomedical tourism, fostering professional *chamanismo* also among Shipibo women."

8. Nevertheless, this is how Shipibo-Konibo shamanism is sold to tourists to satisfy their expectations of "authenticity," which paradoxically is compromised by their own presence.

9. An important literature exists on this subject. See, in particular, Gow (1994) and Labate and Cavnar (2014).

10. This regional term is poorly translated as "métis" or "mixed race," but in fact refers to Indigenous Amazonians who no longer speak their language or that of Andean immigrants (Gow 1994).

11. Belaunde (2012) provides a similar argument in relation to the transformations of the *kéne* designs in the sale of craftwork to foreigners. This anthropologist also paints a fine and complex picture of the Shipibo-Konibo female shaman Herlinda (Belaunde 2015).

12. I also learned that a deceased female relative of Lucio, Camila, had been a renowned shaman. Lucio acknowledged this fact unperturbed after denying the existence of female shamans to me.

13. For more detailed accounts, see Colpron (2004, 2005).

14. Regionally called *pela cara* or *pela piel*, this mythic figure of Andean origin sucks the fat and peels the skin of his victims (Cardenas 1989; Morin 1998; Roe 1982; Gow 2001). The *gringos* are often associated with this anthropophagic killer.

15. Not scientifically identified and called *palo volador* in regional Spanish, this tree possesses a great mythical importance. It is present in the origin story of the *Cháikoni*, privileged auxiliaries of the shamans.

16. What distinguishes the use of *ráo* by the uninitiated from that of the *onánya* is not so much a difference in principle as one of degree, with the *onánya* prolonging and accumulating apprenticeships. The aim is also different, since the *onánya* seeks to contact the masters of the *ráo* by taking *ayahuasca*, which is generally feared by the uninitiated.

17. For Shipibo examples of the couvade, see Morin (1998) and Colpron (2004, 2006).

18. The name *yoshín báke* evokes different degrees of alterity depending on context. During a miscarriage, the inhuman appearance of the fetus, resembling a small snake for example, allows the genitor to be identified and the child's premature death to be explained. The most common paters of *yoshín báke* are the giant otter *Neíno* (*Pteronura brasiliensi*), the freshwater pink dolphin *Coshóshca* (*Inia geoffrensis*), and the forest master *Cháikoni*.

19. Kopenawa and Bruce (2010) give a similar explanation in a Yanomami context: the daughters of shamans are born from the sperm of spirits and are already "other." This predisposes them to become shamans.

20. On this subject, see Arévalo (1986).

21. Elsewhere (Colpron 2013), I further explain how—from the shaman's perspective—the forest encompasses *all* possible knowledge, even that of *gringos*.

22. Ethnologists, including myself, have played a role in the visibility of Shipibo-Konibo female shamans. In the early 2000s, many of us became interested in this possibility and asked questions about them.

23. Fotiou (2016) deplores the personal initiatives of shamanic tourism, regretting a lost collective value, and encourages instead community enterprises. Making shamanism a community project seems to be a Western ideal, however, that has little in common with the local logic of this practice. The *onánya* highlight the difficulty of the privations and the dangers incurred when taking *ayahuasca* to justify the economic compensation.

24. Not sharing with relatives is considered a rejection of kinship, an individualist act that is strongly criticized and stigmatized, as Frédéric Laugrand (this volume) points out in his Inuit case study.

25. Presenting the appropriation of *ayahuasca* in the Xingu region, Lima (2018) reports the sentence of a young Yudjá man who echoes this idea: "[T]he past is not in the past." *Ayahuasca* creates a political affect allowing a resumption of past practices that makes the future conceivable.

References

Arévalo, Guillermo. 1986. "El ayahuasca y el curandero Shipibo-Conibo del Ucayali." *América indígena* 46 (1): 147–61.

Belaunde, Luisa Elvira. 2012. "Diseños materiales e inmateriales: la patrimonialización del kené shipibo-konibo y de la ayahuasca en el Perú." *Mundo Amazónico* (3): 123–46. https://revistas.unal.edu.co/index.php/imanimundo/article/view/28715

———. 2015. "'Revivir a la gente': Herlinda Agustín, onaya del pueblo Shipibo-Konibo." *Mundo amazónico* 6 (2): 131–46. https://doi.org/10.15446/ma.v6n2.54498

Brabec de Mori, Bernd. 2014. "From the Native's Point of View: How Shipibo-Konibo Experience and Interpret Ayahuasca Drinking with Gringos." In *Ayahuasca Shamanism in the Amazon and Beyond*, edited by Beatriz C. Labate and Clancy Canvar, 206–30. New York: Oxford University Press.

Brabec de Mori, Bernd, and Laida Mori Silvano de Brabec. 2009. "La corona de la inspiración: los diseños geométricos de los Shipibo-Konibo y sus relaciones con cosmovisión y música." *Indian* 26: 105–34. https://doi.org/10.18441/ind.v26i0.105-134

Cardenas, Clara. 1989. *Los unaya y su mundo: aproximación al sistema medico de los Shipibo-Conibo del rio Ucayali.* Lima: Instituto Indigenista Peruano; CAAAP.

Chaumeil, Jean-Pierre. 2009. "El comercio de la cultura: el caso de los pueblos amazónicos." *Bulletin de l'institut Français d'Études Andines.* 38 (1): 61–74. https://doi.org/10.4000/bifea.2822

Colpron, Anne-Marie. 2004. "Dichotomies sexuelles dans l'étude du chamanisme: le contre-exemple des femmes chamanes shipibo-conibo." PHD dissertation, Université de Montréal.

———. 2005. "Monopólio masculino do xamanismo amazônico: o contra-exemplo das mulheres xamãs shipibo-conibo." *Mana* 11 (1): 95–128. https://doi.org/10.1590/S0104-93132005000100004

———. 2006. "Chamanisme féminin contre-nature? Menstruation, gestation et femmes chamanes parmi les Shipibo de l'Amazonie Occidentale." *Journal de la Société des américanistes* 92 (2): 95–128. https://doi.org/10.4000/jsa.3181

———. 2012. "Fluctuations et persistances chamaniques: le cas shipibo-conibo de l'Amazonie occidentale." In *Dynamiques religieuses des autochtones des Amériques*, edited by Robert Crépeau and Marie-Pierre Bousquet, 391–420. Paris: Éditions Karthala.

———. 2013. "Contact Crisis: Shamanic Explorations of Virtual and Possible Worlds." *Anthropologica* 55 (2): 373–83. https://www.jstor.org/stable/24467343

Fotiou, Evgenia. 2016. "The Globalization of Ayahuasca Shamanism and the Erasure of Indigenous Shamanism." *Anthropology of Consciousness* 27 (2): 151–79. https://doi.org/10.1111/anoc.12056

Gonzáles, María Eugenia. 2002. "In Search for Curing Knowledge—The Story of a Female Health Specialist among the Shipibo-Conibo in the Peruvian Amazon." *Anales Nueva Época* 5 (12): 109–41. https://gupea.ub.gu.se/bitstream/2077/3237/1/anales_5_gonzalez.pdf

Gow, Peter. 1994. "River People: Shamanism and History in Western Amazonia." In *Shamanism, History and the State*, edited by Nicholas Thomas and Caroline Humphrey, 90–113. Michigan: The University of Michigan Press.

———. 2001. *An Amazonian Myth and Its History.* Oxford: Oxford University Press.

Heise, Maria, Liliam Landeo, and Astrid Bant. 1999. *Relaciones de género en la Amazonia peruana.* Lima: CAAAP.

Herbert, Andrea. 2010. "Female Ayahuasca Healers Among the Shipibo-Konibo (Ucayali, Peru) in the Context of Spiritual Tourism." *Núcleo de Estudos*

Interdisciplinares (NEIP). http://neip.info/novo/wp-content/uploads/2015/04/
herbert_female_ayahuasca_healers_shipibo_spiritual_tourism.pdf

Kopenawa, Davi, and Bruce Albert. 2010. *La Chute du ciel: paroles d'un chaman Yanomami*. Paris: Plon.

Labate, Beatriz C., and Clancy Canvar. 2014. *Ayahuasca Shamanism in the Amazon and Beyond*. New York: Oxford University Press.

Laugrand, Frédéric, and Robert Crépeau. 2015. "Shamanisms, Religious Networks and Empowerment in Indigenous Societies of the Americas." *Anthropologica* 57 (2): 289–98. https://www.jstor.org/stable/26350441

Lima, Tânia Stolze. 2018. "Plant Regained: An Account of the *Ayahuasca* Encounter with the Yudjá People." *Revista do Instituto de Estudos Brasileiros* (69): 118–36. https://doi.org/10.11606/issn.2316-901x.v0i69p118-136

Morin, Françoise. 1998. *Los Shipibo-Conibo*. Vol. 3, *Guía etnográfica de la Alta Amazonia*, edited by F. Santos Granero and F. Barclay. Quito: Abya Yala.

——. 2015. "Résilience et flexibilité du chamanisme Shipibo-Konibo (Pérou)." *Anthropologica* 57 (2): 353–66. https://www.jstor.org/stable/26350446

Poirier, Sylvie. 2008. "Reflections on Indigenous Cosmopolitics—Poetics." *Anthropologica* 50 (1): 75–85. https://www.jstor.org/stable/25605390

Roe, Peter. 1982. *The Cosmic Zygote*. New Jersey: Rutgers University Press.

——. 1988. "The Josho Nahuanbo Are All Wet and Undercook: Shipibo Views of the Whiteman and the Incas in Myth, Legend, and History." In *Rethinking History and Myth: Indigenous South American Perspectives on the Past*, edited by Jonathan D. Hill, 106–35. Chicago: University of Illinois Press.

Vilaça, Aparecida. 2000. "O que significa tornar-se outro? Xamanismo e contato interétnico na Amazônia." *Revista brasileira de ciências sociais* 15 (44): 56–72. http://dx.doi.org/10.1590/S0102-69092000000300003

Viveiros de Castro, Eduardo. 2004. "Exchanging Perspectives: The Transformation of Objects into Subjects in Amerindian Ontologies." *Common Knowledge* 10 (3): 463–84.

7

TYING DOWN THE SOUL OF A POTATO IN THE SOUTHERN PERUVIAN ANDES

Performance and Frictions

INGRID HALL

IN THE PISAC POTATO PARK, Peru, the celebration of the National Potato Day has been named *Papa Watay*, a name taken from a ritual used to "tie down" the soul contained in the tubers of a new harvest, according to local views. This event also celebrates the importance of the potato in the Andes, as well as the 7000-year-old role of Andean *campesinos* (peasants)[1] in the domestication of this tuber and in the selection and conservation of its nearly 3000 Andean landraces. On National Potato Day, the formerly domestic *Papa Watay* ritual is now performed in the Potato Park in a collective and public context in front of an external audience of visitors from Lima and even from abroad (figure 7.1).

In this chapter, I explore how Indigenous religiosity is entangled with biodiversity conservation policies. I analyze the implications of these entanglements through the ethnography of the *Papa Watay*, focusing on how and why people of the Potato Park perform their ritual in this new context. I will show how, due to the presence of an international audience, a global understanding of Indigenous religiosity is stressed and performed as an alternative to Western ontology. This type of performance provides the opportunity for the people of

FIGURE 7.1. Various offerings surrounded by delegations from each community, visitors, and journalists. (Photograph by Ingrid Hall, 2015.)

the Potato Park to articulate an important political statement: We are Indigenous, as you expect us to be. As we will see, however, the "we" in this statement must be thoroughly analyzed. Moreover, in a contested religious context, the performance also engenders a local rethinking of customs (*costumbres*). This, in turn, contributes to a reevaluation of the place of *campesinos* both in Peruvian society and more globally according to international standards.

Various authors have demonstrated the relevance of performance in addressing issues of identity politics, especially for Indigenous people (Dussart 2000, 2004; Glowczewski and Henry 2007; Graham 2005). In these cases, performance is considered a way of adjusting local interest within national and/or international contexts. As far as the Andes are concerned, this kind of approach has been applied mainly in Bolivia, where Andean indigeneity is now at the heart of the national political project (Canessa 2018; Fabricant and Postero 2018). In Peru, where Andean indigeneity is not the object of institutional recognition in the same way (Raymond and Arcé 2013), the emergence of indigeneity results from various initiatives often linked to environmental conflicts, particularly regarding mining (F. Li 2013; Salazar-Soler 2009). In this chapter, I propose to explore one such initiative, the Potato Park, which mobilizes a more international understanding of indigeneity.

Like many scholars, I understand indigeneity to be dynamic and political (Dussart and Poirier 2017, this volume; Comaroff and Comaroff 2009; T. Li 2000; Povinelli 1997; Glowczewski and Henry 2007; Graham 2005). As Dussart and Poirier (this volume) have argued, indigeneity is a process *"in the making"* that has to be understood in its contemporaneity. Furthermore, local practices are interconnected with national and global logics and dynamics, often through interactions. The local, national, and global are, thus, "entangled," as Dussart and Poirier point out (this volume, 2017; see also, this volume: Colpron; Pimenova). The negotiations (Dussart and Poirier 2017) or frictions (Tsing 2005) generated by these entanglements shape the way indigeneity is understood and lived. In this chapter, I focus on these interactions among different actors, and understand the *Papa Watay* ritual as a place and moment of negotiating the politics of difference.

I mobilize Elizabeth Povinelli's (1997, 20) proposed distinction between "recognition" and "identification," which is here especially relevant as it accounts for both internal and external processes of self-recognition while also acknowledging the importance of third-party perceptions and actions. This allows me to analyze both how these populations self-identify and how they are identified by other (national and international) actors. It also allows me to see how the frictions generated by and in the interactions between actors shape these processes of identification and integration. The importance of the *Papa Watay*, in this specific case, is the outcome of such a negotiation as it stresses the figure of a ritualized, globalized Indigenous person (also called an "ecological Indian" by Krech [1999] or a "hyperreal Indian" by Ramos [1994]). In this specific situation, religiosity then really appears to "pragmatically engage the definition of [Indigenous peoples'] own contemporaneity" (Dussart and Poirier, this volume).

The data analyzed in this article were collected between 2012 and 2018 in the context of a research project on policies and practices for the conservation of biodiversity in Pisac Potato Park. I attended the *Papa Watay* twice in this context, in 2015 and 2017, while also following up on festivities in other years. Alongside these observations, I carried out interviews with the various actors present, including the members of the Peruvian NGO Asociación para la Naturaleza y el Desarrollo Sostenible (ANDES) that coordinates conservation activities in the Park, representatives of the International Potato Centre (Centro Internacional de la Papa, or CIP), and members of the public (both locals and outsiders) who attended the celebrations.

This chapter is divided in two sections. First, I outline what the *Papa Watay* is—in terms of meaning, practices, and perceptions—for the different groups of actors present. I then give an account of the frictions caused by the co-existence of contrasting points of view, examining the impacts of performing the ritual in the context of Peruvian National Potato Day.

Different Understandings of the *Papa Watay*

From the Domestic to the Public Sphere

Pisac Potato Park in Cusco, Peru (figure 7.2) was created in 1998 on the initiative of ANDES in order to promote conservation of potato landraces. Since then, it has become a landmark, both nationally and internationally, in terms of in situ conservation led by local communities (Graddy 2014). Through its biocultural approach, the Park illustrates the importance of local and Indigenous peoples in biodiversity conservation and advocates for the rights of these populations to living resources.

It was on the initiative of the *campesinos* from the Park that National Potato Day was established in 2005. The request, one year before, for this day to be institutionalized had led to a performance of the first public *Papa Watay*.

Papa Watay—literally, "tying down the potato" in Quechua—is the name of a domestic ritual in the agricultural calendar. This ritual is carried out to ensure that the new harvest keeps well so that families have enough food throughout the year and so that they have enough

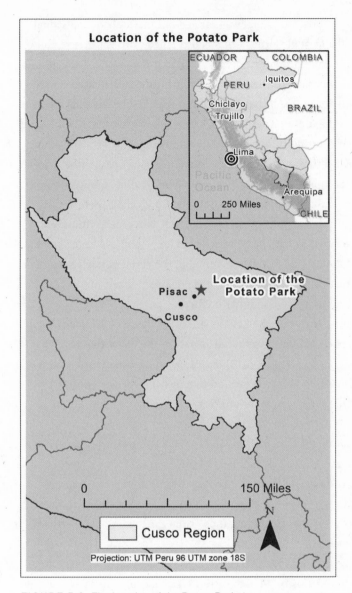

FIGURE 7.2. The location of the Potato Park. (Alejandra Uribe-Albornoz, 2020)

seed potatoes to sow the following year.[2] Potatoes are considered to have a soul (*animu*),[3] and so it is important to ensure that this soul is well attached to the tubers. If it escapes or becomes detached, the tubers will be negatively affected and household food supplies—of which the potato is the staple—could be significantly reduced.

Until the 2000s, this ritual was carried out privately by individual families on the feast of Corpus Christi (also called Corpus Christi locally), 60 days after Easter Sunday; in other words, it was part of the Catholic calendar. By this date, the harvest is usually finished. The ritual consists in protecting it. As with other agricultural rituals (like the offering to the earth on the first of August), it is a syncretic ritual, inscribed within a Catholic and agricultural calendar, whereby the entities involved in reproductive activities are invoked—including Pachamama (the Andean earth mother) and the *apu* (entities, usually masculine, embodied in the mountain summits)—alongside the Catholic God (called Tayta locally) (figure 7.3). In this chapter, I am not so much concerned with interpreting this ritual as with the way in which it is mobilized in the context of National Potato Day festivities; although the ritual in itself has not changed drastically in this context, its instrumentalization has, and this is critical in terms of identity politics.

Since 2005, the year when National Potato Day was initiated, *Papa Watay* has been publicly celebrated as part of the festivities organized in the Potato Park. ANDES (2018) indicated on its website under the section about *Papa Watay* (a section that has since been removed) that the aim of this ritual is to make offerings to Pachamama in order to thank her for her generosity. The festivities are organized mainly by the Park Association, by local experts, and by the *Papa Arariwa* (guardians of potato diversity), who are members of the communities involved in the committee responsible for in situ conservation activities. ANDES helps in several ways: it organizes various activities in advance, raises funds, coordinates any visits (including those from the media), and partakes in certain events.

Primarily, the *Papa Watay* seems to be about ritual and religiosity—a very ancient religiosity. Nonetheless, it is largely entangled with current political and legal issues—specifically, the recognition of *campesinos* and of their rights to seeds.

The Ritual Performance

During the public performances carried out in the Park on National Potato Day, the ritual aspect of the event is emphasized for the attending visitors (*visitadores*). (Indeed, ANDES calls this celebration *Papa Watay* rather than National Potato Day.) Here, I turn my attention to what is shown to these *visitadores* in order to underline this ritual dimension. Within the category of *visitadores*, we can distinguish the staff of ANDES and its usual partners (including researchers such as anthropologists and biologists who work on a regular basis in the Park) from more exceptional visitors that are called *invitados* (guests) by the *campesinos* and ANDES. To give an idea of the size of the event and the people that it mobilizes, in 2015 *invitados* numbered around 10 (including Brazilian journalists), while ANDES members and partners numbered around 20 (including international volunteers, researchers working in the Park, and members of the CIP). As for *campesinos* from local communities, these numbered around 200. In terms of numbers, then, the event concerns first and foremost the local population.

The *invitados* are often prestigious and come mostly from abroad. They are often researchers, important figures in national and (more often) international governance of plant resources, or even international media. They may also be officials at a national or a regional level. Usually, they have heard of the Park and are interested in the biocultural approach it deploys.[4] A particularity of this approach is that it values the cultural diversity that is closely linked to successful biodiversity conservation.

When guests visit the Park, their trip is coordinated by ANDES. Since the Park is situated at an altitude of over 3600 metres and lodgings are basic, guests generally stay in Cusco and make a day trip to the Park. With more than two hours of transport between Cusco and the Park, the schedule on site is limited and guests basically attend those activities directly associated with the *Papa Watay*. Thus, it is significant that, for these actors, National Potato Day in the Park is named after the *Papa Watay* ritual: the celebrations are presented to them as a relatively linear succession of events culminating in a collective ritual.

The following description lays out how the day proceeded in 2017; however, this is, in large part, how it has also transpired in other years. A committee of *campesinos* welcomed the *invitados* as they got out of their bus with the sound of flute (*quena*) and drum music. The women

FIGURE 7.3. The park offering set up in the centre of the stage/ritual space at the beginning of the *Papa Watay*. A gathering of participants from one community appears in the background. (Photograph by Ingrid Hall, 2015.)

showed off their layered, coloured dresses, ornamentally trimmed jackets, hats (*monteras*), and woven shawls (*lliklla*). The men matched them with their ponchos, coloured jackets, and woollen hats (*chullo/ch'ullu*). The *invitados* were led towards arches made of branches and decorated with flowers while women showered flower petals on each of their heads. Once they passed this plant threshold, they came out into a large space (the football pitch of the receiving community) in the middle of which was a pile of potatoes that would be the object of the ritual to come (figure 7.3). A number of *campesinos* were already installed in groups in the four corners of the soon-to-be stage and ritual space, each community forming a colourful cluster.

The day was officially opened by a *técnico*[5] from a local community, who guided the day's proceedings over the microphone. He introduced the president of the Potato Park, then a representative of ANDES, each of whom spoke briefly. Other than a few words of welcome in Spanish, most interventions were in Quechua, and it was in this language that information was given concerning the day's activities. Most of the guests didn't understand this language. While they understood that activities were beginning, they didn't know the details. It was clear that the event was not meant primarily for them.

The *Papa Watay* celebrations, both in 2015 and 2017, began with a procession by the four communities present. Each community's delegates set out from the corner where they had been waiting and followed a spiral trajectory that led them close to the potato pile, marking out the ritual space. Each delegation was accompanied by a group of musicians (with drums and *quena*) who set themselves up near the microphones. The number of participants varied from one community to another, but was generally between thirty and fifty, including men, women, and children of all ages. For its performance, each delegation was organized in three groups: an offerings group, a dance group, and a group of other members of the community. These processions have a specific name: *qashwa*, a Quechua word that means "a collective dance." This group organization is influenced both by Catholic processions and different kinds of performances representing Inca festivals (*raymis* such as the *Inti Raymi,* which is a main event in Cusco). For each delegation's performance, the first group brought the offerings, which consisted mainly of potatoes. The actions of the participants were, in general, carefully orchestrated; the agricultural and ritual objects presented facilitated the staging of both the procession and the offering. Following the offerings group, a group of dancers arrived, alternating simple dance movements moving forward and more elaborate choreography on the spot. Finally, the rest of the community delegates followed the dancers with simplified, common dance steps. Each community finished its procession with a final presentation of the complete choreography; meanwhile, the rest of the community made the offering visible in the centre of the ritual space and eventually concluded the performance by miming the ritual.

Communities do not actually perform the *Papa Watay* ritual at this point. The actual ritual action takes place later, after the completion of each community performance. This shows very clearly that the processions just described are performances for an audience and are not themselves rituals.

Once all of the communities carried out their procession, a pair of ritual specialists (*yachaq*)—a man and a woman—moved towards the centre of the ritual space where the five offerings had been placed: one from each of the four communities, plus one from the Park itself that had been placed there before the event started. In 2015, the man who presided over the ritual was well-known locally as well as in Cusco and even elsewhere in Peru. He gave a brief comment in Spanish to explain that the ritual is dedicated to Pachamama and the *apu* (a similar statement was given in 2017), but this generality did little to clarify the ritual proceedings that followed.

During the ritual, which lasted almost an hour, the two ceremony-holders unpacked the various items they brought and proceeded with the ritual. Since these activities weren't amplified by any sound system and the line of sight was blocked by the mass of delegations surrounding the ritual specialists, the visitors were not able see or hear what was happening. This posed a challenge for the visitors who could not understand what was happening, and for the television crews who could not easily film the proceedings.[6]

The activities finished around one o'clock in the afternoon, at which point everyone was invited to take a midday break. After an early start, the journey, the altitude, and the burning sun of late May, this was welcome. The *campesinos* gathered with their community and ate their meals. Depending on their status, the guests were either offered a potato-based meal on site or a much more elaborate Andean-style buffet prepared at the Park's restaurant a few miles away in an amazing environment. The *invitados* then set off back to Cusco, possibly stopping on the way to see the conservation activities carried out in the Park (especially in the cold chamber and the greenhouses).

Interviews I have carried out with international guests have shown that they greatly appreciated the colourful and festive aspects of the *Papa Watay*. They assume that it hasn't much changed across time and they are impressed by the respect that local people show towards the potatoes and Pachamama. The lack of contextualization and explanation doesn't seem to bother them much; rather, it is taken as a clue that the event is not meant for tourists, and as some proof of authenticity.

The performance of the ritual stresses the importance of cultural differences, which in turn show the relevance of the Park's biocultural approach. It also shows how the perception of external actors is important. The global context of nature conservation policies and Indigenous rights at the international level are relevant, and the importance of the concept of the sacred becomes especially interesting. In fact, the concept of a sacred site proposed by the International Union for Conservation of Nature (IUCN) is one of the most used concepts in nature conservation with regard to protecting Indigenous rights on their territory. In the 1970s and 1980s, the creation of such rhetorical devices went hand-in-hand with the increasingly powerful image of "ecological Indians" (Krech 1999), guardians of a nature with which they have a spiritual relationship (Ramos 1994). The performance of *Papa Watay* must thus be considered within this broader, international discourse—a discourse, moreover, that guests are familiar with and to which they generally adhere. An Andean touch is added via the reference to Pachamama, who is legally recognized by Bolivia in its 2009 constitution—a fact that the country never fails to mention in these same international forums.

For the *invitados*, and from an analytical point of view, two intertwined processes of recognition and identification take place. By foregrounding the importance of culture for the people of the Park, the latter are recognized by outsiders as an Andean version of a globalized Indigenous People (Poupeau 2011). This recognition, largely depending on the performance of the *Papa Watay* at hand, also implies a process of identification. Through the category of Indigenous peoples and local communities (IPLCs) acknowledged by the United Nations and the Convention on Biological Diversity, the *campesinos* from the Park are identified as Indigenous. Presenting the people from the Park in this way contributes to making the Park an emblem of the work carried out in these international initiatives, which in turn facilitates the reinforcement of strategic alliances and the acquisition of funds.

The emphasis on religiosity reflects the attempts of external and globalized actors who expect local populations to behave like "hyperreal" Indigenous people (Ramos 1994), which means, for example, considering nature in a holistic and ritualistic way. The performance of the *Papa Watay*, and the framing chosen for the *invitados*, fulfill such an expectation.

The Institutional Event

I will now consider the perspective of the Park inhabitants who are numerically in the majority at this event. In presenting this contrast, my objective is not to critique the possible gullibility of the *invitados* described above. My purpose is not, that is, to identify a kind of authenticity— Rountree (this volume) shows the limits of such a concept. Moreover, local practices cannot be understood at a local level only (Dussart and Poirier, this volume; Colpron, this volume). My purpose is, rather, to take into account contrasting visions of religiosity in order to better understand the frictions that they generate—frictions that I analyze in the last section of the chapter.

For the local people, the ritual dimension of the day's proceedings is relatively marginal. In fact, the commentary in Quechua at the beginning of the day presents the day's events as the anniversary of the Asociación de Comunidades del Parque de la Papa (the association of the communities belonging to the Potato Park), the local institution that encompasses the Park.[7] As is the norm in the context of institutional anniversaries (e.g., community anniversaries,[8] agricultural contests), the day basically consists in a succession of contests, among which the most prestigious and significant are the processions mentioned above. This observation, however, is too restricted to fully address local understandings of the day. It is necessary to take account of the whole day's schedule. All these institutional events share the imprints of an external administrative culture (whether that of an NGO or of the Peruvian state), which is based on a methodology designed to engage local people in development projects (Asensio 2016). International development organizations have stressed competition, which has met with great success in the Andes. Indeed, competition has been at the heart of social and cultural life in the Andes for a long time: during previous ethnographic research at a similar site in the same province, I discovered that, before the 1960s, men had to show their speed and dexterity during collective agricultural work[9]—a way defining their masculinity according to social norms. This cultural phenomenon seems to have been reactivated recently under the influence of development organizations, both governmental and nongovernmental. As a matter of fact, during the festivities of National Potato Day in the Park, there is a contest dedicated to men's ploughing abilities.

The institutional dimension of the proceedings is evident in another way, too: taking part in National Potato Day is considered a duty by *campesinos*. In fact, given the governance structure in place in the Park,[10] when the association of the Park's member communities decides to organize the event, it is expected that all families from the Park's different communities take part. The event is understood as a community work party (*faena*), almost like the clearing of canals, agricultural work on communal land, or the upkeep of paths.[11] As is the norm, each family's participation is sanctioned economically by their community. Usually, their absence entails a financial penalty equivalent to a day's salary (PEN 24 in 2018, or around CAD 9). In some communities, members' presence is rewarded by an equivalent salary.

The dances (*qashwas*) presented by each community are the first and most important of the contests. This contest involves the biggest prizes, the most people, and the greatest preparation (and hence investment of time and energy). Since the results of the contest are not made public until the end of the day, the competitive dimension of the event largely passes under the radar of the visitors.

The *Papa Watay* ritual that follows the *qashwas* is carried out with great seriousness by the ritual specialists, and the transgressions of certain journalists in 2014 were not at all appreciated.[12] During the hour-long ritual, a respectful circle forms around the ritual specialists. Children who are naughty or not dressed in traditional clothing are taken away. Representatives of each community are sought for the final blessing. In fact, this ritual seems to be understood by the *campesinos* as a propitiatory ritual for the Park itself, in the image of the public rituals that take place nowadays in various institutions such as municipalities, universities, or companies in Peru. The ritual appears relatively unchanged, but it has acquired a new purpose in a new context.

Following the *qashwa* contest and the *Papa Watay* ritual, a myriad of other contests take place. These involve: the peeling of the *qhachun waqachi* potato[13] (figure 7.4); the contest regarding knowledge about native potatoes; running races (for both men and women); *harawi* (poems, often recited by children); earth oven (*watya*) construction; culinary contests; and men working the earth with the Andean foot spade (*chaki taklla*). Each year there are certain variations, and efforts are made to include the youth in the *harawi* contests and running races in particular.

During both the National Potato Day festivities that I attended in 2015 and 2017, the hope of winning prizes turned out to be a fundamental motivation for the participants, and even a source of conflict. The prizes are significant, particularly for the *qashwa* contest, and can total nearly CAD 1250. This is an occasion for redistributing a portion of the profits made from the various activities related to the Park. Ten percent of the profit made through the activities linked to the Park (especially the groups selling food, medicinal plant products, and handicrafts, as well as those dedicated to lodging and guiding tourists) is systematically fed into an operating fund, which is redistributed to the communities in two ways: by financing activities such as the *Papa Watay* (the prizes and various other costs), and via an intercommunity redistribution mechanism through which each community executes a project of its choice. The winners of each contest are given a prize: cash for the most prestigious and significant contests, and goods (rice, sugar, oil, etc.) for less prestigious ones. These prizes are then redistributed within each community by calculating the portion due to each

FIGURE 7.4. A small pile of *qhachun waqachi* potatoes, which "make daughters-in-law cry." (Photograph by Ingrid Hall, 2015.)

person. The economic dimension is thus significant for local people. Losing the main prizes is a serious matter, as I was able to perceive on both occasions in which I served as a member of the jury for the *Papa Watay*.[14]

If we contrast the *visitadores'* point of view with that of the *campesinos*, it is clear that there are radical differences between the perceptions of the actors present. For the former group, the proceedings are mainly ritual and cultural events; for the latter, they are mainly institutional events linked to economic interests. This reflects the fact that the latter group considers themselves primarily (and here Povinelli's [1997, 20] concept of recognition is pertinent) to be *campesinos*, adhering to a value system that gives great importance to communal obligations, collective work, and competition among individuals and households. Besides this, they identify themselves as members of a *campesino* community according to a legal status that governs their place in Peruvian national society and their relationship to the land. Simply foregrounding these contrasts, however, is not in itself enough to understand the full significance of the *Papa Watay*, for reasons we shall now explore.

The *campesinos* do not consider this public performance to be simply religious. This does not mean the *Papa Watay* ritual is irrelevant for the *campesinos*. Indeed, those—particularly Catholic families—for whom the ritual is still relevant may continue to perform the ceremony privately in its domestic form during the feast of Corpus Christi. Still, the public form of the ritual performed during the National Potato Day festivities in the Park shifts the ritual's purpose as, in this instantiation, it is mainly devoted to the Park (and not simply the tubers). Moreover, the performance of *Papa Watay* during National Potato Day reveals the importance of economic interests and the necessity to strengthen the partnerships among the communities themselves, between the communities and ANDES, and between the communities and the CIP.

Frictions While Performing the *Papa Watay*

The driving forces behind the performance of the *Papa Watay* are complex. Local people's involvement should be understood in terms of a local logic, partially shaped by external actors such as NGOs. It is this logic that we will focus on here. I will detail the frictions generated by the organization of the event in order to grasp how the processes of recognition and identification are affected by the staging of this ritual in front of an external public.

The institutional importance associated with celebrating National Potato Day and its economic implications impose a certain logic upon the performance. In order to have a chance of winning the *qashwa* contest, each community thinks carefully about what dance(s) to stage. Insofar as there is no choreography linked to the domestic ritual, the contest requires that people innovate. Thus, in 2017, one community chose a dance associated with the flowering of potato plants, while another tried to highlight the importance of wild potato varieties.

Valorizing "Andean Cosmovision"

The *campesinos* feel encouraged to refer to the past, to *costumbres*, whether in terms of choreography, clothing, or choice of ritual and agricultural objects. This stresses the importance of showing some Andean cultural specificity in the performance of the *Papa Watay*, or what ANDES usually calls the *Cosmovisión Andina* (Andean Cosmovision) following a whole tradition of publications on the topic. In the Guatemalan context, MacKenzie (this volume) shows the importance of Maya spirituality," while Pimenova (this volume) evokes a similar process in Siberia. This is supposed to meet the expectations of both for the international *visitadores* and most of the regional *mestizo* and urban population attending the event.

Since we are dealing with a contest, it is essential to take account of the criteria by which performances are evaluated. The *campesinos* require that jury members be outsiders to the communities in question, and thus they seek out ANDES staff, representatives of the CIP, and others who work with these organizations. For those who occupy key positions, this is a delicate task. It was in this context that I was asked to serve as a jury member for the *qashwa* contest both in 2015 and 2017. In 2016, for the anniversary of the CIP organized in the Park, the jury decision had generated tension among the communities and negatively impacted the relationship between them and the two organizations, ANDES and the CIP. Consequently, in 2017, significant tensions were still in the air and people from the Park—as well as those from ANDES and the CIP—were very cautious. In the 2017 jury, as in 2015, we emphasized the music, the costumes, the choreography, the staging, and the objects used. We appreciated the performance as a spectacle. But the results we agreed on as a jury were contested, debated, and negotiated. The *técnicos locales* from the Park in charge of the event's organization wanted to see the criteria of local people better accounted for, namely the number of participants and the enthusiasm that they showed. Our first choice was impossible in their eyes, as the chosen delegation was unable to skillfully handle the llama they had brought for the *qashwa*. For these herders, this lack of mastery was a major fault. These discussions around the criteria that should be relevant to the jury decision illustrate the differences among the points of view of the different actors involved.

The *visitadores* usually expect to see typical manifestations of the local culture. Their expectations may vary according to their background and their knowledge of the local populations, which typically hinges upon two figures. The first is a globalized Indigenous protector of nature (Krech 1999; Ramos 1994), and the second is the figure of the Andean man that emerged during the twentieth century in Peru with the *indigenismo* movement (Mendoza 2006; Herrera 1980) and is currently being refashioned by the Bolivian state (Canessa 2018; Poupeau 2011). In general, the local population is relatively familiar with the politically motivated use of the Andean figure in Peru and Bolivia. They are, however, less familiar with the global Indigenous figure, except for ten or so individuals who frequent international events such as the climate-focused Conferences of the Parties (held in Paris, Lima, or Bonn), and who have thus become aware of what "being Indigenous" means globally. Performances are thus designed with regard to these two external figures of indigeneity, which are remote for most locals. In fact, it seems that it is through the performances that the local population becomes more familiar with these figures and has to take a position regarding them. It is noteworthy that this is not a deliberately assertive act by the local population, as seems to be true in the cases mentioned above (Glowczewski and Henry 2007; Dussart 2004; Graham 2005).

To illustrate how the outsider's gaze affects choices made locally, let us now focus on a specific performance, namely the *Machu Papa*, the dance presented in 2016 and 2017 by the community of Chahuaytiri. The middle-aged men who made this choice of dance and who work with ANDES explained that they have saved (*rescatado*) a dance that they witnessed in their childhood. The dancers, dressed up as elderly hunchbacks, wear leather masks with the woollen side facing outwards (figure 7.5). The characters of the *Machu Papa* symbolize the wild varieties of potato, the term *machu* meaning "old" or "ancestral" in Quechua.[15] The *qashwa* contest has caused people to reevaluate different kind of dances, which were not originally linked to the *Papa Watay* ritual.

The choice of the *Machu Papa* dance should be understood within the logic of nature conservation policies. "Wild ancestors" of the mainly edible potato species cultivated by humans are critical for the

FIGURE 7.5. The *Machu Papa* dance. (Photograph by Ingrid Hall, 2017.)

development of climate-change-adapted varieties. It is therefore significant that the *Machu Papa* choreography was chosen in 2016 for the 45th anniversary of the CIP, an organization that houses the world's largest collection of these varieties and also develops new varieties from them. The emphasis on certain cultural traits is thus intertwined with an international agenda of biodiversity conservation and the use of genetic resources. Moreover, one of the objectives of the NGO is to acknowledge and valorize the role of Andean *campesinos* in the creation and conservation of these resources. For this reason, too, the *Machu Papa* dance is a perfect match.

The performance is thus designed with regard to present-day issues, taking into account the Park's various partners as well as international biodiversity governance policies.[16] The choice of choreographies, which is considered to be an act of local safeguarding of customs, is largely influenced by the presence of external actors and the gaze that they introduce. This translates as well to the emphasis placed on Pachamama and the *apu* during the *Papa Watay*. Their importance is broadcasted over the loudspeakers throughout the performance; references to the Catholic faith, on the other hand, are avoided. Thus, the meaning of Andean Cosmovision is co-produced throughout the *Papa Watay* by everyone in attendance. Whether they are conscious of their role or not, they are all actors who influence the production of Andean Cosmovision, and whose perception of it is, in turn, influenced by this process.

Eluding the Religious Dimension

This desire to emphasize Andean Cosmovision generates frictions locally.[17] For the Catholics and Evangelists, it means occulting their main deity. For Evangelist converts, who represent nearly half the population, this erasure is critical.[18] Conversion means renouncing Pachamama, who is equated with the devil (*Satanás*), renouncing the *apu*, and stopping dancing. In such a context, as I observed during previous field research, showing belief in the existence of Pachamama (particularly in public) may cast doubt on the sincerity of one's conversion. My interlocutors indicated that converts usually refuse to actively participate in activities in the Park that involve Pachamama or the *apu* (i.e., Andean Cosmovision) and prefer instead to take on secondary roles. They do not take part in offerings or in dances, generally being content to pad out the retinue that follows after each delegation. Consequently, although ANDES by no means refuses to work with converts, the fact that it promotes Andean Cosmovision strongly discourages the converted from involving themselves in the performances and more broadly in the Park.

According to some of my interlocutors, this situation has led to significant changes. Ten years ago, the practice of *Papa Watay* was disappearing as it was associated with indigeneity and was considered shameful at the time. This tendency was accentuated over the last three decades by the growing influence of Evangelical churches. Nevertheless, several interviews showed that since the public *Papa Watay* performance began, Catholics are more at ease regarding the domestic performance of the ritual. Families that tended to disregard the ritual within their household on the feast of Corpus Christi now practice it again with renewed fervour. The public event has allowed a ritual revival at a domestic level, and sometimes for tourists.

All of this applies to those who identify themselves as "Catholics,"[19] but also extends beyond the boundaries of this group. For the Park's *técnicos,* the *Papa Watay* is an opportunity to transmit customs, dances, stories, rituals, and other forms of knowledge to the youth. In this regard, the commentary accompanying the peeling of the *qhachun waqachi* potatoes is exemplary. In 2015, while the various teams set to work laboriously peeling these tubers with their intricate curves (figure 7.4), a commentator recounted that, in the olden days, a young woman about to marry would have to peel this potato under the gaze of her mother-in-law in order to show that she was, in fact, ready to marry (Hall 2020). It is supposed to have been a kind of female initiation ritual. Organized in the context of *Papa Watay,* the contest thus becomes an opportunity to transmit this knowledge, which the youth have never received because only a few elders alive today actually experienced this in person. Numerous such comments in Quechua, which punctuate National Potato Day, serve as reminders of certain practices, transmitting them to youth who have never been exposed to them either because of their parents' religion, or because the occasion has never arisen. The desire to valorize and transmit this knowledge takes precedence over the ritual significance of the event, and also over issues concerning international governance of natural resources.

Negotiating Identity

Erasing the Catholic dimension of the *Papa Watay* favours the cultural valorization of this ritual by glossing over delicate issues, among which the most emblematic is people's relationship to Pachamama and the *apu.* This process is, moreover, encouraged by the development of a tourist industry in the Park. As ecotourism grows, it is not uncommon for families, even those of converts, to organize rituals to Pachamama for visitors. Andean Cosmovision, like crafts or natural medicine, is the object of a process of commodification (Comaroff and Comaroff, 2009; Appadurai 1986).[20]

This context contributes to a space of reflection on what it means to be *campesino* in the Andes for the people concerned, which can be understood as an internal form of recognition (following the categories of recognition and identification proposed by Povinelli [1997]). Under the gaze of the *visitadores*, customs and rituals are reevaluated, leading to an internal negotiation of what is to be judged relevant. For example, the contests that come after the *Papa Watay* ritual emphasize physical endurance,[21] mastery of the main agricultural tools, or dexterity with a knife in peeling potatoes. These skills are all essential for daily life in a rural community of the Andes but must also be understood in a practical and a moral way. They are essential for the *campesinos* in that they define who they are: *runa* in Quechua (Robin Azevedo, 2004), *jaqi* in Aymara (Canessa 2012) (both terms mean, literally, "human"). Thus, even if the *Papa Watay* highlights a globalized Indigenous figure for the *visitadores*, it allows local people to valorize a particular perception that the *campesinos* have of themselves, which draws from a socially and culturally specific logic. This is an instance of what Canessa (2018, 331) calls "symbolic indigeneity," which "can index a distinct lifestyle and cultural difference." For Catholics, the reciprocity with Pachamama and the *apu* is also part of this cultural specificity, though for Evangelists— at least theoretically—this is not the case. This process of recognition, moreover, takes place in a religious and economic context that is undoubtedly contemporary; in other words, one that takes account of Evangelical churches, new economic opportunities, and so on. The process of internal recognition induced by these performances thus traces the outline of a local, contemporary Indigenous figure negotiated in relation to its global counterparts (both Andean and beyond).

These processes of internal and external recognition, which mutually influence each other, seem to allow the Park's *campesinos* to reconsider the place that they have occupied in national society hitherto. The *campesinos* notice that, by participating in various campaigns orchestrated by ANDES, the Peruvian government now takes them into consideration (on several occasions, they have sent delegations to Lima, especially to the Ministry of the Environment). Thus, the *campesinos* are inclined to reposition themselves vis-à-vis other sectors of society. For example, as I witnessed, some of them now dare to refuse mistreatments such as being offered derisory prices for their products. (Of course, other dynamics are also at work, but these refusals were not common twenty years ago when I started fieldwork in neighbouring communities, and constitute a major change.)

Conclusion

Peruvian National Potato Day, as celebrated in Pisac Potato Park, is an event that prompts *campesinos* of the local communities to orient themselves with regard to the globalized Indigenous figure introduced by international institutions. This figure is made visible to visitors in the context of the *Papa Watay* via the NGO ANDES, with the active collaboration of the *campesinos* who represent it locally. This creates a challenge, however, since the *campesinos*, for the most part, have quite a different image of their cultural specificity: they consider themselves not as Indigenous, but as *campesinos* or *runa* within their national framework.

Carrying out the *Papa Watay* for an external public is an imposed activity and entails a certain amount of negotiation locally. The emphasis on a globalized Indigenous figure becomes problematic because of the role allocated to Andean Cosmovision on the one hand, and Christian religion on the other. Holding the event gives rise to negotiations resulting in the valorization of the ritual and of certain customs. In the public performance, the ritual dimension is emphasized but also chan-nelled to fit the expectations of the visitors. This is also coherent with the commodification of culture that is prevalent in the Park—and more generally in the region of Cusco—through tourism. This process, however, induces a rupture between the ritual and its religious dimension (contested locally), eluding the Catholic influences and stressing the importance of Pachamama. Doing so, it generates conflicts inside the local community as Pachamama is considered to be *Satanás* (the devil) by the numerous Protestants. Paradoxically, this rupture simultaneously allows some kind of cultural valorization of an idealized Andean religiosity, and the reval-orization of Catholicism (and Catholics), which is otherwise dismissed.

In this hall of mirrors, the *campesinos* are encouraged to reflect on how they define themselves (i.e., recognition as defined by Povinelli [1997]). The external gaze, although it gives rise to this reflection, does not determine it completely; it is negotiated locally among and between the various groups of community actors. In fact, in the absence of the visitors' gaze (they are not present the whole day), a number of individual and collective morals specific to the communities are affirmed, such as the importance of community organization, work, and competition. Thus, the reflection goes beyond the framework imposed by external actors (who are generally not aware of it and who may know little about it).

Let us return to the concepts proposed by Povinelli (1997). Regarding recognition, the external valorization of Andean Cosmovision prompts the cultural valorization of certain customs locally. The organization and execution of the performance, however, also allow for the affirmation of specific social values. In terms of identification, the fact that *campesinos* find themselves in a paradigm of international governance of plant and genetic resources during the *Papa Watay* (external identification) causes people to reposition themselves in their relationship with the Peruvian government (internal identification). In this process, the presence and support of international observers is crucial, both in terms of their mere presence and through their financial or political support for the Park at an international level. The various successes achieved in the name of the Park, among which are the institutionalization of National Potato Day in Peru and the national ban against GMOs, allow the *campesinos* to appreciate the effectiveness and relevance of this external identification. The performance of the ritual, then, becomes a mostly political tool, a way to negotiate some kind of political recognition in international and national arenas.

In this way, the celebration of Peruvian National Potato Day creates the conditions for local people to demand rights that are largely inspired by the perspective of international plant resource governance. The visitors' recognition of the specific characteristics of the local population (politics of difference) stimulates not only a global reflection on the rights of Indigenous peoples, but also a local reflection on the way that people of the Potato Park define themselves (recognition), including on the values that are essential to them. As a result of this, local people begin to think that their place in Peruvian society should be reconsidered (identification). Religiosity, then, appears to be a very political and contemporary matter, entangled with social claims and environmental policies at different levels, from the local to the national and even the international.

Author's Note

First of all, I want to thank the different partners who facilitated this work and made it possible: the *campesinos* from the Park and especially the *técnicos locales* and *Papa Arariwa*, the members of ANDES, and the members of the CIP, especially from the Bank of Germplasm. This would not have been possible without their help and their patience. This chapter is the outcome of a reflection presented in July 2017 in a panel co-organized by Sylvie Poirier and Françoise Dussart at the 34th Conference of the International Society for the Sociology of Religion in Lausanne, Switzerland. I want to thank them for this stimulating encounter and the way they contributed to this chapter. Last but not least, I want to thank the Fonds de recherche du Québec—Société et culture (FRQSC) and the Social Sciences and Humanities Research Council of Canada (SSHRC) for their financial support.

Notes

1. I use the local Spanish term *campesino* to refer to the members of the communities of the Potato Park. In fact, in Peru, the assimilation of *campesinos* with Indigenous people is not obvious and is even controversial. On the one hand, the category of Indigenous people, as used locally, mostly refers to Amazonian people and stresses their difference from Andean people. They tend to consider themselves to be "human" (*runa* in Quechua [Robin-Azevedo 2004], *jaqi* in Aymara [Canessa 2012]), which entails a rural way of life and the importance of reciprocity among humans and different kinds of entities such as Pachamama and the mountains (*apu*). On the other hand, the Peruvian state itself tends to deny the status of Indigenous people to *campesinos* except in the context of the law on consultation (Castillo Castañeda and Santos Peralta 2015). In this context, a more international definition of Indigeneity is often used—for instance, in dealing with environmental conflicts (mostly mining conflicts), or in specific projects (such as the Potato Park), which are entangled with

international politics. This strategy is a way to protect *campesinos'* rights by referring to international laws concerning Indigenous Peoples (e.g., UNDRIP).

2. Potatoes are clones; they are not grown from seed as such, but from small, sprouting tubers.

3. The concept of *animu* is used in reference both to humans (La Riva Gonzalez 2005) and nonhumans, such as potatoes (Hall 2018; Arnold and Yapita 1996; Allen 1982).

4. For more information on the biocultural approach, see Argumedo and Wong (2010), Hall (2019), and Graddy (2013).

5. This term refers to *campesinos* who participate in the conservation activities of ANDES.

6. This led to difficulties in 2014, when crews interfered with the ritual. In 2015, the ritual space was delimited with chalk and clear instructions was given to the film crew. A suitable spot had also been found previously to film the whole event.

7. This association allows for the participation of local communities and their representatives in the Park. As the Park had no official recognition from the Peruvian government until spring 2020, this association has also been the official and administrative face of the Park until recently.

8. These celebrate the date of a *campesino* community's official registration, and thereby their acquisition of a land title. These celebrations are particularly important in communities recognized after the agricultural reform of 1969, which is the case for different communities from the Park that were previously private estates (*haciendas*).

9. The term *wachu* (furrow) in Quechua designates both an agricultural practice and the sociopolitical journey of a man, as Beatriz Pérez Galán (2004) has shown regarding one of the Park's member communities.

10. See Argumedo and Stenner (2008) on the governance principles of the Park.

11. It is very important that community members take part in these events to be recognized as true members of the community (Hall 2014).

12. The media team made its way in between the participants in order to film better, which was experienced by the communities as an unwelcome intrusion. This was exacerbated by the fact that, more generally, the journalists were expecting to be treated with great regard, which has been badly interpreted by the *campesinos*.

13. The name of this potato literally means "that which makes the daughter-in-law cry" because it is so hard to peel such a bumpy potato.

14. As a close collaborator of ANDES known by the *técnicos locales*, I was solicited on both occasions that I've attended the event and could not refuse to

participate, as we will see later. This put me in a position to experience the bitter disillusionment of the members of the community that hosted me.

15. The term *machu* in Quechua can be used to refer to human ancestors as well as wild potato varieties; on this point, see Hall (2018).

16. For example, the concept of the sacred, as recognized by the IUCN through the category of the sacred site, is particularly important and relevant for Indigenous peoples defending their territories.

17. Numerous works on the Andes point out the influences of the Catholic Church in Andean beliefs and practices (see, e.g., Canessa 2012; Robin Azevedo 2008).

18. See MacKenzie (this volume) for a more detailed discussion of this subject in the Guatemalan context.

19. I use this term here by default, for lack of a better one, to designate those who haven't converted to a neo-Protestant church.

20. For a discussion on the importance of tourism among the Shipibo-Konibo, see Colpron (this volume).

21. It is noteworthy that the running race, which is a favorite among young adults, reminds the latter of the great endurance possessed by their elders working in the fields.

References

Allen, Catherine J. 1982. "Body and Soul in Quechua Thought." *Journal of Latin American Lore* 8 (2): 179–96.

ANDES. 2018. "Papa Watay." Accessed December 18, 2018. http://www.andes.org.pe/event-papa-watay (webpage discontinued).

Appadurai, Arjun, ed. 1986. *The Social Life of Things: Commodities in Cultural Perspective*. Cambridge: Cambridge University Press.

Argumedo, Alejandro, and Tammy Stenner. 2008. *Conserving Indigenous Biocultural Heritage in Peru*. No. 137a, *Gatekeeper*. London: IIED Publications. http://pubs.iied.org/14567IIED/

Argumedo, Alejandro, and Bernard Wong. 2010. "The Ayllu System of the Potato Park, Cusco, Peru: United Nations University Institute of Advanced Studies." *Case Studies* (blog), Satoyama Initiative. May 3, 2010. http://satoyama-initiative.org/en/the-ayllu-system-of-the-potato-park/

Arnold, Denise Y., and Juan de Dios Yapita, eds. 1996. *Madre Melliza y sus crias: Ispall Mama Wawampi*. La Paz: Hisbol.

Asensio, Raúl Hernández. 2016. *Los nuevos Incas: la economía política del desarrollo rural andino en Quispicanchi (2000–2010)*. Lima: IEP.

Canessa, Andrew. 2012. *Intimate Indigeneities: Race, Sex, and History in the Small Spaces of Andean Life*. Durham: Duke University Press.

——. 2018. "Indigenous Conflict in Bolivia Explored through an African Lens: Towards a Comparative Analysis of Indigeneity." *Comparative Studies in Society and History* 60 (2): 308–37. https://doi.org/10.1017/S0010417518000063

Castillo Castañeda, Pedro, and Lucía Santos Peralta. 2015. "Las artimañas del gobierno ara evadir el proceso de consulta sobre temas de minería." *La revista agraria* 171: 10–12.

Comaroff, John L., and Jean Comaroff. 2009. *Ethnicity, Inc.* Chicago: University of Chicago Press.

Dussart, Françoise. 2000. "The Politics of Representation: Kinship and Gender in the Performance of Public Ritual." In *The Oxford Companion to Aboriginal Art and Culture*, edited by Sylvia Kleinert and Margo Neale, 75–78. Oxford: Oxford University Press.

——. 2004. "Montrer sans partager, présenter sans proférer: redéfinition de l'identité rituelle chez les interprètes rituelles Warlpiri." *Anthropologie et sociétés* 28 (1): 67. https://doi.org/10.7202/008571ar

Dussart, Françoise, and Sylvie Poirier, eds. 2017. *Entangled Territorialities: Negotiating Indigenous Lands in Australia and Canada*. Toronto: University of Toronto Press.

Fabricant, Nicole, and Nancy Postero. 2018. "Performing Indigeneity in Bolivia: The Struggle Over the TIPNIS." *Anthropological Quarterly* 91 (3): 905–36. https://doi.org/10.1353/anq.2018.0044

Galán, Beatriz Pérez. 2004. *Somos como Incas: autoridades tradicionales en los Andes peruanos, Cuzco*. Madrid: Iberoamericana.

Glowczewski, Barbara, and Rosita Henry, eds. 2007. *Le défi indigène: entre spectacle et politique*. Montreuil: Aux lieux d'être.

Graddy, T. Garrett. 2013. "Regarding Biocultural Heritage: In Situ Political Ecology of Agricultural Biodiversity in the Peruvian Andes." *Agriculture and Human Values* 30 (4): 587–604. https://doi.org/10.1007/s10460-013-9428-8

——. 2014. "Situating In Situ: A Critical Geography of Agricultural Biodiversity Conservation in the Peruvian Andes and Beyond." *Antipode* 46 (2): 426–54. https://doi.org/10.1111/anti.12045

Graham, Laura R. 2005. "Image and Instrumentality in a Xavante Politics of Existential Recognition: The Public Outreach Work of EtÉnhiritipa Pimentel Barbosa." *American Ethnologist* 32 (4): 622–41. https://doi.org/10.1525/ae.2005.32.4.622

Hall, Ingrid. 2014. "Compter les journées de travail, classer les individus et ordonner la société dans une communauté des Andes sud-péruviennes." *Ethnographiques.org* 29, n.p. http://www.ethnographiques.org/2014/Hall

——. 2018. "Les Ancêtres au prisme des pommes de terre non domestiquées: une perspective andine." *Frontières* 29 (2). https://doi.org/10.7202/1044161ar

——. 2019. "Le 'bien vivre ' (*sumaq kawsay*) et les pommes de terre natives: du délicat exercice de la diplomatie ontologique." *Anthropologie et sociétés* 43 (3): 217–44.

——. 2020. "Du concours au rituel, épluchage et transmission." In *Regards croisés sur la transmission: actes du 2ème colloque annuel du département d'anthropologie à l'UdeM (CADA), 2019* edited by M. Chateauneuf and A. Haroun, 47–64. Université de Montréal, Département d'anthropologie.

Herrera, José Tamayo. 1980. *História del indigenismo cuzqueño, siglos XVI-XX*. Lima: Instituto Nacional de Cultura.

Krech, Shepard. 1999. *The Ecological Indian: Myth and History*. New York: W.W. Norton & Company.

La Riva Gonzalez, Palmira. 2005. "Las representaciones del animu en los Andes del Sur Peruano." *Revista andina* 41: 63–88. http://revistaandinacbc.com/wp-content/uploads/2016/ra41/ra-41-2005-02.pdf

Li, Fabiana. 2013. "Relating Divergent Worlds: Mines, Aquifers and Sacred Mountains in Peru." *Anthropologica* 55 (2): 399–411. https://www.jstor.org/stable/24467345

Li, Tania Murray. 2000. "Locating Indigenous Environmental Knowledge in Indonesia." In *Indigenous Environmental Knowledge and Its Transformations: Critical Anthropological Perspectives*, edited by Roy F. Ellen, Peter Parkes, and Alan Bicker, 121–49. London: Routledge.

Mendoza, Zoila S. 2006. *Crear y sentir lo nuestro: folclor, identidad regional y nacional en el Cuzco, siglo XX*. Lima: Pontificia Universidad Católica del Perú, Fondo Editorial.

Poupeau, Franck. 2011. "L'eau de la Pachamama." *L'homme: revue française d'anthropologie* (198–199): 247–76. https://doi.org/10.4000/lhomme.22781

Povinelli, Elizabeth A. 1997. "Reading Ruptures, Rupturing Readings: Mabo and the Cultural Politics of Activism." *Social Analysis: The International Journal of Social and Cultural Practice* 41 (2): 20–28. https://www.jstor.org/stable/23171717

Ramos, Alcida. 1994. "The Hyperreal Indian—Alcida Rita Ramos, 1994." *Critique of Anthropology* 14 (2): 153–71. https://doi.org/10.1177/0308275X9401400203

Raymond, Christopher, and Moisés Arcé. 2013. "The Politicization of Indigenous Identities in Peru." *Party Politics* 19 (4): 555–76. https://doi.org/10.1177/1354068811407597

Robin Azevedo, Valérie. 2008. *Miroirs de l'autre vie: pratiques rituelles et discours sur les morts dans les Andes de Cuzco, Pérou*. Nanterre: Société d'ethnologie.

———. 2004. "Indiens, Quechuas ou paysans?" *Amérique latine histoire et mémoire: Les cahiers ALHIM* 10. https://doi.org/10.4000/alhim.98

Salazar-Soler, Carmen. 2009. "Los tesoros del Inca y la Mardre Naturaleza: etnoecología y lucha contra las companias mineras en el norte del Perú." In *El regreso de lo indígena: retos, problemas y perspectivas*, edited by Valérie Robin Azevedo and Carmen Salazar-Soler, 183–210. Lima: IFEA; Cuzco: CBC; MASCIPO; Centre d'anthropologie sociale; Lima: Cooperación Regional para los Países Andinos.

Tsing, Anna Lowenhaupt. 2005. *Friction: An Ethnography of Global Connection*. Princeton: Princeton University Press.

8

NEGOTIATING INDIGENOUS-GLOBAL RELATIONSHIPS IN CONTEMPORARY SHAMANISM

The Case of Malta

KATHRYN ROUNTREE

Introduction

We live in a globalized world and, as Robert Schreiter (2011, 26) has pointed out, while "globalization on the one hand homogenizes the world, wiping out local difference," on the other it may "provoke the resistance of the local, thereby re-invigorating the local. This creates a dialectic between the global and the local." A poignant example of this dialectic is contemporary shamanism. In this instance, the dialectic within the global cultural economy with its disjunctive cultural flows (Appadurai 1990) is complicated further because of the difficulties of distinguishing local Indigenous shamanisms from eclectic globalized varieties: Indigenous shamanisms from neo-shamanisms, contemporary Indigenous shamanisms from traditional Indigenous shamanisms, and contemporary Indigenous shamanic practitioners from non-Indigenous ones who share similar systems of belief and practice (often because the former have taught the latter) but have different ethnic and cultural heritages and may live in different countries. This chapter argues that, with regard to the possibility of disentangling such categories and making neat this-or-that distinctions, the horse has irretrievably bolted. The mixing of, or overlap between, once more or less separate shamanisms has increased to the point that it is now often difficult to distinguish between "neo" and "traditional," Indigenous and non-Indigenous, or local and global shamanisms.

It is not only the globalized contemporary context that creates these conundrums. The term *shamanism* has never been a single phenomenon, being always a capacious umbrella term that came to be applied to enormously diverse sets of practices in diverse geographical, sociocultural, and historical contexts (Harvey and Wallis 2007; Wallis 2003). Ronald Hutton (2006, 209) goes so far as to say: "What is very clear is that the only common factor in the study of shamanism consists of Western scholarship. It is this that created the term,[1] produced the studies that embody its different meanings, and transmitted enthusiasm for it to audiences within its own homelands" (see also Hutton 2002). Nor, for that matter, would such superficially culture-specific terms as *Native American shaman* have made meaningful sense in the precolonial past. As James Mackay and David Stirrup (2012, 182) say: "Native American peoples did not and indeed could not have conceived of themselves as forming a single race distinct from other races before the arrival of the forces of discovery and conquest. 'The' Indian, therefore, is a Euro-American invention." The same is true for New Zealand Māori, who also saw their tribal groups as separate peoples and only used the term *Māori*, meaning "normal, usual, ordinary" (Williams 1975, 179), to distinguish themselves from foreign, "different" Europeans.

The chapter begins by looking at definitions and discussing the awkward term *neo-shamanism* and its connection with debates about what constitutes "authentic" shamanic practice. I then discuss recent developments in Indigenous and pan-Indigenous shamanic projects and endeavours, and the increasing entanglement of local and global shamanisms in the contemporary hyperconnected world. Such developments have been accompanied by a shift in the debate about the appropriation of Indigenous cultural knowledge and spirituality by non-Indigenous people around the world wanting to learn about and practice shamanism. It is important, however, not to overstate the changes in this debate; although it is now generally less acrimonious than it was in the final decades of the twentieth century, there is still a range of strongly held opinion. In the final section of the chapter, I discuss my fieldwork in Malta with three groups of people involved in exploring shamanism. I conducted fieldwork with them in 2015 and in several follow-up visits in the years since. On one hand, these people seek "authentic" teaching about Indigenous shamanic practices from foreign sources. On the other, they are happy to creatively adapt these Indigenous practices to the local Maltese context as they see fit, while also claiming that they want eventually to uncover or rediscover an Indigenous (but historically unrecorded) Maltese shamanism.

Definitions of Shamanism

The rationale for terming all these systems "shamanism" calls for an attempt at a definition, although any definition that is not banal because of its breadth is bound to trigger the citing of examples that do not fit. Eliade (1964, 3), leaning mostly on his knowledge of Siberian shamanism, saw the shaman as "possessing magico-religious powers," a medicine man who could cure and perform miracles and was sometimes also a priest, mystic, and poet. Above all, the shaman is "the great master of ecstasy" (4), capable of magical soul flight by entering trances and journeying to the sky or underworld to meet, or be in the company of, spirits with whom he has a special relationship. Graham Harvey (2003, 1) emphasizes the shaman's role as a community leader trained to work on the community's behalf "by engaging with other-than-human persons," a term coined by Alfred Irving Hallowell (1960) in dialogue with the Indigenous Ojibwe/Anishinaabeg of Berens River, Manitoba. Harvey prefers Hallowell's term (*other-than-human persons*) to Eliade's (1964, x) *spirits*, arguing it gives agency to other-than-human persons in accordance with an Ojibwe worldview and acknowledges the Indigenous conception of a vast web of social relationships in which all persons are dynamically connected. Harvey regards the term *spirit* to be inadequate to capture the range of beings with whom shamans work; while shamans do engage with unseen entities, they also engage with other-than-human persons such as trees, animals, rocks, and clouds, which are not beyond sensual experience as the term *spirit* might suggest. Hutton (2006, 211) leans towards

Eliade's (1964, x) focus on "techniques of ecstasy" as the identifying characteristic of shamans, saying:

> *If we are to attempt to map out the former extent of shamanism as a traditional mode of spirituality, we are not looking for trance states in general, or specific kinds of trance, or relationships with spirits, but a dramatic ritualized performance as a means of working with spirits to achieve results in the human world.*

Caroline Humphrey (Humphrey and Onon 1996), who undertook research in Siberia, Mongolia, India, Nepal, and Manchuria, also emphasizes performance as critical to shamanism.

Two broad points emerge amid the diversity of practices termed shamanism and the debate over the definition of this term. First, shamanic practice typically (but not necessarily) involves entering an altered state of consciousness and journeying within a multilayered cosmos to meet spirits or other-than-humans for a variety of purposes, most commonly to seek healing, protection, assistance, or knowledge. Traditionally, the healing was sought by the shaman on behalf of the community at large or a patient or client within the community (Bernstein 2006). Today, especially in the non-Indigenous context, the healing—often psychological or emotional and closer to what is now called self-development—tends to be sought for oneself. Secondly, this goal-focused practice is founded in animist cosmologies in which the seen and unseen worlds, along with the agentic beings of all kinds who inhabit them, are connected in a web of relationships and are capable of mutual influence and, sometimes, cooperation. Beyond these commonalities, a plethora of culture-, time-, and place-specific beliefs and ritual practices gather. It is these that help make shamanism look different from one setting to another. Moreover, within any particular setting, shamanism may also evolve over time.

What distinguishes the phenomenon of shamanism today are the increasingly blurred boundaries between once unique, discrete sets of local and culturally specific practices that went under various names in different societies—for example, *noaidi* among the Sámi, *tohunga* among the Māori, *machi* among the Mapuche, *oiun* among the Yakut. This blurring is taking place through conscious and unconscious borrowing between them and increasingly evident creative developments. Of course, cultural borrowing in all areas of cultural life has always occurred, with cultural elements being picked up, appropriated, exchanged, transformed, and reinterpreted locally in creative ways. In today's global context, such cultural borrowing has expanded and accelerated. More and more, Indigenous and non-Indigenous people seem to be co-creating contemporary forms of shamanism—sometimes consciously and/or deliberately, sometimes not. The process often involves those usually referred to as "Westerners" learning (some would say appropriating) from Indigenous traditions and making creative additions and modifications. There are instances of Indigenous people in turn learning from these same non-Indigenous "shamans" and making further changes to their traditions based on research into their local heritages as well as by co-opting elements from other Indigenous shamanisms and from global New Age resources (Sanson 2017; Kraft 2015; Fonneland 2017; Peers 2015). These reconstructed practices are then passed on, taught, and sold at workshops, courses, healing centres, sweat lodges, retreats, festivals, and, increasingly, online to other Indigenous and non-Indigenous people.

Neo-shamanism and the Question of Authenticity

This raises the question of whether such hybridized versions should be called neo-shamanism rather than Indigenous shamanism or simply shamanism. Conversely, one might perhaps argue that, given the amount of eclecticism, syncretism, and creativity being employed by contemporary Indigenous and non-Indigenous shamans alike, the term *neo-shamanism* has become almost meaningless: all forms of shamanism are just diverse instantiations of the same broad phenomenon. The labels *neo-shaman* and *neo-shamanism* tend to be rejected by those (usually non-Indigenous) people to whom some scholars apply such terms because they lack an Indigenous heritage connecting them to "traditional" shamans and traditional cultural channels for shamanic learning. Some argue that the ability to be a shaman is a "potential enshrined in all humans" (Fonneland 2017, 9),[2] and that world-view, beliefs, and practices matter more than heredity and ethnicity. Nevertheless, Indigenous shamans are deeply respected and—in the case of the three strands of shamanic practitioners with whom I conducted research in Malta—somewhat romanticized and idealized.

The charge of inauthentic practice has also been applied to Indigenous shamans. In 1984, Sun Bear and Black Elk were condemned as inauthentic by the American Indian Movement, in particular because they charged clients to participate in sweat lodges and other sacred ceremonies (Harvey and Wallis 2007, 36, 216). Sun Bear responded that "cooperation, sharing, and global harmony were more important than what he saw as parochialism and meanness" (Harvey and Wallis 2007, 216).

As well as the question of whether it is necessary to be an Indigenous person in order to practise authentic shamanism, there is the issue of the importance of the connection between the shaman and place. Shamanic practices were traditionally developed in relationship with particular local places, emerging from a group's embeddedness in a place and deep engagement with the local spirits, beings, and natural forces, seen and unseen, that shared the place. One might therefore ask whether those practices can be "authentically" relocated to globally distant places with different constellations of characteristics, beings, and forces. How transferable are these practices to landscapes where the other-than-human beings are different, even if it is an Indigenous person doing the transferring? There are different positions on this. For anthropologist Peter Sutton (2010, 81), Aboriginal Australians' relationship with "an intimately and empirically well-known local world of places, animals, plants, seasons, ceremonial performances, objects, groups of people and their political economy…is barely portable and never universalisable." Nonetheless, Indigenous shamans, including some from Australia, are sharing their knowledge with non-Indigenous people locally and globally. If spirit beings can accompany Indigenous migrants around the world and become relocalized in exotic locations, can shamanic knowledge and practices also be relocated "authentically" from an Indigenous to a non-Indigenous person? In my fieldwork in Malta, those who eschew the label *neo-shaman* are less concerned with the ethnic, cultural, or geographical provenance of the practitioner than they are with the practices, even if these have mixed provenances. In the Maltese environment, practices may be creatively adapted or added to without fear of losing authenticity.

The evolving, syncretic process of constructing shamanism in the contemporary hyperconnected, mobile, and globalized world may go through multiple cycles, with the result resembling a hall of mirrors where questions of what "real" and "authentic," let alone "traditional," shamanism is become ever more difficult to decipher and are arguably fruitless. As Françoise Dussart and Sylvie Poirier (this volume) say, "while scholars have often stressed the so-called Indigenous attachment to their 'traditions,' Indigenous peoples' cosmological and ritual expressions have nevertheless been characterized by a fair degree of openness, flexibility, and creativity, and thus anchored in dynamic modes of trans-actions and trans-formations." Anne-Marie Colpron (this volume) emphasizes that Shipibo-Konibo shamanism is relational by definition, and that the involvement of non-Indigenous social actors does not make its practice inauthentic. I suggest that this point is more widely generalizable. From an emic, Indigenous perspective, authentic traditions—shamanic or otherwise—are not static artifacts ossified in "pure" past forms impregnable to change in modern times. Like all aspects of a culture, they are dynamic, socially constructed forms of behaviour and belief, perennially and inevitably subject to transformation over time by the humans who live and engage with them and for whom they matter. Cultures are always changing; as an aspect of culture, we might well expect shamanisms to change, also.

More arguable, I have suggested, is the degree to which the "authentic" practice of shamanism today requires those engaging with it to be the biological and cultural descendants of the original Indigenous practitioners and to inhabit the same local territory as the original practitioners. In short, "blood and soil" are now less likely to be regarded as critical to the authenticity of either shamanic practices or practitioners. There has been a sea change in this discourse during the twenty-first century, although a range of voices and positions still exists.

Indigenous and Pan-Indigenous, Local and Global Shamanisms

In recent decades, especially since the 1970s, shamanism has burgeoned in Indigenous communities in connection with projects of cultural retrieval and reclamation, ethnic revival, and the strengthening of Indigenous identities in a global context of protest against the technologies, ethos, and longstanding, devastating legacies of colonialism (Sanson 2017; Kraft 2015; Peers 2015; Fonneland 2017). Indigenous American examples are the best known outside and inside the academy (Castaneda 1968; Black Elk and Lyon 1990; Crow Dog and Erdoes 1995; Grim 1983; Hallowell 1960; Harner 1984; Handelman 1967; Joralemon and Sharon 1993; Myerhoff 1974; Villoldo and Jendresen 1990). However, there are other notable examples. The revival of Sámi shamanism in Norway is connected to nation-building, consciousness-raising, and a revalorization of ethnic identity among a new generation of Sámi who grew up with little knowledge of Sámi culture and language and previously experienced their ethnicity as a social stigma (Kraft 2015, 27). Even while it is uniquely local, the practices of contemporary Sámi shamans are diverse and have resulted in a "hybrid style Sámi shamanism" (Fonneland 2017, 170), whereby the local is woven into global discourses on shamanism, with new forms of practices and worldviews emerging (Fonneland 2018).

Eleanor Peers (2015, 110) describes the shamanic revival taking place in the Republic of Sakha (Yakutia) in northeastern Siberia, which is rooted in the pre-Soviet shamanic tradition but has adapted to the contemporary "social context that stands at the intersection of shifting nationalist, colonialist and globalizing power dynamics, in common with the shamanic revivals that are occurring in other parts of Siberia." Like the Sámi shamans, Sakha shamans mesh global neo-shamanisms, local identity politics, and Indigenous shamanic belief. Galina Lindquist (2006), prefiguring Robert Schreiter's (2011) dialectic, describes this local-global entanglement in post-Soviet Siberia as a postmodern religious movement enmeshed in global structures and processes (such as escalating migration, tourism, and internet use facilitating global communication and access to knowledge). Lindquist claims that it is only in this global context that a local tradition can be revitalized and recharged with meaning.

Thomas Alberts (2016) has pointed out that sometimes the revival of local shamanic knowledge is hitched to contemporary global environmental concerns, a process that in turn legitimates local Indigenous claims. While the global concern about climate change and environmental destruction may be relatively recent for non-Indigenous peoples, the natural world has typically been at the heart of Indigenous lifeways, subsistence strategies, geopolitics, and cosmologies. Indigenous shamanisms have now overflowed their traditional geocultural borders and become increasingly transcultural and deterritorialized in the globalized world (Torre 2011, 154). This has occurred as a result both of swathes of non-Indigenous New Agers seeking out Indigenous shamans, often but not always in their local Indigenous contexts, to learn their techniques; and of Indigenous people themselves forming transnational, pan-Indigenous movements and taking shamanism to the world, including the non-Indigenous world.

Thus, the revival of Indigenous shamanisms has contributed not only to local cultural revival, but also to cross-cultural sharing via multiethnic endeavours including online social networking, international festivals, workshops, tours, conferences, ecological projects, and business entrepreneurship. Norway's Isogaisa festival, first held in 2010, is one such endeavour where "shamans from all over the world gather annually to perform ceremonies and exchange knowledge" (Fonneland 2017, 121), taking inspiration from one another and from other sources including Wicca, Celtic, and Northern European traditions. As Torre (2011, 153) points out, not only have New Age ideas been appropriated in Indigenous revivals and the reconfiguring of pre-Hispanic traditions, but also the connections with New Age seekers have helped spark revivals in Indigenous traditions.

Dawne Sanson (2017, 224) describes contemporary Māori shamans in New Zealand as "cosmopolitan *bricoleurs*" who revive and disseminate traditional sacred knowledge, synthesize it with global Indigenous and non-Indigenous knowledges including New Age ideas, and create new shamanic forms which they believe the world urgently needs. Some Aboriginal Australians are also drawing on New Age ideology and practices. David Waldron and Janice Newton (2012, 65) point to convergences and collaborations between Indigenous and non-Indigenous practitioners, claiming that "there are signs of a shift away from absolute condemnation of cultural borrowing." However, condemnation, if not absolute condemnation, is still present (Sutton 2010).

Some Indigenous shamans, and some claiming to be Indigenous, have become "spiritual entrepreneurs" (Lindquist 2006; Alberts 2016; Fonneland 2017) sharing their knowledge with non-Indigenous people who subsequently pursue these ostensibly "Indigenous" practices in their own non-Indigenous home settings far from the practices' geographic and cultural origins. *Ayahuasca* shamanism is well documented in academic and popular literature and in online advertising, in relation to both the trips made by Westerners to retreat centres in the Peruvian Amazon, and the exportation of such shamanism around the world by Indigenous and non-Indigenous people (Valentish 2018; Holman 2011; Fotiou 2014; Labate and Cavnar 2018; Kavenská and Simonová 2015). Thus, the terms *local* and *Indigenous*, while remaining valorized, have become uncoupled, and *Indigenous* may mean a cocktail of different Indigenous practices variously combined and adapted within local environments globally. Openness, innovation, and fluidity characterize Indigenous perspectives and practices as they always have; what is different now is the global nature of negotiations in the expression of shamanisms as Indigenous identities are affirmed and reproduced. As Colpron (this volume) points out in her chapter on Shipibo-Konibo shamanism, "the singularity of this practice is to create bridges between different worlds and temporalities, constructing itself through these relations with others, whether forest entities, neighbouring ethnic groups, *mestizos* from the towns, or foreign tourists. Shipibo-Konibo shamanic do not precede the relationships that forge them; they are, rather, constituted by these relations of difference."

New Voices in the Cultural Appropriation Debate

The condemnation of cultural borrowing from Indigenous spiritual traditions—often called cultural appropriation or imperialism—was common from the 1980s through to the first decade of the twenty-first century (Wallis 2003; Hobson 2002; Aldred 2000; Rose 1992; Sutton 2010). Some Indigenous people and scholars alike decried it as a form of cultural theft that "continues the uncritical essentialism and subjugation of colonialism" (Waldron and Newton 2012, 65). Even then, however, there was a variety of Indigenous American opinion. Some "genuine" medicine people actively encouraged neo-shamans, others "waged 'war' on neo-Shamanic appropriation" (Wallis 2003, xvi), and still others claimed to be Indigenous but had dubious ancestry. One-time anthropologist Michael Harner, the founder of Core Shamanism and the California-based Foundation for Shamanic Studies,[3] has often been accused of appropriation, as have a number of other non-Indigenous teachers. Wallis (2003, 49) summarizes the charges made against Harner and his ilk: they decontextualize shamanic practices from their local cultural settings; they universalize, psychologize, individualize, and romanticize Indigenous shamanisms; and they reproduce notions of cultural primitivism.

The ground of cultural politics—in particular, relationships between Indigenous and non-Indigenous people—has gradually shifted in the twenty-first century and "a simple dichotomy of cultural theft by exploitative New Agers from good but suffering Indigenous peoples is [now] inadequate to explain the complex and multiple levels of interaction between the two groups" (Waldron and Newton 2012, 65). In his foreword to *The Expanding World Ayahuasca Diaspora*, Oscar Calavia Saez (2018, xii) notes that Indigenous shamanism was traditionally "characterized by widespread borrowing and experimentation," writing:

> *The contrast between a primitive authenticity and New Age inventions has become of less and less interest. The professionals and amateurs of anthropology have little by little abandoned their belligerence against neo-shamanism...Moreover the subjects who*

supposedly represented the purest tradition—Indigenous shamans—
had been directly involved in openly hybrid ventures.

The concept—and condemnation—of cultural appropriation depends
on the idea that cultures are discrete, essentialized, self-generative
things with a perennial, inalienable, incontestable authenticity. This
idea is increasingly hard to sustain in a globalized world characterized
by hyperconnectivity and mobility. Amid lingering antagonisms generated by decades of debate about neo-shamanic cultural imperialism,
the Western appetite for shamanism continues to grow, along with
those—Indigenous and non-Indigenous—offering to teach it (Csordas
2007).

Contemporary Shamanism in Malta

The rest of this chapter examines the interplay of the local and global
in the case of contemporary shamanic practice in Malta. Alongside my
field research among shamans in the country between 2015 and 2018,
I have kept in touch with individuals through Facebook groups (an open
group called *"Temazcal* Malta" and a secret group called "Our Tribe")
and private messaging. I refer to "shamans in Malta" rather than "Maltese
shamans," because around a third of those I met and spent time with
are not of Maltese ethnicity or nationality, despite living permanently
or temporarily in Malta. I consider how these shamans negotiate the
local-global and Indigenous—non-Indigenous nexus as they adapt
purportedly Indigenous American shamanic ideas and practices to the
cultural and natural landscapes of Malta.

My research concentrated on three strands of shamanism, loosely
interwoven at the local level with strong global connections. In 2017,
I learned that *ayahuasca* had made its way to Malta, particularly to the
smaller island of Gozo, and visiting shamans, Indigenous and non-
Indigenous, were offering *ayahuasca* experiences at weekend retreats
and calling it shamanism. I talked with people who had attended such
sessions but did no fieldwork at them and therefore do not include
them in this discussion.

One of the strands I focused on is a loose network of people who participate in sweat lodges, or *Temazcals*,[4] run twice a year by a Maltese woman named Kimimila,[5] assisted by a visiting Argentinian shaman, Carlos, a self-described political refugee who now resides in Spain when he is not facilitating sweat lodges in various places in Europe.[6] Carlos received his shamanic training in Mexico from an Indigenous shaman who was already synthesizing elements from different Indigenous shamanic traditions. Carlos told me:

> *My lineage is a mixture of Mexican pre-Hispanic culture and the Lakota[7] because of the man I got my patronage from. When he was young, he learned from men in Mexico, then after some years they sent him to meet the Lakota people in the United States.*
> *(per. comm., 2 October 2015)*

In October 2015, I participated in a weekend camp dedicated to two *Temazcals*. The preparations for the sweat lodge and sacred space began on the previous Thursday and were undertaken by a handful of men and women[8] under the direction of Carlos before most participants arrived. The ground (a farmer's field hired for the weekend) was cleared of weeds and debris and raked flat, a roughly circular frame for the lodge was constructed from wooden pallets, a firepit for receiving the red-hot stones was dug in the centre of the lodge (figure 8.1), and blankets were laid over the top of the frame to enclose the space. Outside the doorway, a heart-shaped altar was created from mounded earth and decorated with flowers and crystals (figure 8.2). Several metres away, in line with the altar and doorway, a fireplace was constructed for heating twenty-eight stones.[9] Several metres beyond the fireplace and perpendicular to the axis connecting the fireplace, altar, and doorway, a raised arc of earth was decorated with red, blue, and yellow flowers in the shape of a double helix. This arc symbolized the sky (figure 8.3).

During the afternoon before the first sweat lodge, held on Friday night, Carlos led several rituals. These included passing a tobacco pipe around the circle of participants and individuals and offering pinches

Counterclockwise from top left:

FIGURE 8.1. Preparing the sweat lodge. The frame of lodge is visible, with a hollowed-out fire pit inside and a heart-shaped altar of mounded soil outside, prior to its decoration. (Photograph by Kathryn Rountree, 2015.)

FIGURE 8.2. The heart-shaped altar decorated with flowers and crystals, with shaman's tobacco and tools alongside. (Photograph by Kathryn Rountree, 2015.)

FIGURE 8.3. Sacred fire heating stones, which would be carried into the sweat lodge later. A raised arc of soil symbolizing the sky is decorated with flowers in the shape of a double helix. (Photograph by Kathryn Rountree, 2015.)

FIGURE 8.4. Foreground: Tobacco-filled prayer bundles ready to be hung inside the lodge. Left side: The lodge covered with blankets. Right side: The altar. (Photograph by Kathryn Rountree, 2015.)

of tobacco to the fire with requests for what they wished to receive from the sweat lodge experience. Tobacco-filled prayer bundles were made and hung inside the lodge (figure 8.4); there were prayers to bless the sacred stones, and a ceremony to present the stones to the fire (figure 8.5).

FIGURE 8.5. A ritual presentation of stones. Carlos, the shaman, receives a stone from each participant and places them on the pyre.

(Photograph by Kathryn Rountree, 2015.)

The stones were heated in a roaring fire for several hours, tended by two fire-keepers who stoked and guarded it. Around 9 PM, participants—wearing sarongs and no jewellery[10] and having consumed a lot of water—lined up at the doorway, processed inside, and sat in a circle around the firepit. The fire-keepers removed the red-hot stones from the fire with a pitchfork, brushed away clinging embers with a bunch of herbs, and carried the stones very carefully to the entrance of the lodge. Carlos, seated near the entrance, received the stones and placed them in the firepit. When the first seven stones were in the pit, the door of the lodge (a couple of blankets) was pulled shut. Steam was created by Carlos casting water on the stones from time to time.

The sweat lodge was divided into four "doors" or sessions, each lasting around half an hour. During this time, participants were free to talk, pray, sing, sit in silence, share visions, ask questions, and voice opinions, doubts, and dreams. After each session the door was opened for a few minutes so that fresh air could enter to give brief respite to participants. Then the fire-keepers brought in another seven stones to add to those in the pit for the second "door." The process continued for four "doors," at which point there were twenty-eight stones inside the lodge and the heat reached its peak. Around 11 PM, Carlos cried, "Open the door!" for the fourth time and the first *Temazcal* of the weekend concluded. I recorded in my field diary: "Everyone staggered out, dripping with sweat and one at a time were squirted with cold water from a hose. They wandered around quietly, occasionally hugging, went to their tents to dress, stood by the now-dying fire." The second *Temazcal* was held the following night.

Between *Temazcal* weekends, connections in this network are maintained by informal socializing, online networking, and a Facebook page. I interviewed Carlos twice during the weekend camp and he quickly launched into an explanation of his shamanic worldview, drawing in quantum physics, phenomenology, and the ills of an anthropocentric cosmology. Later, he set down for me in an email (25 January 2017) his ideas on the question of "adaptation, translation or update" of Indigenous shamanic practice. He placed what he does outside any specific culture, people, or time period, describing the source as the "Mythos"—a timeless, acultural oneness—while "respecting the essence of the designs and instructions given to [him] by the [Indigenous] Elders" who trained him in shamanic thinking and techniques in Mexico. He wrote:

It is not about connecting with the past, but with a dimension of consciousness. We do not deal with a regression, but with a reactivation from the depths of our consciousness of the Mythos that flows to our personal, social and cultural reality, a reaffirmation of the eternal from which we come. The Temazcal *offers us an enriched conception of the "sacred" and a questioning of our understanding of the world and of ourselves. Opening to a more fluid and dynamic conception, and with it a new philosophical and ontological conception of our presence and responsibility in the face of current challenges, and how the answers we give will affect future generations.*

While the *Temazcals* in Malta undoubtedly have an exotic cultural source, structure, and appearance, they are gradually being adapted to the local Maltese environment in a process Carlos supports. "As long as it works, no problem!" he told me. For example, he said that at sweat lodges in North America, the altar is made in the shape of a turtle—a reference to Turtle Island, the name given by some Indigenous groups to North America. Carlos used to create the *Temazcal* altar in the shape of a turtle when in Europe,[11] but has changed the shape to a heart, which he says is a universal symbol representing the heart of Mother Earth; the turtle symbolism is out of place in Europe. In Malta, where pliable branches are unavailable for building the frame of the sweat lodge, wooden pallets are used instead.

As noted above, the local organizer of the *Temazcals* is a woman called Kimimila. Her story illustrates the cosmopolitan nature and global connections typical of shamans in Malta. She was introduced to shamanism by a Maltese ex-Jesuit priest called Francis, who, through his spirit guides, opened Kimimila to the knowledge that in a past life she had belonged to the Lakota tribe. At first, she thought, "This is crazy!" but gradually came to embrace the identity and sought to learn more about those she now considers "her people." In 2012, she travelled to South Dakota to visit the sacred places of the Lakota and met a Medicine Man and Sundance Chief who, upon hearing her describe visions of an earlier life as a Lakota woman, endorsed her Indigenous Lakota identity. Arriving back in Malta, Kimimila heard about a sweat lodge due to be held in Spain, so travelled with a friend to Spain and had her first *Temazcal* experience. She met Carlos and in 2013 invited him to come and facilitate a weekend of sweat lodges in Malta, the first of many. Kimimila has returned to Spain to undertake four Vision Quests over four years, each involving four days of solitary fasting outdoors confined to a circle two metres in diameter. She travels from Malta to Mount Etna in Sicily to get the volcanic rocks needed for the *Temazcal*[12] fire because there are none suitable in Malta. She described "inviting" the rocks to come and to bring their energy, thereby apparently attributing them with agency to accept the invitation to travel and participate. After the rocks have been used several times, Kimimila said, their energy is exhausted and they cannot be used again; fresh rocks are sought.

Kimimila's global connections are strong. For her, Lakota shamanism is not an exotic tradition appropriated from an Indigenous people in a distant place; it is *her* tradition because of the connection she traces to it via her past lives, affirmed by her visit to South Dakota in this life. However, she does not identify solely as Lakota. She is adamantly and proudly Maltese and committed to developing a local shamanism that functions independently of overseas experts once she and her local collaborators have learned enough from Carlos and others. This Maltese version would draw on what Kimimila and her friends have learned from foreign sources, with local adaptations:

> There will come a time when Carlos will leave us to do things on our own. We are Maltese! We've always been colonized! Why don't we have our own things? Why does someone always come and do everything for us? We've been shamans from the beginning! We never really needed foreigners to come, but lately everyone wants to get to Malta. (per. comm., 31 July 2015)

In the last sentence, Kimimila was referring to the various high-profile Indigenous and non-Indigenous shamans circulating in Europe at the time, looking for new "markets" to introduce shamanism. The quote above is interesting in that Kimimila identifies as Maltese and Indigenous and refers to Malta's long history of being colonized. She does not see that in taking up the *Temazcal* and shamanic rituals taught by Carlos, she could be seen as appropriating the sacred traditions of Indigenous peoples in the Americas.

A second strand of shamanism in Malta consists of a group of around forty women who refer to themselves as a "sistren" and "tribe." They meet on full moons and special occasions (such as a birthday or the visit of shamans from abroad) in one another's homes, at beaches, or in other natural places for shamanic rituals. These typically involve trance journeys induced by drumming and guided meditation conducted by one or other of the group members to meet spirit guides, normally in the form of animals though they may include ancestors and other spirit beings. The purpose of a trance journey largely has to do with the individual woman: healing, insight, support, knowledge, empowerment, comfort, assistance with achieving a goal, and so on. I attended ceremonies where the purpose was to send healing and love to other people (for example, during the refugee crisis in Europe) and to the environment. Between meetings, group members keep in constant touch through a closed Facebook group; they have formed strong friendships.

The sistren formed following a series of workshops taught by three visiting shamans from the United Kingdom (one of whom was a Maltese woman) who themselves had studied with the Four Winds School of Shamanic Healing founded by Alberto Villoldo. Villoldo claims to have learned his shamanic techniques over a period of ten years from Indigenous shamans. The Four Winds School (n.d., under "About Alberto Villoldo, PHD") describes these Indigenous shamans as "jungle medicine people" whom Villoldo found "scattered throughout the Andes and Amazon." The Four Winds School (under "About Us") claims to have trained more than 10,000 students in shamanic energy medicine over the last twenty-five years through its online program and at residential campuses in the United States, Germany, and Chile. The sistren have also worked together through a recorded training course on self-directed healing and spiritual growth conducted by American shaman Sandra Ingerman,[13] and they regularly participate in webinars advertised through various global shamanic networks (for example, The Shift Network: https://theshiftnetwork.com/).

A significant number—around half—of the women in this group are not Maltese by birth and about a quarter live overseas and visit Malta occasionally. Most are professional or retired women who travel extensively, have lived and worked in many parts of the world (two worked for the United Nations), and have explored a wide range of spiritual practices in the course of their lives in such places as Peru, the United States, Australia, Scandinavia, Britain, Ireland, and many parts of Europe, Africa, and India. One woman commented during a focus group interview to which I invited the sistren (30 September 2015): "Shamanism encompasses all the spiritual practices that I've come to know and be. That's who I am right now." Although they follow the basic ritual structure taught by Villoldo, they freely invent and improvise, combining what they have learned from diverse sources with their own intuition and whim. The local and global are interwoven effortlessly and exuberantly. While their summertime full moon meetings are often held on a rocky hillside close to Malta's Neolithic temples,[14] thus invoking a connection with these important, local sacred places, none of the animal spirits they invoke for the cardinal directions in that setting are found locally: serpent, jaguar, hummingbird, and eagle belong to the context of Indigenous people in the Americas. Furthermore, the animal spirits they meet in their shamanic journeys represent a global menagerie. While these spirits and guardians are regarded as having roots in particular cultures, histories, and landscapes, they are not regarded as restricted or *belonging* to those geocultural spaces. To use Csordas's (2007, 264) term, spirits "travel well" beyond local boundaries, as do the shamans who journey to meet them.

When the sistren met with me to share their stories in the group interview (30 September 2015), a common thread in their narratives was the centrality of nature to their lives from a young age and the strong connection they felt with the Earth, animals, and plants. "Nature is the true divine for me," said one Maltese woman, who had once lived in Peru for three years surrounded by Indigenous shamanic activity. Her empathy for animals as a child was such that she "did not feel any more important than a chameleon or a caterpillar." Another Maltese woman who had visited Peru for a nine-day retreat with an Inca shaman told me, "Nature is my everything! Mother Earth heals you; Mother Earth loves you." Another described trying out many spiritual practices, but it was through shamanism that she "became aware of the power of earth. It is the same thing anywhere in the world...the same Mother Earth." This connection to the Earth and nature was the constant in the women's lives irrespective of where they had lived or travelled, or from whom they had learned. The repeated maxim was: There is only one Mother Earth, one Father Sky, one Grandmother Moon, and one Grandfather Sun. This is not to say that local places do not matter. They were not talking about "a One-World placelessness" like the one Klein (2000, 117) suggests is produced by the global consumer culture. In their worldview, the place where one lives is a unique, multispecies community with whom one daily experiences an intimate, embodied connection. However, that local connection does not provide the grounds for political claims related to cultural chauvinism.

Other themes in the women's stories were the importance of healing and working with energy (especially for a doctor in the group), connecting with alternate realities and "a bigger world" via the shamanic journey, and an enormous appreciation for the social and spiritual connections provided by the group itself. One woman, a British permanent resident in Malta who had explored a large variety of spiritual practices and trained with shamans during her travels in many parts of the world, said in terms reminiscent of those used by Carlos (although she had not engaged with him or the *Temazcal* network discussed above):

> *I came to realize the sameness in all practices, whether it was Druidism in Wales and Devon and Cornwall, or whether it was the Native American, or whether it was in Peru, or in Russia, or Australia... with all the Indigenous people there was such a similarity. I thought to follow the thread of truth that runs through all of that. When*

I look back at the history of my path, it was learning more about
love, understanding my love connections to the earth, the stars, as
well as all other realities and all of us. (per. comm., 30 September 2015)

A third strand of shamanism in Malta clusters around a Maltese man named Francis, who figured in Kimimila's journey with shamanism. Formerly a Jesuit priest for thirty years, many of which spent in missions abroad, Francis has spent the last two decades facilitating people's explorations of spirituality in diverse quarters. He runs three spirituality centres hosting an eclectic range of activities related to wellness, healing, and holistic living as well as spirituality, interweaving Catholic, New Age, and shamanic elements. "We do everything here!" he said. "This is like a supermarket" (per. comm., 6 August 2015). The shamanic group he facilitates has been together about seven years. Francis's own journey with shamanism began in England, training (like the sistren) with Villoldo's Four Winds School, as well as with Caitlin Matthews, an authority on Celtic Wisdom and the ancestral traditions of Britain and Europe. He then branched into Core Shamanism, making contact with an Austrian group, but became disenchanted with the money-making preoccupation of this and other such schools on the international circuit.

Therefore, Francis and a likeminded group in Malta decided to start their own practice using their intuition, experimentation, and reading. "The most important thing," he told me, "is to revive a very ancient shamanic experience here in Malta. And to do that you need to practise, you need to open yourself up to it, and you need to link with the land" (per. comm., 6 August 2015). He is not interested in the "romance" of exotic rituals from distant cultures; they are "out of context" in Malta. The manufacturing of authenticity built on exotic Indigeneity is not for him. He says to seekers of shamanism he meets: "You're not in Peru; you're in Malta! Why do you imitate a culture which is not yours and is totally foreign to your experience?"

Of all those I have met, Francis is the most focused on "reviving" an Indigenous (but historically unknown) Maltese shamanism, but he is happy to share it with the multiethnic group that meets at his centre to meditate, explore past lives, and embark on shamanic journeys to meet the spirits assisted by drumming and rattle-shaking. He believes that many thousands of years ago there was a powerful shamanic practice in Malta associated with the country's Neolithic temples. He thinks this knowledge "is still alive in the land and in the collective unconscious" and that people today can link to it and reexperience what their ancestors experienced. Thus, his meandering exploration of Indigenous shamanic traditions and Harner's eclectic Core Shamanism has ended up at home in Malta.

Shamans in Malta participate in constantly shifting local communities and global networks and proclaim a strong sense of living in "one world." However, they do so in local places—often multiple local places because they are highly mobile—which they treasure and with which they are intimate in their everyday lives. They tell me that Mother Earth cannot be dismembered according to human political, cultural, ethnic, or national maps. Mother Earth's destiny is the destiny of all people and all beings. The participants of all three strands of contemporary shamanism in Malta share the two common characteristics of shamanism identified near the beginning of this chapter. Their ritual practice involves entering altered states of consciousness and journeying within a multi-layered cosmos to meet spirits and commonly to seek healing (personal or planetary). Their ritual practice and everyday lives are founded in an animist worldview. Their animism is clearly not the same as that of traditional, Indigenous hunting and gathering peoples (Rountree 2012). It is an elective, somewhat intellectualized, and romantic ideology held by mostly urban-dwelling people rather than a taken-for-granted way of living in the world inherited from their culture. However, they are motivated by a deep concern to decentre humans' position in the ecosystem, and they fervently articulate a belief that attributes spirit, agency, and interconnectedness to all human and other-than-human beings with whom they share the world.

Conclusion

In the contemporary globalized world characterized by hypermobility and hyperconnectivity, notions of "ours" and "theirs" are increasingly difficult to sustain and boundaries between the local and global become ever more porous. Indigenous shamans and shamanisms retain their reputation and value as sources of culturally derived spiritual wisdom and healing and as touchstones for ethnic identity and revitalization. However, they are increasingly seen not just by non-Indigenous spiritual seekers and neo-shamans, but also by Indigenous peoples themselves, as having global relevance in a troubled, globalized world. These Indigenous shamanisms themselves are increasingly cocktails of old and new practices drawn from within and outside the original "traditional" culture.

The once virulent scholarly and Indigenous tendency to analyze Western neo-shamans as cultural appropriators of Indigenous traditions following an all-too-familiar colonial model is today less prevalent. A new discourse is emerging among shamans themselves that spans the local-global, Indigenous–non-Indigenous divide. The importance of cultural roots and identity is retained, but the concept of cultural ownership has less currency. It emphasizes the interdependence of all peoples and cultures and all forms of existence: the oneness of the world and singularity of its destiny. Indigeneity, ethnicity, and cultural origins are increasingly conceptualized and used by modern shamans as a bridge between people and a conduit for sharing, rather than as cultural or geographical boundary markers and grounds for separation. In Carlos's words: "We are here to recognize the other, that we are sons and daughters of the same Father Sun, the same Mother Earth. We are made of the same water and sustained by the same earth, the sacred one that gives life. Beyond culture and biographical stuff." (per. comm., 2 October 2015) In a globalized world facing serious environmental challenges, the common wellbeing and destiny of all beings increasingly takes precedence over traditional cultural, ethnic, or national maps.

Author's Note

My heartfelt gratitude to the shaman communities in Malta who so warmly welcomed and taught me, patiently answered my questions, corrected my misunderstandings, shared their rituals with me, and went out of their way to help in many other ways. Your thoughtfulness, humility, generosity, and love are deeply appreciated. Ho!

Notes

1. The word *shaman* comes from the Tungus šaman, most famously reported in Mircea Eliade's (1964) classic study of Siberian shamanism.
2. I have also often heard claims to this effect among shamans in Malta.
3. The Foundation for Shamanic Studies' (n.d.) website explains Harner's approach:

   > Core Shamanism consists of the universal, near-universal, and common features of shamanism, together with journeys to other worlds, a distinguishing feature of shamanism. As originated, researched, and developed by Michael Harner, the principles of Core Shamanism are not bound to any specific cultural group or perspective. Since the West overwhelmingly lost its shamanic knowledge centuries ago due to religious oppression, the Foundation's programs in Core Shamanism are particularly intended for Westerners to reacquire access to their rightful spiritual heritage through quality workshops and training courses.

4. A *Temazcal*, so named in the Nahuatl language of central Mexico, is a type of sweat lodge that originated in Mesoamerica and is being revived in Mexico and Central America as a religio-therapeutic tool for purifying, healing, and renewing the mind, body, and spirit. The term has migrated outside Mexico along with migrating shamans. Sweat lodges elsewhere in the Americas have different local names.
5. This is the name she wishes to be known by in my research. *Kimimila* is the Lakota word for "butterfly."
6. Carlos was dismissive of the *ayahuasca* weekend retreats being held in Malta, saying: "Here in Malta there are people who pay 150 euros for one night to drink *ayahuasca*. You get the trip but you can't integrate it in your life."
7. The Lakota are a Native American tribe—one of the three Sioux tribes of the Plains in North America—whose current lands are in North and South Dakota.
8. The participants were mostly Maltese and all were resident in Malta.

9. I was told that the lodge represented the womb of Mother Earth and the fire symbolized the masculine energy.

10. This was a safety measure. There was a risk that jewellery could become hot enough in the sweat lodge to burn the skin.

11. The term *Turtle Island* was not traditionally used in Mexico. However, Carlos's shaman teacher synthesized Lakota and Mexican traditions.

12. Kimimila's special affinity is with the Lakota, who would not refer to the sweat lodge as a *Temazcal*. By doing so, she is following Carlos's terminology.

13. Sandra Ingerman was educational director at Michael Harner's Foundation for Shamanic Studies, has taught shamanism internationally for over thirty years, and is the author of 12 books on shamanism (https://sandraingermanbooks.com/).

14. Malta's Neolithic temples, of which there are at least 23 spread fairly uniformly throughout the islands, were built of megalithic limestone blocks between 3600 BCE and 2500 BCE. Constructed in groups of two or three, they comprise distinctive rounded chambers that, from an aerial view, resemble the shape of an ample human body. Six of these temple complexes are UNESCO World Heritage sites (Rountree 2002).

References

Alberts, Thomas. 2016. *Shamanism, Discourse, Modernity*. London: Routledge.

Aldred, Lisa. 2000. "Plastic Shamans and Astroturf Sun Dances: New Age Commercialization of Native American Spirituality." *American Indian Quarterly* 24 (3): 329–52.

Appadurai, Arjun. 1990. "Disjuncture and Difference in the Global Cultural Economy." *Theory Culture and Society* 7: 295–310. https://www.jstor.org/stable/1185908

Bernstein, Anya, dir. 2006. *In Pursuit of the Siberian Shaman*. Watertown: Documentary Educational Resources. Digital film in Russian and Buryat with English subtitles, 75 min.

Black Elk, Wallace, and William Lyon.1990. *Black Elk: The Sacred Ways of a Lakota*. New York: Harper & Row.

Castaneda, Carlos. 1968. *The Teachings of Don Juan: A Yaqui Way of Knowledge*. Berkeley: University of California Press.

Crow Dog, Leonard, and Richard Erdoes. 1995. *Crow Dog: Four Generations of Sioux Medicine Men*. New York: HarperCollins.

Csordas, Thomas. 2007. "Introduction: Modalities of Transnational Transcendence." *Anthropological Theory* 7 (3): 259–72. https://doi.org/10.1177/1463499607080188

Torre, Renée, de la. 2011. "Les rendez-vous manqués de l'anthropologie et du chamanisme." *Archives de sciences sociales des religions* 153 (January–March): 145–58. https://doi.org/10.4000/assr.22798

Eliade, Mircea. 1964. *Shamanism: Archaic Techniques of Ecstasy*. Translated by Willard R. Trask. Princeton: Princeton University Press.

Fonneland, Trude. 2017. *Contemporary Shamanisms in Norway: Religion, Entrepreneurship and Politics*. Oxford: Oxford University Press.

——. 2018. "Shamanism in Contemporary Norway." *Religions* 9 (7): 233. https://doi. org/ 10.3390/rel9070223

Fotiou, Evgenia. 2014. "On the Uneasiness of Tourism: Considerations on Shamanic Tourism in Western Amazonia." In *Ayahuasca Shamanism in the Amazon and Beyond*, edited by Beatriz C. Labate and Clancy Cavnar, 159–81. New York: Oxford University Press.

Foundation for Shamanic Studies. n.d. "Core Shamanism." Accessed March 21, 2021. https://www.shamanism.org/workshops/coreshamanism.html

Four Winds, The (website). n.d. Accessed March 21, 2021. https://thefourwinds.com

Grim, John. 1983. *The Shaman: Patterns of Religious Healing among the Ojibway Indians*. Norman: University of Oklahoma Press.

Hallowell, A. Irving. 1960. "Ojibwa Ontology, Behavior and World View." In *Culture in History*, edited by S. Diamond, 19–52. New York: Columbia University Press.

Handelman, Donald. 1967. "The Development of a Washo Shaman." *Ethnology* 6 (4): 444–64. https://doi.org/10.2307/3772830

Harner, Michael. 1984. *The Jivaro: People of the Sacred Waterfalls*. Berkeley: University of California Press.

Harvey, Graham. 2003. "General Introduction." In *Shamanism: A Reader*, edited by Graham Harvey, 1–23. London: Routledge.

Harvey, Graham, and Robert Wallis. 2007. *Historical Dictionary of Shamanism*. Lanham: Roman and Littlefield.

Hobson, Geary. 2002. "The Rise of the White Shaman: Twenty-Five Years Later." *Studies in American Indian Literatures* 14 (2/3): 1–11. https://www.jstor.org/stable/20737138

Holman, Christine. 2011. "Surfing for a Shaman: Analysing an Ayahuasca Website." *Annals of Tourism Research* 38 (1): 90–109. https://doi.org/10.1016/j.annals.2010.05.005

Humphrey, Caroline, and Urgunge Onon. 1996. *Shamans and Elders: Experience, Knowledge and Power among the Daur Mongols*. Oxford: Oxford University Press.

Hutton, Ronald. 2002. *Shamans: Siberian Spirituality and the Western Imagination*. London: Hambledon.

———. 2006. "Shamanism: Mapping the Boundaries." *Magic, Ritual and Witchcraft* 1 (2): 209–13. https://muse.jhu.edu/article/236470

Joraleman, Donald, and Douglas Sharon. 1993. *Sorcery and Shamanism: Curanderos and Clients in Northern Peru*. Salt Lake City: University of Utah Press.

Kavenská, Veronika, and Hana Simonová. 2015. "Ayahuasca Tourism: Participants in Shamanic Rituals and their Personality Styles, Motivation, Benefits and Risks." *Journal of Psychoactive Drugs* 47 (5): 351–59. https://doi.org/10.1080/02791072.2015.1094590

Klein, Naomi. 2000. *No Logo*. London: Flamingo.

Kraft, Siv Ellen. 2015. "Sámi Neo-Shamanism in Norway: Colonial Grounds, Ethnic Revival and Pagan Pathways." In *Contemporary Pagan and Native Faith Movements in Europe: Colonialist and Nationalist Impulses*, edited by Kathryn Rountree, 25–42, Oxford: Berghahn.

Labate, Beatriz Caiuby, and Clancy Cavnar, eds. 2018. *The Expanding World Ayahuasca Diaspora: Appropriation, Integration and Legislation*. London: Routledge.

Lindquist, Galina. 2006. *The Quest for the Authentic Shaman: Multiple Meanings of Shamanism on a Siberian Journey*. Stockholm: Almqvist and Wiksell International.

Mackay, James, and David Stirrup. 2012. "Introduction: Native Americans in Europe in the Twentieth Century." *European Journal of American Culture* 31 (3): 181–86. https://doi.org/10.1386/ejac.31.3.181_2

Myerhoff, Barbara. 1974. *The Peyote Hunt: The Sacred Journey of the Huichol Indians*. Ithaca: Cornell University Press.

Peers, Eleanor. 2015. "Soviet-Era Discourse and Siberian Shamanic Revivalism: How Area Spirits Speak through Academia." In *Contemporary Pagan and Native Faith Movements in Europe: Colonialist and Nationalist Impulses*, edited by Kathryn Rountree, 100–19. Oxford: Berghahn.

Rose, Wendy. 1992. "The Great Pretenders: Further Reflections on White Shamanism." In *The State of Native America*, edited by M. Annette Jaimes, 403–21. Boston: South End Press.

Rountree, Kathryn. 2002. "Re-inventing Malta's Neolithic Temples: Contemporary Interpretations and Agendas." *History and Anthropology* 13 (1): 31–51. Published online 2010. https://doi.org/10.1080/13537903.2012.675746

———. 2012. "Neo-Paganism, Animism and Kinship with Nature." *Journal of Contemporary Religion* 27 (2): 305–20. https://doi.org/10.1080/02757200290002879

Saez, Oscar Calavia. 2018. "Foreword: Ayahuasca and Its Controversies." In *The Expanding World Ayahuasca Diaspora: Appropriation, Integration and Legislation*, edited by Beatriz Caiuby Labate and Clancy Cavnar, xii–xvii. London: Routledge.

Sanson, Dawne. 2017. "Cosmopolitanism, Neo-Shamans and Contemporary Māori Healers in New Zealand." In *Cosmopolitanism, Nationalism and Modern Paganism*, edited by Kathryn Rountree, 221–43. New York: Palgrave Macmillan.

Schreiter, Robert. 2011. "Cosmopolitanism, Hybrid Identities, and Religion." *Exchange* 40 (1): 19–34. https://doi.org/10.1163/157254311X550713

Sutton, Peter. 2010. "Aboriginal Spirituality in a New Age." *The Australian Journal of Anthropology* 21 (1): 71–89.

Valentish, Jenny. 2018. "Ayahuasca is the New Frontier for 'Psychedelic Feminism'." *ABC News*, August 4, 2018. https://mobile.abc.net.au/news/2018-08-05/ ayahuasca-psychedelic-feminism/10069880. Consulted the 01 September 2020.

Villoldo, Alberto, and Erik Jendresen. 1990. *The Four Winds: A Shaman's Journey into the Amazon*. New York: Harper & Row.

Waldron, David, and Janice Newton. 2012. "Rethinking Appropriation of the Indigenous: A Critique of the Romanticist Approach." *Nova Religio: The Journal of Alternative and Emergent Religions* 16 (2): 64–85. https://doi.org/10.1525/ nr.2012.16.2.64

Wallis, Robert. 2003. *Shamans/Neo-Shamans: Ecstasy, Alternative Archaeology and Contemporary Pagans*. London: Routledge.

Williams, Herbert. 1975. *A Dictionary of the Māori Language.* Wellington: Government Printer.

9

INDIGENOUS COSMOLOGIES AND SOCIAL MEDIA

Creativity, Self-Representation, and Power of the Image
for First Nations Women Artists

CAROLINE NEPTON HOTTE & LAURENT JÉRÔME

IN CANADA, the 1960s marked a turning point for First Nations women who, in the wake of the feminist movement and postcolonial critique, launched mass mobilization and militant actions to denounce the inequalities they were facing. Inspired by the intersectional reflection of third-wave feminism in the 1980s (see Crenshaw and Bonis 2005), as well as decolonial and anticolonial movements today (Smith 1999; Anderson 2000; Green 2007; LaRoque 2009; Simpson 2011, 2014, 2017), First Nations women are becoming more visible and influential across academic and research communities. Through sustained militant action, they remain at the root of most key political mobilizations, as shown by the Idle No More movement launched by First Nations women's groups in English Canada (led by Jessica Gordon, Sylvia McAdam, Sheelah McLean, and Nina Wilson) and Quebec (led by Mélissa Mollen Dupuis and Widia Larivière).[1] In Quebec, for example, their aspirations and conceptions of the world are expressed through various projects and media including literature and poetry (Joséphine Bacon, Marie-Andrée Gill) and film (Alanis Obomsawin, Kim O'Bomsawin), as well as mobilization and political action (Ellen Gabriel). In the last few years, this movement of affirmation has gained further traction thanks to, among other factors, the emergence of social network sites and the wide media coverage of the Idle No More movement (George and Lupien 2012; Tupper 2014; Jérôme 2015; Sioui Durand 2016; Simpson 2011, 2017).

Social network sites have also led to a broader dissemination of Indigenous people's actions, projects, and claims. Self-disclosure through the sharing of photos, videos, and political views is now rapidly and widely broadcast via social network sites, thus benefiting from greater media, cultural, and sociopolitical clout within the public sphere. These alternative mediation networks provide a space of resistance for Indigenous people. These sites are used for increasingly diverse aims (Alexander et al. 2009): transmitting knowledge; (re)affirming social and family ties; extending invitations to community dinners, rituals and ceremonies; and broadcasting information about artistic, cultural, and recreational events (e.g., music festivals, powwows, and bingos, respectively). As Petronella Vaarzon-Morel (this volume) writes, we are far from that past where "Indigenous cosmologies were characterized as localized, holistic, and closed as opposed to the universalizing and 'open' world religions."

In this chapter, we reflect on the relationship between artistic production, cosmologies, and the power of First Nations women in the digital age (Adelson 2012; Escobar et al. 1994; Iseke-Barnes 2002; Jérôme and Veilleux 2014; Leavy et al. 2007). Sociologist and art critic Guy Sioui Durand (2016, 4) noted that, in 2016, we were witnessing an "Indigenous assertion through art...mainly driven by female artists in communities (reserves) as well as in urban settings" (our translation). In this chapter, we want to focus more specifically on the media art practice and production of two Quebec artists: the Innu poet and activist Natasha Kanapé Fontaine and Kanien'kehá:ka visual artist Skawennati Fragnito (known simply as Skawennati). Natasha Kanapé Fontaine is part of a movement that celebrates a diversity of worldviews and actions transforming relations with and within contemporary Quebec society. Skawennati, through her multiple references to history, Haudenosaunee values and creation myths, and the founding figures of the various Indigenous traditions, also describes her actions as part of the complex process of resurgence and affirmation online. Today, these processes take on various forms: dictionaries and interactive online training courses on Indigenous languages, mapping apps, virtual museums, heritage protection websites, videogames inspired by traditional stories, and so on. All are in line with traditional Indigenous knowledge and worldviews that are central to the wellbeing of the members of a group or nation. As Dene scholar Glen Sean Coulthard (2014) explains, these embodied worldviews, or this "grounded normativity," were transferred to the next generation through language, stories, and skills, and by living on the land (see also Simpson 2017; K. Wilson 2005; S. Wilson 2008; Kermoal and Altamirano-Jimenez 2016). These contemporary processes participate actively in the continuity of these worldviews. Both artists question a number of representations related to non-Indigenous society, including power dynamics, self-determination, and agency of Indigenous people in different domains (e.g., education, art, the economy, and politics). By exploring new creation platforms, they create hyperspaces for Indigenous celebration and resurgence (Simpson 2011, 2017) through text, art, videogames, and virtual worlds.

Whereas Natasha Kanapé Fontaine showcases her production in the form of photographs, videos, and texts on the expression platform Facebook (Dalsgaard 2016), Skawennati uses the online creation platform Second Life (Boellstorff 2013), in which users also act as content producers and creators by making "user generated content," or UGC. Although they belong to different generations and have divergent career paths, both artists' actions are linked by their use of the social web as a vehicle for representation, discourse, aspirations, and worldview (Proulx, Millette, and Heaton 2012; Millerand, Proulx, and Rueff 2010).

Cyberspace has become an essential place of expression for Indigenous identities and cosmologies. Following science historian Donna Haraway (1991), we are interested in the ties between human and "machine," and we propose to (re)introduce gender dimensions in our exploration of Indigenous cosmologies and cyberspace. We consider Indigenous women to be "multiply heterogeneous, inhomogeneous, accountable, and connected human agents" (Haraway 1991, 3). This is why, when examining the online practices, careers, and works of these two artists, we ask ourselves: What are the various ways in which the social web could be considered a dynamic tool for the (re)construction and (re)affirmation of Indigenous cosmologies, especially for Indigenous women artists?

First, we present the key concept of our argument, namely the idea of a *media cosmology*, which we believe allows for the articulation of the relationship between pragmatic actions and Indigenous cosmology. Our approach adopts a gender perspective to explore the discourse on these digital platforms. We then present a reflection on the notions of self-presentation and visibility on Facebook by examining photos posted by poet Natasha Kanapé Fontaine, whose use of the platform is rooted in her everyday life. In the last section of our chapter, we discuss a few aspects of the work of artist Skawennati in the virtual worlds of the social web and show how self-representation, understood here in the collective sense, can at once draw inspiration from a revisiting of historical events and yield new and original interpretations of prospects for the future.

Media Cosmologies

In order to articulate our discourse around the concepts of cosmologies and pragmatic actions, we use the term *media cosmology,* first suggested by the Kanien'kehá:ka (Mohawk, Quebec) intellectual, curator, and artist Steven Loft (2014). Director of the Aboriginal Arts Office of the Canada Council for the Arts and, in the 1990s, the First Nations curator at the Art Gallery of Hamilton, Loft was appointed director of the Indigenous artist-run centre Urban Shaman Gallery (Winnipeg). In 2007, he was Curator-in-Residence of Indigenous Art at the National Gallery of Canada. In his work, Loft emphasizes the idea of a technical, scientific, relational, ritual, and communicational continuity between traditional Indigenous forms and knowledge and the virtual world. Far from seeing in it a rupture, Loft considers the use of internet and sociodigital platforms as a way of updating Indigenous conceptions of the world, maintaining relations (in a kinship sense)[2] with the broader community of humans and nonhumans,[3] and sharing stories within a collective memory space. Following Loft's perspective, along with other non-Indigenous anthropologists who consider the body to be the main mode of expression of Indigenous cosmologies (Laugrand 2013; Viveiros de Castro 2009; Descola 1993, 2005, 2006), we see the internet and the social network sites as spaces populated by the ancestors' voices, Indigenous stories, and memory, and as tools of communication and mediation (De Largy Healy 2013; Warschauer 1998; Wachowich and Scobie 2010), especially for First Nations women. The concept of media cosmology entwined with analyses of the importance of women in the transmission of knowledge, the declaration of identity, and the reproduction of kinship relations, prove to be helpful when we consider practices and strategies of assertion, self-representation, and "patrimonialisation" (heritage in the making), as developed by the artists Natasha Kanapé Fontaine and Skawennati.

Through its fluidity, the concept of religiosity embraces a large scope of Indigenous practices, worldviews, and rituals. In contrast to religion, which focuses on specific dogmas, "religiosity focuses instead on experiential and performative dimensions" and "further evokes a dynamic process always *in the making*...[It] acknowledges the openness and fluidity of Indigenous perspectives and practices" (Dussart and Poirier, this volume). In this chapter, we use the concept of cosmology for the same arguments, but in a more specific way: to engage in the power shift initiated by Indigenous academics through various scientific conferences, articles, and essays. The way Indigenous scholar Loft elaborated a media cosmology theory is based on Indigenous epistemologies and ontologies at the core of the Indigenous paradigm (S. Wilson 2008; Hart 2010; Rice 2005). As Loft (2014, 175) says: "That hardware technology has made it accessible through a tactile regime in no way diminishes its power as a spiritual, cosmological, and mythical 'realm.'" Referring to cosmology in our analysis of Indigenous mediation online reflects the knowledge shared by Loft and his teachings regarding the notion of "Indigenous cosmological thought." It is, for us, a way to stress the link between the two concepts of religiosity and cosmology, as well as an ethical choice that valorizes the concepts used by Indigenous scholars (Sinclair 2009; Smith 1999).

By *cosmology*, we mean a conception of the world that organizes space and time, structures rituals and stories, carries the memory and voices of the human and nonhuman ancestors, and frames practices of relationships and reciprocity with the agency of the land and the entities dwelling in it (Ingold 2000). The concept of an Indigenous cosmology refers to a conception of the world based on presence, exchange, and sharing that allows for the constant weaving of a web of relationships and responsibilities towards every living thing (Poirier 2016; Kohn 2013). As Gerdine Van Woudenberg (2004, 76) mentions, the oral traditions of the Wabanaki people speak, for example, of "the interconnection amongst all people in the universe" (our translation), including the earth and the land, which are seen as living and "sacred" beings.

Following Frédéric Laugrand (2013), we argue that cosmologies are first and foremost constructed, sustained, and passed on via the body. We also consider them to be gendered: tethered to the social roles of First Nations women (Basile 2017; Van Woudenberg 2004). During a public presentation in 2017, Atikamekw artist Meky Ottawa reminded us that the expression *to remember* in the Atikamekw language is *nimikow-iwin*, literally translated as "to have in one's blood."[4] The process of transmitting cosmologies is thus accomplished through "blood," a process reminiscent of two key ceremonial events, birth and menstruation. Take, for example, the ceremony of the first menstrual period, the moon ceremony, or the ceremony of the burial of the placenta carried out in many First Nations. Filmmaker Alanis Obomsawin (1977), in her film *Mother of Many Children,* focused particularly on the words spoken by women and the link between gender, cosmology, and the land: "From earth—from water our people grow to love each other in this manner. For in all our languages there is no she or he. We are the children of the earth and of the sea."

The omnipresence of internet and digital media in Indigenous people's lives highlights, as Anne-Marie Colpron (this volume) notes in relation to shamanism, "how the contemporary appropriations of these women are linked to the practices of the past."[5] Artists, like shamans, "create bridges between different worlds and temporalities, constructing [themselves] through these relations with others, whether forest entities, *mestizos* from the towns, or foreign tourists" (Colpron, this volume). Like Colpron, we are also interested in how their "audacious innovations" are making sense through their creative relational logic, taking into account Indigenous internationalism (Simpson, 2017) between and among Indigenous Nations, and in extension with other Nations.

Social network sites are spaces for creative transformation and transmission along with the production of some visual documentaries. Such spaces support the current transmission, patrimonialisation, and affirmation processes related to Indigenous cosmological knowledges and their renewal. Video games and social web environments such as Second Life illuminate the development of a new visual culture. Video games such as *Never Alone* (Inuit), *Skahiòn:hati:, Rise of the Kanien'kehá:ka Legends* (Kanien'kehá:ka), and *Tshakapesh* (Innu), which feature cultural heroes with special powers that increase as the game progresses, are illustrations of such processes. In this chapter, we examine the online worlds (Boellstorff et al. 2012; Hine 2000, 2015) in which two Indigenous female artists represent themselves and their worldviews and participate in these processes.

Natasha Kanapé Fontaine: Self-Representation and Connecting Identities

Kanapé Fontaine, born in 1991, is from the Pessamit community of Quebec's Côte-Nord region. She grew up mainly in the town of Baie-Comeau near her community and graduated from postsecondary studies in Rimouski before pursuing her career as a writer and poet in Montreal, where she has lived since 2013. Her four published collections of poems have all received critical acclaim: *N'entre pas dans mon âme avec tes chaussures* (2012), *Manifeste Assi* (2014), *Bleuets et abricots* (2016), and, more recently, *Nanimissuat: Île-Tonnerre* (2018). As a poet-performer, actor, visual artist, and activist for Indigenous and environmental rights, she often draws her inspiration from Innu cosmology. In her exploration of cosmological themes and issues, she highlights the relationships among "Mother Earth" (in her own words), her body, her sexuality, and colonization—key concepts of Indigenous and Innu cosmologies (see Havard and Laugrand 2014). She also evokes the power of dreams and drums and the relationships with animal worlds, nature, and water (Armitage 1992; Van Woudenberg 2004; Poirier 2008; Watts 2013), which are key in the protection and the transmission of Innu cultural heritage. For Kanapé Fontaine, it is essential to share her experience as an Innu woman through her art, as well as to raise awareness among Indigenous peoples young and old about political, environmental, and spiritual issues.

Our analysis of how Kanapé Fontaine navigates self-representation with regard to the land and the construction of social networks shows that it is anchored on a shared sense of kin belonging. The artist uses the social network site Facebook on a weekly basis in a manner that is reminiscent of strategies observed in other contexts:

> Facebook is for many Indigenous users a site where they can explore identity, both their own and others. It is a vehicle for agency in self-representation that offers opportunities to shed skin, so to speak, and don a new "cyber-skin," a mode of Indigenous identity that moves between the spaces of computer-generated identities as an embodied subject actively creating an identity. (Lumby 2010, 69)

Kanapé Fontaine resorts to various strategies of online representation in order to build her digital identity (boyd and Ellison 2007). Her profile contains different forms of self-expression, online presence, and exposure and traces (Coutant and Stenger 2013). What interests us in this specific case is the space reserved on her public artist Facebook page for the range of picture galleries and slideshows, consumed by over 26,000 followers.[6] She created this page in 2012, on top of her private Facebook profile. Any user can access the public profile simply by creating their own account. Here, we are focusing solely on Kanapé Fontaine's public persona and the context or background of the photos and interactions she has posted there as self-representation.[7]

These images, taken between 2012 and 2020, feature various types of posting practices, including close-up selfies and both staged and impromptu photos. Today, she performs this diversification of identity

FIGURE 9.1. Natasha Kanapé Fontaine. (© Sébastien Raboin, 2013)

utterances on several platforms: Facebook, Instagram, and Twitter (Miller et al. 2016).

The practice of self-representation is not new to First Nations in Canada (Vigneault 2017), as demonstrated by pictographs, birch bark scrolls, and, more recently, self-portraits in oils. For example, in the mid-nineteenth century, Zacharie Vincent Tehariolin, a Huron-Wendat chief, painted twelve self-portraits documenting his aging process and his own people before being totally engulfed by colonization.

Representations—more specifically, self-representations—are attempts at (re)appropriation of an image too often distorted by the dominant society (Bernier 2017; Drache, Fletcher, and Voss 2016). This is especially true in the case of Indigenous women (Vigneault 2017; Simpson 2017; Jérôme 2015; Jérôme, Biroté, and Coocoo 2018). Kanapé Fontaine's digital identity is as much about what she is trying to hide as it is about what she is trying to show (Cardon 2009), whether the images are captured by herself or someone else (figures 9.1 and 9.2). Through a series of portraits and selfies—some of which are not dissimilar from self-portraits by other women artists—we can appreciate the evolution and transformations of her body, but also her movement in space and her routes through Innu territory (Innu Assi) and urban territory, the latter thought and lived as an extension of Innu Assi.

Between 2012 and 2013, following the publication of her first book, Kanapé Fontaine redoubled her call for activism and multiplied her participation in public representations. The first pictures she posted show her as an activist for the Idle No More movement: arms in the air, assertive, walking in demonstrations while waving the Mohawk Warrior flag and looking straight at the camera, or smiling softly and swaying from side to side (figure 9.3). Her empowered and militant Indigenous woman image was broadcast on social network sites. Her Indigenousness (i.e., her Innu-ness) was then performed and very publicly asserted, and her self-representations evolved. Unlike the work of well-known artist Cindy Sherman,[8] Kanapé Fontaine seemed at first to focus on aesthetics rather than gender boundaries. However, like other Indigenous women artists, everything on her profile seemed to say *"je suis une femme"* (I am a woman): comfortable with her own

FIGURE 9.2. Natasha Kanapé Fontaine. (© Jean-François Lemire, Shoot Studio, 2014)

FIGURE 9.3. Natasha Kanapé Fontaine. (© Jérémie Battaglia, 2013)

Figure 9.4. Natasha Kanapé Fontaine.

(© Alexandra Guelil, *L'Itinéraire*, 15 August 2017)

sensuality but assertive of her role as a protector of Mother Earth through the Idle no More movement (Toulouse 2017; Maracle 1996). Incidentally, many images posted on her main Facebook page from 2012 to 2013 include photo shoots of urban flash mobs (quick and spontaneous public gatherings) and an icon on a red background that appears to be a silhouette of an Indigenous woman or man wearing two feathers.[9] This image is one of the logos of the Idle No More—One Stolen Sister Is Too Many movement, which Kanapé Fontaine used for a while as her profile picture. This movement denounced the disappearance of Indigenous women in Canada before the National Inquiry into Missing and Murdered Indigenous Women and Girls launched in 2016.[10]

From 2014 to 2015, the artist began a series of performances and international lectures bringing together key Indigenous intellectuals such as Innu poet Joséphine Bacon. Kanapé Fontaine travelled across Quebec and Canada to fight for environmental issues and for Mother Earth. She is considered a nomadic artist by Sioui Durand (2014).

Such expression of a body in motion mirrors a physical transformation, typical of contemporary strategies in identity assertion, celebration of Indigenous cosmologies, and recognition in the media. In 2017, Kanapé Fontaine championed traditional tattoos on her arms, highlighted by a photo published in the magazine *L'Itinéraire* (figure 9.4).

Here, the artist chose to mark her body with traditional Innu patterns: double-curved flower and plant-like motifs done in red ink. This is a significant example of an embodied proclamation of an Innu woman's identity. Tattoos are literal embodied traces and evidence of a creative and transformative presence (Gell 2009) made possible by various gestures and actions within the places her body inhabits—for example, in the picture taken of the artist near a bridge in Tiohtià:ke (Montreal), asserting her presence and that of Indigenous people in this urban territory. It is also a (re)assertion of traditional art practices (Lacroix 2012). Sharing pictures via the Facebook platform leads to instant connection—at least in Canada's large urban centres and, more and more, in many remote communities—thus shrinking geographical and time constraints, eliminating imaginary colonial boundaries between city and forest, and (re)actualizing friendships and family relationships (Wood 2015). The poet can maintain relationships by introducing herself as an agent of political change on land recognized as Indigenous and under the process of a land claim agreement.[11] As Leanne Simpson (2014, 23) remarks: "The beauty of culturally inherent resurgence is that it challenges settler colonial dissections of our territories and our bodies into reserve/city or rural/urban dichotomies."

Perhaps the body, as expressed through selfies, enters into an immanent, rather than transcendent, relation with the land.[12] Although the native forest remains central for Indigenous people, their presence in online spaces (re)affirms their physicality as it relates to their manifold relationships—a crucial element of identity-building for Indigenous women. In her online performances, Kanapé Fontaine embodies the space by asserting her presence in the world through her body, thus transcending both the device and the technology. She carves her presence within what Haida artist Michael Nicoll Yahgulanaas (n.d.) underlines as a space between Indigenousness and the nation-state— between the categories of understanding, values, and respective ontologies—in order to better grasp social dynamics and relationships.

Skawennati: Self-Representation through Virtual Creation

Skawennati is a Kanien'kehá:ka multimedia artist who was born in Kahnawake Kanien'kehá:ka reserve in Quebec and grew up in the suburb of Châteauguay. In 1992, she earned a BFA in design arts and, in 1995, a graduate diploma in institutional administration with an art speciality at Concordia University in Montreal, Quebec. She is currently the head of Aboriginal Territories in Cyberspace (AbTeC), a network of artists and researchers who develop creative virtual worlds inspired by Indigenous history, memory, and cosmologies. In 2015, AbTeC started IIF (Initiative for Indigenous Futures), through which they host "Skins" workshops. According to IFF (n.d.), these workshops are structured around Indigenous narrative traditions and cover the development of experimental media practices as a way of fostering creativity in Indigenous youth. The work of Skawennati and her team is not limited to the mobilization of Indigenous history and memory. She frames Indigenous cosmologies as creative and dynamic processes by developing stories and adventures, as well as critical documentary pieces on colonial histories. Her project, entitled *Time Traveller* (2008–2013), is composed of nine "machinima" (from *machine* and *cinema*, a term used to describe virtual filmmaking) episodes[13] and is the continuation of two earlier projects, namely *CyberPowWow* (1997–2004) and *Imagining Indians in the 25th Century* (2001).

Indigenous video and interactive digital animation projects are still so new in Quebec that for some the presence of Indigenous people in these productions remains stereotyped (Lewis 2014). *Time Traveller* features the virtual character Hunter, a Kanien'kehá:ka man who can travel through time. In several episodes, Skawennati makes Hunter narrate important events in the history of First Nations in Quebec such as the Oka Crisis (1990).[14] Through the voice of Hunter, Skawennati gives a perspective from within the Kanien'kehá:ka nation where she is from, thus contributing to the transformation of how this event is understood. In other episodes of *Time Traveller*, Skawennati's perspective on religious plurality highlights the canonization of Kanien'kehá:ka thaumaturge Kateri Tekakwitha—the first Indigenous person, a woman, to achieve sainthood—as well as the presence of powwows, which have been growing in popularity in Quebec in the last few decades. Her machinimas present the viewer with a *mise en abyme*: We (the viewers) are watching a video on a screen in which Hunter leaves his own reality to enter a virtual one. We travel through time with Hunter to various historical periods marked by the presence or actions of important cultural figures. As Jason Edward Lewis (2014, 70) explains,

> *[m]achinima relies on real-time engines from video games and virtual worlds to create cinematic computer animations that are captured to video. The artist then takes the output from these processes and creates the artwork, which can be as varied as linear video clips, recorded game sessions, or live performances. Its emergence is as an offshoot of the explosive growth of digital gaming and virtual environments.*

Lewis adds that the low-resolution graphics in Second Life (the online platform used to create *Time Traveller*) give the piece a retrofuturistic look: "a visual feel that serves as subtextual commentary on the relationship between actual and imagined futures" (70). Similarly, the work of anthropologist Faye Ginsburg (1994, 2018; Ginsburg and Myers 2006) sheds light on how Aboriginal artists in Australia have engaged with new forms of media expression since the 1970s to develop and secure a cultural future both for themselves and for Aboriginal society as a whole in its ties to non-Aboriginal society. This cyberspace can be interpreted as a "third-space" (Bhabha 1994) where imaginaries and identities are (re)negotiated, (re)mediated, juxtaposed, or/and superimposed. Hunter, the hero of Skawennati's machinima, travels through different historic spaces and periods but also through imagined futures that refer to different processes of affirmation and resistance. This is called "remediation": the process of incorporating images, representations, and discourses of past and future media technology into present-day, online spaces and platforms. For example, Skawennati offers an Indigenous perspective of the Minnesota Massacre of 1862 (figure 9.5), which affected many Indigenous people around the Great Lakes. Here, Skawennati (re)negotiates worldviews of the history of colonization and, by extension, spaces of expressions, relationships, and creativity.

Unlike Facebook representations, which often showcase life events and reflections of a living person with whom we have a friendly relationship, *Time Traveller* invites viewers to develop a relationship within a fictional, virtual world. In such a virtual environment, Indigenous representations are often embodied by historical figures. This self-representation within cyberspace is similar to the strategies adopted by ethnocultural minorities, some of whose online communities seem to gravitate around worldviews of a generally shared origin: "People use the Internet to both form and reaffirm individual racial identity and seek out communities based on race and racial understandings of the world" (Daniels 2013, 698). The character of Hunter created by Skawennati signals a broader process of indigenization (Dussart and Poirier 2017; Sahlins 1993) of virtual worlds through the celebration of signs, symbols, acts, or qualities that are recognized and shared by various Indigenous societies. As Hunter travels to different moments in history—sometimes dressed as a Kanien'kehá:ka hunter—he lives alongside other Indigenous peoples and acts within their universe without actually being part of it, akin to an Indigenous visitor. He adopts a new way of doing things or interacting with people depending on whether he is in the past or future, recontextualizing historical events within an Indigenous perspective.

The *machinimas* are an opportunity to show a contemporary Indigenous version of history through, for example, a decolonized vision of the Sioux war of 1862. Hunter learns that by moving through spacetime—a form of embodied knowledge—he can flip the depiction of Indigenous people showing how Indigenous perspectives can respect and celebrate their cosmologies. This perspective uses the body as a place of creativity, continuity, and dynamism (e.g., by donning traditional

FIGURE 9.5. "Dakotas Raise Weapons" (2010), from episode 2 of *Time Traveller*. Hunter (back) travelling to the Minnesota Massacre (1862), also known as the Sioux Uprising. (Used with permission from Skawennati.)

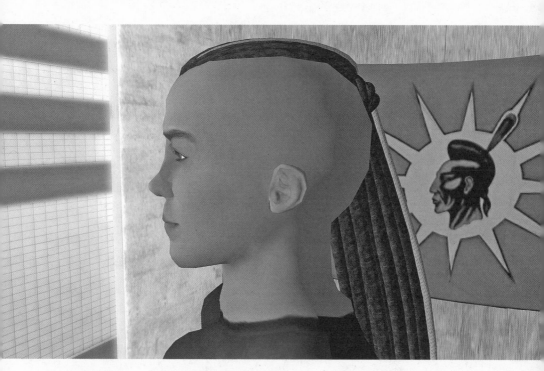

FIGURE 9.6. "Hunter Reflects" (2017), from episode 6 of *Time Traveller*. (Used with permission from Skawennati.)

FIGURE 9.7. "Jingle Dancers Assembled" (2011), from episode 4 of *Time Traveller*. (Used with permission from Skawennati.)

FIGURE 9.8. "Kateri and Karahkwenhàwi–BFFs" (n.d.), from episode 5 of T*ime Traveller*. Kateri Tekakwitha (left) and Karahkwenhawi, Hunter's girlfriend (right) talking with missionaries. (Used with permission from Skawennati.)

or futuristic clothes, or by physically and freely moving through different historical periods).

Daniel Heath Justice (2008, 161) reminds us that "native bodies are sites of both colonial conflict and passionate decolonization." In *Time Traveller*, Hunter provides a different perspective on Indigenous history in relation to both past events and yet-to-be-written futures.

The episode in which Hunter encounters Kateri Tekakwitha lets the viewer visualize Tekakwitha's body and her movements, hear her voice, and follow her actions and gestures, thus giving a tangible existence to this lost historical figure surrounded by missionaries of the time. Here, viewers are invited to experience Indigenous history.

Another jump forward in time allows viewers to visit an imagined future in which Indigenous people are the majority. It is as though Skawennati had answered Cheryl L'Hirondelle's (2014, 152) invitation:

> *Our connection to the land is what makes us Indigenous, and yet as we move forward into virtual domains we too are sneaking up and setting up camp—making this virtual and technologically mediated domain our own. However, we stake a claim here too as being intrinsic part of this place—the very roots, or more appropriately route. So, let's use our collective Indigenous unconscious to remember our contributions and the physical beginnings that were pivotal in how this virtual reality was constructed.*

By investing cyberspace with a reappropriated history, stories still told today, lore and life skills, conceptions of the world, and individuals as bodies moving in spacetime such as the famous Anishinaabe trickster Nanabush,[15] Indigenous cosmologies are at once passed on, preserved, celebrated, and (re)affirmed in the present.

Skawennati suggests we consider this engagement in cyberspace as a possibility of linking past, present, and future history: "The majority of images I saw of Native people were in the past, unhappy-looking, and unnamed. I want us to be there, in the future, alive and kicking and thriving," Skawennati says as she explains the power of storytelling in cyberspace (quoted in Laurence 2016, para. 20). Even though, as Lewis

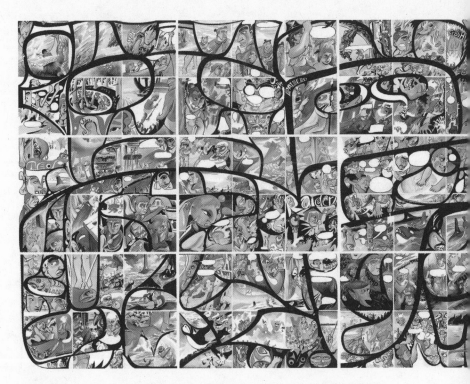

FIGURE 9.9. Image from *Red: A Haida Manga*, by Haida artist Michael Nicoll Yahgulanaas. (Used with permission from Michael Nicoll Yahgulanaas, https://mny.ca.)

(2014) maintains, Indigenous people have yet to create their own digital software and digital languages, we must nevertheless recognize the potential of cyberspace for creative transformation by and for Indigenous peoples, and as an interstice to negotiate all identities as users/viewers (Bhabha 1994).

Indigenous Cosmologies in the Virtual World: Between Spaces and Interstices

In order to show the relationship between social network sites, self-representation, and the power of images (Deger 2006, 2012, 2013, 2016) in the transformative creativities linked with Indigenous cosmologies, we conclude with a note from *Red: A Haida Manga* by Haida artist Michael Nicoll Yahgulanaas.

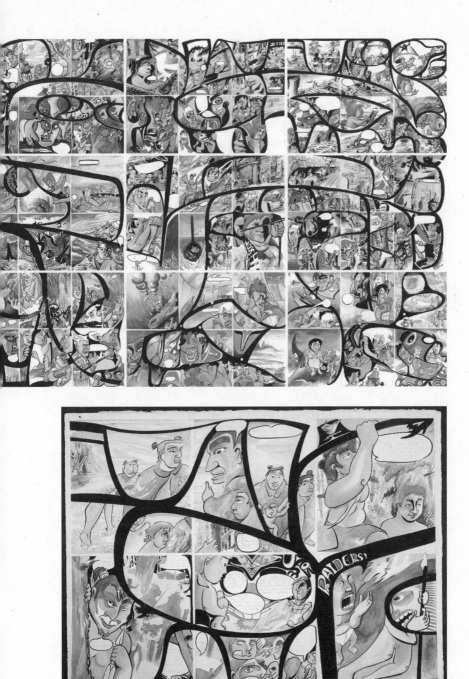

FIGURE 9.10. Detail from *Red: A Haida Manga* by Haida artist Michael Nicoll Yahgulanaas. (Used with permission from Michael Nicoll Yahgulanaas, https://mny.ca)

In his online lecture entitled *Art Opens Windows to the Space between,* Yahgulanaas (2015) maintains that his work is a reflection about the spaces that form and can be formulated between people's semantic spaces. In his production, he explains that the black outline separating each panel in the manga—the "gutter"—is not empty, but rather filled with knowledge, representations, practices, and stories that refer to a broader, vaster cosmology (Harrison 2016). His work illustrates the notion that all living beings and existents, humans and nonhumans, animals and plants, men and women, young people and Elders, are linked together as part of an interrelated whole. It is a way to affirm the presence and the influence of Elders as "cosmological foundation." As Vaarzon-Morel (this volume) writes, "in the face of change, Elders were determined to maintain cultural and community autonomy." Furthermore, these outlines are a direct reference to Haida imagery with its aesthetics and motifs that interconnect to create larger drawings with different meanings that superimpose themselves on the pages' panels. His proposition is similar to Homi K. Bhabha's (1994) concept of interstice: a space of negotiation of identities, cultured, gendered, and so on. Bhabha writes:

> These "in-between" spaces provide the terrain for elaborating strat-
> egies of selfhood—singular or communal—that initiate new signs of
> identity, and innovative sites of collaboration, and contestation, in
> the act of defining the idea of society itself. (1–2)

In his lecture, Yahgulanaas invites us to step into the space between expressive, representative, and semantic spaces to connect with other human and nonhuman beings. Likewise, we believe that this is what artists—women artists more specifically—achieve when working with digital technology.

Kanapé Fontaine takes her militant writing—a vehicle for her political aspirations and her vision of Innu cosmology—to the Facebook platform by exploiting the effects and strategies of self-representation with her images. Without having a systematic preference for selfies, she nevertheless uses photography, including selfies and other images, and affirms a presence on the land by sharing her own conception of the world—a social context that includes cultural and gendered issues—on social network sites. Skawennati uses documentary to revisit a collective history, either by materializing past historical figures and events or by creating a vision for the future inspired by collective memory. In both cases, these artists explore online territories. They shift from the contemporary to the virtual—two equally real modalities (Proulx and Latzko-Toth 2000)—and from the virtual to the fictional as a way of illustrating the complexity of different versions of history. For example, as Skawennati revisits Kateri Tekakwitha's story, she explains that Tekakwitha was often seen and represented in historiography as performing acts of self-mortification (see, e.g., Shoemaker 1995). But the narrative in Skawennati's machinima shapes a different version that involves a traditional ritual shared by many Indigenous groups in Quebec and Canada known as the cedar cleansing ceremony. Therefore, several possible layers of analysis allow the user/viewer to play with, rethink, and decolonize the various categories of knowledge that make up Indigenous cosmologies and rituals by following a form of multidimensional, emotional geography in which women regain power and traditional healing knowledge that act to distance the user/viewer from stereotypes. Here, one can subvert appearances in the physical world and act upon the virtual territory online by presenting and constructing a new worldview populated by Indigenous ontologies and interiorities. From the artists' perspective, self-representation is built through a process of decolonizing their respective realities and cosmologies, memories and visions. By investing the public sphere with incarnations—in the sense of "embodiments"—of their selves in the forms of photographs and videos on the social web, the artists Kanapé Fontaine and Skawennati ensure the presence of Innu and Kanien'kehá:ka cosmologies within different realms.

Conclusion

Cyberspace as a territory is particularly invested by First Nations women artists who maintain a unique rapport with the land in their constant (re)affirmation of relationships still marked by the manipulations of colonization. These relationships superimpose themselves onto and juxtaposed themselves with society today. As (re)imagined by First Nations women, this poetic territory can be seen as a matrix for various ecosystems of Indigenous relationships (Alaimo 2008), a territory within which identities and cosmologies are constructed, expressed, lived, and (re)imagined via the body. Cybertext as body can feature in a relation of transcendence with the land by allowing artists to get rid of geographical and temporal boundaries. For artists and users, dynamic exercise of self-representation online could provide another form of decolonization as cyberspace becomes a medium of agency for Indigenous ontologies.

Authors' Note

This research was supported by the Social Sciences and Humanities Research Council of Canada (SSHRC) Joseph-Armand Bombardier Canada Graduate Scholarship (Caroline Nepton Hotte, 2018–2021), Insight Development Grant (Laurent Jérôme, 2018–2020), and Partnership Engage Grant (Laurent Jérôme, 2017–2018). We are grateful for the support of the Nishkatsh Upahuatsh program, part of the Secteur du développement de l'éducation et de la main-d'oeuvre of the Pekuakamiulnuatsh Takuhikan of Mashtéuiatsh. Finally, we would also like to express our sincere gratitude to Sylvie Poirier and Françoise Dussart and to all of the Elders, artists, colleagues, and research partners (Indigenous and non-Indigenous) who inspired this chapter.

Notes

1. Idle No More is one of the largest Indigenous political movements of resistance in Canadian history and was built principally through social media. It was initiated in November 2012 when Jessica Gordon, Sylvia McAdam, Sheelah McLean, and Nina Wilson, four Indigenous women from Saskatoon, Saskatchewan, denounced the federal omnibus bill C-45 (passed by a government led by Prime Minister Stephen Harper) that included the removal of the Navigable Water Protection Act, 1882. For more details, see https://idlenomore.ca/about-the-movement/.

2. Theresa Halsey, a Dakota woman among the Great Plains Peoples, points out that their concept of kinship is different from the traditional Western one. She states: "When we live in our community, it is called a *tiyospaye*, [or a] group of tipis. This community was very important to us because that is where we found our strength and knowledge of knowing who we are and where we come from.

We no longer live in tipis but still believe in this concept" (per. comm., 2002). Halsey quotes Ella Deloria's ethnographic book *Waterlily* on traditional Dakota living: "Any family could maintain itself adequately as long as the father was a good hunter and the mother an industrious woman" (quoted in Guerrero 2003, 63–64).

3.   Here, we are referring to the whole of nonhuman entities with whom humans interact in Indigenous cosmologies and ontologies (game, fish, bodies of water, plants, ancestors, astral bodies, spirits, etc.).

4.   We are aware that readers may think that this expression refers to the concept of "Indian blood" or "pure blood" and the passing down of Indian status as formulated in the 1876 Indian Act. However, since the Atikamekw language existed before this colonial concept, in our view, *nimikowiwin* refers, instead, to the flesh and blood (i.e., placenta) of the mother that nourishes the child, and by extension to breastfeeding (Simpson, 2017).

5.   For a discussion of this in the context of the hypermediatization of Shibo-Kinibo female shamanism in Brazil, see Colpron (this volume).

6.   Kanapé Fontaine's Facebook artist page can be found at https://www.facebook.com/natashakanapefontaine.

7.   We are not considering reception theories or discourse analyses, nor are we following interactions with the public, texts she has posted, or conversations she might have had.

8.   To learn more about Cindy Sherman's work, see, e.g., https://www.moma.org/artists/5392.

9.   Created by the Cree and Métis artist Aaron Paquette, this image was originally entitled *Sisters, Daughters, Mothers*. Kanapé Fontaine included three hashtags when she posted the image to her public page: #Not1More, #MMIW (i.e., Murdered and Missing Indigenous Women), and #StolenSisters (Facebook post, 22 September 2014).

10. To learn more about the inquiry and read the final report, visit the National Inquiry into Missing and Murdered Indigenous Women and Girls website (https://mmiwg-ffada.ca/).

11. Like the majority of First Nations in Canada, the Innu Nation has never ceded or surrendered their ancestral lands and continues to assert its rights on Nitassinan, their ancestral territory. Indigenous ancestral titles and rights are recognized under section 35 of the Constitution Act (1982). The Innu Nation has been engaged for the last forty years in land right negotiations with the federal and the provincial governments under the Comprehensive Land Claims Policy.

12. Philippe Descola (2007) and others have studied continuities between human and nonhuman entities. He notes:

Animism is based on the idea that humans and many non-humans have an interiority of the same nature, which allows for person-to-person relationships, while they are distinguished by their body envelopes. Speaking of body envelopes, we must take seriously the usual way to designate the body in these animist systems, the local term being "clothing." It is the idea that the interiorities, which are thought of as human inwardness, are covered with a garment, which is a body that can be undone at will. (para. 15; our translation)

13. Watch the episodes of *Time Traveller* at http://www.timetravellertm.com/ episodes/.

14. This event took place in the province of Quebec during the summer of 1990. After many years of land claims processes, the Mohawk of Kanehsatake, near Montreal, resisted a development project being considered by the mayor of the neighbouring municipality, Oka. He wanted to extend a golf course and introduce a condominium complex in the Pine sector, a land considered sacred by the Kanien'kehá:ka. The Native community set up a peaceful barricade to contest this development. The protests became violent when Sûreté du Quebec, the province's police force, raided the barricade and protest camp. A police officer was killed. The Canadian army intervened. The siege lasted ninety days that summer and is known for setting a precedent in the Americas and inspiring Indigenous movements around the world. On the Oka crisis, see Trudel (2009) and Obomsawin's (1993) film *Kanehsatake: 275 Years of Resistance*.

15. Nanabush, as other tricksters from various Indigenous cosmologies (Dembrick 2010; Slater 1994; Radin 1956), can appear and disappear at will and travel over long distances to meet humans and nonhumans, following a circular cosmological temporality.

References

Adelson, Naomi. 2012. "Reflecting on the Future: New Technologies, New Frontiers." In *Aboriginal History: A Reader,* edited by Burnett Kristin and Read Geoff, 264–75. Don Mills: Oxford University Press.

Alaimo, Stacy. 2008. "Trans-corporeal Feminisms and the Ethical Space of Nature." In *Material Feminisms*, edited by Alaimo Stacy and Susan Hekman, 237–64. Bloomington: Indiana University Press.

Alexander, Cynthia J., Agar Adamson, Graham Daborn, John Houston, and Victor Tootoo. 2009. "Inuit Cyberspace: The Struggle for Access for Inuit Qaujimajatuqangit." *Journal of Canadian Studies / Revue d'études canadiennes* 43 (2): 220–49. Published online 2016. https://doi.org/10.3138/jcs.43.2.220

Anderson, Kim. 2000. *A Recognition of Being: Reconstructing Native Womanhood*. Toronto: Second Story Press.

Armitage, Peter. 1992. "Religious Ideology Among the Innu of Eastern Quebec and Labrador." *Religiologiques* 6 (4): 64–110. http://www.religiologiques.uqam.ca/no6/armit.pdf

Basile, Suzy. 2017. "Le rôle et la place des femmes atikamekw dans la gouvernance du territoire et des ressources naturelles." PHD thesis, Université du Québec en Abitibi-Témiscamingue. Depositum. https://depositum.uqat.ca/id/eprint/703/

Bernier, Andréanne. 2017. "Au-delà de Pocahontas: logique et effets de la représentation médiatique des femmes autochtones." Master's thesis, University of Ottawa. uO Research. https://ruor.uottawa.ca/handle/10393/36579

Bhabha, Homi K. 1994. *Location of Culture*. London: Routledge.

Boellstorff, Tom. 2013. *Un anthropologue dans Second Life: une expérience de l'humanité virtuelle*. Ottignies-Louvain-la-Neuve: Academia-l'Harmattan.

Boellstorff, Tom, Bonnie Nardi, Celia Pearce, and T.L. Taylor. 2012. *Ethnography and Virtual Worlds: A Handbook of Method*. Princeton: Princeton University Press.

boyd, danah m., and Nicole B. Ellison. 2007. "Social Network Sites: Definition, History, and Scholarship." *Journal of Computer-Mediated Communication* 13 (1): 210–30. https://doi.org/10.1111/j.1083-6101.2007.00393.x

Cardon, D. 2009. "L'identité comme stratégie relationnelle." *Hermès, la revue* 53 (1): 61–6. https://doi.org/10.4267/2042/31477

Coulthard, Glen Sean. 2014. *Red Skin, White Masks: Rejecting the Colonial Politics of Recognition*. Minneapolis: University of Minnesota Press.

Crenshaw, Kimberlé Williams, and Oristelle Bonis. 2005. "Cartographies des marges: intersectionnalité, politique de l'identité et violences contre les femmes de couleur." *Cahiers du genre* 39 (2): 51–82. https://doi.org/10.3917/cdge.039.0051

Dalsgaard, Steffen. 2016. "The Ethnographic Use of Facebook in Everyday Life." *Anthropological Forum: A Journal of Social Anthropology and Comparative Sociology* 26 (1): 96–114. https://doi.org/10.1080/00664677.2016.1148011

Daniels, Jessie. 2013. "Race and Racism in Internet Studies: A Review and Critique." *New Media & Society* 15 (5): 695–719. https://doi.org/10.1177/1461444812462849

Deger, Jennifer. 2006. *Shimmering Screens: Making Media in an Aboriginal Community*. Minneapolis: Minnesota University Press.

——. 2012. *Art/Emergence: Crossing Cultures: The Owen and Wagner Collection of Contemporary Australian Aboriginal Art*. Hanover: Hood Museum of Art.

——. 2013. "The Jolt of the New: Making Video Art in Arnhem Land." *Culture, Theory and Critique* 54 (3): 355–71. https://doi.org/10.1080/14735784.2013.818277

———. 2016. "Thick Photography." *Journal of Material Culture* 21 (1): 111–32. https://doi.org/10.1177/1359183515623312

De Largy Healy, Jessica. 2014. "Remediating Sacred Imagery on Screens: Yolngu Experiments with New Media Technology." In *Australian Aboriginal Anthropology Today: Critical Perspectives from Europe*, edited by Laurent Verger, Barbara Glowczewski, Laurent Dousset, Marika Moisseeff, and Jessica De Largy Healy, Vol. 4, *Les actes de colloques du Musée du quai Branly Jacques Chirac*. Paris: Musée de Quai Branly. https://doi.org/10.4000/actesbranly.577

Dembrick, Matt. 2010. *Trickster: Native American Tales, A Graphic Collection*. Wheat Ridge: Fulcrum Publishing

Descola, Philippe. 1993. *Les lances du crépuscule: relations jivaros, Haute-Amazonie*. Paris: Plon.

———. 2005, *Par-delà nature et culture*. Paris: Gallimard.

———. 2006. "La fabrique des images." *Anthropologies et sociétés* 30 (3): 167–82. Published online 2007. https://doi.org/10.7202/014932ar

———. 2007. "À propos de *Par-delà nature et culture*." *Tracés: revue de sciences humaines* 12 (May): 231–52. https://doi.org/10.4000/traces.229

Drache, Daniel, Fred Fletcher, and Coral Voss. 2016. *What the Canadian Public Is Being Told about the More Than 1200 Missing & Murdered Indigenous Women and First Nations Issues: A Content and Context Analysis of Major Mainstream Canadian Media, 2014–2015*. Toronto: York University.

Dussart, Françoise, and Sylvie Poirier. 2017. "Knowing and Managing the Land: The Conundrum of Coexistence and Entanglement." In *Entangled Territorialities: Negotiating Indigenous Lands in Australia and Canada*, edited by Françoise Dussart and Sylvie Poirier, 3–24. Toronto: University of Toronto Press.

Escobar, Arturo, David Hess, Isabel Licha, Will Sibley, Marilyn Strathern, and Judith Sutz. 1994. "Welcome to Cyberia: Notes on the Anthropology of Cyberculture." *Current Anthropology* 35 (3): 211–31. https://www.jstor.org/stable/2744194

Gell, Alfred. 2009. *L'art et ses agents: une théorie anthropologique de l'art*. Fabula Collection. Dijon: Les presses du réel.

George, Éric, and Philippe-Antoine Lupien. 2012. "Internet, nouvel eldorado pour la circulation de la production audiovisuelle autochtone?" *Recherches amérindiennes au Québec* 42 (1): 31–40. https://doi.org/10.7202/1023718ar

Ginsburg, Faye. 1994. "Embedded Aesthetics: Creating a Discursive Space for Indigenous Media." *Cultural Anthropology* 9 (3): 365–82. https://doi.org/10.1525/can.1994.9.3.02a00080

———. 2018. "The Indigenous Uncanny: Accounting for Ghosts in Recent Indigenous Australian Experimental Media." *Visual Anthropology Review* 34 (1): 67–76. https://doi.org/10.1111/var.12154

Ginsburg, Faye, and Fred Myers. 2006. "A History of Indigenous Futures: Accounting for Indigenous Art and Media." *Aboriginal History* 30: 95–110. https://doi.org/10.22459/ah.30.2011.08

Green, Joyce. 2007. *Making Space for Indigenous Feminism*. Black Point: Fernwood Publishing.

Guerrero, Jaimes M.A. 2003. "'Patriarchal Colonialism' and Indigenism: Implications for Native Feminist Spirituality and Native Womanism." *Hypatia* 18 (2): 58–69. Published online 2020. https://doi.org/10.1111/j.1527-2001.2003.tb00801.x

Haraway, Donna. 1991. *Simians, Cyborgs and Women: The Reinvention of Nature*. London: Free Association Books.

Harrison, Richard. 2016. "Seeing and Nothingness: Michael Nicoll Yahgulanaas, Haida Manga, and a Critique of the Gutter." *Canadian Review of Comparative Literature / Revue Canadienne de Littérature Comparée* 43 (1): 51–74. https://doi.org/10.1353/crc.2016.0009

Hart, Michael Anthony. 2010. "Indigenous Worldviews, Knowledge, and Research: The Development of an Indigenous Research Paradigm." *Journal of Indigenous Voices in Social Work* 1 (1): 1–16. http://136.159.200.199/index.php/jisd/article/view/63043/46988

Havard, Gilles, and Frédéric Laugrand. 2014. *Éros et tabou: sexualité et genre chez amérindiens et les Inuit*. Quebec: Septentrion

Hine, Christine. 2000. *Virtual Ethnography*. London: SAGE.

———. 2015. *Ethnography for the Internet: Embedded, Embodied and Everyday*. London: Bloomsbury.

IFF (Initiative for Indigenous Futures). n.d. "Workshops" (webpage). Accessed March 17, 2021. http://indigenousfutures.net/workshops/

Ingold, Tim. 2000. *The Perception of the Environment: Essays in Livelihood, Dwelling and Skill*. London: Routledge.

Iseke-Barnes, Judy. 2002. "Aboriginal and Indigenous People's Resistance, the Internet, and Education." *Race Ethnicity and Education* 5 (July): 171–98. https://doi.org/10.1080/13613320220139617

Jérôme, Laurent. 2015. "Les cosmologies autochtones et la ville: sens et appropriation des lieux à Montréal." *Anthropologica* 57 (2): 327–39. https://www.jstor.org/stable/26350444

Jérôme, Laurent, Biroté Christiane, and Jeanette Coocoo. 2018. "Images de la mort et ritualisation du deuil sur les réseaux socionumériques: des usages de Facebook en contexte autochtone." *Frontières* 29 (2): article 1044165. https://doi.org/10.7202/1044165ar

Jérôme, Laurent, and Vicky Veilleux. 2014. "Witamowikok, 'dire' le territoire atikamekw nehirowisiw aujourd'hui: territoires de l'oralité et nouveaux médias

autochtones." *Recherches amérindiennes au Québec* 44 (1): 11–22. https://doi.
org/10.7202/1027876ar

Justice, Daniel Heath. 2008. "'Go Away Water!': Kinship Criticism and the
Decolonization Imperative." In *Reasoning Together: The Native Critics Collection,*
edited by Daniel Heath Justice, Christopher B. Teuton, and Craig S. Womack,
147–68. Norman: University of Oklahoma Press.

Kermoal, Nathalie, and Isabel Altamirano-Jimérez. 2016. "Introduction: Indigenous
Women and Knowledge." In *Living on the Land: Indigenous Women's
Understanding of Place,* edited by Nathalie Kermoal and Isabel Altamirano-
Jimérez, 3–17. Edmonton: Athabasca University Press.

Kohn, Eduardo. 2013. *How Forests Think: Toward an Anthropology Beyond the Human*,
Berkeley: University of California Press.

Lacroix, Laurier. (2012). "L'Art des Huronnes vu par le frère récollet Gabriel Sagard
en 1623–1624." *Cahiers des dix* 66, 323–38. https://doi.org/10.7202/1015077ar

LaRocque, Emma. 2009. "Reflections on Cultural Continuity through Aboriginal
Women's Writings." In *Restoring the Balance: First Nations Women, Community,
and Culture,* edited by Gail Guthrie Valaskakis, Madeleine Dion Stout, and Eric
Guimond, 149–74. Winnipeg: University of Manitoba Press.

Laugrand, Frédéric. 2013. "Pour en finir avec la spiritualité: l'esprit du corps dans les
cosmologies autochtones du Québec." In *Les autochtones et le Québec: Des
Premiers contacts au Plan Nord,* edited by Alain Beaulieu, Stéphan Gervais, and
Martin Papillon, 213–32. Montreal: Presses de l'Université de Montréal.

Laurence, Robin. 2016. "Skawennati Takes Aboriginal Storytelling into Cyberspace."
Straight, 24 August 2016. https://www.straight.com/arts/764706/
skawennati-takes-aboriginal-storytelling-cyberspace

Leavy, Brett, Theodor G. Wyeld, Joti Carroll, Craig Gibbons, and James Hills. 2007.
"Evaluating the Digital Songlines Game Engine for Australian Indigenous
Storytelling." In *Proceedings of the 13th International Conference on Virtual
Systems and Multimedia,* edited by Theodor G. Wyeld, Sarah Kenderdine, and
Michael Docherty, 162–71. Berlin: Springer.

Lewis, Jason Edward. 2014. "A Better Dance and Better Prayers: Systems, Structures,
and the Future Imaginary in Aboriginal New Media." In *Coded Territories:
Tracing Indigenous Pathways in New Media Art,* edited by Steven Loft and Kerry
Swanson, 49–77. Calgary: University of Calgary Press.

L'Hirondelle, Cheryl. 2014. "Code Talkers Recounting Signals of Survival." In *Coded
Territories: Tracing Indigenous Pathways in New Media Art,* edited by Steven Loft
and Kerry Swanson, 138–68. Calgary: University of Calgary Press.

Loft, Steven. 2014. "Mediacosmology." In *Coded Territories: Tracing Indigenous Pathways in New Media Art,* edited by Steven Loft and Kerry Swanson, 170–186. Calgary: University of Calgary Press.

Lumby, Bronwyn. 2010. "Cyber-Indigeneity: Urban Indigenous Identity on Facebook." *The Australian Journal of Indigenous Education* 39 (S1): 68–75. https://doi.org/10.1375/S1326011100001150

Maracle, Lee. 1996. *I Am Woman: A Native Perspective on Sociology and Feminism.* Global Professional Publishing.

Miller, Daniel, Elisabetta Costa, Nell Haynes, Tom McDonald, Razvan Nicolescu, Jolynna Sinanan, Juliano Spyer, Shriram Venkatraman, and Xinyuan Wang. 2016. *How the World Changed Social Media.* London: UCL Press.

Millerand, Florence, Serge Proulx, and Julien Rueff, eds. 2010. *Web social: mutation de la communication.* Quebec: Presses de l'Université du Québec.

Obomsawin, Alanis, dir. 1977. *Mother of Many Children.* Montreal: National Film Board, digital film, 57 min. https://www.nfb.ca/film/mother_of_many_children/

Poirier, Sylvie. 2008. "Reflections on Indigenous Cosmopolitics—Poetics." *Anthropologica* 50 (1): 75–85. https://www.jstor.org/stable/25605390

———. 2016. "Ontologies." In *Anthropen.org*. Paris: Éditions des archives contemporaines. https://doi.org/10.17184/eac.anthropen.035

Proulx, Serge, and Guillaume Latzko-Toth. 2000. "La virtualité comme catégorie pour penser le social: l'usage de la notion de communauté virtuelle." *Sociologie et sociétés* 32 (2): 99–122. https://doi.org/10.7202/001598ar

Proulx, Serge, Mélanie Millette, and Lorna Heaton, eds. 2012. *Médias sociaux: enjeux pour la communication.* Quebec: Presses de l'Université du Québec.

Radin, Paul. 1956. *The Trickster: A Study in American Indian Mythology.* London: Routledge; K. Paul.

Rice, Brian. 2005. *Seeing the World with Aboriginal Eyes: A Four Directional Perspective on Human and Non-human Values, Cultures and Relationships on Turle Island.* Winnipeg: Aboriginal Issues Press.

Sahlins, Marshall. 1993. "Goodbye to Tristes Tropes: Ethnography in the Context of Modern World History." *The Journal of Modern History* 65 (1): 1–25. https://doi.org/10.1086/244606

Shoemaker, Nancy. 1995. "Kateri Tekakwitha's Tortuous Path to Sainthood." In *Negotiators of Change: Historical Perspectives on Native American Women*, edited by Nancy Shoemaker, 49–71. New York: Routledge.

Simpson, Leanne Betasamosake. 2011. *Dancing on Our Turtle's Back: Stories of Nishnaabeg Re-creation, Resurgence, and a New Emergence.* Winnipeg: ARP Book.

————. 2014. "Land as Pedagogy: Nishnaabeg Intelligence and Rebellious Transformation." *Decolonization: Indigeneity, Education & Society* 3 (3): 1–25. https://jps.library.utoronto.ca/index.php/des/article/view/22170/17985

————. 2017. *As We Have Always Done: Indigenous Freedom through Radical Resistance.* Minneapolis: University of Minnesota Press.

Sinclair, Raven. 2009. "Identity or Racism? Aboriginal Transracial Adoption." In *Wicihitowin: Aboriginal Social Work in Canada,* edited by Raven Sinclair, Michael Anthony Hart, and Gord Bruyere, 89–113. Winnipeg: Fernwood Publishing.

Sioui Durand, Guy. 2014. "Un Wendat nomade sur la piste des musées: pour des archives vivantes." *Anthropologie et sociétés* 38 (3): 271–88. https://doi.org/10.7202/1029028ar

————. 2016. "L'Onderha." In "Affirmation autochtone." Special issue, *Inter, art actuel* 122: 4–19. https://www.sodep.qc.ca/wp-content/uploads/2017/03/Inter-Guy-Sioui-Durand.pdf

Slater, Candace. 1994. *Dance of the Dolphin: Transformation and Disenchantment in the Amazonian Imagination.* Chicago: University of Chicago.

Smith, Tuhiwai L. 1999. *Decolonizing Methodologies: Research and Indigenous Peoples.* London: Zed Books.

Stenger, Thomas, and Alexandre Coutant. 2013. "Médias sociaux: clarification et cartographie. Pour une approche sociotechnique." *Décisions marketing* 70: 107–17. https://www.jstor.org/stable/24582919

Toulouse, Léa. 2017. "I Am Woman: The Decolonial Process of Indigenous Feminist Art / Je suis femme: le projet décolonial de l'art féministe autochtone." *Esse* 90: 52–59.

Tupper, Jennifer. 2014. "Social Media and the Idle No More Movement: Citizenship, Activism and Dissent in Canada." *Journal of Social Science Education* 13 (4): 87–94. https://doi.org/10.2390/jsse-v13-i4-1354

Trudel, Pierre. 2009. "La crise d'Oka de 1990: retour sur les événements du 11 juillet." *Recherches amérindiennes au Québec* 39 (1–2): 129–35. Published online 2010. https://doi.org/10.7202/045005ar

Van Woudenberg, Gerdine. 2004. "Des Femmes et de la territorialité: début d'un dialogue sur la nature sexuée des droits des autochtones." *Recherches amérindiennes au Québec* 34 (3): 75–86.

Vigneault, Louise. 2017. "Repenser le temps et l'espace, du wampum au selfie." *RACAR: Revue d'art canadienne / Canadian Art Review* 42 (2): 87–99. Published online 2018. https://doi.org/10.7202/1042948ar

Viveiros de Castro, Eduardo. 2009. *Métaphysiques cannibales: lignes d'anthropologie post-structurales.* Paris: PUF.

Wachowich, Nancy, and Willow Scobie. 2010. "Uploading Selves: Inuit Digital Storytelling on YouTube." Études/Inuit/Studies 34 (2): 81–105. https://doi.org/10.7202/1003966ar

Warschauer, Mark. 1998. "Technology and Indigenous Language Revitalization: Analyzing the Experience of Hawai'i." *The Canadian Modern Language Review* 55 (1): 139–59. https://doi.org/10.3138/cmlr.55.1.139

Watts, Vanessa. 2013. "Indigenous Place-Thought and Agency Amongst Humans and Non-humans (First Woman and Sky Woman Go on a European World Tour!)." *Decolonization: Indigeneity, Education, & Society 2* (1): 20–34. https://jps.library.utoronto.ca/index.php/des/article/view/19145

Wilson, Kathi. 2005. "Ecofeminism and First Nations Peoples in Canada: Linking Culture, Gender and Nature." *Gender, Place & Culture: A Journal of Feminist Geography* 12: 333–55. Published online 2006. https://doi.org/10.1080/09663690500202574

Wilson, Shawn. 2008. *Research Is Ceremony: Indigenous Research Methods*. Halifax: Fernwood Publishing.

Wood, Lesley J. 2015. "Idle No More, Facebook and Diffusion." *Social Movement Studies* 14 (5): 615–21. https://doi.org/10.1080/14742837.2015.1037262

Yahgulanaas, Michael Nicoll. n.d. "Speaking." Michael Nicoll Yahgulanaas (website). Accessed July 17, 2018. http://mny.ca/en/speaking

——. 2015. "Art Opens Windows to Space Between Ourselves." Filmed November 14, 2015 at TEDxVancouver, Vancouver, BC. Video, 14:25. https://youtu.be/u1R_-3wzYEQ

10

HUMAN REMAINS AND INDIGENOUS RELIGIOSITY
IN THE MUSEUM SPACE

*Ritual Relations to the Altaian Mummy in the
Anokhin National Museum of the Altai Republic, Russia*

KSENIA PIMENOVA

THE RETURN OF HUMAN REMAINS from museums to Indigenous
populations as a part of broader processes of postcolonial transformations has attracted a growing body of research in anthropology. Most
of these studies have focused on the phase *preceding* the return, in
particular on the colonial history of collections, the evolution of legal
frames of repatriation, or Indigenous activism and ceremonies of repatriation (Bray 2001; Curtis 2008; Fforde, Hubert, and Turnbull 2002;
Gagné 2013; Nakamura 2018; Turnbull and Pickering 2010). Longer
effects of the repatriation of human remains on Indigenous societies
have somehow not been the focus of this literature, as if repatriation
does not raise internal debates within Indigenous societies—as if these
often complicated stories always have happy endings. This chapter is
an ethnographic contribution to the study of the *post-return* phase from
a religious and ritual angle. It is organized around two main questions:
First, does the return of archaeological human remains that are considered ancestors of Indigenous populations trigger transformations
within Indigenous religiosities?[1] Second, when reburial is impossible
for various reasons and is replaced by museification on Indigenous

lands, how do local museums contextualize human remains and how do they manage the agencies of these unburied dead?

In this chapter, I show how human remains are powerful actors of cosmopolitics that include human and other-than-human beings in a common collective of co-existing subjects (Dussart and Poirier, this volume; Latour 1999; Stengers 2003; S. Poirier 2008). The approach to human remains is also inspired by Katherine Verdery's (1999) seminal work on the political lives of dead bodies that became symbolic vehicles for political and moral change in Eastern Europe after socialism (post-1999). The ancient human remains claimed for return are political symbols, too, since they perfectly embody the conceptions of ancestrality, kinship, and locality, and thus allow for the modelling and remodelling of ethnic, cultural, and religious identities. Yet, as we shall see, human remains and dead persons are more than symbols; they are actors and partners within various ritual practices that evolve in the museums, which become new places of cosmopolitics and ritual creativity.

This chapter begins with a brief outline of the history of the discovery of the Altai Princess mummy and her recontextualization in the Anokhin National Museum of the Altai Republic after her return to Altai. I then move on to an overview of the complex Altaian ethnic and religious funerary traditions, followed by an analysis of lay ritual relations towards the Princess that reveal her complex ontological status. I then draw upon individuals' experiences of communication with the Princess to analyze her role in new ritual careers before shifting my focus to the Anokhin Museum itself as a material and institutional environment that encourages multiple readings of the Princess's persona and ritual relations towards her. The chapter's conclusion outlines the role of the museum as a new space of cosmological reconfigurations and ritual transformations.

Return of Human Remains and Indigenous Cosmopolitics in the Museum

This chapter draws upon the story of the Altai Princess,[2] a 2500-year-old female mummy found in 1993 by Russian archaeologists in an ice-filled grave in the Altai Republic in Southern Siberia, Russia. After the excavations, she was transferred to the Institute of Archaeology and Ethnography (Russian Academy of Sciences in Novosibirsk,

Russia's third largest city and capital of Western Siberia). There, she was studied and displayed for about twenty years. The mummy belongs to the Pazyryk archaeological culture (sixth to third centuries BCE), a branch of the Scythian people of mostly Iranian origins who lived in the Eurasian steppes during the Iron Age. Russian academic archaeologists do not consider contemporary Altaian people to be heirs of the Pazyryk and deny cultural and genetic continuity between these two populations. For them, this particularly well-preserved mummy was a valuable find because of her exceptional state of conservation, which shed new light on the art of tattooing, techniques of mummification, genetics, lifestyles, and commercial networks of the Pazyryk (Molodin, Polosmak, and Tchikicheva 2000). For the Altaian people, however, the Princess was one of them, an unburied ancestor from the sacred land of Altai where, they claimed, she belonged. This entanglement of ancestrality, kinship, and locality is the main feature of the importance of the Princess for the Altaian people, and allows for comparison with other, different uses in the past to affirm and reshape contemporary cultural identities around the globe (see, this volume: Laugrand; Tassinari; Vaarzon-Morel).

In 2012, after almost two decades of protests, the Altai Princess mummy was returned to Gorno-Altaysk, the capital of the Altai Republic. In this problematic return process (Plets et al. 2013), Altaian requests for reburial were rebuffed by academic archaeologists and denied due to her legal status as heritage of the Russian Federation. The museification in Altai was therefore a negotiated compromise to respond to both the claims for her return and the heritage conservation logic. Anokhin National Museum of the Altai Republic in Gorno-Altaysk (figure 10.1) became the repository of the mummy for an indefinite period of time. Today, several years after her return, some Altaian people recognize the museum as a place where she can be both preserved for future science and *at home in Altai*. However, most—including several religious leaders in particular—consider the museification to be only a temporary solution and express a strong wish to see the mummy reburied. Apocalyptic oral narratives continue to depict her as an angry and a vindictive entity who asks for reburial according to Altaian funerary

FIGURE 10.1. The Anokhin National Museum of the Altai Republic in Gorno-Altaisk (Siberia, Russia). The sloped-roof addition on the right side of the building houses the Ukok Plateau exhibition space where the Altai Princess lies. (Photograph by Ksenia Pimenova, 2017.)

traditions and who will send diseases, deaths, and natural disasters such as earthquakes and floods until her wish is granted (Doronin 2016; Pimenova 2019; see also Halemba 2008). These claims for reburial tightly connect human actions to the other-than-human realm, reminding us that Indigenous discourses about the end of times reactivate moral norms.[3] In other words, the return of the Princess to the Altaian museum has been perceived as a good step forward in the recognition of Indigenous cultural rights. For the Altaian people, however, the return of the Princess in this manner failed to entirely measure up to their moral and religious values.

One of the purposes of the ethnographic fieldwork I have carried out in the Anokhin Museum[4] was to understand how visitors and employees relate to the presence of the Altai Princess's body and what meanings they attribute to her persona. Initially, I did not expect to find many ritual practices in the museum since Altaian people have multiple taboos concerning dead people and death itself and do not worship ancestral remains. Neither do they imbue them with any positive power of protection, as Catholics or Orthodox Christians do with the relics of saints. On the contrary, dead bodies and any material traces of death are considered dangerous for the living. The same concerns people's souls—in particular the souls of recently dead people—which can turn into dangerous ghosts who may take the lives of their relatives. Only ritual specialists can deal with the souls of the dead through rituals that aim to expel the souls of the dead from the world of the living. Lay people are not supposed to interact with these beings and should avoid any contact with them. Yet I found that the Princess in the museum attracted a broad spectrum of ritual attitudes and practices. These included strategies of avoidance, but also more positive actions such as verbal communication with the mummy, different ritual gestures, and elaborate offerings.

These gestures and formulas (normally used in other ritual contexts) can be analyzed as processes of establishing relations to the Princess, signs of ongoing ritual transformations. One way to explain this phenomenon is that her presence in the museum challenges Altaian traditions that assume the burials of all remains and their concealment from the public eye. People therefore feel the need to address the Princess in the museum but cannot draw upon funerary traditions. The complex status of the Princess's persona is another way to understand these ritual relations. Since her discovery in 1993, the inhabitants of Altai Republic have considered the Princess to be, at one and the same time, an ancestor of the Altaian nation and a powerful, dangerous, and vindictive dead soul. While establishing their own ritual attitudes toward her body, people also seek to solve complexities and contradictions of her ontological status. Drawing on the relational approach to the ritual (Houseman 2006; Houseman and Severi 2009), I argue here that ritual practices reflect both the complex status of the Princess and the lack of traditional ritualization of the unburied dead person.

The Anokhin Museum also plays an active role in these transformations. It not only recognizes the legitimacy of Altaian interpretations of the Princess's persona but also actively reproduces them. The concept of media cosmology developed by Nepton Hotte and Jérôme (this volume) is helpful here since it "allows for the articulation...between pragmatic actions and Indigenous cosmology." Indeed, the museum takes decisions on exhibition settings and makes implicit and explicit rules of visiting and behaving next to the Princess's remains; cosmological conceptions can here take the shape of material displays and precise actions.

This role of the Anokhin Museum has something to do with its particular nature as a "museum of Self" (*musée de Soi*) using the term proposed by Benoît de l'Estoile (2007). Museums of Self represent and construct the identity of the community (or several communities) in which they are located, in contrast to "museums of Others" (*musées des Autres*), which represent Indigenous cultures as seen by former colonial empires. Western museums of ethnography, most of which fall into the second category, try to fulfill a function of "contact zones," to use James Clifford's (1997) expression, between their mostly Western audiences and the source communities. They have developed a sense of guardianship, implemented Indigenous protocols for the curation of objects, and have also become more receptive to repatriation claims (Morphy 2010; C. Poirier 2011). However, the participative projects within Western museums often encounter limits in the representation of Indigenous meanings (Jérôme and Kaine 2014) and are criticized for reproducing the dissymmetry between the "Western us" and "others" (Boast 2011).

Unlike Western museums of ethnography, the Anokhin Museum is an Indigenous institution, linked to (and dependent on) other cultural and political institutions such as the Ministry of Culture of the Altai Republic. The scenography of the Princess after her return to Altai in 2012 did not actually result from any collaboration with external Indigenous groups. Rather, it stemmed from two converging factors: first, the personal habitus of the employees, most of whom are Altaians or Altaian-born Russians; and second, the instrumentalization of the museum within local political agendas of construction and representation of local ethnic identities. Although Anokhin is bound by Russian heritage law to curate the Princess's remains that Altaian people would rather rebury, these two converging factors informed the museum's recontextualization of the mummy (Myers 2001; Thomas 1991). While recontextualizing the Princess, the museum took into consideration contemporary Altaian perspectives and allowed for the creation of ritual relationships with her within the museum space. In doing so, I argue, the museum has become not only a new location for ritual practices but also an institutional actor that maintains the Princess's religious meanings and shapes ritual change.

Altaian Funerary Traditions:
The Princess between Ghosts and Ancestors

Altai is a Central Asian crossroads located in the southwestern part of Siberia on the borders of Russia, Mongolia, China, and Kazakhstan. The territory of the contemporary Altai Republic has been a Russian colony since the eighteenth century. It is populated nowadays by a majority of Russians, by the Turkic-speaking Altaians (approximately 35%), and by a significant minority of Kazakhs (6%) who live mostly in southern Altai next to the Kazakh border (Russian Federal State Statistic Service 2010). The Altaian people all-together number about 70,000 individuals and are composed of several close ethnic groups who speak dominant southern Altaian languages (Altai-kizhi and Telengits) and other northern ones. The relative unity of different Altaian groups has been shaped by Russian imperial and Soviet policies, though southern and northern groups still display economic, cultural, and ritual differences. Although all the inhabitants of Altai—including the Russians and the Kazakhs—were concerned with the fate of the Princess (Halemba 2008), her story has embodied specific Altaian ethical conceptions and ideas of spiritual power.

Nowadays the main religions practised by the Altaian people are shamanism, the *Ak Jang* (White Faith) movement, and Tibetan Buddhism. These overlap in many ritual areas, but also compete for the role of defining Altaian identity (Halemba 2003). Shamanism is represented in Altai by individual shamans (*kamdar*) and other "inspirational" specialists such as *neme biler ulus* (people who know something) who are able to see or sense the spirits. They all claim a connection with different other-than-human beings that may include evil spirits and souls of the dead. Some Altaian shamans and *neme biler ulus* communicate with the Princess and transmit her messages (Doronin 2016). The contemporary *Ak Jang* religious networks draw upon the legacy of the messianic *Ak Jang* movement (known also as *burkhanism*) that appeared in 1904 and had an anticolonial (i.e., anti-Russian) and antishamanistic dimension. It aimed at reestablishing morality and purifying the Altaian ritual practice and faith from the worship of malevolent entities (Znamenski 2005). Today's *Ak Jang* promotes regular collective rituals, the respect of morality, and customs as the bases of the "Altaian way of life." Some *Ak Jang* leaders have been particularly active in claiming the return of the Princess and her reburial. Buddhism, for its part, is supported in particular by Altaian intelligentsia as an institutionalized religion with clear ritual and moral rules: a quality that puts it in competition with the *Ak Jang* movement (Halemba 2003), but does not exclude shamans and *neme biler ulus,* as they may be inspired by Buddhist ideas and ritual practices or be part of Buddhist networks.

It is important to stress at this point that lay discourses and simple rituals represent a rich domain of spiritual life beyond these three denominations with their specific religious authorities. Lay persons can either endorse or contest discourses and practices of religious leaders. They are traditionally granted the ability to perform simple rituals. While the story of the Altai Princess pushed Altaian shamans and *Ak Jang* leaders to take moral stances and to develop new ritual practices, it also triggered lay ritual agency in, for instance, museums.

The attitude towards dead bodies and death is a point of convergence between these different denominations and between ritual specialists and lay people. Like other Indigenous populations of Siberia and Mongolia (D'jakonova 1975; Delaplace 2008), the Altaians transported their dead to isolated places and put them in shallow graves or left them on the ground to be eaten by wild animals (Toshakova 1978). These burial sites were known and avoided. Soviet funerary reforms introduced the obligation to bury the dead in cemeteries in deep, Russian-style graves, yet traditional conceptualizations of death persisted. Unlike Russians who regularly decorate tombs of their dead relatives, Altaians do not visit cemeteries or burial sites. Contemporary cemeteries, ancient burial places, and sites of fatal road accidents are sites of avoidance.

Regardless of personal affinities with shamanism, Buddhism, or *Ak Jang,* death is tightly linked with the notion of danger. The souls of the dead are believed to wander on earth for a certain period of time and turn into ghosts or evil spirits (*körmös*). They are particularly dangerous for their relatives and neighbours but may also attack persons who are not their kin (Broz 2018). There are numerous techniques poised to disconnect the bond between the deceased and their family. To prevent the return of the dead soul, shamanic rituals called "last meals" are of crucial importance. They are organized forty days after a death. Shamans speak to the deceased and then send the souls away for good from the world of the living to deactivate their danger. The attachment of the dead to the living—and in particular to the living kin—explains why ghosts are the most important figures in the Altaian relationship to death. The concept of ancestors, on the other hand, is much less elaborated and seems to apply only to those remote dead whose memory is pacified by time.

With regard to this distinction, archaeological human remains such as the Altai Princess occupy a complex and uncertain position. They are unburied bodies, and no one knows what rituals (if any) have been performed for their souls. They are perceived, therefore, as animate, still in our world, and gifted with harmful agencies. From this perspective, archaeological digs disturbed the Princess who then became a great danger for all inhabitants of Altai, especially those who live in southern Altai next to the Ukok Plateau.

Her persona, however, has been more positively interpreted by some as an emblem of cultural identity. After the fall of the USSR in 1991, Altaian nationalism appropriated the Pazyryks as a deep history of the Altaians (Mikhajlov 2013). The latter now perceive the former as their ancestors and predecessors either in a narrow genetic sense or more broadly in terms of historic and cultural continuity (Broz 2009). Since the Princess lived and was buried in the sacred land of Altai, she thus shares the mystic essence of "Altaian-ness" with its contemporary inhabitants regardless of their ethnic origins.

These two contrasting perspectives converge towards reburial as a respectful way of treating the Princess as an ancestor and as a way of deactivating the danger she represents as a *körmös*. Since the reburial remains impossible for legal reasons, the presence of the dead body in the museum continuously challenges Altaian funerary conceptions and fosters new ritualizations that reflect the plurality of the Princess's meanings.

Ritual Creativity and Relations with the Princess

Françoise Dussart and Sylvie Poirier (this volume) rightly remind us that "cosmologies are reproduced, transformed, and legitimated through people's experiences, which include dream experiences, rituals, and pragmatic actions." Rituals, rather than beliefs, are therefore one of the main domains of life where the entanglement of cosmological continuities and change can be observed anthropologically. In the studies of rituals, a growing body of research does not consider rituals to be stable and unchanging events, but rather focuses on ritual invention and creativity (see, e.g., Bell 2009; Fedele 2013; Grimes 2000). Forms of ritual creativity can be observed in different confessional and ethnic contexts. This creativity can express itself as an adjustment of existing ritual techniques and tools in political contexts that repress religion, as was the case in Soviet Siberia where pieces of fabric were used as substitutes for shamanic drums (Znamenski 2007, 342). It allows for the new contents created by an individual (e.g., in a dream) to be introduced into existing community rituals (Dussart 2000, 139–76). Ritual creativity is also a means of addressing unprecedented situations of individual or collective life for which no ritual model exists. For example, in Western countries, rituals can emerge when people feel a need for new *rites de passage*, or as a way to relate to the disasters for which no one could be prepared (Grimes 2000, 2003). Other newly invented rituals can also fill in the lack of religious conceptualization, as, for instance, in the case of women's bodily experiences in Christianity (Fedele 2013; Houseman 2007).

The concept of ritual creativity can help us understand how both the Princess's polysemic agencies and the lack of preexisting ritual models in dealing with the excavation of her buried body foster multiple ritual gestures and attitudes. Yet ritual creativity does not mean boundless invention, since rituals are always created from the standpoints of the performers and enact relationships between performers and nonhuman entities. These relationships, as Houseman (2006, 415) puts it, are "an ongoing reciprocal involvement between subjects implying... the attendant qualities of agency, interaction, intentionality, affect and accountability." In other words, when people elaborate attitudes and practices towards the Princess, they classify her as belonging to a certain category of Altaian ontology: dangerous souls of the dead, venerated ancestors, or even entities similar to shamanic spirit-helpers. Relations with the Princess are also reflexive since they build the performers' ritual positions as lay persons or ritual specialists.

Most lay persons engage with three types of ritual relationships with the Princess: avoidance strategies, verbal formulas, and small offerings. Strategies of avoidance correlate with the conception of the Princess as a negative, dark entity, similar to souls of the dead. The degree and form of avoidance are matters of individual decision. Some of the Altaian visitors simply avoid the Ukok Plateau exhibition space where the mummy lies while they enjoy other parts of the museum. Other visitors use different tactics. I observed one visitor, an old woman, move while in the exhibition space in such a way so as to never turn her back to the Princess because it would be "disrespectful and dangerous."

The Altaian employees of the museum display avoidance strategies as well, even though they adapt them to their professional duties. For example, in addition to their daily work, employees take on shifts to switch the lights on and off and to lock and unlock the rooms. Some of them dread when they are assigned to the Ukok Plateau exhibit. In these cases, according to museum guard Anna Meketchinova, some try "to check everything quickly, without looking around much" while others "try not to make any noise while walking."[5] Larissa Tel'denova, a museum curator, reported:

Once during my shift, I just felt unable to open this door and cross the threshold [of the Ukok Plateau exhibition]. I felt as though there were a lump of darkness over there, and that it concerned me personally, like She was angry with me.

When asked what she did in this case, Tel'denova responded:

I waited for the employees of the cleaning service. We usually open all the rooms to let them wash the floor. They entered, cleaned the floor. By the time they finished, I no longer had that dreadful feeling and could do my job.

Another example comes from the manager of the museum shop, A. Yakoyakova, who provides a more detailed account of avoiding the Princess. Although she sells Altaian arts and crafts just over the wall from the Ukok Plateau exhibition space, she has only once ventured in there. Her explanation points to the link between the materiality of death and its danger:

I will never want to be curious. If we, the Telengits [Southern Altaians], know that there is a burial place somewhere, we never approach it. The room feels like a tomb. This is why I will never see the exhibition and won't let my kids go there...Yet I have been asked once to lock the room. I tried not to look around and to do every-thing quickly, then I rushed toward the exit. I got goose bumps! I don't know what I am afraid of. But I do believe the shamans. They say that She is a wandering soul that has not found peace.

This narrative is an example of the typical attitude of Altaian lay persons toward the dead as unhappy and dangerous ghosts who should be avoided at all costs. Yet avoidance is not the only form of lay rela-tions towards the Princess. Museum employees and certain visitors also address her with verbal formulas that they have elaborated. Such communications are unilateral: People do not ask the Princess for favours or active protection and do not expect her to answer. Rather, they acknowledge her presence with the hope that she will not harm them. As Rimma Erkinova, the director of the Anokhin Museum, explained:

> *We, the museum employees, all have a particular attitude to the room. I always say "Hello" [to the Princess]. Not that I speak to Her continuously, as some other employees do, but I greet Her in my thoughts, silently. Some people apologize to Her for the disturbance.*

Small offerings are the third type of lay attitude towards the Altai Princess. They suggest that her status goes beyond the dark and dangerous entity that should be avoided. Some visitors sprinkle milk or spread a few crumbs of the Altaian cheese *kurut* in front of her sarcophagus; others discretely leave coins on the floor. These offerings can be compared to the lay rituals performed for the spirits of the middle world. Like other Indigenous peoples in Siberia, Altaian people venerate different spirits who inhabit the landscape—mountain passes, lakes, springs— and are generically called *jer-su* (earth-water) (D'jakonova 1976). These spirits are not always benevolent; they can be responsible for bad weather, unsuccessful hunting, or car accidents. Yet unlike the dangerous souls of the deceased, no one is scared of them nor would they try to avoid them. They are, rather, seen as partners: capricious yet receptive to respectful offerings such as pieces of coloured fabric (*jalama*), milk, or food. From the perspective of ritual relationships, making an offering to the Princess means that she is seen as a spiritual partner able to restrain her anger in exchange for gifts.

Spiritual Communication, Ritual Reflexivity, and Shamanic Careers

The aforementioned examples of avoidance, verbal formulas, and small offerings define the performers as lay persons with limited ritual competences. They acknowledge the power of the Princess, but do not pretend to communicate with her. The following examples highlight how she can reveal information both to the lay persons and to ritual specialists. They show that in today's Altaian religious landscape, the controlled bilateral communication with the Princess reflexively defines the status of a ritual specialist (rather than a lay person) and can be used as a narrative tool in the construction of such a specialist's ritual career.

In southern Siberian discourses on spiritual power, there is a fundamental difference between shamans (or other inspirational specialists) and lay people. The former are supposed to have something that the latter will never have: a quality known as "origin" or "essence" (Hamayon 1990; Stépanoff 2015). This essence underlies shamans' exclusive connection to their hereditary spirits: the ability to see other spiritual beings and to ask their assistance on behalf of the community. Yet lay persons could become shamans through apprenticeship (Dyrenkova 1930) or after encounters with particular kinds of nonhereditary spirits (Kenin-Lopsan 1987). Lay persons are also able to dream, see, hear, or sense the spirits, though this communication is usually described as frightening, uncontrollable, and incomplete, involving only one sensory channel (Broz 2018; Tyukhteneva 2006; Delaplace 2008). In other words, experiences of sensing the spiritual world can be lived by both lay persons and ritual specialists. For the latter, however, the quality of these experiences and the control over communication with spirits are particularly important since they define the person as a specialist with extraordinary abilities useful for the community.

Three types of experiences with the Princess have been reported to me. They include spontaneous sensations that neither change ritual position of lay persons nor have a practical use, extraordinary experiences that do not change ritual positions of lay persons but have practical uses, and extraordinary experiences that have practical use and correlate with a change of ritual position. Most of the lay visitors and the employees of the museum fall into the first category: when they are inside the museum, they may feel a cold draft, tingling in the body, or the desire to scratch, or they may hear voices and cries. These experiences are perceived usually as negative, correlate with avoidance strategies described earlier, and reflexively confirm these people's definition as lay persons.

The dream of the Altaian lay artist and craftsman Vladimir Monosov falls into the second category. Monosov has been making copies of archaeological objects for the Anokhin Museum for years, and this proximity with the Princess made him particularly sensitive to her ambiguous power:

> *I usually work in my storage room at night... When I was working on the copy of an egret [a hair accessory for a mannequin of the Princess], I fell asleep on the sofa. I don't know if I was really asleep, since I heard dogs barking outside. Suddenly, the door creaked and She entered. She was tall, Her face was blurry and in the dark...She spoke to me in an unknown language. Yet I understood that She was talking about Her egret; it seems that I was copying it wrong. I wanted to wake up, but I couldn't. I got cold from fear. When I finally woke up, there was nobody there and the door was wide open.*

In Vladimir Monosov's dream, the Princess suggested how to correctly copy the egret, and the artist used her advice to modify the accessory. This information not only helped Monosov in his professional activity, but also informed the shape of a museum object, making the Princess's agency more positive and tangible. Yet this experience of communication did not change Monosov's ritual position, and his reaction to her apparition is described, as is typical for lay persons, as frightening and confusing.

Finally, ritual specialists display other emotional reactions to the communication with the Princess and establish with her relations that they claim to control. The following example illustrates how a ritual specialist in the early phase of her career conceptualizes the Princess as a helping entity and establishes with her a personal connection.

I met Karakys,[6] an Altaian woman in her thirties, in the Ukok Plateau room in contemplation in front of the Princess's body. Karakys stated: "I am here on Her request. She is staying next to me right now...She has tears on Her face and is smiling at the same time. She is the spirit of this place, She continuously goes back and forth in the room, and everyone is afraid of Her." As many other Altaians, Karakys was convinced that the Princess should one day be reburied, and never had a wish to visit the museum before. Yet she recently dreamed of the Princess asking her: "Why does everyone come to see me, except you? Come and visit me in the museum!" In the dream, the Princess offered Karakys a hawk that she later tattooed on her shoulder as a way of materially representing this gift. While in the museum, Karakys was surprised to see a stuffed hawk at the feet of the mannequin representing the Princess (figure 10.4) and interpreted this coincidence as more proof of their deep connection. Many features of this report are reminiscent of the relationship between shamans and their helping spirits in Siberian traditions, which comprises interaction, reception of the spirits' messages and gift, and the spirit's materialization, as well as pilgrimages to sites where the spirits could be easily encountered.

Her fearless contact with the Princess is part of the bigger pattern of Karakys's attitude toward the dead. According to her autobiographic narrative, she acquired the capacity to see the dead in the first days of her life. Her mother had a terrible car accident just before delivery, and the baby—Karakys—was wrongly declared dead. She remained in the morgue for a few days. By chance, an Elder preparing her body for burial realized that she was alive. Her miraculous rescue made Karakys sensitive to the presence of the dead. Karakys has seen them since her early childhood and played with them "as they were my best friends." Yet she rejects the identity of shaman (*kam*) because she does not perform most shamanic rituals and does not have shamans among her ancestors. Karakys instead defines herself as a "person who sees other persons" (*kizhi köör kizhi*) whose speciality is to connect the living and the dead.

Karakys has recently met with people who wanted to hear from their dead relatives. Her clients are often relatives of those who died a violent death, and did not find answers in shamanic funerary rituals, the last meals. During these rituals, shamans communicate with the souls of the deceased and transmit their messages to the family, then send them away from the world of the living to prevent their return. In contrast, Karakys's technique is a reconfiguration of Altaian funerary tradition. Rather than making a ritual fire in the countryside, she calls out dead people at her kitchen table and speaks to them while drawing tiny circles and lines on a sheet of paper that her clients burn after the consultation. Karakys's consultations are confidential and follow her clients' own wish to communicate with their relatives outside the framework of collective shamanic rituals. Karakys also invokes the Princess, but only for important matters and only for herself: "The Princess does not like to be bothered with everyday matters." This affirmation is another way to stress both the importance of the Princess's ambiguous power and Karakys's ability to initiate the communication.

Through these ritual relationships, the Princess appears as a multi-faceted entity that oscillates between different categories of Altaian ontology. She is a frightening ghost for some lay persons, a spirit-like entity for others, and, for ritual specialists, a sort of helping spirit embedded into their self-presentations and practices. In ritual pragmatics, her figure is used both to confirm ritual statuses and to transform them in the process of constructing ritual careers.

Multiple Meanings of the Princess in the Museum

Most of the experiences and practices described above are related to the presence of the Princess's body in the Anokhin Museum and take place within its walls. It is therefore legitimate to question the role of the museum both with regard to the materiality and the agencies of the Princess's archaeological human remains and in terms of how it shapes religious meanings and practices. The problematic of religion in museums has attracted a growing literature, in particular on the representation of religious meanings of objects in museums and on living religions in museum spaces (Grimes 1992; Paine 2013; Buggeln, Paine, and Plate 2017). Archaeological displays may raise questions of whose religion they represent: past cultures or present populations (Zuani 2017)? The Anokhin Museum, for instance, builds its scenography on ideas related to contemporary Altaian identity and cosmology rather than on information about Pazyryk funeral practices. In this section,

FIGURE 10.2. The entrance to the Ukok Plateau exhibition space at the Anokhin National Museum. (Photograph by Ksenia Pimenova, 2017.)

I show how a medium (here a museum) can materialize cosmological ideas through its particular actions and decisions, as well as its material settings such as architecture and scenography.[7]

When the Altai Princess returned to Gorno-Altaysk in 2012, the Anokhin Museum committed itself to the legal obligation of preserving her body as scientific evidence for future research, but also produced a scenography coherent with the Altaian interpretations of her persona. This double task of recontextualization was all the more complicated since the material presence of the body is in contradiction with Altaian funerary traditions described earlier. The museum acknowledged the importance of the funerary issues at the early stages of the negotiations preceding the return of the Princess from Novosibirsk in 2012. A particular architectural space called Ukok Plateau was purpose-built within the permanent exhibition between 2008 and 2011. It occupies an entire side wing of the museum and serves as the Princess's mausoleum (Erkinova 2013). In contrast with the other parts of the permanent exhibition, which have clear pedagogical aims, the setting of the Ukok Plateau[8] keeps the academic explanations of Pazyryk archaeology to a minimum. Instead, it provides visitors with an experiential context and gives them relative freedom of interpretation. To access the Ukok Plateau exhibition space, visitors have to take a long staircase leading down to the exhibition (figure 10.2). The space is dark and silent (with the exception of mysterious, soft music playing in the background) and extremely cold. As Sergei Kireev, the Altai-born Russian archaeologist and museum curator who conceived of the space, explained, this is "both to guarantee the conservation of the body and as a means of museology." The descent to a darker place and the sense of cold create the feeling of being underground.

Further on, the visitors can observe an impressive diorama of a mannequin (representing the dead Princess) in a coffin and a man (representing a ritualist) standing nearby. The scene, as visitors can imagine, takes place a few minutes before the tomb is closed. It can be best seen from above, as if they were observing her funeral from the edge of her burial mound (figure 10.3). Visitors can read the scene either as an archaeological reconstruction or as a ritual action. In this latter perspective, the Ukok Plateau exhibit space enacts the reburial of the Princess that many Altaians still wish for.

The museum also acknowledges the Altaian ideas about the link between the archaeological past and the present. Two mannequins—one representing the Princess dead, the other alive (figure 10.3)—have slightly Asian features and black hair, as contemporary Altaians do, and Altaian visitors identify with the Princess as their ancestor. These materialized ideas of continuity are in sharp contrast with the prevalent academic arguments that consider the Princess to be a European-looking woman of Indo-Iranian descent.

The public display of the Princess's body has been a political issue since her return to the Altai Republic. Before her return in 2012, discussions on the possibility of displaying the mummy to the visitors

FIGURE 10.3. Mannequins of the Altai Princess representing her dead and alive. The reconstructions of the Princess's features suggest her physical resemblance to contemporary Altaians. (Photographs by Ksenia Pimenova, 2017.)

involved Altaian Elders and high-ranking politicians from the Ministry of Culture of the Altai Republic. They concluded that public display was against Altaian funerary traditions. Many museum employees shared this point of view, and between 2012 and 2016 only the closed sarcophagus containing the mummy was available for public viewing (figure 10.4). Yet in 2016, under the double pressure of Russian tourists who wanted to see the mummy and some Altaians who doubted her return,[9] the Anokhin Museum (n.d., para. 6) decided to soften its policy in order "to respect the constitutional right of citizens to access objects of cultural heritage of the Russian Federation" (my translation). Now the sarcophagus is open on certain dates advertised in advance on the museum website, but *exclusively* on the crescent moon. The visitors thus have a choice of satisfying their curiosity or avoiding the spectacle of the dead body.

The display on the crescent moon has been an attempt to find a compromise between universalist values of heritage and local traditions. Many Altaian rituals follow the lunar calendar so that ritual specialists address benevolent entities on the crescent moon and ambiguous and dangerous entities on the waning moon. This double temporality reflects the activity of nonhuman entities: benevolent spirits are supposed to be more receptive to human demands at the beginning of lunar cycle, while dangerous ones are more receptive, and also more harmful, at the end. The decision of the museum to display the Princess on the crescent moon stresses her positive qualities. It also means concealing her body on the waning moon; thus, the museum implicitly reproduces Altaian interpretations of the Princess as a dangerous entity whose agency has to be contained. It also creates new, unsolvable issues with regard to funerary traditions since lunar cycles do not apply to human remains, which are the objects of permanent prohibitions. The Princess's display creates a conundrum between different areas of Altaian ritual traditions (funerary versus others) and reveals the limits of a compromise between heritage values and religious logic.

The recontextualization of the Princess according to religious ideas also concerns the way employees mediate visitors' attitudes toward the mummy. The museum does not formulate any explicit rules in the Ukok

FIGURE 10.4. The closed sarcophagus of the Altai Princess.
(Photograph by Ksenia Pimenova, 2017.)

Plateau room so that different ritual and nonritual behaviours are,
in principle, possible. Yet some of the visitors' attitudes are marked as
inappropriate. Anna Meketchinova, the attendant of the room and an
Altaian woman in her sixties, prevents long and close observation of the
mummy, laughing, loud comments, and quick movements, which are
considered disrespectful. She sometimes expresses concerns for visitors'
safety, disapproving of children's presence and recommending that
pregnant women cover their head. These two groups are indeed seen as
vulnerable and are expected to avoid dangerous rituals or to take

FIGURE 10.5. Alena Argokova, an employee of the Anokhin National Museum, shows the silk and felt outfit donated to the Altai Princess by a visitor from Kazakhstan. (Photograph by Ksenia Pimenova, 2017.)

precautions. The attendant has a permanent appointment in the Ukok Plateau room and implements the museum's implicit policy of visitors' interactions with the mummy. Her personality and her attitude are reminiscent of the figure of an Altaian Elder whose role is to guarantee the respect of authority, morality, gender roles, and customs.

Conversely, museum employees encourage expressions of ritual creativity by visitors as long as they are considered respectful. The attendant and other employees of the museum are curious of the visitors' narratives and take time to discuss with those who perform rituals to the Princess. The director and the curators have invited ritual specialists—shamans and *Ak Jang* representatives—to purify the museum space and to perform rituals of pacification. They also carefully store some of the visitors' ritual offerings to the Princess, such as coloured silk fabrics (a traditional ritual gift to highly venerated persons) and a beautiful female outfit donated by a visitor who discovered his extraordinary abilities and felt that spirits were pushing him to make a rich offering to the Princess (figure 10.5).

A visit to the museum can therefore generate different experiences: one can participate in the Princess's (re)burial, identify with her as an ancestor, and feel grief and compassion, but also danger. Different ritual relations are also possible such as avoidance, offerings, and communication. The museum leaves the choice of interpretation and ritual relation to visitors, and thus maintains and reproduces the polysemy of the Princess. On the other hand, the museum limits external interpretations of the Princess. It clearly gives priority to various (and sometimes contradictory) Altaian interpretations of the mummy rather than to scientific discourse on Pazyryk culture produced within Russian academic networks. This implicit hierarchy of meanings informs the museum's architecture and scenography and continues to shape Altaian perceptions of the Princess.

Conclusion

This chapter explored the fate of the Altai Princess mummy after her return to local museums and the longer effects of this repatriation on Altaian religiosity. From this point of view, the Anokhin Museum can be compared to Te Papa Tongarewa Museum in New Zealand, which hosts repatriated Māori remains that cannot be identified with any particular kin group and thus cannot be reburied (Alderton 2014). Indeed, both museums preserve human remains to keep future research possible and integrate Indigenous values into their settings. Te Papa, for instance, provided a sacred space with restricted access for ancestral remains to respect Māori conceptions of kinship and vital energy within remains. The Anokhin Museum followed a similar, yet less radical, path, conceiving of the Ukok Plateau space as a public mausoleum for the Princess and restricting the visibility of her body instead of access to the whole space. In both cases, the repatriation fostered public reflection on cultural rights and positively impacted Indigenous identities.

Both cases, however, also reveal the limits of compromises between Indigenous ethics and the universalist values of museums in contemporary societies: in the Anokhin case, tensions focus on the public access to heritage; in the Te Papa case, they are concerned with women's access and issues of gender equality (Alderton 2014). The anthropological interest in repatriations of human remains can therefore contribute to a better understanding of the philosophical, ethical, and practical challenges that face different museums when they deal with religiosity as a living phenomenon. These interactions and frictions between Altaian cosmology and the cultural logic of heritage preservation can be seen as examples of what Dussart and Poirier (this volume) call "'entangled religiosity' as the local co-existence and management of plurality." Such entanglements question the nature of the museum as a secular, presumably "religiously neutral" institution and show on the contrary the reenchantment of the museum.

The Princess's return was motivated by preexisting Altaian ethical ideas, traditions, and interpretations of the Princess's persona. Yet the material presence of her body in the museum has triggered ritual creativity, pushing people to further elaborate relationships with the Princess. What this elaboration looks like depends on their perception of her agencies and their own ritual status. The examples analyzed here show how lay persons and ritual specialists materialize, through their gestures and discourses, the Princess's shifting conceptualizations as a respected ancestor, a dangerous being, or a helping entity.

As a result, the custody of the Princess's body transformed the museum into a new centre of religious life, a place of ambiguous pilgrimage attracting some Altaians and repelling others. If the Anokhin Museum remains a public cultural institution and does not pretend to have religious authority, this very quality paradoxically makes it an actor of ritual and cosmological transformations. Indeed, the museum avoids any fixed religious discourses and endorses multiple meanings of the Princess. The Ukok Plateau exhibit space is conceived in a way that generates various experiences and practices, forms of perception, identification, and appropriation of the Princess as an Altaian treasure. Rather than keeping the religion as an ethnographic object in display cases, it becomes a new actor in the evolution of practices and conceptions of spiritual power.

Author's Note

In Altai Republic, I would like to thank the director of the Anokhin National Museum, Rimma Erkinova, as well as museum visitors and employees who accepted my presence and became my research partners: in particular, Sergei Kireev, Emilija Belekova, Vera Kydyeva, Alena Argokova, and Anna Meketchinova. This fieldwork has been supported by the Musée du quai Branly (Paris). This chapter was finalized thanks to the post-doctoral grant of the Fonds de la Recherche Scientifique (F.R.S.-FNRS Belgium). I am grateful to my colleagues Frédéric Keck, Jessica De Largy Healy, Grégory Delaplace, Felicity Bodenstein, Pierre Petit, and Manon Istasse, with whom I discussed earlier versions of this chapter. My sincere gratitude as well to Sylvie Poirier and Françoise Dussart for their helpful insights and suggestions, which greatly improved the text.

Notes

1. Like Françoise Dussart and Sylvie Poirier (this volume), I prefer the concept of religiosity over that of religion because it better refers to dynamic changes and creativity in ritual and cosmological domains. Religion, on the other hand, is reserved to more or less institutionalized bodies of ritual specialists.

2. "Altai Princess" is a colloquial yet inaccurate name for the mummy. There is indeed no archaeological evidence of royalty, and the precise social role of this relatively wealthy woman remains unknown. Here, I follow my Altaian informants from the museum who prefer the Russian name *Princess* as a respectful way of referring to the remains. The Altaian names *Ak Kadyn* (White River Kadyn, after the main Altaian river) and *Otchi-bala* (a woman-warrior from Altaian epic) are also broadly used in Altaian-speaking religious milieus outside the museum.

3. For a discussion of end-of-time narratives among the Kaingang of southern Brazil, see Crépeau (this volume).

4. Ethnographic interviews in this chapter were conducted in Gorno-Altaisk in March 2017 among the museum employees and visitors, Altaian officials, and ritual specialists.

5. I have translated this and all other personal communications from Russian.

6. The name has been changed at the request of the informant.

7. For an account of this subject in the context of online and digital media, see Nepton Hotte and Jérôme (this volume).

8. The setting of the Ukok Plateau was conceived by Altai-born Russian archaeologist and curator Sergei Kireev.

9. Some of Altaian visitors asked, "How we can be sure that She returned if we can't see Her body?"

References

Alderton, Zoe. 2014. "The Secular Sacred Gallery: Religion at Te Papa Tongarewa." In *Secularisation: New Historical Perspectives*, edited by Christopher Hartney, 251–79. Newcastle upon Tyne: Cambridge Scholars Press Publishing.

Anokhin Museum. n.d. "Eksponirovanie mumii" (Displaying the mummy; webpage). Accessed April 20, 2021. http://musey-anohina.ru/index.php/component/k2/item/403

Bell, Catherine. 2009. *Ritual: Perspectives and Dimensions*. New York: Oxford University Press.

Boast, Robin. 2011."Neocolonial Collaboration: Museum as Contact Zone Revisited." *Museum Anthropology* 34 (1): 56–70. https://doi.org/10.1111/j.1548-1379.2010.01107.x

Bray, Tamara L., ed. 2001. *The Future of the Past: Archaeologists, Native Americans, and Repatriation*. New York: Garland.

Broz, Ludek. 2009. "Substance, Conduct and History: 'Altaianness' in the 21 Century." *Sibirica: Interdisciplinary journal of Siberian studies* 8 (2): 43–70. https://doi.org/10.3167/sib.2009.080202

———. 2018. "Ghost and the Other: Dangerous Commensalities and Twisted Becomings." *Terrain* 69 (April). https://doi.org/10.4000/terrain.16623

Buggeln, Gretchen, Crispin Paine, and Brent Plate. 2017. *Religion in Museums: Global and Multidisciplinary Perspectives*. London: Bloomsbury.

Clifford, James. 1997. *Routes: Travel and Translation in the Late Twentieth Century*. Cambridge: Harvard University Press.

Curtis, Neil. 2008. "Thinking about the Right Home: Repatriation and the University of Aberdeen." In *Utimut: Past Heritages—Future Partnerships: Discussions on Repatriation in the 21st Century*, edited by Mille Gabriel and Jens Dahl, 44–54. Copenhagen: Greenland National Museum & Archives.

D'jakonova, Vera. 1975. *Pogrebal'nyj obrjad tuvincev kak istoriko-ètnografičeskij istočnik* (Funerary ritual of the Tuvans as historical and ethnographic source). Leningrad: Nauka.

———. 1976. "Religioznye predstavlenija altajcev i tuvincev o prirode i čeloveke" (Altaian and Tuvan religious representations of nature and human being). In *Priroda i čelovek v religioznyx predstavlenijax narodov Sibiri i Severa*, edited by I.S. Vdovin, 268–91. Leningrad: Nauka.

de l'Estoile, Benoît. 2007. *Le goût des autres: de l'exposition coloniale aux arts premiers*. Paris: Flammarion.

Delaplace, Grégory. 2008. *L'invention des morts:* sépultures, fantômes et photographie en Mongolie contemporaine. Paris: EPHE.

Doronin, Dmitry. 2016. "Chto opyat' ne tak s 'altajskoj printsessoj'? Novye fakty iz njuslornoj biografii Ak Kadyn" (What is wrong again with the "Altaian Princess"? New facts from the newslore biography of Ak Kadyn). *Sibirskie istoritcheskie issledovanija* 1: 74–104.

Dussart, Françoise. 2000. *The Politics of Ritual in an Aboriginal Settlement: Kinship, Gender and the Currency of Knowledge*. Washington: Smithsonian Institution.

Dyrenkova, Nadezhda. 1930. "Polučenije šamanskogo dara po vozzrenijam tureckix plemen" (Acquiring the shamanic gift according to representations of Turkic populations). *Sbornik Muzeja Antropologii i Ètnografii pri Rossijskoj Akademii Nauk* 9: 267–91.

Erkinova, Rimma. 2013. "Iz istorii nacional'nogo muzeja: Kak pomogla Princessa Ukoka" (On the history of the national museum: How the Ukok Princess helped us). In *Anokhinskie tchtenija*, edited by Rimma Erkinova, Emilija Belekova, and Tatiana Polteva, 132–36. Gorno-Altaïsk: Muzei Anokhina

Fedele, Anna. 2013. *Looking for Mary Magdalene: Alternative Pilgrimages and Ritual Creativity at Catholic Shrines in France*. Oxford: Oxford University Press.

Fforde, Cressida, Jane Hubert, and Paul Turnbull. 2002. *The Dead and Their Possessions: Repatriations in Principle, Policy and Practice*. New York: Routledge.

Gagné, Natacha. 2013. "Musées et restes humains: analyses comparées de cérémonies maori de rapatriement en sols québécois et français." *Journal de la Société des Océanistes* 1–2 (136–37): 77–88. https://doi.org/10.4000/jso.6984

Grimes, Ronald. 1992. "Sacred Objects in Museum Spaces." *Studies in Religion / Sciences religieuses* 21 (4): 419–30.

———. 2000. *Deeply into the Bone: Re-inventing Rites of Passage*. Berkeley: University of California Press.

———. 2003. "Ritualizing September 11." In *Disaster Rituals: Explorations of an Emerging Ritual Repertoire,* edited by Paul G.J. Post, Ronald L. Grimes, Albertina Nugteren, P. Pettersson, and Hessel J. Zondag, 199–13. Leuven: Peeters.

Halemba, Agnieszka. 2003. "Contemporary Religious Life in the Republic of Altai: The Interaction of Buddhism and Shamanism." *Sibirica* 3 (2): 165–82. https://doi.org/10.1080/1361736042000245295

——. 2008. "What Does It Feel Like When Your Religion Moves Under Your Feet? Religion, Earthquakes and National Unity in the Republic of Altai, Russian Federation." *Zeitschrift für Ethnologie* 133 (1): 283–99. https://www.jstor.org/stable/25843151

Hamayon, Roberte. 1990. *La Chasse à l'âme: esquisse d'une théorie du chamanisme sibérien*. Nanterre: Société d'ethnologie.

Houseman, Michael. 2006. "Relationality." In *Theorizing Rituals: Issues, Topics, Approaches, Concepts*, edited by Jens Kreinath, Jan Snoek, and Michael Stausberg, 413–28. Leiden: Brill.

——. 2007. "Menstrual Slaps and First Blood Celebrations: Inference, Simulation and the Learning of Ritual." In *Learning Religion: Anthropological Approaches*, edited by David Berliner and R. Sarro, 31-48. Oxford: Berghahn Books.

Houseman, Michael, and Carlo Severi. 2009. *Naven ou le donner à voir: essaie d'interprétation de l'action rituelle*. Paris: CNRS-Éditions, Éditions MSH.

Jérôme, Laurent, and Elisabeth Kaine. 2014. "Représentations de soi et décolonisation dans les musées: quelles voix pour les objets de l'exposition C'est notre histoire. Premières Nations et Inuit du XXIe siècle (Québec)?" *Anthropologie et sociétés* 38 (3): 231–52. https://doi.org/10.7202/1029026ar

Kenin-Lopsan, Mongush. 1987. *Obrjadovaja praktika i fol'klor tuvinskogo šamanstva: konec XIX – načalo XX veka* (Ritual practices and folklore of the Tuvan shamanism: End of XIX – beginning of XX century). Novosibirsk: Nauka.

Latour, Bruno. 1999. *Politiques de la nature*. Paris: La Découverte.

Mikhailov, Dmitrii. 2013. "Altai Nationalism and Archeology." *Anthropology & Archeology of Eurasia* 52 (2): 33–50. Published online 2014. https://doi.org/10.2753/AAE1061-1959520203

Molodin, V.I., N.V. Polosmak, and T.A. Tchikicheva. 2000. *Fenomen altajskikh mumij* (Phenomenon of the Altaian mummies). Novosibirsk: Institut arkheologii i ètnografii SO RAN.

Morphy, Howard. 2010. "Scientific Knowledge and Rights in Skeletal Remains: Dilemmas in the Curation of 'Other' Peoples' Bones." In *The Long Way Home: The Meaning and Values of Repatriation*, edited by Paul Turnbull and Michael Pickering, 147–62. New York: Berghahn Books.

Myers, Fred. 2001. "Introduction: The Empire of Things." In *The Empire of Things: Regimes of Value and Material Culture*, edited by Fred Myers, 3–64. Santa Fé: School of American Research Press.

Nakamura, Naohiro. 2018. "Redressing Injustice of the Past: The Repatriation of Ainu Human Remains." *Japan Forum* 31 (3): 358–77. https://doi.org/10.1080/09555803.2018.1441168

Paine, Crispin. 2013. *Religious Objects in Museums: Public Lives and Public Duties*. London: Bloomsbury.

Pimenova, Ksenia. 2019. "Un paradis à reconquérir: critique sociale et utopie traditionnaliste dans les discours sur la 'Princesse altaïenne'." In *La Sibérie comme paradis*, edited by Samson Normand, Dominique de Chambourg, and Dany Savelli, 271–96. Paris: Centre d'Etudes Mongoles et Sibériennes.

Plets, Gertjan, Nikita Konstantinov, Vassili Soenov, and Erick Robinson. 2013. "Repatriation, Doxa, and Contested Heritages: The Return of the Altai Princess in an International Perspective." *Anthropology & Archeology of Eurasia* 52 (2): 73–98. https://doi.org/10.2753/AAE1061-1959520205

Poirier, Claire. 2011. "Drawing Lines in the Museum: Plains Cree Ontology as Political Practice." *Anthropologica* 53 (2): 291–303. https://www.jstor.org/stable/41473880

Poirier, Sylvie. 2008. "Reflections on Indigenous Cosmopolitics—Poetics." *Anthropologica* 50 (1): 75–85.

Russian Federal State Statistic Service. 2010. "Vserossijskaja perepis' naselenija – 2010" (All-Russia census – 2010). http://www.gks.ru/free_doc/new_site/perepis2010/croc/perepis_itogi1612.htm

Stengers, Isabelle. 2003. *Cosmopolitiques II*. Paris: La Découverte.

Stépanoff, Charles. 2015. "Transsingularities: The Cognitive Foundations of Shamanism in Northern Asia." *Social Anthropology / Anthropologie Sociale* 23 (2): 169–85. https://doi.org/10.1111/1469-8676.12108

Thomas, Nicholas. 1991. *Entangled Objects: Exchange, Material Culture, and Colonialism in the Pacific*. Cambridge: Harvard University Press.

Toshakova, E.M. 1978. *Tradicionnye tcherty narodnoj kul'tury altajcev (XIX – nachalo XX v.)* (Traditional features of the popular culture of the Altaians [XIX – beginning of XX centuries]). Novosibirsk: Nauka.

Turnbull, Paul, and Michael Pickering. 2010. *The Long Way Home: The Meaning and Values of Repatriation*. New York: Berghahn Books.

Tyukhteneva, Svetlana. 2006. "Zemlya moego snovidenija" (The land of my dream). *Etnografitcheskoe obozrenie* 6: 31–37.

Verdery, Katherine. 1999. *The Political Lives of Dead Bodies: Reburial and Postsocialist Change*. New York: Columbia University Press.

Znamenski, Andrei. 2005. "Power of Myth: Popular Ethnonationalism and Nationality Building in Mountain Altai, 1904–1922." *Acta Slavica Iaponica* 22: 25–52.

———. 2007. *The Beauty of the Primitive: Shamanism and the Western Imagination*. Oxford: Oxford University Press.

Zuani, Chiara. 2017. "Archaeological Displays: Ancient Objects, Current Beliefs." In
    Religion in Museums: Global and Multidisciplinary Perspectives, edited by
    Gretchen Buggeln, Crispin Paine, and Brent Plate, 63–70. London: Bloomsbury.

11

SHAMAN, CHRISTIAN, BUREAUCRAT, COP

Maya Responses to Modern Entanglements

C. JAMES MACKENZIE

Introduction

On January 18, 2002, about a year into my doctoral fieldwork in
Guatemala, customs officials saw fit to separate me from my car (or
"research vehicle," as I referred to it in the formal correspondence and
paperwork that followed). Up until that point, I had been making regular
trips to the border—a few hours from my field site of San Andrés Xecul
in the Western Highlands—to renew the monthly permissions that
customs habitually extended to my well-travelled 1990 Toyota 4Runner.
Each permission would take up a full page in my passport by way of a
complex stamp festooned with numbers, sundry declarations, and
signatures. My initial worry was that I would run out of pages in my
passport before my research period concluded, but on this day, apparently, the jig was up. My car had been in the country too long, I was
informed, and I must either leave with it for good or pay the corresponding import taxes, which amounted to its full Kelley Blue Book
value (about USD 5000), with no reference to its general condition or
mileage. I was also given the option to leave it impounded and try to
sort out an exemption. After discussions with the head customs official
at the border in which I tried to impress upon him the arbitrariness
and various irrationalities of this rule (while obliquely determining if a

bribe might be in order), I embarked upon my bureaucratic quest for special consideration.

This lasted twelve weeks, during which time I assembled an impressive dossier comprised of letters of support from various institutions and a growing stack of paperwork that attached itself to my petition as it wound its way through sundry government offices. I spent much time in Guatemala City and the regional customs office in Quetzaltenango navigating a byzantine officialdom and attempting to shore up support from other ministries: Migration approved a student visa, which, I reasoned, solidified my claims concerning the "research vehicle." Midlevel officials from INGUAT (Instituto Guatemalteco de Turísmo, the national tourism institute) lent a sympathetic ear and promised to do what they could in the interest of preventing other foreign visitors from suffering such travesties. All was, alas, for naught as the final ruling simply ordered me to pay the taxes forthwith, offering no further explanation. Choosing to ignore this decree and brandishing instead an earlier piece of official paper which said, conversely, that I could take the car out of the country rather than pay the assessed duties, I headed back to the border. My "research vehicle" spent seven months in Mexico until I managed to successfully bring it back (through a different border crossing) for a final month at the end of my fieldwork, just in time for my return to Canada.

When discussing these problems with Xuan Chuc Chan,[1] a respected shaman[2] and key consultant for my research in Xecul, I mused that perhaps Guatemala's then-president, Alfonso Portillo, was behind it all. "Couldn't we do a little witchcraft to mess with him?" I joked. "Of course we could!" came the immediate—and wholly sincere—reply. I gently protested, reminding Xuan that he had always assured me that he never dabbled in what he called, in K'iche' Maya, *itzb'al* (sorcery). He quickly clarified things, noting that the ceremony would be by the books—if a bit more robust than usual—arguing that an offensive approach was in order because my cause was clearly just. "Besides," he added, "Portillo probably has dozens of witches working for him."

Before long, plans were in place for us to head to the powerful *encanto*[3] of Juan No'j, located in the volcanic landscape of Cerro

Quemado near Quetzaltenango. On the appropriate day, we headed to the site: a long tunnel that ends in a steep cliff plunging to uncertain depths, the eponymous home of a powerful and capricious Earth Lord (*rajaw juyub'*). Carving out space for a fire ceremony[4] along the length of the tunnel, Xuan prayed confidently for my Toyota, invoking a whole range of deities: Indigenous, such as Uk'ux kaj (Heart of Sky) and Uk'ux ulew (Heart of Earth); Catholic, such as Jesucristo and the Celestial Father; and, it would seem, bureaucratic, including Secretario Mundo (Secretary of the Holy World), helpful especially for petitioners such as myself. President Portillo did get a critical mention: "This guy has millions, this evil president! What is he trying to do anyway? So, give us some strength and do us a favour!" After an hour or so, we made our way back into the sunlight, bathed in waxy smoke from copal incense fires. While we were too late with the ceremony to influence the outcome of my initial petition, Xuan encouraged me to consider the long game: he was certain the way was clear for me to bring the car back into the country temporarily when it was time for me to leave Guatemala. And so it was.

This event has led me to consider more broadly the ways Indigenous Guatemalans confront bureaucratization through religious techniques. A number of anthropologists have called for renewed attention to bureaucracy, with recent research focusing on civil servants and their procedural cultures, intersections with citizens, and the paperwork itself (Bernstein and Mertz 2011; Heyman 2012; Hull 2012; Mathur 2015; Vohnsen 2017).[5] The ideas of Max Weber remain central in these and related discussions, especially those that explore the promises, failures, and ambiguities of modernity as it takes hold in particular contexts. Weber, of course, considered the ideal-typical modern bureaucracy as operating under a formal-rational legal authority characterized by depersonalization, which arises with the separation of the office (the "means of administration") from the officeholder. More fundamentally, he defined this form of organization as "domination through knowledge" (Weber 1978, 225). While the modern bureaucrat may not be free to change the rules in order to serve their personal interests, their unique experience with the workings of the system, acquired over time, culminates in a personalized knowledge that can be deployed in ways that, at a minimum, guarantee or advance their own position and status, making substantive change in the system difficult or impossible. This was the "rule of officialdom" that Weber (2005, 206) warned about, made possible through bureaucracy's congenital obsession with secrecy. While he considered this form of organization the most technically efficient and in a basic sense necessary to modern capitalism and the state, he also saw it as the hardest to kill, with only the entrepreneur and politician cast as potential forces to check its dominance (Swedberg 2005, 20). In this version of modernity, religion is no match for such awesome powers.[6]

Still, I want to suggest some elective affinities between bureaucracy and religion, which help frame the perspectives of the Indigenous Guatemalans I consider below. While few would express an overt love of bureaucratic procedures, as David Graeber (2015, 205) has argued, there is an appeal in the utopian model of "a world where everyone knows the rules, everyone plays by the rules, and—even more—where people who play by the rules can actually still win." Of course, as both Weber and Graeber document in detail, this is not how actual bureaucracies tend to operate, much less in a place like Guatemala. While Weber emphasized the importance of the "office secret" to bureaucratic domination (such that everyone clearly does *not* know the rules, or at least not all of them), Graeber (2015, 185–86) suggests the effects of secrecy are paradoxically reproduced in the very transparency of contemporary bureaucratic procedures (the "fine print") given that they are presented in a language few can understand, and at such length that they seem designed to be ignored. In short, this world—for all its utopian appeal—depends upon and generates incomprehensibility and stupidity (Weber 1978, 993). Still, it does not seem a stretch to detect an air of transcendence in a system that formally enshrines impartiality, equality, and fairness, promoting the public good and limiting self-interest: a utopian model of and for our modern reality.

In the contexts I explore below, a critique emerges that speaks to the heart of the experience of modern bureaucracy—in particular how its goals and values often seem arbitrary, or at the very least incontestable in terms that might take into account one's own circumstances. The two vignettes I share below feature Xeculenses who, in different ways, adopt an ambivalent relationship to modernity as expressed in the concept of entangled religiosities theorized by Dussart and Poirier (this volume). In short, their perspectives are less likely to routinely assume the instrumental effectiveness of Weberian formal-rational or rule-oriented behaviour, opting instead for persuasive action, which can involve direct, personalized appeals to, and relationships with, powerful figures—often divinities of some description who may be approached through embodied ritual and dreams—to achieve pragmatic, particular, and collective ends. These appeals also draw upon secret knowledge derived from one's cumulative experience interpreting the hidden signs that dot the landscape of daily sociability with human and nonhuman subjects or persons, alerting the attentive to all manner of danger and opportunity including ways to conjure spaces of freedom from modern bureaucratic entanglements. Traditionalists, or *costumbristas* as they generally self-identify, are most explicit about the value of *secretos* (secrets) and use this term most generally to describe virtually any practice, formula, or experience that is thought to have some concrete and pragmatic effect in achieving a particular goal.[7]

Before presenting these cases, it may be useful to review the nature of the religious landscape in Guatemala, and in San Andrés Xecul in particular. At least since the 1950s, the institutional hegemony of the Catholic Church has been challenged by the growth of Protestantism (Garrard-Burnett 1998). In response, the Catholic hierarchy began a program of "reevangelization" from the 1950s through to the 1970s, relying in particular upon lay organizations—primarily Catholic Action—with an aim to establish a more orthodox version of Catholicism, often targeting practitioners of traditional religion, called *costumbre* (custom) (Brintnall 1979). This religion, which includes aspects of Catholic cere-monialism (including saint worship), is the product of centuries of ambivalent exposure to Christianity. While often characterized as "syncretic," it is generally thought to have strong roots in pre-Hispanic Maya cosmology and practice, including shamanism (Carlsen 2011; Cook 2000), and reflects the sort of cosmological openness that

Dussart and Poirier (this volume) discuss. Historically, it also under-girded the so-called cargo system or civil-religious hierarchy—common throughout Mesoamerica—which consisted of a series of ranked offices who saw people, especially men, serving a year in a saint society followed by a year in the local government (Mongahan 2000, 40–41). The arrival of Protestantism and more orthodox versions of Catholicism in Indigenous communities represented more than a strictly religious transformation, challenging these local authority structures.

In San Andrés Xecul, the religious landscape at present includes a number of competing and overlapping factions (MacKenzie 2016). *Costumbristas* remain strong and maintain an ambivalent relationship with Catholicism. Most Xeculenses, including shamans, identify as Catholic, and though not all self-identifying Catholics approve of the work of shamans or *costumbre* in its strongest form, there is greater tolerance among non-Charismatic Catholics for these practices.[8] Protestantism is expressed through various forms of Pentecostalism, with the Charismatic Renewal and some related movements within the Catholic church encouraging a comparable spiritually "enthusiastic" (MacKenzie 2016, 121–72) style of praise.[9] The position of the local Catholic church towards these sorts of movements varies depending on the sensibilities of the resident parish priest, though the tendency through the years has been to offer cautious support rather than actively encourage their growth. Xecul was also the site of a somewhat unique experiment in Catholic evangelization from the mid-1970s to the mid-1980s, a period that bookends the genocidal violence of the state's counterinsurgency campaign. The resident priest at this time, himself K'iche' Maya, sought to include aspects of *costumbre* and Maya culture and spirituality in the local liturgy through a theological program that has since been labelled "inculturation." Practitioners of traditional religion in recent decades have been presented with an additional choice: to reject any connection with Christianity by adopting an anti-syncretic version of their faith generally referred to as "Maya Spirituality." A growing number of Xeculenses are sympathetic to this rationalized and "purified" version of shamanism, and can find legitimation through some small, local organizations and larger national-level associations of *Sacerdotes Mayas* (Maya Priests), as leaders in this movement usually identify (MacKenzie 2016, 221–66). With this thumbnail sketch of the religious landscape in place, I turn now to my first case study.

The Shaman and the Health Inspector

Octaviano is a farmer, merchant, and shaman in his seventies who has long been active in community and religious associations in Xecul, serving on a number of Catholic saint societies as well as municipal development committees. When we spoke in the Fall of 2014, he described how he came to accept his shamanic vocation—commonly referred to as a "cross," likening this fate to Christ's burden—due to troubles with alcohol that led to near constant fights with his wife. After consulting with local shamans, a consensus emerged that he needed to accept this destiny if he wanted to live a tolerable life. Following his apprenticeship in the early 1970s, which included a number of ceremonies at particular mountainside altars, Octaviano received his divining bundle, cross,[10] and incense burner on the Maya calendar date 8 B'atz, after a midnight ceremony at the town's public altar, *Calwar* (Calvary). This was followed by a morning visit to the Catholic church, where additional prayers were offered and the church bell was struck in a particular pattern in public recognition of the event. He regretted that this didn't happen anymore—a consequence of, as he put it, "all the religions," referencing the emergence of the plural religious landscape sketched above.

As Octaviano described it, while his public initiation marked the start of his shamanic career, much remained to be learned. Most importantly, his mentor only explained the rudiments of divination to him on the final day of his initiation. Subsequently, it took him a good deal of time and experimentation to learn to effectively count the calendar days using the red *tz'ite'* seeds[11] from his diviner's bundle and interpret what his blood was telling him during these divinations, through twitches and shudders in various parts of his body.[12] Through the years, he came to better understand the nature of his "cross" and perhaps how it differed from that of other shamans, some of whom he suggested dabbled in witchcraft. He noted that in his case he has maintained a very strict concern with purity and righteousness. This stance, he reasoned, has made for a mutually beneficial relationship with the *nawales*[13] who send him dreams, which offer signs that help him to avoid traps and court good luck in his waking life. Octaviano's experience mirrors that of most other shamans of his age and background I have known, in particular his insistence that constant vigilance is needed to detect signs (*señas*) that signal potential misfortune in dreams or in daily life. As he explained,

> *A disaster can come. For example, with a rabbit. If it goes by on the left, it's bad, but if it goes to the right it's nothing—just passing by. It's important to pay attention to whatever animal that comes and crosses your path...It's got meaning. Also, with dogs: if a dog comes along and it defecates in front of you, you have to be careful as there's a disaster coming.*

This concern with uncovering the hidden meanings and signals behind otherwise innocuous experiences is widespread among *costumbristas*, reflecting a Maya variant of the perspectivist cosmological system documented in other parts of the Americas (Viveiros de Castro 1998; Pitarch 2010; Vilaça and Wright 2009; MacKenzie 2016).

A basic tenet of perspectivism holds that different subjects or persons derive their outward appearance from the perspective of the person who is doing the viewing. This is typified in the Amazonian view that jaguars see each other as humans, and see "humans" as prey, with "bodies" more generally often likened to clothing (this volume: Colpron, Tassinari). Indeed, according to Viveiros de Castro (1998, 482), "clothing is a body." Concern is thus lavished upon "what these clothes do rather than what they hide." Indeed, what they "hide"—a common human subjectivity—is not the subject of much attention. Rather, what is of interest is a person's surface body, which is "their distinctive equipment, endowed with the affects and capacities which define each animal" (Viveiros de Castro 1998, 482).[14] In this relational cosmology, bodies and appearances are not, however, stable (Tassinari, this volume). *Costumbristas*, like Octaviano, share this point of view, often noting that the messages they receive from animals are right there on the surface and are noteworthy either because they conform to communicative behaviour established by precedent (and codified as a *seña* or *secreto*) or because they differ in some way from the expected behaviour of the subject. In many cases, the meaning of an encounter with an animal exhibiting unexpected behaviour is further revealed through dreams in which the erstwhile nonhuman person will appear as a human and communicate their message in more straightforward terms (MacKenzie 2016, 70–72). *"Tiene su secreto"* (It has its secret) is a common way these meanings—potentially offered by a range of persons (including, most commonly, saint images), particular stones, and aspects of the natural landscape (including certain animals)—are signalled. Secrets in the *costumbrista* context, however, are designed to be revealed, openly discussed, and continually revisited as important tools to interpret shifting intersubjective encounters with a broad range of beings.[15] While contemporary shamans are most often concerned with managing these relationships for individual clients,[16] *costumbre* also has a communal dimension, where the fate and protection of the town as a whole is the objective of ritual labour.

While such communal practices were more institutionalized in the past—and in particular communities such as Momostenango where shamans occupy official positions that carry public ritual responsibilities (Tedlock [1981] 1992)—it is not uncommon for contemporary *costumbristas* to conflate the wellbeing of individual clients with that of broader collectives. As Octaviano suggested:

> *It's not just for us, but for all the neighbours and the people and the municipality and the department and the Capital. So that violence calms down and ends. That's the work we do. We don't just* pedir *[petition/pray] for our own things or for our families, forgetting the others; it's not that way. You have to* pedir *for the town and everyone. This is it. This is the ceremony we do. First, we say what it is we've dreamed, then we'll pray for others right up to the Capital so that there will be peace. This is our work.*

Still, the Guatemalan state—glossed here as "the Capital," or Guatemala City, which is the seat of national government—and its officials of various stripes are more likely than not considered agents of discord, disruption, and straightforward violence in the daily lives of Xeculenses. Octaviano described how local shamans would regularly organize and pray together during the genocidal violence of the late 1970s and early 1980s, to help protect their youth from forced military recruitment, and the town itself from pretty much any questionable encroachment by the Government. "The Government" is not, however, considered a faceless abstraction, but is made concrete and embodied in specific powerful persons:

> Sometimes the president comes, or the governor, whoever...So, they arrive. But the Sacerdotes Mayas, they get together and do a ceremony so that these people don't enter the town or the neighbourhood. This way they aren't permitted to grab the young men to make them soldiers. Because in the past, they would come and beat people up...So the Sacerdotes Mayas would get together and do a little k'otzij [ceremony] with candles and everything, and ask the ajaw [owner, lord] that this not be permitted, so that the military people forget things, and don't arrive. So, whatever the situation is as I've been told, when these people come and they have it in their mind that they're going to plant something here, or build something, or do whatever it is that they want—whatever thing the government or Governor of Totonicapán is thinking—the shamans hear this and they say, "No, it isn't good that this situation should arise. Let's do a little k'otzij so that these people calm down and they don't think about it again." So, they do this so that people don't enter the town and neighbourhood.

This led Octaviano straight into a more specific story he had been told, linking the overt violence of the state with the violence inherent in its more daily bureaucratic functions. Enter the health inspector:

Before, you used to slaughter cows in your own house to sell locally when the animal was ready to butcher. So, there are some animals that aren't as good—there are different grades here, right? So, the health inspector [sanidad] comes along and takes the meat and throws it to the dogs. He doesn't allow it to be sold. What he does is really troubling. So, then people thought, "This isn't good. We've got money in this, and they throw our money away! Who cares if there's just a little dirt on the meat? What should you do? Just wash it! But they'll grab you and throw you in jail and say it's not good." So, with meat, with just a little defect they throw it out. So, the people said, "We should do a ceremony for this." So, they'd do a little ceremony. And when these guys [health inspectors] came over the mountains, the dogs came out and mauled them. They turned around right there on the path and they didn't come back! That calmed things down! So, the ceremony works. It's not just nothing. There are lots of religions that have arrived and say that we're just throwing our money away,[17] that this stuff doesn't work. But it depends on the person.

As Graeber (2015, 61) notes, in most of the rural places where anthropologists have tended to study, modern state bureaucracy is often viewed as an alien and violent imposition—sometimes benevolent, but generally coercive. Its attentions are likewise often sporadic and unpredictable. In Mesoamerica, Eric Wolf's (1957) much discussed closed corporate peasant community model was conceived as a historical response to and buffer against colonial power, which included the development of local bureaucratic institutions (the civil-religious hierarchy mentioned above) that shaped local lives while engaging with (and ideally minimizing) extractive demands of state government and private enterprises.[18] The coercive power of civil governments of decades past is strongly remembered in Xecul. "*Te pasó la muni?*" (Did the town hall stop by?) is still a common joking refrain that men will hear after getting a haircut—particularly a short one—referencing those times past when local authorities, scissors in hand, might accost an unlucky resident to ensure their tonsorial appearance reflected community standards. Still, this sort of coercion and violence is understood differently from that of the state in its various incursions into Xecul.[19] Receiving an unexpected haircut, being obliged to work cleaning the streets, painting public buildings, or being jailed and fined for anything from public drunkenness to a refusal to take on a civil or religious cargo mandated by the local hierarchy: these are all coercive acts, but they tend to be remembered by Xeculenses as reasonable, or at least comprehensible, given the ostensibly shared nature of the values these actions enforced. These acts aimed to produce particular kinds of humans: those oriented towards each other and the broader natural and spiritual ecology (including animals, saints, and ancestors) in ways that would help guarantee the existential continuity of their town through respect for custom (Carlsen 2011; Cook 2000).

Of course, custom and tradition doesn't serve everyone's interests equally, and few Xeculenses these days would put up with a forced haircut or mandatory "volunteer" service for religious or civil authorities. Political and religious pluralism and increased cosmopolitanism—lumped into a bundle of processes Xeculenses themselves gloss as "modern"—have not, however, displaced attachments to Xecul as the prime site for the kind of interpretive labour that defines most social relationships in both their harmonious and conflictive dimensions. Such relations demand "a constant and often subtle work of imagination, of endlessly trying to see the world from the others' points of view" (Graeber 2015, 68). As Graeber (2015, 67) notes, a key goal of modern bureaucracies is to replace this difficult (but productive) work of imagination with a system that formally detaches means from ends and effectively replaces imagination and communication with the threat of force.

Thus, Xeculenses saw no point in dealing with health inspectors or other state officials in the same way they may have dealt with their neighbours (human, animal, or divine) or even their own bodies as potential sources for concealed information that might be marshalled to influence relationships. As typifies situations of structural inequality, those who are dominated do not expect their oppressors to see the world from their point of view and must find more oblique ways to influence matters (Graeber 2015, 69–72). This may include, as Octaviano suggests, engaging potentially sympathetic divinities who can help make it so the oppressor doesn't see you at all: either forgetting you exist or deciding you're just not worth a confrontation with an aggressive pack of dogs. In either case, what is sought is the kind of relative autonomy that Dussart and Poirier (this volume) discuss. But Xeculenses, of course, are not nearly so parochial that cutting off the rest of the world is seriously entertained in more general terms. As with Indigenous people throughout the Guatemalan highlands, they have long been involved in extralocal networks of trade, economic migration, pilgrimage, and, increasingly, education and tourism, not to mention all manner of engagement with global popular culture through the expected channels (Carlsen 2011, 171–87; MacKenzie 2016, 269–313). So how might bureaucratic entanglements be managed beyond one's community?

The Christian and the Traffic Cop

One solution emerged from a somewhat unexpected source, during an interview in 2014 with Gerardino, a shop owner in his fifties who converted to Pentecostalism in his early teens after being orphaned and raised by his older brother (who had converted previously). His late father, a shaman, had left his divining bundle and related paraphernalia with Gerardino, who—not knowing what to do with this stuff—stored it under the roof of the house he had inherited. While nominally religious through his teens, he dropped his Christian beliefs as a young adult in a pique of independence defined by a brief period of debauchery, but soon returned, repentant, to his congregation. Though reconciled with his church, Gerardino—as with many other Pentecostal converts who shared their testimonies with me—found that the devil wasn't finished with him. He was subjected to persistent and terrifying visits by a *sub'enel*: a term that tends to refer to either a shape-shifting witch or some other malevolent spirit that generally appears as an animal. In his case, it took the form of a cat that tormented his family at night and proved impossible to catch. Following a prayer session with the congregation gathering at his house, he was finally able to catch the animal and kill it with repeated blows to the head and a stick inserted in its anus—such being a traditional *secreto* to dispatch these creatures, who, he noted, have their heart in that part of their body. He threw the corpse in a nearby ravine but was worried when it was no longer there in the morning.

While his family experienced peace for a couple of weeks, the problems began again with strange sounds emanating from the ceiling of his home. They put up with the noises for a while, but as things got worse—tables and chairs moving around and sewing machines working on their own at night—he consigned his fate to God and organized another domestic prayer session with his church to help divine the cause of these attacks. Three days prior to this ceremony, Gerardino received a dream from God, which revealed the source of his problems. He dreamed of a tiny image of Ximón, also known as Maximón or San Simón—a popular saint strongly associated with witchcraft by Christians as well as some *costumbristas* (MacKenzie 2009)—hidden in the rafters of his house. He confronted this image in his dream, declaring that he owed it nothing and that it had no right to bother him. Still dreaming, he brought the Ximón effigy to his patio and sat on it, after which it disappeared. A few days later, following the prayer meeting at his home, the pastor asked if there might be some object in his home causing these problems. Remembering his father's divinatory paraphernalia, he delivered it to church leaders for proper disposal. With this, he reported three decades of domestic peace, aided by his ability to detect otherwise hidden messages from God that protect him from difficulties and ensure his family's health.[20] For Gerardino, the pragmatics of his faith are highlighted through the instrumentally effective power of sincere Christian prayer, experienced corporeally—including, as with shamans, through dreams. Indeed, the notion that dreams are important occasions for communication with deities is broadly accepted in Xecul, across confessional lines.[21] As Dussart and Poirier (this volume) say, dreams represent one of a number of "sources of knowledge, power and change...for dealing with the imponderables of life."

Other parallels between Pentecostal and shamanic worldviews are, of course, rather clear here. Indeed, Gerardino's tale of an attack by a *sub'enel* is one of the most detailed and dynamic examples I have recorded in Xecul. The encompassment of traditional ideas like this within a Pentecostal framework may be understood as a kind of "ontological preservation" in Joel Robbins's (2004, 128–29) terms, though the way religion is experienced here—particularly the attention paid to bodies and the interpretive work put into identifying threats to one's relationships and wellbeing—suggests other affinities with some aspects of *costumbrista* cosmology. In explaining the global rise in Pentecostal and Charismatic Christianity, especially in the context of Indigenous (or animist/shamanic) communities, it has been common to highlight such correspondences or interpret religious conversion in terms that stress the indigenization, and hence local differentiation, of this form of Christianity, downplaying its more global features (Robbins 2004, 118; Martin 1990, 140). Still, as Robbins (2004, 126–27) rightly cautions, a lack of precision often accompanies such searches for correspondences, which, if overstated, can downplay the very real cultural transformations that conversion provokes. The obvious point is, not least, that while Pentecostals may accept the ontological reality of key aspects of traditional cosmology, they do not accept the "normative presuppositions" (Robbins 2004, 128) of that world—for example, the possibility that good results can be obtained from petitioning *nawales* (Earth Lords and Saints)—and instead routinely demonize it. Still, as concerns possible continuities with *costumbrista* sensibilities, a shared stress on an embodied (rather than overtly theologized or rationalized) experience of divinity combined with pragmatic expectations concerning prayer and ritual—especially in the context of health and familial wellbeing—forms a common substrate between these cosmologies and a shared basis for dispute (MacKenzie 2016, 161–64). These religiosities are thus "entangled" as Dussart and Poirier (this volume) theorize, with the specific grounds of entanglement experienced and contested largely in corporeal terms.

In the case of *sub'enel*, it is worth noting that these beings are also considered malevolent in the shamanic context, and Gerardino's methods in dealing with the intruder were thoroughly traditional, employing *costumbrista* "*secretos*." Of course, as the subsequent problems with his late father's divining paraphernalia reveal, the demonization of *costumbre* is much more thoroughgoing, and was expanded to include a general rejection of public Catholic ceremonialism, especially the veneration of saint images. This is a very common, perhaps universal, aspect of Pentecostal discourse in Xecul, with the treatment of saints marking a key boundary defining their affiliation. While, as noted above, Catholics may themselves be either supportive of or ambivalent towards shamanism, Pentecostals have less cause to make sharp distinctions between these religions. The construction of a strong boundary in these terms was key aspect of Gerardino's experience of Pentecostalism, which demands a radically dualistic[22] and repeatedly ritualized rupture with previous social and cultural worlds (Robbins 2004, 127). The Pentecostal life requires continuous maintenance in individual terms (maintaining a stringent moral asceticism) but is also defined by a generally heightened participation in and material support of communal church activities, which amounts to a reconfiguration of one's relation with key subjectivities—including human and nonhuman persons—and a sacralization of time in dualistic terms, positing a sharp "before" and "after" that define the conversion experience. Christopher Chiapparri (2015, 130–31) argues that in the Pentecostal context these nonhuman persons include key Christian divinities (deities of the Trinity as well as Satan) and, in certain contexts, autochthonous "Territorial Spirits" (for those who practise Spiritual Warfare) and the Bible itself (to the extent that it is given agency to "speak" to adherents and effect transformations in their lives). The dualistic sacralization of time[23]—the need to live a life of "constant prayer," a commonly stated goal among Pentecostals and Charismatic Catholics in Xecul—is rewarded by familial and social peace and good health.[24] In this respect, the ritual techniques of Pentecostalism are framed as instrumentally effective, with success interpreted as proof of one's salvation.

This brings us to the ways these rituals can be marshalled to decidedly more mundane and pragmatic ends outside the boundaries of the community and its particular social and religious entanglements.

Gerardino followed up his story about shape-shifting witches and revelatory dreams with the following narrative:

There was a time when I was driving [a motorbike] without a licence, and in the newspaper there was something saying that there's a 500 quetzal[25] fine for this. One day at a corner there was a check stop, right there! I didn't have a licence: I had an expired one about a year old. When I came around the corner, I was right in the middle of the road, and I couldn't go back. What to do? "God! God help me. You know how I am, you will help me." So, I said this to God: just that he help me.

I came to the check stop and they said "Stop." Fine, I stopped. I had my helmet, my gloves, and my goggles, and I took them off. I started to open my jacket to take out my papers. The policeman came and said, "Do you have papers?" "Yes," I said. "You can continue."

Who did this work, at this moment, if it wasn't God? When this happened, and they said I could continue, I felt that I had just had a cool refreshing drink—I felt this way, because I knew how it was with my papers.

The next time...well, as we get lazy sometimes, I hadn't dealt with the paperwork. In a couple of weeks, the same thing happened to me, and I thought, "This time I'm not going to say, 'My God, help me!' and let's see what happens." How did this go? I figured they'd just let me go like they did before, because I had my helmet and gloves and such. I thought, "They'll let me by." But this time? Forget it! "Stop! Get off your bike and get your papers ready!" I waited until the last minute when I had to take out the papers, and they said, "You've forgotten to bring your licence. You don't have your licence." So, forget it. They fined me 300 quetzals. I trusted in the helmet, but not in God. So, the first time I believed in God and said, "Lord, help me! You know how I am, and I know you'll help me." And the Lord helped me in that moment. But it depends on our faith with him. Whatever moment and place he'll be with you, whatever instant and whatever place, he'll always be with us.

Even a brief, sincere Christian prayer like "God help me" leaves a bodily trace when its effects are registered—akin to a cool refreshing drink—though the magic that was worked on the regulation-enforcing cop suggests a further critique of bureaucratic logic. Gerardino knew that the laws had changed, that valid licences were now required, and that fines would be issued should one fail to comply. I did not get the sense, however, that he felt a licence itself was personally necessary or particularly useful—he knew perfectly well how to drive a motorbike, and how to do so safely with his goggles, gloves, and helmet. Rather, this was just another more or less arbitrary law resulting in more paperwork and the potential for fines—not unlike Octaviano's assessment of the stupidity of regulations concerning proper hygiene for home butchers. What we have when the policeman decides, with a nudge from God, to simply trust that Gerardino possessed the correct paperwork is an unexpected case of a bureaucrat doing a little interpretive labour rather than coldly and impersonally enforcing a rule.[26] Gerardino, after all, wasn't breaking any obvious laws—he was dressed as a motorcyclist should and, we can assume, not driving dangerously. By choosing to simply trust that the paperwork was in order, the cop treated this encounter as a fleeting kind of social relationship—granted, one with clear positive benefits for his interlocutor, but a relationship nonetheless, based on communication. In effect, in a small way he "knew" Gerardino in the same way God knew him—as an honest, hardworking, and good man who could be trusted. God, of course, also knew that he didn't have a valid licence, and while it may be expected that this close call might motivate him to get one, Gerardino's interpretation of the encounter suggests otherwise.

The real magic here was the pragmatic effectiveness of prayer in transforming a bureaucratic relationship into something more recognizably human, approximating to a certain degree the relations of care that Vaarzon-Morel (this volume) describes for the Warlpiri. As noted above, Pentecostals widely consider Christian prayer in instrumental and pragmatic terms, especially when it addresses issues of health and familial security. That Gerardino eventually got caught up by the cops is not explained as a punishment from God for failing to get his paperwork in order after a divinely ordained second chance. Rather, it is rooted in his failure to believe in and call upon God that second time. Relying upon his appearance alone—helmet, goggles, and gloves— to produce a similar effect, he found himself instead dealing with a regular old bureaucrat asking for a piece of identification and issuing steep fines. Xeculenses (and many other Guatemalans) have rarely entertained a positive image of police, though they have managed to limit their influence and potential disruption within the town itself: kicking them out for a year, monitoring them closely since, and doing much of the basic work of law enforcement themselves through volun- tary security committees.[27] When venturing outside the community, as most Xeculenses do regularly, the potential to influence or otherwise reason with police is of course reduced, though as Gerardino's expe- rience suggests, where reason and talk may fail, pragmatic Christian prayer can succeed in securing some "relative autonomy" (Dussart and Poirier, this volume; Keane 1997).

Conclusion

In short, we have here two cases where the seemingly arbitrary and absolute power of bureaucracy is either diffused or transformed through the application of spiritual techniques. It seems that the experiences that bureaucracy produces are particularly susceptible to these sorts of efforts. As noted above, both shamans and Evangelicals are, in some- what different ways, concerned with interpreting signs the world provides to ward off hidden dangers and help secure one's safety and health, as well as that of important relations. This takes place through interactions with nonhuman persons who are, like them, concerned with producing concrete results. That the perils of bureaucracy are readily counted among such dangers by two otherwise mutually antag- onistic religions may relate to the opacity and mystery that bureaucracy generates. Again, as Weber (1978, 992) stressed, a central aspect of bureaucracy, in a disenchanted world of modernity, is the professional control of information: "Bureaucratic administration always tends to exclude the public, to hide its knowledge and action from criticism as well as it can." In this light, Octaviano's and Gerardino's experiences

can be seen as a critique or reenchantment of this state of affairs, realized with ritualized feats of imaginative labour. The imaginative quality
of this work makes it no less real; rather, the work is directed, as Graeber
(2015, 68) notes, towards considering, and ideally influencing, the
perspectives of powerful, if professionally indifferent, Others. Clearly,
bureaucrats are not the only ones who deal in secrecy, though both
shamans and Pentecostals understand that a secret is only useful once
shared. It is in sharing and communication more generally—among
costumbristas discussing various strategies and techniques useful in
navigating a cosmos where fates and subjectivities are endlessly tangled,
and among Pentecostals who narrate testimonies that record their more
absolute spiritual victories, both cosmic and mundane—that subjectivities are formed and reformed through relations with key human and
nonhuman persons. That both shamans and Pentecostals highlight
the value of dreams in their spiritual labour is worth noting, as dreams
seem to represent a key embodied resource in the imaginative
construction of more human worlds, however those are conceived.

| Xuan died in 2006, before I had a chance to see him again after I
safely entered and left the country with my Toyota one final time in
2002. Fate did, indeed, catch up to then-president Alfonso Portillo,
who ended up serving prison terms in Guatemala and the United
States after fleeing to Mexico to evade corruption charges immediately following his presidential term. Curious about the fortune of the
less famous officials I had unsuccessfully petitioned during my own
bureaucratic struggles, a web search informed me that several had
likewise been imprisoned on corruption charges. I can picture Xuan
smiling: "You see! This stuff works!"

Author's Note

Some of the materials developed in this chapter were first presented in a paper at the
American Anthropological Association meeting in Denver, Colorado in November
2015. I am grateful for the thoughtful comments of the editors of this volume,
Françoise Dussart and Sylvie Poirier, who helped both reframe the argument in
important ways and clarify the ethnographic data. The key ideas I develop here were

inspired through my participation in the conference session "Indigenous Contemporary Religiosities: Between Solidarity, Contestation, Convergence and Renewal" organized by the editors, which took place in Lausanne, Switzerland as part of the 34th meeting of the International Society for the Sociology of Religion. Funding for the research upon which this chapter is based was provided by the University of Lethbridge Research Fund.

Notes

1. As I note below, Xuan has since died, but he expressed his wish to be named in my work. I provide pseudonyms for other consultants whose perspectives I consider below.

2. In Mayanist literature, *shaman* is a common gloss for a type of religious specialist familiar with the workings of the 260-day sacred calendar used in divination through sortilege of *tz'ite'* (coral tree) seeds and during fire ceremonies performed at various sacred locations (often in natural settings). In K'iche', these specialists tend to be referred to as *ajq'ijab'*—often translated as "daykeepers" in reference to the centrality of calendrics in their practice. In recent years, with the rise of Maya cultural activism, these specialists are commonly called *guias espirituales* (spiritual guides) or *Sacerdotes Mayas* (Maya Priests) in Spanish.

3. This is a common Spanish gloss used by Maya for key sacred sites in the landscape generally marked by stone altars where ceremonies are held. They are more generally referred to as *mundos*—the dwelling places of chthonic deities or Earth Lords who are considered owners of resources, animals, and wealth (Cook 1986, 141).

4. The immolation of copal incense and a variety of other offerings is a standard of Maya ceremonialism in Guatemala. In K'iche', these rituals are referred to as *k'otzij* (offerings; flowers) and tend to take place at mountainside or more public community altars, depending on the location. While the form of these ceremonies varies, they tend to be considered occasions during which deities are fed and petitions for particular causes are presented (MacKenzie 2016, 98–107)

5. Pimenova (this volume) describes a comparable case where museum bureaucracy and protocols in a Russian context are modified to adapt to the interests of a diverse set of Indigenous perspectives, which minimized, in that case, the erstwhile hegemonic scientific discourse to create an emergent and flexible ritual space for repatriated remains.

6. The tendency for religion itself to become bureaucratized through the "routinization of charisma" and the ascendance of the priest over the prophet is a well-known aspect of Weber's thought. Indeed, Bourdieu (1991, 22–31),

applying his field theory to religion, takes up the tension Weber establishes between the prophet and the priest, characterizing the former as spiritual entrepreneurs and the latter as bureaucrats.

7. These goals can be as mundane as keeping a pet kitten from running away (*secreto*: snip some of its whiskers and place them under your stove) or as important as attracting a spouse (*secreto*: get an image of Saint Anthony, stand it on its head, and make your petition).

8. A survey I conducted in 2002 identified 78.2% of Xeculenses as Catholics. Among Catholics who were not themselves also shamans, opinions on the work of these religious specialists were split between positive (42.5%) and neutral (44.2%), with only 13.3% characterizing their practices as unambiguously evil.

9. My survey identified 22.3% of Xeculenses as Pentecostals and another 13.1% of Catholics identified as members of movements such as the Charismatic Renewal. While in some contexts Charismatic Catholicism is described as more accepting of certain autochthonous cultural expressions, such is not the case in Xecul or more broadly in Guatemala—at least as far as explicit valuation of key aspects of *costumbre* is concerned. Indeed, as I note elsewhere (MacKenzie 2016, 169n23), official publications from the Guatemalan Catholic Charismatic Renewal are explicit in their satanization of shamans, diviners, Maximón (see "The Christian and the Traffic Cop," this chapter), and particular sacred altars that are key in shamanic practice. This is also reflected in my survey, where rejection of shamanism as unambiguously evil was much stronger among Catholic members of the Charismatic Renewal and associated movements (70.4%) and Pentecostals (82.2%) than among Catholics in general (see note 8, above).

10. In addition to its use as a metaphor for a shamanic vocation, many shamans in Xecul receive a small, wooden cross image, which they keep on their home altar following their initiation.

11. See note 2, above.

12. See Tedlock ([1981] 1992, 47–74) for a detailed discussion of the recruitment and training of shamans in Momostenango in the 1970s. The initiation she describes is much more thorough than what Octaviano reports in Xecul, though basic similarities—including prayers in the Church following public initiation—remain. Unlike other highland Maya communities, shamanism has maintained a relatively strong public and institutional presence in Momostenango.

13. This is a complex and somewhat contested term in the Mayanist literature. Derived from Nahuatl, in Mesoamerica more generally it tends to refer to shape-shifting witches or to "co-essential" animal familiars acquired by humans at birth. In Guatemala, its meanings are extended to a range of objects, animals, and segments of time. Elsewhere I suggest this breadth of usage signals, in the most general

terms, subjecthood in the context of a multinatural perspectivist cosmology (MacKenzie 2016, 68–71).

14. Monaghan (2000, 29) notes how a focus on surfaces, appearances, and skin itself as the source of divine power (not a mask or external representation of some deeper, sacred essence) is common in Mesoamerican religions.

15. In this sense, *secretos* bear a certain resemblance to the *ráo* described by Colpron (this volume) in Shipibo-Konibo shamanism.

16. Shamans in Xecul are part-time religious specialists, though some are more active or have a larger client base than others. Conducting fire ceremonies at mountainside or other altars is the most complex and spiritually demanding aspect of their work. The busiest shamans I knew might perform a few of these ceremonies a week—perhaps more if they use a home altar—with or without the presence of the client. Divinations using *tz'ite'* seeds are performed more often and are more perfunctory in nature, and may or may not result in a diagnosis requiring further ritual action.

17. Shamans typically charge for their services in addition to the cost of the materials used in a given ceremony. The amount varies depending on the age and experience of the shaman and their relationship to the client. I have been charged between GTQ 20 and 100 (CAD 5–20; see also note 25, below) for ceremonies performed on my behalf over the years, in addition to materials, while some ceremonies were offered for free. See Little (2008) for a discussion of the economics of shamanic practice in Guatemala.

18. In a related argument, Nader (1996) has suggested that the legal and procedural culture of dispute resolution in some Mesoamerican communities, which emphasizes harmony and restoring the balance among neighbours rather than simply determining guilt or innocence, may have emerged as a response to colonialism. Specifically, she notes that an ideological focus on harmony at the local level avoids attracting the attention of the state.

19. See MacKenzie (2016, 36–43) for more detail on the history of relations between the state and community in Xecul, including responses to state violence.

20. In a comparative vein, Harding (2000, 228–46) notes how Fundamentalist Christians routinely probe the meaning of current events for hidden evidence for the fulfillment of Biblical prophecies. In the Pentecostal Maya context I am describing here, however, this reading of signs is not explicitly oriented to an apocalyptic future, but to pragmatic concerns of the present.

21. In my survey (note 8, above), 65.2% of Catholics and 71.1% of Protestants report having had a dream that they believed provided signs from God. Furthermore, only 5.7% of Catholics and 8.9% of Protestants suggested that they do not believe that dreams carry such signs.

22. Unlike most *costumbristas* who tend to be less convinced about the absolute separation of good and evil (as with Xuan's suggestion above that we might do some "good" witchcraft), Pentecostals are much more thoroughly dualistic in this context. Striving after a kind of transcendent (though embodied rather than highly intellectualized) state of perfection on Earth (and anticipating as much in the world to come) is common among Pentecostals I have known, who are also clear on the divide between this state and the state of fallenness, sin, worldliness, and evil.

23. As suggested above, in the *costumbrista* context, time is also sacralized, but in a manner that stresses multiplicity rather than duality (good/evil). The 260 days of the sacred calendar are considered *nawales*, as noted, though the effects of these on individual human subjectivities serve to introduce considerable diversity into the relational field, with no corresponding push to reduce this to something more manageable. Plurality, in perspectivist cosmologies, is ontological (Viveiros de Castro 2004, 482).

24. Vaarzon-Morel (this volume) describes a comparable pragmatic association between corporeal health and Christian practice in the Warlpiri context.

25. The quetzal (GTQ) is the currency of Guatemala. At the time of writing, GTQ 500 is approximately CAD 90.

26. What is missing here, of course, is the actual experience or perspective of the bureaucrat in question. As noted above, recent ethnographies of bureaucracy have focused upon these actors, seeking to trace the cultural dimensions of their role. Whether or not the cop saw the encounter the same way (Was he exercising discretion due to a fundamental trust in Gerardino? Was he bored with his work and resisting the professional expectations for thoroughness with which he was charged?) cannot, of course, be answered here.

27. As I note elsewhere (MacKenzie 2016, 327–28), Xeculenses kicked out the local police detachment—sacking the station and hounding the officers out of town— in August of 2011, accusing them of supporting a pair of young presumed-delinquents who were captured by the community and accused of ambushing vehicles outside of the town. Locals managed their security autonomously for about a year before agreeing to the return of the police, though they remain highly critical of police efforts (or lack thereof).

References

Bernstein, Anya, and Elizabeth Mertz. 2011. "Introduction: Bureaucracy: Ethnography of the State in Everyday Life." *PoLAR: Political & Legal Anthropology Review* 34 (1): 6–10. https://doi.org/10.1111/j.1555-2934.2011.01135.x

Bourdieu, Pierre. 1991. "Genesis and Structure of the Religious Field." *Comparative Social Research* 13 (1): 1–44.

Brintnall, Douglas. 1979. *Revolt Against the Dead: The Modernization of a Mayan Community in the Highlands of Guatemala*. New York: Gordon and Breach.

Carlsen, Robert S. 2011. *The War for the Heart and Soul of a Highland Maya Town*. Revised edition. Austin: University of Texas Press.

Chiappari, Christopher L. 2015. "De ánimas al animismo: subjetividad y poder en la espiritualidad maya y la religión evangélica en Guatemala." *Revista Sendas* 3 (3): 113–15.

Cook, Garrett W. 1986. "Quichean Folk Theology and Southern Maya Supernaturalism." In *Symbol and Meaning Beyond the Closed Community: Essays in Mesoamerican Ideas*, edited by G.H. Gossen, 139–53. Albany: Institute for Mesoamerican Studies.

———. 2000. *Renewing the Maya World: Expressive Culture in a Highland Town*. Austin: University of Texas Press.

Garrard-Burnett, Virginia. 1998. *Protestantism in Guatemala: Living in the New Jerusalem*. Austin: University of Texas Press.

Graeber, David. 2015. *The Utopia of Rules: On Technology, Stupidity, and the Secret Joys of Bureaucracy*. Brooklyn: Melville House.

Harding, Susan Friend. 2000. *The Book of Jerry Falwell: Fundamentalist Language and Politics*. Princeton: Princeton University Press.

Heyman, Josiah. 2012. "Deepening the Anthropology of Bureaucracy." *Anthropological Quarterly* 85 (4): 1269–77. https://doi.org/10.1353/anq.2012.0067

Hull, Matthew S. 2012. *Government of Paper: The Materiality of Bureaucracy in Urban Pakistan*. Berkeley: University of California Press.

Keane, Webb. 1997. *Signs of Recognition: Powers and Hazards of Representation in an Indonesian Society*. Berkeley: University of California Press.

Little, Walter E. 2008. "Maya Daykeepers: New Spiritual Clients and the Morality of Making Money." In *Economics and Morality: Anthropological Approaches*, edited by Katherine E. Brown and B. Lynne Milgram, 77–97. New York: Altamira Press.

MacKenzie, C. James. 2009. "Judas off the Noose: Sacerdotes Mayas, Costumbristas, and the Politics of Purity in the Tradition of San Simón in Guatemala." *The Journal of Latin American and Caribbean Anthropology* 14 (2): 355–81. https://doi.org/10.1111/j.1935-4940.2009.01052.x

———. 2016. *Indigenous Bodies, Maya Minds: Religion and Modernity in a Transnational K'iche' Community*. Boulder: University of Colorado Press.

Martin, David. 1990. *Tongues of Fire: The Explosion of Protestantism in Latin America*. Oxford: Basil Blackwell.

Mathur, Nayanika. 2015. *Paper Tiger: Law, Bureaucracy and the Developmental State in Himalayan India*. Cambridge: Cambridge University Press.

Monaghan, John. 2000. "Theology and History in the Study of Mesoamerican Religions." In *Ethnology*. Vol. 6, *Supplement to the Handbook of Middle American Indians,* edited by John Monaghan, 24–49. Austin: University of Texas Press.

Nader, Laura. 1996. "Coercive Harmony: The Political Economy of Legal Models." *Kroeber Anthropological Society Papers* 80: 1–13.

Pitarch, Pedro. 2010. *The Jaguar and the Priest: An Ethnography of Tzeltal Souls*. Austin: University of Texas Press.

Robbins, Joel. 2004. "The Globalization of Pentecostal and Charismatic Christianity." *Annual Review of Anthropology* 33: 117–43. https://doi.org/10.1146/annurev. anthro.32.061002.093421

Swedberg, Richard. 2005. *The Max Weber Dictionary: Key Words and Central Concepts*. Stanford: Stanford University Press.

Tedlock, Barbara. (1981) 1992. *Time and the Highland Maya*. Revised edition. Albuquerque: University of New Mexico Press.

Vilaça, Aparecida, and Robin M. Wright. 2009. *Native Christians: Modes and Effects of Christianity Among Indigenous Peoples of the Americas*. London: Ashgate Publishing Company.

Viveiros de Castro, Eduardo. 1998. "Cosmological Deixis and Amerindian Perspectivism." *The Journal of the Royal Anthropological Institute* 4 (3): 469–88. https://doi.org/10.2307/3034157

———. 2004. "Exchanging Perspectives: The Transformation of Objects into Subjects in Amerindian Ontologies." *Common Knowledge* 10 (3): 463–84. http://film.ncu. edu.tw/word/Exchanging_perspectives.pdf

Vohnsen, Nina Holm. 2017. *The Absurdity of Bureaucracy: How Implementation Works*. Manchester: Manchester University Press.

Weber, Max. 1978. *Economy and Society: An Outline of Interpretive Sociology*. Edited by Guenther Roth and Claus Wittich. Berkeley: University of California Press.

———. 2005. *Max Weber: Readings and Commentary on Modernity*. Edited by Stephen Kalberg. Oxford: Blackwell.

Wolf, Eric R. 1957. "Closed Corporate Peasant Communities in Mesoamerica and Java." *Southwestern Journal of Anthropology* 13 (1): 1–18. https://www.jstor.org/stable/3629154

ANNE-MARIE COLPRON is Associate Professor in Residence in the Department of Religious Sciences at the Université du Québec à Montréal (UQAM). She conducts research with Indigenous Peoples of the Amazon on shamanism, cosmologies, and gender. She has published articles on shamanic practices and their transformations as well as Indigenous conceptualizations of gender and personhood, including "Contact Crisis: Shamanic Explorations of Virtual and Possible Worlds" (*Anthropologica* 55, no. 2 [2013]) and "Chamanisme féminin contre-nature? Menstruation, gestation et femmes chamanes parmi les Shipibo de l'Amazonie Occidentales" (*Journal de la Société des Américanistes* 92, no. 1/2 [2006]). She has been conducting field research among the Shipibo-Konibo of the Western Amazon since 1996. She is a member of the funded research groups Centre interuniversitaire d'études et de recherches autochtones (CIÉRA) and l'Équipe de recherche sur les cosmopolitiques autochtones (ERCA).

ROBERT R. CRÉPEAU is Professor of Anthropology at the Université de Montréal. He has conducted research in Quebec as well as in South America with the Achuar of Amazonia in Peru and the Kaingang of Southern Brazil on different topics including rituals, myths, shamanism, and cosmology. He has published many papers and has edited, with Solange Lefebvre, *Les religions sur la scène mondiale* (Presses de l'Université Laval 2010), and with Marie-Pierre Bousquet, *Dynamiques religieuses des autochtones des Amériques: vers de Nouvelles méthodes / Religious*

Dynamics of Indigenous People of the Americas: Towards New Methods (Karthala 2012).

FRANÇOISE DUSSART is Professor of Anthropology and Women's, Gender, and Sexuality Studies at the University of Connecticut. Her specialties in social anthropology include: Australian Aboriginal visual systems; Indigenous rights; various expressions of gender, ritual, and performance; health; and citizenship. In 2015–2016, she curated a major presentation of contemporary Aboriginal and Torres Strait Islander arts from Australia at the Musée de la Civilisation in Quebec City (Canada). She is the author of *La peinture des aborigènes d'Australie* (Parenthèses 1993) and *The Politics of Ritual in an Aboriginal Settlement: Kinship, Gender and the Currency of Knowledge* (Smithsonian Institution Press 2000). She has also edited several volumes on media and religion: *Media Matters: Representations of the Social in Aboriginal Australia* (VAR 2006), *Christianity in Aboriginal Australia Revisited* (TAJA 2010, with Carolyn Schwarz), and *Entangled Territorialities* (UTP 2017, with Sylvie Poirier).

INGRID HALL is Associate Professor at the Université de Montréal with research expertise in environmental anthropology. She does fieldwork mostly in the Peruvian Andes, focusing on the conservation of the biodiversity of potatoes. In this line, she co-edited the volume *Savoirs locaux en situation: retour sur une notion plurielle et dynamique* (Quae 2019), in which she published the chapter "Le Parc de la pomme de terre, conservation *in situ* et valorisation des savoirs locaux au Pérou" as well as the conclusion. She also published "Le 'bien vivre' (*sumaq kawsay*) et les pommes de terre paysannes: du délicat exercice de la diplomatie ontologique" (*Anthropologie et sociétés* 43, no. 3 [2019]) and "Les ancêtres au prisme des pommes de terre non domestiquées: une perspective andine" (*Frontières* 29, no. 2 [2018]). She is interested in the sociopolitical organization of rural communities of the Peruvian Andes and has published several papers on this subject, including "Propriété collective, gestion des communs et structuration sociale" (*Revue internationale des études du développement* 234 [2018]), "Parole et hiérarchie dans les Andes du Sud du Pérou" (*Autrepart*, no. 73 [2016]), and "La reforma agraria, entre memoria y olvido (Andes sur peruanos)" (*Anthropologica* 31 [2013]).

LAURENT JÉRÔME is an anthropologist, Associate Professor of Religious Sciences, and Director of Indigenous Studies programs at the Université du Québec à Montréal (UQAM). He is interested in the politics of identity and culture in Indigenous contexts in Quebec and Brazil, as well as in the processes of enhancement, protection, and transmission of tangible and intangible Indigenous heritage. He has published several papers on Indigenous youth, Indigenous cosmologies, and decolonization processes. He currently leads the Research Group on Indigenous Cosmopolitics (ERCA), which aims to document and analyze the political and legal dimensions of Indigenous cosmologies. He has recently published the chapter "'Mediacosmologies': The Convergence and Renewal of Indigenous Religiosities in Cyberspace" in the *Routledge International Handbook of Religion in Global Society* (Routledge 2021).

FRÉDÉRIC LAUGRAND is Professor of Anthropology at Université catholique de Louvain (Belgium) and Director of the Laboratoire d'études prospectives (LAAP), with research expertise in Indigenous cosmologies, human-animal relationships, and Christianization. He is the author of *Mourir et renaître: la réception du christianisme par les Inuit de l'Arctique de l'Est canadien* (PUL/CNWS 2002). He has co-edited many books in different collections with Jarich Oosten, including *Nunavut Arctic College Interviewing Inuit Elders*, *Inuit Perspectives of the Twentieth Century*, and *Memory and History in Nunavut*. He is also co-author (with Oosten) of *The Sea Woman* (Alaska University Press 2009), *Inuit Shamanism and Christianity: Transitions and Transformations in the Twentieth Century* (MQUP 2010), *Hunters, Predators and Prey: Inuit Perceptions of Animals* (Berghahn Books 2014), and *Inuit, Oblate Missionaries and Grey Nuns in the Keewatin* (MQUP 2019); and (with Emmanuel Luce) of *Pelly Bay Album (1939–1954): Franz Van de Velde Photographic Codex* (Presses universitaires de Louvain 2019).

C. JAMES MACKENZIE is Associate Professor and Chair of Anthropology at the University of Lethbridge, with research expertise in the anthropology of religion, ethnic politics, transnationalism, migration, and popular culture. His work draws on ongoing, long-term fieldwork in Maya communities in Guatemala, which he has conducted since the mid-1990s. He is the author of the monograph *Indigenous Bodies, Maya Minds: Religion and Modernity in a Transnational K'iche' Community* (University Press of Colorado 2016) and has published in the *International Journal of Latin American Religions*, *Nova Religio, Anthropos, Latin American and Caribbean Ethnic Studies,* and the *Journal of Latin American and Caribbean Anthropology,* among others.

CAROLINE NEPTON HOTTE is a doctoral student in the Department of Religious Sciences and Professor of Art History at Université du Québec à Montréal (UQAM). She is a member of the ilnu community of Mashteuiatsh (Quebec) and has been interested in Aboriginal issues for over twenty years, particularly issues concerning First Nations women. Drawing inspiration from feminist critical theories and reflections on Indigenous epistemologies, she documents and analyzes the continuities and transformations of expressions of Aboriginal identities and cosmologies through the works of Aboriginal women, particularly artistic practices integrating digital technologies. She has worked for more than ten years in public relations in institutions managed by and for First Nations. She worked as a journalist at Radio-Canada/CBC for over nine years. Now transposing her reflections into a scientific approach, she has published in the *Cahiers du Centre interuniversitaire d'études et de recherches autochtones* and has organized numerous scientific conferences.

KSENIA PIMENOVA is a Fonds de la Recherche Scientifique postdoctoral researcher and a lecturer at the Université libre de Bruxelles (Belgium). She holds a PHD in sociology from École des Hautes Études en Sciences Sociales (Paris). Her research expertise lies in the anthropology of religion with a focus on Siberian shamanism and Buddhism, as well as in the anthropology of museums and repatriation. She directed a documentary on Siberian shamanism: *Spirits of the Three Peaks* (CNRS Images 2017). Her recent publications include: "Muséographie de réappropriations: la momie de la Princesse altaïenne dans un musée sibérien" in *Valeurs et matérialité: approches anthropologiques* (Éditions rue d'Ulm 2019); "Un paradis à reconquérir: critique sociale et utopie traditionnaliste dans les discours sur la 'Princesse altaïenne'" in *La Sibérie comme paradis* (Centre d'Etudes Mongoles et Sibériennes—École Pratique des Hautes Études 2019); and "Traditions et emprunts dans un miroir chamanique: réflexions autour d'un nouveau rituel touva" (*Ethnographiques.org* 33 [2016]).

SYLVIE POIRIER is Professor of Anthropology at Université Laval. She is currently Editor-in-Chief of *Anthropologie et sociétés*. She has conducted research with Indigenous people in the Australian Western Desert and with the Atikamekw Nehirowisiwok, a First Nation in north-central Quebec, on a range of issues pertaining to land, knowledge, and transmission. In addition to numerous articles and thematic issues, she is the author of *A World of Relationships: Itineraries, Dreams and Events in the Australian Western Desert* (UTP 2004), co-editor of *Figured Worlds: Ontological Obstacles in Intercultural Relations* (UTP 2004, with John Clammer and Eric Schwimmer), and co-editor of *Entangled Territorialities: Negotiating Indigenous Lands in Australia and Canada* (UTP 2017, with Françoise Dussart).

KATHRYN ROUNTREE is Professor Emeritus of Anthropology at Massey University (New Zealand). She has published widely on aspects of contemporary Paganism and shamanism, pilgrimage and embodiment, the contestation of sacred sites, feminist spirituality, and animism. She has conducted ethnographic research in Malta, Turkey, Ireland, and New Zealand. Recent edited books include: *Cosmopolitanism, Nationalism and Modern Paganism* (Palgrave Macmillan 2017), *Contemporary Pagan and Native Faith Movements in Europe* (Berghahn 2015), and *Archaeology of Spiritualities* (Springer 2012, with Christine Morris and Alan A.D.

Peatfield). Monographs include: *Crafting Contemporary Pagan Identities in a Catholic Society* (Ashgate 2010) and *Embracing the Witch and the Goddess* (Routledge 2004).

ANTONELLA TASSINARI received her PHD in anthropology from the University of São Paulo in 1998. She has been Professor of Anthropology at University of Santa Catarina (Brazil) since 1999, where she coordinates a researcher team at the Núcleo de Estudos de Populações Indígenas. Working with Indigenous Peoples in Uaçá Basin, North Brazil, she has been writing about their festivals, rituals, history, social organization, Indigenous education, schooling, and childhood since 1990. She is the author of several articles, co-editor of four volumes, and author of one monograph, *No bom da festa* (EDUSP 2003). She has also directed the ethographic film *Creating the Body in Kumarumã* (2013) and has been writing the ethnographic blog *Memórias do Oiapoque* since 2014.

PETRONELLA VAARZON-MOREL is Honorary Research Associate at The University of Sydney and is a sessional lecturer in anthropology at New York University Sydney. She has undertaken long-term research with Indigenous people in Australia on projects related to the environment, land and native title rights, social justice, media, infrastructure, and history. Her research interests include personhood, multispecies relations, religion, visual and sound cultures, Indigenous mapping, and materiality. She is co-editor of *Archival Returns: Central Australia and Beyond* (Sydney University Press 2020, with Linda Barwick and Jennifer Green) and editor of *Warlpiri Women's Voices: Our Lives Our History* (IAD Press 1995). Her other recent publications include "Enlivening People and Country: The Lander Warlpiri Cultural Mapping Project" in *Archival Returns* (with Luke Kelly); "Reconfiguring Relational Personhood among Lander Warlpiri" in *People and Change in Indigenous Australia* (University of Hawai'i Press 2018); and, with Linda Barwick and Jennifer Green, "Sharing and Storing Digital Cultural Records in Central Australian Indigenous Communities" (*New Media & Society* 23, no. 4 [2021]).

124–25, 129n13. *See also*
Kaingang people, Brazil; Karipuna
people, Brazil; Shipibo-Konibo
people, Amazonia
Buddhism and Altaian people, 259–61
Buliard, Joseph, 40–44, 53–54,
55n10
bureaucracies: domination through
knowledge, 303–04; power
relations, 287–88, 295–97,
301–04; secrets, 288–89;
spiritual strategies (prayers),
301–03. *See also* Mayan people,
Guatemala
burkhanism *(Ak Jang)*, 259–61, 276

Canada, Indigenous peoples: about,
219–22; Anglican missionaries,
33–37; constitutional recognition,
243n11; decolonization, 219,
228–30, *229*, 241; digital media,
220–22; Idle No More movement,
219–20, 228–30, *229*, 242n1;
Indian Act, 243n4; land rights,
243n11; media cosmology,
222–25; Missing and Murdered
Indigenous Women and Girls,
230, 243nn9–10; resistance,
220–23; self-representations,
225–32, *227*, *229–30*; social
media, 242n1; Turtle Island, as
term, 205, 214n11. *See also* Haida
people; Innu people; Inuit; Inuit,
Anglican conversions; Inuit,
Catholic conversions;
Kanien'kehá:ka people
Canada, Indigenous women artists,
219–25. *See also* Kanapé Fontaine,
Natasha; Skawennati
Canessa, Andrew, 178
care and relationality: about, 5, 12,
15–16, 23–25; ancestrality, 15–16;

Christians, 15–16, 71;
contemporary shamanism, 212;
customary cosmology, 18;
entanglements, 15–16, 18; land,
12, 15–16; relationality, 4–5, 12.
See also relationality; Warlpiri
people, Lander region, Australia
Catholics: ancestrality, 11; celibacy,
34–35, 44–46, 48, 51–54;
contemporary shamanism, 210;
Inuit conversions, 17–18, 33–35,
40; Jesuits, 49, 89–90, 116, 205;
Oblates, 40–54; saints, 11, 233;
Tekakwitha, 233, *236*, 237, 241.
See also Andean people, Peru,
religiosity; Inuit, Catholic
conversions; Kaingang people,
religious plurality; Karipuna
people, religiosity and Catholics;
Mayan people, religious pluralism
ceremonies and rituals: about, 7–8,
262–63; authenticity, 8–9;
cosmologies, 7–8, 262–63;
entanglements, 8–10, 262–63;
funeral rituals, 20; ontological
turn, 5–6; power relations, 6,
7–8; pragmatism, 7–8; ritual
plurality, 8–9, 262–63. *See also*
Mayan people, Guatemala;
religiosities; Warlpiri people,
Lander region, Australia
Choque, Charles, 42, 47, 51
Christians: agency, 80; care and
relationality, 15–16, 71;
entanglements, 13–16; identity as
fluid, 9; individualism, 17, 35, 73,
79; locality, 17–18; personhood, 9.
See also Anglicans; Baptists;
Catholics; Evangelicals;
Lutherans; Pentecostals; religion;
religiosities

Christians, conversion process, 9,
33–36, 300. *See also* Inuit,
Anglican conversions; Inuit,
Catholic conversions
cinema. *See* film and video
Codonho, Camila, 99
Coelho, João Xê, 121–22, 125
Colpron, Anne-Marie, 16, 20–21,
133–56, 193, 196, 224–25, 311
Comaroff, Jean and John, 9, 14
contemporaneity vs. modernity,
25n4. *See also* modernity
contemporary shamanism. *See* Malta,
contemporary shamanism; New
Age cosmologies; shamanic
tourism; shamanism,
contemporary
corporeity: about, 87–88; animism,
190, 211, 243n12; decolonization,
241–42; media cosmology,
222–25, 241–42; perspectivism,
292–93; scholarship on, 88, 223;
self-representations, 226–32, *227*;
shamanic adornments, 147–48;
tattoos, *230*, 231, 268; wellness, 4,
83n15, 99–101. *See also* gender;
Karipuna people, personhood and
corporeity; repatriation of human
remains
cosmologies: about, 2–3, 6–7, 24–25;
concept of, 6–9, 224;
entanglements, 8, 10, 13–16,
24–25; media cosmology, 221–25;
narratives of, 6–7; ontological,
5–8; openness to plurality, 1–3,
7–8; perspectivism, 292–93;
pragmatism, 7–8; as process *in
the making,* 1, 6–9, 63, 135–36,
159; reappropriated history,
237–38, 241; relationality, 3–4,
6–8, 224; risks in, 24; tricksters,
66, 112, 237, 244n15. *See also*

indigeneity; personhood;
relationality; religiosities
Crépeau, Robert R., 9, 13, 17, 19–20,
111–32, 311–12
cultural borrowing and appropriation,
188–89, 191, 196–98, 206–07,
212. *See also* authenticity
cultural tourism, shamanic. *See*
shamanic tourism
Cusco, Peru, 160, *161,* 163. *See also*
Andean people, Peru
customary religiosity. *See* religiosities
cyberspace. *See* digital media; Kanapé
Fontaine, Natasha; Skawennati

Dakota people, *235,* 242n2
D'Angelis, Wilmar, 116
Danowski, Déborah, 19, 112
decolonization. *See* resistance and
decolonization
Delâge, Denys, 9
Deloria, Ella, 242n2
Deloria, Vine, Jr., 26n9
Descola, Philippe, 5, 243n12
digital media: about, 22; arts media,
220–21; hyperconnectivity, 25n2;
identity negotiation, 240–41;
machinima (machine and cinema),
232–37, *235–36,* 241; manga,
238–39, 238–40; media
cosmology, 22, 221–25; political
activism, 242n1; recontextualizing
of history, 233–37, *235,* 241;
religiosity, 223; self-
representation, 226, 228, 234;
shamanic tourism, 20, 198, 204,
207–08, 210; shamanism, 211–12;
social media, 134, 198, 204, 207,
221–22, 225, 226, 230–31, 234,
240; user generated content
(Second Life), 221, 225, 233; video
games, 225; webinars, 208;

women artists, 22, 221–22, 226. *See also* Kanapé Fontaine, Natasha; Skawennati

dividual (multiple) vs. individual (autonomous), 26n7. *See also* personhood

Dreaming. *See* Warlpiri people, customary cosmology

dreams: communication with deities, 298, 300–01; cosmologies, 8, 298; Karipuna shamans, 19, 93, 94–95, 103–04; knowledge source, 298, 304; Mayan religiosity, 289, 292–93, 298, 301, 304, 307n21

dualism vs. relationality, 4. *See also* relationality

Dussart, Françoise, 1–32, 64–65, 312

Eliade, Mircea, 189–90, 213n1

end of times. *See* narratives, end of times and new worlds

entanglements: about, 1–4, 10; ancestrality, 10–12, 15–16; care and relationality, 15–16, 18; Christianity, 13–16; globalization, 20–25; indigeneity, 13–16; Indigenous cosmologies, 8, 10, 13–16, 24–25; kinship, 11, 15–16; modernity, 13–14; other-than-human realms, 15–16; political sphere, 12–13; as process *in the making*, 1, 3, 6–9, 14–16, 87, 135–36, 159; religiosities, 4, 8–16, 24–25, 60, 277; shamanism, 13, 21–22, 191, 194–96, 205–09, 211–12

environment: biodiversity in Andean potatoes, 21; contemporary shamanism, 195, 211; "ecological Indians," 21, 159, 167–68, 174; ecotourism, 177; end of times and

new worlds, 126–27; indigeneity and conflicts, 159; Innu women activists, 230–31; sacred sites, 167

Eriksen, Annelin, 72–73

Erkinova, Rimma, 265

ERSAI (Équipe de recherche sur les spiritualités amérindiennes et Inuit), 3, 25n1

ethnography. *See* anthropology; museums of ethnography

Evangelicals: conversion process, 9, 300. *See also* Andean people, Peru, religiosity; Christians; Kaingang people, religious plurality; Pentecostals

females. *See* women

film and video: machinima (machine and cinema), 232–37, *235–36*, 241; *Time Traveller*, 232–37, *235–36*, 244n13; video games, 225. *See also* digital media

First Nations. *See* Canada, Indigenous peoples

Fotiou, Evgenia, 154n23

Four Winds School of Shamanism, 207, 210

Fragnito, Skawennati, 220. *See also* Skawennati

Frazer, James George, 113

Friedman, Jonathan, 25n4

gender: Christian conversions, 33–34; media cosmology, 222–24; women's self-representations, 225–32, *227, 229–30*. *See also* women

Ginsburg, Faye, 233

globalization: consumer culture, 209; cultural borrowing, 191; dialectic with local, 187–91, 194–98, 211–12; entanglements, 20–25;

shamanism, 187–91, 194–98. *See
also* digital media; shamanism,
contemporary; shamanic tourism
Gorno-Altaysk, Russia, 255, *256. See
also* Altai Princess, Anokhin
National Museum, Russia
Graeber, David, 288, 295, 296–97,
304
Greenshield, Edgar William Tyler, 36
Grey Nuns, 33, 35, 49, 52, 52n2
Guatemala. *See* Mayan people,
Guatemala
Gurvitch, G., 128n2

Haida people, *238–39,* 238–40
Hall, Ingrid, 14, 20, 21, 157–86,
312–13
Hallowell, A. Irving, 5, 189
Halsey, Theresa, 242n2
Harner, Michael, 197, 210–11, 213n3,
214n13
Harvey, Graham, 3, 189
Haudenosaunee people, 220–21. *See
also* Skawennati
human body. *See* corporeity
human remains. *See* Altai Princess;
repatriation of human remains
Huron-Wendat people, 228
Hutton, Ronald, 188, 189–90

identity: about, 159; "ecological
Indians," 21, 159, 167–68, 174;
identity politics, 158–59;
performance, 158–59; recognition
vs. identification, 159, 172, 178,
180. *See also* indigeneity;
personhood
Idle No More movement, 219–20,
228–30, *229,* 242n1
Idlout, Paul, 38–40
Inca as shamanic auxiliaries, 139,
145–46, 148, 150

indigeneity: about, 2–3; authenticity,
8–9; entanglements, 13–16;
media cosmology, 222–25;
ontologies, 5–6; as process *in the
making,* 1, 3, 6–9, 14–16, 87,
135–36, 159; relationality, 2–3;
self-representation, 226, 228;
symbolic indigeneity, 178. *See also*
cosmologies; entanglements;
locality; relationality
individualism, Western: dividual
(multiple) vs. individual
(autonomous), 26n7, 87–88; vs.
Indigenous relationality, 3;
resistance to, 17. *See also*
personhood
Ingerman, Sandra, 208, 214n13
Innu people: cosmologies, 225–26,
231; environmental activism,
230–31; land, 243n11; video
games, 225; women artists and
writers, 220, 225, 230. *See also*
Kanapé Fontaine, Natasha;
Skawennati
International Society for the
Sociology of Religion (ISSR),
Lausanne conference (2017), 3–4
internet. *See* digital media
Inuit: about, 17–18, 33–35, 52–54;
ancestrality, 18, 35, 44, 52–53;
artists and writers, 47, 50–51;
caring and relationality, 37, 39,
51–53; kinship and marriage,
17–18, 34–36, 40, 51–53; naming
system, 44, 52; *qallunaat* (White
people), 35, 47, 52, 54;
relationality, 17–18, 34–36,
39–40, 52–53; resistance to
individualism, 35, 52; video
games, 225; women, 33–34,
37–38, 52

Malta, contemporary shamanism: about, 21–22, 198–212; acultural timeless oneness, 204–05, 208–12; ancestrality, 205–07; authenticity, 188–89, 191–94, 197–98, 210–11; *ayahuasca* use, 22, 196, 198, 213n6; Carlos (shaman), 199, *203*, 203–10, 212, 213n6, 214n10, 214n12; digital media, 21–22, 198, 204, 207; entanglements, 22, 205–12; Francis (ex-priest), 205, 210–11; Kimimila (organizer), 199, 205–07, 210, 213n5, 214n12; Neolithic culture, 208, 211, 214n14; purposes, 209, 211; research project, 198–99; rituals, 22, 207; sweat lodges *(Temazcals)*, 22, 199–206, *200–03*, 213n4, 214n12, 214nn9–10; women ("sistren"), 207–10. *See also* shamanism, contemporary; shamanic tourism

Manernaluk, Anthony, 40–47, 55n10, 55n22

manga, *238–39*, 238–40

Māori people: shamanism, 191, 195–96; Te Papa Tongarewa Museum, 276–77; as term, 188

marginalized peoples, 11–14, 24–25, 26n10

Matthews, Caitlin, 210

Mauss, Marcel, 30n7, 87, 128n3

Mayan people, Guatemala: about, 23, 287–91; bureaucracies, 23, 285–89, 294–97, 301–04, 308nn26–27; calendars, 308n23; care and relationality, 23; cosmological openness, 289–90; demographics, 306nn8–9; dispute resolution, 307n18; entanglements, 289, 299;

historical background, 294; modernity, 296–97; perspectivism, 292–93; research projects, 285–86, 306nn8–9; San Andrés Xecul, 285, 289, 290–91; state/community relations, 23, 290, 293–96, 307nn18–19

Mayan people, religious pluralism: about, 289–91, 306n9; bureaucracies, 287, 301–04; Catholics, 289–91, 299–300, 306nn8–9, 307n21; ceremonies and rituals, 287, 289, 291, 293–95, 300, 305nn3–4; dreams, 289, 292–93, 298, 301, 304, 307n21; entanglements, 289, 299; Gerardino (Pentecostal), 297–304; good and evil, 300; hidden meanings, 292–93, 298, 307n20; individual vs. collective values, 293; other-than-human beings, 300; Pentecostals, 289–90, 297–304, 306n9, 307n20, 308n22; perspectivism, 292–93; petitions/prayers, 292–93, 297–98, 300–03; Protestants, 307n21; religious pluralism, 306n9; sacred sites *(encanto)*, 286–87, 305n3; saints, 289, 298, 300; in San Andrés Xecul, 306nn8–9; secrets *(secretos)*, 288–89, 293, 298, 299–300, 304, 306n7, 307n15; traditionalists *(costumbristas)*, 289–93, 298–300, 304, 305nn2–4, 306n9

Mayan people, shamanism: about, 23, 289–97, 305n2, 306n9; calendars, 291, 305n2; as Catholics, 290–91, 300, 306nn8–9; ceremonies and rituals, 293–95, 305nn2–4,

306nn9–10, 307nn16–17;
dreams, 292–93, 304; fees,
307n17; hidden meanings,
292–93, 298, 307n20; individual
vs collective, 293; initiations,
306n12; *nawales* (Earth Lords and
Saints), 287, 292, 299, 305n3,
306n13, 308n23; Octaviano
(shaman), 291–97, 302, 303–04;
petitions/prayers, 298–99;
religious specialists, 305n2,
307n16; sorcery and witchcraft
(itzb'al), 286, 291–92, 297–301;
spiritual guides *(guias
espirituales)*, 305n2; Xuan Chuc
Chan (shaman), 286–87, 304,
305n1, 308n22

Maybury-Lewis, David, 124–25

media cosmology and women artists,
22, 222–25, 241–42, 258. *See also*
digital media; Kanapé Fontaine,
Natasha; Skawennati

Meketchinova, Anna, 263–64, 274–75

Melucto, John and Moses, 35–36

Merlan, Francesca, 2

Mexico, 199, 204, 213n4

Minnesota Massacre (1862), 234–36,
235

modernity: vs. contemporaneity,
25n4; dualistic ontology, 3;
entanglements, 13–14; as local
diversity, 9. *See also* digital media;
globalization; Kaingang people,
Brazil; shamanism, contemporary;
shamanic tourism; Warlpiri
people, Lander region, Australia

Monaghan, John, 307n14

Monnier, Alain, 113–14, 128n4

Monosov, Vladimir, 267

Morin, Françoise, 137

Morphy, Howard and Frances, 12–13

Mother of Many Children (film), 224

museums of ethnography: flexibility
in ritual space, 305n5; Indigenous
vs. universalist values, 277;
museums of Self vs. Others, 258;
representation of religions,
269–70, 277. *See also* Altai
Princess, Anokhin National
Museum, Russia; repatriation of
human remains

mutuality and care. *See* care and
relationality

Myers, Fred, 60

mythologies. *See* narratives

Nakamurra (Warlpiri), 72

naming systems, 44, 52, 124–25

Nampijinpa, Violet, 68, 75, 79, 80

Nangala, M. (Warlpiri), 65–66

Napangardi (Warlpiri), 75, 77, 78

narratives: in anthropology, 7–8;
apocalypses, 19, 112, 255–56; of
cosmologies, 6–7, 237–41;
creation *(Jukurrpa)*, 61;
Indigenous control, 237–38;
manga, *238–39*, 238–40; moral
order foundation in, 113–15;
recontextualizing of history,
232–38, 241; *Time Traveller*,
232–37, *235–36*, 244n13;
tricksters, 66, 112, 237, 244n15;
video games, 225. *See also* digital
media; Skawennati

narratives, end of times and new
worlds: about, 19–20, 111–12,
126–27; Altai Princess, 255–56;
apocalypse narratives, 19, 112,
255–56; climate change, 19, 112;
disasters, 128n4; fire stories,
112–13; flood stories, 20, 111–14;
new legal and moral order,
112–14, 125–27, 256; retribution,
113, 128n2; scholarship on,

112–14; *Time Traveller,* 232–37, 235–36, 244n13. *See also* Kaingang people, end of times and new worlds

Nasook, Noah and Martha, 37

National Potato Day, 157. *See also* Andean people, Peru, *Papa Watay* celebration

natives. *See* indigeneity

nature conservation. *See* environment

neo-shamanism, as term, 188, 191–93. *See also* Malta, contemporary shamanism; shamanism, contemporary; shamanic tourism

Nepton Hotte, Caroline, 13, 16, 20, 22, 219–51, 258, 314

New Age cosmologies: about, 13; authenticity, 197–98; cultural borrowing and appropriation, 188–89, 197–98, 206–07, 212; entanglements, 13, 197; power relations, 14; relationality, 16; revival of indigeneity, 195–96; shamanism, 22, 191, 195–98, 210. *See also* shamanism, contemporary; shamanic tourism

new media. *See* digital media

Newton, Janice, 196

new worlds. *See* narratives, end of times and new worlds

New Zealand. *See* Māori people

nonhuman beings. *See* other-than-human realms

Norway: shamanism, 190–91, 194, 195

Nutaraaluk, Lucaasie, 37

Oblates, 40–54, 55n7. *See also* Inuit, Catholic conversions

Obomsawin, Alanis, 224

Oka Crisis, 232, 244n14

online spaces. *See* digital media

ontologies, 5–8. *See also* cosmologies; personhood; relationality

oral traditions, 224. *See also* narratives; narratives, end of times and new worlds

other-than-human realms: about, 189–90, 243n3; ancestrality, 10–11; apocalypse narratives, 255–56; continuities with humans, 243n12; defined, 243n3; entanglements, 15–16; ghosts, 257, 261; hidden meanings, 292–93; kinship, 15; locality, 192; relationality, 4–5, 189–90, 240; shamanism, 189–90, 192, 211. *See also* cosmologies; relationality; shamanism

Ottawa, Meky, 224

Overing, Joanna, 106, 107n2

Papa Watay. See Andean people, Peru, *Papa Watay* celebration

Paquette, Aaron, 243n9

Patrick, Jerry Jangala, 67, 82n5

Peck, E.J., 35–37

Peers, Eleanor, 194

Pelagie (Sister), 33, 35, 48, 49, 51, 54, 54n2. *See also* Inuit, Catholic conversions

Pelletier-De Koninck, Marie-Charlotte, 116–17

Pelly Bay, Nunavut, 42, 53, 55nn6–7

Pentecostals: Australia, 15–16, 74; conversion, 299–300; good and evil, 308n22; Kaingang people, 20, 116–19; Mayans, 289–90, 297–304, 306n9, 307n20, 308n22; prayer, 302–03

personhood: about, 18–20, 24–25, 26n7; ancestrality, 10–11; being-in-the-world, 60; concepts

of personhood, 26n7; and
corporeity, 87–88; dividual
(multiple) vs. individual
(autonomous), 11, 26n7, 87–88;
modern self, 11; ontological turn,
5–6; and relationality, 4–6, 11.
See also corporeity; relationality

perspectivism, 292–93

Peru. *See* Andean people, Peru

Peterson, Nicolas, 70–71

Pimenova, Ksenia, 13, 14, 22–23,
253–83, 305n5, 314–15

Pisac Potato Park, Peru, 21, 157, *158,*
160, *161,* 179–81, 182n7. *See also*
Andean people, Peru, *Papa Watay*
celebration

place. *See* land; locality

Poirier, Sylvie, 1–32, 315

political sphere, 12–13, 23. *See also*
bureaucracies; power relations;
resistance and decolonization

Portillo, Alfonso, 286–87, 304

potatoes, 157, 182nn2–3. *See also*
Andean people, Peru, *Papa Watay*
celebration

Povinelli, Elizabeth, 159, 178, 180

power relations: ancestrality, 10–11;
bureaucracies, 287–89, 295–97,
301–04; ceremonies and rituals,
6, 7–8; colonialism, 295;
Indigenous resistance, 23;
marginalized peoples, 11–14;
prayers/petitions, 301–02; in
rituals, 6; strategic relationality,
13–14

production of the person. *See*
personhood

Protestants: Lutherans, 65–67, 74.
See also Anglicans; Baptists;
Christians; Pentecostals

Quebec: Indigenous arts, 219–21; Oka
Crisis, 232, 244n14. *See also* Innu
people; Kanapé Fontaine,
Natasha; Skawennati

Ramos, Rita, 159, 167, 168

Red: A Haida Manga (Yahgulanaas),
238–39, 238–40

relationality: about, 4–8, 24–25, 189;
"all my relatives," 17, 26n9;
ancestrality, 4–5, 11, 15–16;
animism, 190, 211, 243n12, 299;
autonomy, 13, 65; being-in-the-
world, 35, 60, 91; care and
relationality, 5, 12, 15–16, 23–25;
cosmologies, 3–4, 6–8, 224;
Elders as foundation, 240;
entanglements, 15–16, 18;
indigeneity, 2–3; vs.
individualism, 3, 17; kinship, 11,
15–16, 242n2; land, 4–5, 11–12,
15–16, 231; locality, 4–5, 17–18;
media cosmology, 222–25;
other-than-human realms, 4–5,
189–90, 240; personhood, 4–6,
11, 91; as process *in the making,* 1,
6–9, 14–16, 87, 135–36, 159;
shamanism, 20, 150, 189, 212;
wellness, 83n15; vs. Western
duality, 3–4. *See also* Inuit;
Karipuna people, Brazil;
Shipibo-Konibo people, Amazonia

religion: bureaucracies, 288–89,
305n6; entanglements, 13–16; vs.
religiosity, 8, 278n1. *See also*
Christians; Christians, conversion
process; religiosities

religiosities: about, 8–14, 24–25;
conversion and indigenization,
299; cosmologies, 6–7; as
"culture," 75; dynamic processes,
60, 63, 223; entanglements, 4,

8–16, 24–25, 60, 277;
experiential, 8; Indigenous
autonomy, 12, 65, 297; legal
order, 113–15, 124–27; media
cosmology, 222–23; moral order
and narratives, 113–15;
ontological preservation, 299; as
process *in the making,* 1, 6–9,
14–16, 60, 63, 87, 135–36, 159;
relationality, 12; vs. religion, 8,
278n1; religious plurality, 4, 8, 10;
ritual plurality, 8–9; as term, 8,
278n1. *See also* ceremonies and
rituals; narratives, end of times
and new worlds; other-than-
human realms; shamanism;
spirituality
repatriation of human remains:
about, 253–55, 276–77; future
research potential, 270, 276;
human remains as actors, 253–54,
257; Indigenous vs. universalist
values, 275–77; Māori remains,
276–77; museums of Self vs.
Others, 258; religiosity, 277. *See
also* Altai Princess; museums of
ethnography
resistance and decolonization: about,
24–25; to Christian individualism,
17; incorporation of alterity,
24–25; and indigeneity, 2;
Indigenous women artists, 22;
media cosmology, 22, 222–23,
241–42, 258; Oka Crisis, 232,
244n14; recontextualizing of
history, 232–38, 241; self-
representations, 228, 231–32. *See
also* Canada, Indigenous peoples;
repatriation of human remains
Rio, Knut, 72–73
risk in cosmologies, 24–25
rituals. *See* ceremonies and rituals

ritual specialists: Altaian people, 257,
260–61, 266–67, 269, 273,
276–77; *Papa Watay* ritual, 166,
169–70. *See also* religiosities;
shamanism
Robbins, Joel, 23, 299
Roe, Peter, 137–38
Rountree, Kathryn, 16, 20, 21–22,
187–217, 315–16
Russia. *See* Altaian people, Russia

Saez, Oscar Calavia, 197–98
Sahlins, Marshall, 7, 8–9
Sámi shamanism, 190–91, 194
San Andrés Xecul, Guatemala, 285,
289, 290. *See also* Mayan people,
Guatemala
Sanson, Dawne, 195–96
Schaden, Egon, 121–22, 125
Schreiter, Robert, 194–95
Schwarz, Carolyn, 64–65
secular cosmologies. *See* political
sphere
shamanism: about, 21–22; Altaian
people, 259–69, 276; alterity,
20–21, 136, 145–51; ancestrality,
10–11, 145–46, 193–94, 205–07;
animism, 190, 211, 299;
authenticity, 191–94, 197–98;
combat, 147–48; definitions,
188–91, 213n1; dialectic of global
and local, 187–91, 194–98,
211–12; ecstasy, 189–90;
entanglements, 13, 21–22;
globalization, 187–91, 194–98;
individual vs. collective values,
154n23; locality, 192–93;
other-than-human realms,
189–90, 192, 211; purposes, 190,
207, 209; relationality, 20;
relatives as shamans, 138–42,
145–46, 149, 268; role in

Christian conversions, 36; trance-states, 22, 189–90, 207. *See also* digital media; Karipuna people, shamanism; Mayan people, shamanism

shamanism, contemporary: about, 21–22, 187–91, 211–12; acultural timeless oneness, 204–05, 208–12; ancestrality, 205–07; authenticity, 188–89, 191–94, 197–98, 210–11; cultural borrowing and appropriation, 188–89, 196–98, 206–07, 212; definitions, 188–91; dialectic of global and local, 187–91, 194–98, 205, 208, 211–12; entanglements, 194–96, 205–09, 211–12; Harner's Core Shamanism, 197, 210–11, 213n3, 214n13; Lakota shamanism, 199, 205–06, 213n5, 213n7, 214nn11–12; locations, 206–07, 208; nature as central, 208–09; neo-shamanism, as term, 188, 191–93; New Age cosmologies, 22, 191, 195–98, 210; purposes, 190, 207, 209, 211; research project, 189; training, 207–08, 210; transformative continuities, 9, 20, 134–35, 148–52; women shamans, 136–37. *See also* digital media; Malta, contemporary shamanism; New Age cosmologies; shamanic tourism; Shipibo-Konibo, shamans; Shipibo-Konibo, shamanic tourism

shamanic tourism: about, 20–21, 136, 196; authenticity, 135, 188–89, 191–94, 197–98; *ayahuasca* use, 134, 136–37, 147–48, 150, 152n3, 154n25, 196; care and relationality, 20; dialectic of

global and local, 187–91, 194–98, 211–12; economics, 21, 154n23; entanglements, 13, 191; individual vs. collective values, 154n23; online visibility, 134–35, 191; process *in the making*, 135–36; sexual abuse, 152n5; sweat lodges, 22, 199–206, *200–03*, 213n4, 214n12, 214nn9–10; visibility, 149, 151–52; women shamans, 134–36, 137, 140, 143–44, 147–52, 152n5. *See also* digital media; Malta, contemporary shamanism; shamanism, contemporary; Shipibo-Konibo, shamanic tourism

Sherman, Cindy, 228, 243n8

Shipibo-Konibo people, Amazonia: about, 20–21, 133–36, 149–52; alterity and knowledge, 20–21, 145–52, 154n21, 196; couples, 139; economics, 139, 140, 149, 151; kinship, 151; *meráya* (without *ayahuasca*), 137, 146; *mestizo* (mixed), 153n10; *ráo* (medicinal plants and animals), 144; relationality, 20, 135, 146, 150–52, 193; religious affiliations, 139; scholarship on, 133–35, 137, 149; transformative continuities, 9, 20, 134–36, 148–52; visibility, 134–35, 151–52; *yobé* (sorcerer), 137, 141, 151

Shipibo-Konibo, shamans: about, 20–21, 149–52; alterity and knowledge, 20–21, 145–52, 196; ancestrality, 145–46; authenticity, 20, 135, 137, 149–50, 151–52, 193; auxiliaries (Inca), 139, 145–46, 148, 150, 153n15; *ayahuasca* use, 138, 140, 142, 147–48, 150, 152n3, 154n25; body adornments,

Imagining Indians in the 25th Century, 232; machinima, 232–37, *235–36,* 241; media cosmology, 222–23; recontextualizing of history, 232–38, *235,* 241; *Time Traveller,* 232–37, *235–36,* 244n13. *See also* Canada, Indigenous peoples

social media. *See* digital media

South America: alterity as knowledge, 105–06; corporeity and personhood, 87–88; dispute resolution, 307n18; end-of-time narratives, 111–13. *See also* Andes; Andean people, Peru; Kaingang people, Brazil; Karipuna people, Brazil; Shipibo-Konibo people, Amazonia

Soviet Union (Russia). *See* Altaian people, Russia

spirituality: about, 10–11; agency of spirit beings, 11, 26n6; and ancestrality, 10–11; and cosmologies, 6–7; media cosmology, 22, 222–23, 258; vs. other-than-human realms, 189–90; political sphere, 12; relationality, 4–5. *See also* other-than-human realms; religion; religiosities; shamanism

state cosmologies. *See* political sphere

Swain, Tony, 63

Tagoona, Armand, 37–38

Tapardjuk, Louis, 34–35

Tassinari, Antonella, 17, 19, 87–111, 316

technology. *See* digital media

Tekakwitha, Kateri, 233, *236,* 237, 241

Tel'denova, Larissa, 264

Te Papa Tongarewa Museum, New Zealand, 276–77

Thevet, André, 112–13

Time Traveller (Skawennati), 232–37, *235–36,* 244n13

tourism, environmental. *See* Andean people, Peru, *Papa Watay* celebration

tourism, shamanic. *See* shamanic tourism

traditional religiosity. *See* religiosities

Tulugarjuaq, Peter, 36–37

Turtle Island, as term, 205, 214n11

Tylor, Edward Burnett, 113

United States: cultural borrowing and appropriation, 197–98; Lakota shamanism, 199, 205–06, 213n5, 213n7, 214nn11–12; recontextualizing of history, 234–36, *235,* 241; shamanism, 192, 194

universalism, Western/modern: vs. ontological perspective, 5–6

Vaarzon-Morel, Petronella, 14, 17–18, 59–86, 220, 308n24, 1316

Veiga, Juracilda, 116

Verdery, Katherine, 254

Vidal, Lux, 91

video. *See* digital media; film and video

Viertler, Renate, 88

Villoldo, Alberto, 207–08, 210

Viveiros de Castro, Eduardo, 5, 19, 87–88, 107n2, 112, 292

Wabanaki people, 224

Waldron, David, 196

Wallis, Robert, 197–98

Warlpiri people, Lander region, Australia: about, 18, 59–63, *62,* 81–82; assimilation, 64–67, 77, 83n21; demographics, 61, 74–75;

donkeys, 68, 73–74, 79, 82nn8–9; earthquakes, 70–72; entanglements, 15, 18; historical background, 60–61, 64–74, 81–82; the Intervention, 77–78, 81–82, 83n21; land claims, 64, 69, 81, 82n1; location and map, *62*; missionaries, 65–67; modernity, 64–65, 69–71, 73–74, 76–79, 81; new technologies, 76–77; pragmatism, 60; research projects, 82n1; "strange relatives," 60, 63–65, 78, 81–82; "Whitefella business," 64, 68–69, 73–74, 77–78, 81–82; women, 61, 68, 72, 76; youth, 69–71, 73–74

Warlpiri people, settlements: about, 61, *62,* 64–65; Anmatyerr, 65–66, 82n1; Hermannsburg, *62, 65;* Kalkaringi (Wave Hill), *62,* 68; Kunayungku, *62,* 70; Lajamanu (Hooker Creek), *62, 64,* 68, 70; Warrabri (Alekarenge), *62, 64,* 68, 72; Warrego mine, *62,* 70; Willowra, 59–61, *62,* 64–67, 70, 72–82, 82n1; Yuendumu, 15–16, *62, 64,* 67–68, 72

Warlpiri people, customary cosmology: about, 18, 59–61, 74–82; agency and causality, 70–73, 78–81; ancestrality, 15–16, 61, 64, 66–67, 69, 76, 80–81; autonomy, 60, 65, 69, 81–82; care and relationality, 15–16, 18, 59–60, 63, 65, 67, 69, 71–73, 76–82; ceremonies and rituals, 63, 66, 70, 72, 75, 79, 80, 82n7; the Dreaming *(Jukurrpa),* 15–16, 61–63, 66–68, 70, 75, 78–81, 82n2; Elders, 67–69, 73–74, 80–81; entanglements, 15–16, 67–69, 74–82; funerals and

mourning, 66–68, 76; healers *(ngangkayi),* 72; kinship, 15–16, 61–63, 65, 71; land, 59, 61–64; Law *(Jukurrpa),* 61, 63, 71, 73–74, 75, 81; moral order, 69–74, 77–79; naming systems, 67, 76; narratives, 71–72, 75; other-than-human realms, 18, 59–61, 73, 75; personhood, 60, 72–73, 80; relationality, 59–60, 69, 73, 80–81, 83n15; religiosities, 59–61, 74–75; sorcery, 72, 78–80

Warlpiri people, religiosity and Christians: about, 18, 74–82; agency and causality, 18, 72–73, 78–81; Baptists, 15–16, 64–65, 67–68, 74, 77–81, 82n6, 96; biblical texts, 66, 68, 82n5; care and relationality, 59–60, 63, 71, 77–79, 81–82; ceremonies *(purlapas),* 67–69, 72, 77; demographics, 74–75; entanglements, 67–69, 74–82; funerals and mourning, 66–68, 76; God and *Jukurrpa,* 75, 78–82; historical background, 60–65, 81–82; Lutherans, 65–67, 74; non-Indigenous supports, 76, 77–79; Pentecostals, 74; personhood, 72–74, 79–80

Weber, Max, 10, 287–89, 303, 305n6

wellness, 4, 83n15, 99–101. *See also* corporeity; relationality

Willowra, Australia, 59–61, *62,* 64–67, 70, 72–82. *See also* Warlpiri people, Lander region, Australia

Wolf, Eric, 295

women: Canadian artists, 219–25; Indigenous artists, 220–22; Inuit Anglican ministers, 38; Inuit nun (Pelagie), 33, 35, 48, 49, 51, 54,

54n2; media cosmology, 222–25;
self-representation, 226–29, *227*,
228, 231–32. *See also* Kanapé
Fontaine, Natasha; Shipibo-
Konibo, women shamans;
Skawennati

Xecul, Guatemala. *See* Mayan people,
Guatemala
Xuan Chuc Chan, 286–87, 304,
305n1, 308n22

Yahgulanaas, Michael Nicoll, 232,
238–39, 238–40
Yakoyakova, A., 264
Yuendumu Warlpiri people, 15–16,
62, 64, 67–68, 72. *See also*
Warlpiri people, Lander region,
Australia

Other Titles from University of Alberta Press

Traditions, Traps and Trends
Transfer of Knowledge in Arctic Regions
Edited by JARICH OOSTEN and
BARBARA HELEN MILLER
An edited collection that surveys Indigenous knowledge
practices in northern Canada, Greenland, and
Scandinavia.

Idioms of Sámi Health and Healing
Edited by BARBARA HELEN MILLER
Ten experts document the strength of local communities'
using traditional resources for health and prevention.
Patterns of Northern Traditional Healing Series

More information at uap.ualberta.ca